EVERYMAN, I will go with thee,

and be thy guide,

In thy most need to go by thy side

MATTHEW ARNOLD

Born in Middlesex in 1822, son of Thomas Arnold, the headmaster of Rugby. Educated at Rugby and Balliol College, Oxford. Fellowship at Oriel College, 1845; master at Rugby; private secretary to Lord Lansdowne, 1847. Inspector of schools, 1851; elected to chair of poetry at Oxford in 1857. Died in 1888.

Matthew Arnold's Essays in Criticism

FIRST AND SECOND SERIES

INTRODUCTION BY
G. K. CHESTERTON

DENT: LONDON
EVERYMAN'S LIBRARY
DUTTON: NEW YORK

NO. *1115*

SBN: 460 01115 4

CONTENTS

SECOND SERIES

INTRODUCTION

OUR actual obligations to Matthew Arnold are almost beyond expression. His very faults reformed us. The chief of his services may perhaps be stated thus, that he discovered (for the modern English) the purely intellectual importance of humility. He had none of that hot humility which is the fascination of saints and good men. But he had a cold humility which he had discovered to be a mere essential of the intelligence. To see things clearly, he said, you must 'get yourself out of the way'. The weakness of pride lies after all in this: that oneself is a window. It can be a coloured window, if you will; but the more thickly you lay on the colours the less of a window it will be. The two things to be done with a window are to wash it and then forget it. So the truly pious have always said the two things to do personally are to cleanse and to forget oneself.

Matthew Arnold found the window of the English soul opaque with its own purple. The Englishman had painted his own image on the pane so gorgeously that it was practically a dead panel; it had no opening on the world without. He could not see the most obvious and enormous objects outside his own door. The Englishman could not see (for instance) that the French Revolution was a far-reaching, fundamental and most practical and successful change in the whole structure of Europe. He really thought that it was a bloody and futile episode, in weak imitation of an English General Election. The Englishman could not see that the Catholic Church was (at the very least) an immense and enduring Latin civilization, linking us to the lost civilizations of the Mediterranean. He really thought it was a sort of sect. The Englishman could not see that the Franco-Prussian war was the entrance of a new and menacing military age, a terror to England and to all. He really thought it was a little lesson to Louis Napoleon for not reading *The Times*. The most enormous catastrophe was only some kind of symbolic compliment to England. If the sun fell from Heaven it only showed how wise England was in not having much

vii

sunshine. If the waters were turned to blood it was only an advertisement for Bass's Ale or Fry's Cocoa. Such was the weak pride of the English then. One cannot say that is wholly undiscoverable now.

But Arnold made war on it. One excellent point which he made in many places was to this effect: that those very foreign tributes to England which Englishmen quoted as showing their own merit were examples of the particular foreign merit which we did not share. Frenchmen bragged about France and Germans about Germany, doubtless; but they retained just enough of an impartial interest in the mere truth itself to remark upon the more outstanding and obvious of the superiorities of England. Arnold justly complained that when a Frenchman wrote about English political liberty we always thought it a tribute simply to English political liberty. We never thought of it as a tribute to French philosophical liberty. Examples of this are still relevant. A Frenchman wrote some time ago a book called *À quoi tient la supériorité des Anglo-Saxons?* What Englishman dare write a book called 'What causes the Superiority of Frenchmen'? But this lucid abnegation is a power. When a Frenchman calls a book 'What is the Superiority of Englishmen?' we ought to point to that book and say—'this is the superiority of Frenchmen'.

This humility, as I say, was with Arnold a mental need. He was not naturally a humble man; he might even be called a supercilious one. But he was driven to preaching humility merely as a thing to clear the head. He found the virtue which was just then being flung in the mire as fit only for nuns and slaves: and he saw that it was essential to philosophers. The most unpractical merit of ancient piety became the most practical merit of modern investigation. I repeat, he did not understand that headlong and happy humility which belongs to the more beautiful souls of the simpler ages. He did not appreciate the force (nor perhaps the humour) of St Francis of Assisi when he called his own body 'my brother the donkey'. That is to say, he did not realize a certain feeling deep in all mystics in the face of the dual destiny. He did not realize their feeling (full both of fear and laughter) that the body *is* an animal and a very comic animal. Matthew Arnold could never have felt any part of himself to be purely comic—not even his singular whiskers. He would never, like Father Juniper, have 'played see-saw to abase himself'. In a word, he had little sympathy with the old ecstasies of self-effacement. But for this very reason it is all the more important that his main work was an attempt to preach some kind of self-effacement even to his own self-assertive age. He realized that the saints had even understated the case for humility. They had always said that without humility we should never see the better world to come. He realized that without humility we could not even see this world.

Nevertheless, as I have said, a certain tincture of pride was natural to him and prevented him from appreciating some things of great human value. It prevented him, for instance, from having an adequate degree of popular sympathy. He had (what is so rare in England) the sense of the state as one thing, consisting of all its citizens, the *Senatus Populusque Romanus*. But he had not the feeling of familiarity with the loves and hungers of the common man, which is the essence of the egalitarian sentiment. He was a republican, but he was not a democrat. He contemptuously dismissed the wage-earning, beer-drinking, ordinary labourers of England as 'merely populace'. They are not populace; they are merely mankind. If you do not like them you do not like mankind. And when all the role of Arnold's real glories has been told, there always does remain a kind of hovering doubt as to whether he did like mankind.

But of course the key of Arnold in most matters is that he deliberately conceived himself to be a corrective. He prided himself not upon telling the truth but upon telling the unpopular half-truth. He blamed his contemporaries, Carlyle, for instance, not for telling falsehoods but simply for telling popular truths. And certainly in the case of Carlyle and others he was more or less right. Carlyle professed to be a Jeremiah and even a misanthrope. But he was really a demagogue and, in one sense, even a flatterer. He was entirely sincere as all good demagogues are; he merely shared all the peculiar vanities and many of the peculiar illusions of the people to whom he spoke. He told Englishmen that they were Teutons, that they were Vikings, that they were practical politicians—all the things they like to be told they are, all the things that they are not. He told them, indeed, with a dark reproachfulness, that their strengths were lying neglected or inert. Still he reminded them of their strengths; and they liked him. But they did not like Arnold, who placidly reminded them of their weaknesses.

Arnold suffered, however, from thus consenting merely to correct; from thus consenting to tell the half-truth that was neglected. He reached at times a fascination that was all the more extraordinary because it was a fascination of moderation, an intemperance of temperance. This may be seen, I think, in the admirable argument for classical supremacy to which so much of this selection is devoted. He saw and very rightly asserted that the fault of the Mid-Victorian English was that they did not seem to have any sense of definite excellence. Nothing could be better than the way in which he points out in the very important essay on 'The Function of Criticism at the Present Time' that the French admit into intellectual problems the same principle of clearly stated and generally admitted dogmas which all of us in our daily lives admit into moral problems. The French, as he puts it in a good summarizing phrase, have a conscience in literary matters. Upon the opposite English evil he poured perpetual satire. That any man who had money enough to start a paper could start a paper and say it was as good as the *Athenaeum*; that anyone who had money enough to run a school could run a school and say it was as good as Winchester; these marks of the English anarchy he continually denounced. But he hardly sufficiently noticed that if this English extreme of a vulgar and indiscriminate acceptance be most certainly an extreme and something of a madness, it is equally true that his own celebration of excellence when carried past a certain point might become a very considerable madness also; indeed has become such a madness in some of the artistic epochs of the world. It is true that a man is in some danger of becoming a lunatic if he builds a stucco house and says it is as fine as the Parthenon. But surely a man is equally near to a lunatic if he refuses to live in any house except the Parthenon. A frantic hunger for all kinds of inappropriate food may be a mark of a lunatic; but it is also the mark of a lunatic to be fastidious about food.

One of the immense benefits conferred on us by Matthew Arnold lay in the fact that he recalled to us the vital fact that we are Europeans. He had a consciousness of Europe much fuller and firmer than that of any of the great men of his great epoch. For instance, he admired the Germans as Carlyle admired the Germans; perhaps he admired the Germans too much as Carlyle admired the Germans too much. But he was not deluded by any separatist follies about the superiority of a Teutonic race. If he admired the Germans it was for being European, signally and splendidly European. He did not, like Carlyle, admire the Germans for being German. Like Carlyle he relied much on the sagacity of Goethe. But the sagacity of Goethe upon which he relied was not a rugged or cloudy sagacity, the German element in Goethe. It was the Greek element in Goethe: a lucid and equalized sagacity, a moderation and calm such as Carlyle could not have admired, nay, could not even have imagined. Arnold did indeed wish, as every sane European wishes, that the nations that make up Europe should continue to be individual; that the contributions from the nations should be national. But he did wish that the contributions should be contributions, parts, that is, of a common cause and unity, the cause and unity of European civilization. He desired that Germany should be great, so as to make Europe great. He would not have desired that Germany should grow great so as to make Europe small. Anything, however big and formidable, which tended to divide us from the common culture of our continent he would have regarded as a crotchet. Puritanism he regarded at bottom as only an enormous crotchet. The Anglo-Saxon race most certainly he would have regarded as an enormous crotchet.

In this respect it is curious to notice how English public opinion has within our own time contrived to swing from one position to the contrary position without her touching that central position which Arnold loved. He found the English people in a mood which seemed to him unreal and un-European, but this mood was one of smug Radical mediocrity, contemptuous of arts and aims of high policy and of national honour. Ten years after his death the English people were waving Union Jacks and shouting for 'La Revanche'. Yet though they had passed thus rapidly from extreme antimilitarism to extreme militarism they had never touched on the truth that Arnold had to tell. Whether as antimilitarists or as militarists,

they were alike ignorant of the actualities of our Aryan civilization. They have passed from tameness to violence without
touching strength. Whenever they really touch strength they
will (with their wonderful English strength) do a number of
things. One of the things may be to save the world. Another
of the things will certainly be to thank Matthew Arnold.

G. K. CHESTERTON.

NOTE ON THE TEXT

MATTHEW ARNOLD'S *Essays, Literary and Critical* was first
added to Everyman's Library in 1906, and in successive reprints,
the last of which was in 1954, has consisted of (1) *Essays in
Criticism, First Series* (1865), and (2) the Oxford lectures,
On Translating Homer (1861) and *Last Words on Translating
Homer* (1862), together with Francis W. Newman's *Homeric
Translation in Theory and Practice* (1861), of which the chief
interest today is that it stimulated Arnold to a fuller explanation
of his views in *Last Words*. In 1906 the editors of Everyman's
Library were seriously limited in their choice of Arnold's
critical essays because such later work as *Mixed Essays* (1879),
Discourses in America (1885) and *Essays in Criticism, Second
Series* (1888) was still in copyright. Happily this problem no
longer exists, and in the present reprint it has been decided to
take advantage of the changed situation and replace the Homeric
lectures by *Essays in Criticism, Second Series*. At the same time
room has been found for one of Arnold's liveliest and most
attractive pieces of writing in the condensed preface to the
second edition (1869) of *Essays in Criticism, First Series*.

The benefit to the reader of the inclusion of *Essays in
Criticism, Second Series* in the present volume hardly needs to
be pointed out. In *Essays in Criticism, First Series*, which
preceded Arnold's long preoccupation with social and theological issues (exemplified in *Culture and Anarchy* and *Literature
and Dogma*), the critic's primary concern was with the quality of
English civilization—he wished at all costs 'to pull out a few
more stops in that powerful but at present somewhat narrow-
toned organ, the modern Englishman'. The essays are Epistles
to the Philistines and they have a missionary ring. Convinced of
English narrowness and insularity, Arnold allowed himself a
Goethean breadth of display and took for some of his subjects
Marcus Aurelius, Spinoza, the Literary Influence of
Academies, and Pagan and Mediaeval Religious Sentiment. The
book is a landmark in Victorian critical writing and contains

brilliant passages of pure literary criticism, but no essay is
literary criticism and nothing else, and no essay takes an
English writer for its theme. If it were only for these reasons,
Essays in Criticism, Second Series would be compulsory reading
for anyone wishing to understand Arnold as a critic. Coming
as it does at the end of his literary career, it gives us his matured
reflections on life and literature. The first essay, 'The Study
of Poetry', originally written as the general introduction to
T. H. Ward's *The English Poets* (1880), has drawn the fire of
Mr T. S. Eliot and other modern critics, but much of it survives
the severest bombardment, and historically it ranks in importance with Arnold's famous 1853 Preface to his poems and
the first essay of *Essays in Criticism, First Series*, 'The Function
of Criticism at the Present Time'. Other essays in *Essays in
Criticism, Second Series* deal with Milton, Gray, Wordsworth,
Byron, Shelley and Keats, while the essay on Tolstoi shows
Arnold giving one of his rare glances at the modern novel.
Generally speaking, then, Arnold stands or falls as a critic of
English literature by this volume, and a reading of the two
series of *Essays in Criticism* is probably the shortest route to
a real understanding both of his critical powers and of the
range of his literary interests.

The text of *Essays in Criticism, First Series* is from the
revised second edition of 1869; that of *Essays in Criticism,
Second Series* is from the posthumous first edition of 1888.

KENNETH ALLOTT.

1964.

SELECT BIBLIOGRAPHY

COLLECTED WORKS. *The Works of Matthew Arnold* (Edition de luxe),
15 vols., 1903–4; *The Poetical Works*, ed. C. B. Tinker and H. F. Lowry,
1950; *Complete Prose Works*, ed. R. H. Super, 5 vols., 1960–5.

POEMS. *Alaric at Rome* (Rugby Prize poem), 1840; *Cromwell* (Newdigate
Prize), 1843; *The Strayed Reveller, and Other Poems* (*The Forsaken Merman,
Mycerinus*, etc.), 1849; *Empedocles on Etna, and Other Poems* (*Tristram and
Iseult*, etc.), 1852; *Poems* (*Sohrab and Rustum, The Scholar Gipsy*, etc.),
1853, 1854, 1857; *Poems*: Second Series (*Balder Dead*, etc.), 1855; *Merope,
a Tragedy*, 1858; *New Poems* (*Thyrsis, A Southern Night*, etc.), 1867, 1868.

PROSE WORKS. *England and the Italian Question*, 1859; *The Popular Education of France*, 1861; *On Translating Homer*, 1861; *On Translating Homer : Last Words*, 1862; *A French Eton : or Middle-Class Education and the State*, 1864; *Essays in Criticism*, Series I, 1865, 1869, 1875, 1884, etc.; ed. C. A. Miles and L. Smith, 1918; *On the Study of Celtic Literature*, 1867; *Schools and Universities on the Continent*, 1868; *Culture and Anarchy*, 1869, 1875, 1882; ed. J. D. Wilson, 1931; *St Paul and Protestantism*, 1870 (first and second editions); *Friendship's Garland*, 1871; *Literature and Dogma*, 1873; *God and the Bible*, 1875; *Last Essays on Church and Religion*, 1877; *Mixed Essays*, 1879; *Irish Essays and Others*, 1882; *Discourses in America*, 1885, 1889, 1896; *Special Report on Elementary Education Abroad*, 1888; *General Grant : an Estimate*, 1887; *Essays in Criticism*, Series II, 1888, 1889, 1891, 1895, etc.; *Civilization in the United States*, 1888; *Reports on Elementary Schools*, 1852–82; ed. F. S. Marvin, 1908 (this work is in no collected edition); *On Home Rule for Ireland*, 1891; *Essays in Criticism*, Series III, 1910; *Letters of an Old Playgoer*, ed. B. Matthews, 1919; *The Note-Books of Matthew Arnold*, ed. H. F. Lowry, 1952; *Five Uncollected Essays*, ed. K. Allott, 1953; *Essays, Letters and Reviews*, ed. F. Neiman (1960).

LETTERS. *Letters*, 1848–88, ed. G. W. E. Russell, 2 vols., 1895, 1901; *Letters to John Churton Collins*, 1910; *Unpublished Letters*, ed. A. Whitridge, 1923; *Letters to Arthur Hugh Clough*, ed. H. F. Lowry, 1932.

BIOGRAPHY AND CRITICISM. G. Saintsbury, *Matthew Arnold*, 1899; H. W. Paul, *Matthew Arnold*, 1902; G. W. E. Russell, *Matthew Arnold*, 1904; H. Kingsmill, *Matthew Arnold*, 1928; H. W. Garrod, *Poetry and the Criticism of Life*, 1931; T. S. Eliot, *The Use of Poetry and the Use of Criticism*, 1933; I. Sells, *Matthew Arnold and France*, 1935; L. Trilling, *Matthew Arnold*, 1939; C. B. Tinker and H. F. Lowry, *The Poetry of Matthew Arnold, a Commentary*, 1940; E. K. Chambers, *Matthew Arnold*, 1947; L. Bonnerot, *Matthew Arnold, Poète*, 1947; E. K. Brown, *Matthew Arnold, a Study in Conflict*, 1948; W. F. Connell, *The Educational Thought and Influence of Matthew Arnold*, 1950; G. Tillotson, *Criticism and the Nineteenth Century*, 1951; E. D. H. Johnson, *The Alien Vision of Victorian Poetry*, 1952; J. Holloway, *The Victorian Sage*, 1953; J. D. Jump, *Matthew Arnold*, 1955; J. H. Raleigh, *Matthew Arnold and American Culture*, 1957; P. F. Baum, *Ten Studies in the Poetry of Matthew Arnold*, 1958; D. G. James, *Matthew Arnold and the Decline of English Romanticism*, 1961; W. S. Johnson, *The Voices of Matthew Arnold*, 1961; L. Gottfried, *Matthew Arnold and the Romantics*, 1963.

ESSAYS IN CRITICISM

First Series

PREFACE

SEVERAL of the Essays which are here collected and reprinted had the good or the bad fortune to be much criticized at the time of their first appearance. I am not now going to inflict upon the reader a reply to those criticisms; for one or two explanations which are desirable, I shall elsewhere, perhaps, be able some day to find an opportunity; but, indeed, it is not in my nature,— some of my critics would rather say, not in my power,—to dispute on behalf of any opinion, even my own, very obstinately. To try and approach truth on one side after another, not to strive or cry, nor to persist in pressing forward, on any one side, with violence and self-will,—it is only thus, it seems to me, that mortals may hope to gain any vision of the mysterious Goddess, whom we shall never see except in outline, but only thus even in outline. He who will do nothing but fight impetuously towards her on his own, one, favourite, particular line, is inevitably destined to run his head into the folds of the black robe in which she is wrapped.

So it is not to reply to my critics that I write this preface, but to prevent a misunderstanding, of which certain phrases that some of them use make me apprehensive. Mr Wright, one of the many translators of Homer, has published a letter to the Dean of Canterbury, complaining of some remarks of mine, uttered now a long while ago, on his version of the *Iliad*. One cannot be always studying one's own works, and I was really under the impression, till I saw Mr Wright's complaint, that I had spoken of him with all respect. The reader may judge of my astonishment, therefore, at finding, from Mr Wright's pamphlet, that I had 'declared with much solemnity that there is not any proper reason for his existing'. That I never said; but, on looking back at my Lectures on translating Homer, I find that I did say, not that Mr Wright, but that Mr Wright's version of the *Iliad*, repeating in the main the merits and defects of Cowper's version, as Mr Sotheby's repeated those of Pope's version, had, if I might be pardoned for saying so, no proper reason for existing. Elsewhere I expressly spoke of the merit of his version; but I confess that the phrase, qualified as I have shown, about its want

3

of a proper reason for existing, I used. Well, the phrase had, perhaps, too much vivacity; we have all of us a right to exist, we and our works; an unpopular author should be the last person to call in question this right. So I gladly withdraw the offending phrase, and I am sorry for having used it; Mr Wright, however, would perhaps be more indulgent to my vivacity, if he considered that we are none of us likely to be lively much longer. My vivacity is but the last sparkle of flame before we are all in the dark, the last glimpse of colour before we all go into drab,—the drab of the earnest, prosaic, practical, austerely literal future. Yes, the world will soon be the Philistines'! and then, with every voice, not of thunder, silenced, and the whole earth filled and ennobled every morning by the magnificent roaring of the young lions of the *Daily Telegraph*, we shall all yawn in one another's faces with the dismallest, the most unimpeachable gravity.

But I return to my design in writing this Preface. That design was, after apologizing to Mr Wright for my vivacity of five years ago, to beg him and others to let me bear my own burdens, without saddling the great and famous University, to which I have the honour to belong, with any portion of them. What I mean to deprecate is such phrases as, 'his professorial assault', 'his assertions issued *ex cathedrâ*', 'the sanction of his name as the representative of poetry', and so on. Proud as I am of my connection with the University of Oxford,[1] I can truly say, that knowing how unpopular a task one is undertaking when one tries to pull out a few more stops in that powerful but at present somewhat narrow-toned organ, the modern Englishman, I have always sought to stand by myself, and to compromise others as little as possible. Besides this, my native modesty is such, that I have always been shy of assuming the honourable style of Professor, because this is a title I share with so many distinguished men,—Professor Pepper, Professor Anderson, Professor Frickel, and others,—who adorn it, I feel, much more than I do.

However, it is not merely out of modesty that I prefer to stand alone, and to concentrate on myself, as a plain citizen of the republic of letters, and not as an office-bearer in a hierarchy, the whole responsibility for all I write; it is much more out of genuine devotion to the University of Oxford, for which I feel, and always

---

[1] When the above was written the author still had the Chair of Poetry at Oxford, which he has since vacated.

must feel, the fondest, the most reverential attachment. In an epoch of dissolution and transformation, such as that on which we are now entered, habits, ties, and associations are inevitably broken up, the action of individuals becomes more distinct, the shortcomings, errors, heats, disputes, which necessarily attend individual action, are brought into greater prominence. Who would not gladly keep clear, from all these passing clouds, an august institution which was there before they arose, and which will be there when they have blown over?

It is true, the *Saturday Review* maintains that our epoch of transformation is finished; that we have found our philosophy; that the British nation has searched all anchorages for the spirit, and has finally anchored itself, in the fulness of perfected knowledge, on Benthamism. This idea at first made a great impression on me; not only because it it so consoling in itself, but also because it explained a phenomenon which in the summer of last year had, I confess, a good deal troubled me. At that time my avocations led me to travel almost daily on one of the Great Eastern Lines,—the Woodford Branch. Everyone knows that the murderer, Müller, perpetrated his detestable act on the North London Railway, close by. The English middle class, of which I am myself a feeble unit, travel on the Woodford Branch in large numbers. Well, the demoralization of our class,—the class which (the newspapers are constantly saying it, so I may repeat it without vanity) has done all the great things which have ever been done in England,—the demoralization, I say, of our class, caused by the Bow tragedy, was something bewildering. Myself a transcendentalist (as the *Saturday Review* knows), I escaped the infection; and, day after day, I used to ply my agitated fellow travellers with all the consolations which my transcendentalism would naturally suggest to me. I reminded them how Caesar refused to take precautions against assassination, because life was not worth having at the price of an ignoble solicitude for it. I reminded them what insignificant atoms we all are in the life of the world. 'Suppose the worst to happen,' I said, addressing a portly jeweller from Cheapside; 'suppose even yourself to be the victim; *il n'y a pas d'homme nécessaire*. We should miss you for a day or two upon the Woodford Branch; but the great mundane movement would still go on, the gravel walks of your villa would still be rolled, dividends would still be paid at the

Bank, omnibuses would still run, there would still be the old crush at the corner of Fenchurch Street.' All was of no avail. Nothing could moderate, in the bosom of the great English middle class, their passionate, absorbing, almost blood-thirsty clinging to life. At the moment I thought this over-concern a little unworthy; but the *Saturday Review* suggests a touching explanation of it. What I took for the ignoble clinging to life of a comfortable worldling, was, perhaps, only the ardent longing of a faithful Benthamite, traversing an age still dimmed by the last mists of transcendentalism, to be spared long enough to see his religion in the full and final blaze of its triumph. This respectable man, whom I imagined to be going up to London to serve his shop, or to buy shares, or to attend an Exeter Hall meeting, or to assist at the deliberations of the Marylebone Vestry, was, perhaps, in real truth, on a pious pilgrimage, to obtain from Mr Bentham's executors a secret bone of his great, dissected master.

And yet, after all, I cannot but think that the *Saturday Review* has here, for once, fallen a victim to an idea,—a beautiful but deluding idea,—and that the British nation has not yet, so entirely as the reviewer seems to imagine, found the last word of its philosophy. No, we are all seekers still! seekers often make mistakes, and I wish mine to redound to my own discredit only, and not to touch Oxford. Beautiful city! so venerable, so lovely, so unravaged by the fierce intellectual life of our century, so serene!

There are our young barbarians, all at play!

And yet, steeped in sentiment as she lies, spreading her gardens to the moonlight, and whispering from her towers the last enchantments of the Middle Age, who will deny that Oxford, by her ineffable charm, keeps ever calling us nearer to the true goal of all of us, to the ideal, to perfection,—to beauty, in a word, which is only truth seen from another side?—nearer, perhaps, than all the science of Tübingen. Adorable dreamer, whose heart has been so romantic! who hast given thyself so prodigally, given thyself to sides and to heroes not mine, only never to the Philistines! home of lost causes, and forsaken beliefs, and unpopular names, and impossible loyalties! what example could ever so inspire us to keep down the Philistine in ourselves, what teacher could ever so save us from that bondage to which we are all prone, that bondage which Goethe, in his incomparable lines on the death of Schiller, makes it his friend's highest praise (and nobly did Schiller deserve the praise) to have left miles out of sight behind him;—the bondage of '*was uns alle bändigt, DAS GEMEINE!*' She will forgive me, even if I have unwittingly drawn upon her a shot or two aimed at her unworthy son; for she is generous, and the cause in which I fight is, after all, hers. Apparitions of a day, what is our puny warfare against the Philistines, compared with the warfare which this queen of romance has been waging against them for centuries, and will wage after we are gone?

I

THE FUNCTION OF CRITICISM AT THE PRESENT TIME

MANY objections have been made to a proposition which, in some remarks of mine on translating Homer, I ventured to put forth; a proposition about criticism, and its importance at the present day. I said: 'Of the literature of France and Germany, as of the intellect of Europe in general, the main effort, for now many years, has been a critical effort; the endeavour, in all branches of knowledge, theology, philosophy, history, art, science, to see the object as in itself it really is.' I added, that owing to the operation in English literature of certain causes, 'almost the last thing for which one would come to English literature is just that very thing which now Europe most desires,—criticism'; and that the power and value of English literature was thereby impaired. More than one rejoinder declared that the importance I here assigned to criticism was excessive, and asserted the inherent superiority of the creative effort of the human spirit over its critical effort. And the other day, having been led by an excellent notice of Wordsworth [1] published in the *North British Review*, to turn again to his biography, I found, in the words of this great man, whom I, for one, must always listen to with the profoundest respect, a sentence passed on the critic's business, which seems to justify every possible disparagement of it. Wordsworth says in one of his letters:

> The writers in these publications [the Reviews], while they prosecute their inglorious employment, can not be supposed

[1] I cannot help thinking that a practice, common in England during the last century, and still followed in France, of printing a notice of this kind,—a notice by a competent critic,—to serve as an introduction to an eminent author's works, might be revived among us with advantage. To introduce all succeeding editions of Wordsworth, Mr Sharp's notice (it is permitted, I hope, to mention his name) might, it seems to me, excellently serve; it is written from the point of view of an admirer, nay, of a disciple, and that is right; but then the disciple must be also, as in this case he is, a critic, a man of letters, not, as too often happens, some relation or friend with no qualification for his task except affection for his author.

to be in a state of mind very favourable for being affected by the finer influences of a thing so pure as genuine poetry.

And a trustworthy reporter of his conversation quotes a more elaborate judgment to the same effect:

> Wordsworth holds the critical power very low, infinitely lower than the inventive; and he said today that if the quantity of time consumed in writing critiques on the works of others were given to original composition, of whatever kind it might be, it would be much better employed; it would make a man find out sooner his own level, and it would do infinitely less mischief. A false or malicious criticism may do much injury to the minds of others, a stupid invention, either in prose or verse, is quite harmless.

It is almost too much to expect of poor human nature, that a man capable of producing some effect in one line of literature, should, for the greater good of society, voluntarily doom himself to impotence and obscurity in another. Still less is this to be expected from men addicted to the composition of the 'false or malicious criticism', of which Wordsworth speaks. However, everybody would admit that a false or malicious criticism had better never have been written. Everybody, too, would be willing to admit, as a general proposition, that the critical faculty is lower than the inventive. But is it true that criticism is really, in itself, a baneful and injurious employment; is it true that all time given to writing critiques on the works of others would be much better employed if it were given to original composition, of whatever kind this may be? Is it true that Johnson had better have gone on producing more *Irenes* instead of writing his *Lives of the Poets*; nay, is it certain that Wordsworth himself was better employed in making his Ecclesiastical Sonnets than when he made his celebrated Preface, so full of criticism, and criticism of the works of others? Wordsworth was himself a great critic, and it is to be sincerely regretted that he has not left us more criticism; Goethe was one of the greatest of critics, and we may sincerely congratulate ourselves that he has left us so much criticism. Without wasting time over the exaggeration which Wordsworth's judgment on criticism clearly contains, or over an attempt to trace the causes,—not difficult I think to be traced, —which may have led Wordsworth to this exaggeration, a critic may with advantage seize an occasion for trying his own conscience, and for asking himself of what real service, at any given moment, the practice of criticism either is, or may be made, to his own mind and spirit, and to the minds and spirits of others.

The critical power is of lower rank than the creative. True; but in assenting to this proposition, one or two things are to be kept in mind. It is undeniable that the exercise of a creative power, that a free creative activity, is the highest function of man; it is proved to be so by man's finding in it his true happiness. But it is undeniable, also, that men may have the sense of exercising this free creative activity in other ways than in producing great works of literature or art; if it were not so, all but a very few men would be shut out from the true happiness of all men. They may have it in well-doing, they may have it in learning, they may have it even in criticizing. This is one thing to be kept in mind. Another is, that the exercise of the creative power in the production of great works of literature or art, however high this exercise of it may rank, is not at all epochs and under all conditions possible; and that therefore labour may be vainly spent in attempting it, which might with more fruit be used in preparing for it, in rendering it possible. This creative power works with elements, with materials; what if it has not those materials, those elements, ready for its use? In that case it must surely wait till they are ready. Now in literature,—I will limit myself to literature, for it is about literature that the question arises,—the elements with which the creative power works are ideas; the best ideas, on every matter which literature touches, current at the time. At any rate we may lay it down as certain that in modern literature no manifestation of the creative power not working with these can be very important or fruitful. And I say *current* at the time, not merely accessible at the time; for creative literary genius does not principally show itself in discovering new ideas; that is rather the business of the philosopher: the grand work of literary genius is a work of synthesis and exposition, not of analysis and discovery; its gift lies in the faculty of being happily inspired by a certain intellectual and spiritual atmosphere, by a certain order of ideas, when it finds itself in them; of dealing divinely with these ideas, presenting them in the most effective and attractive combinations,—making beautiful works with them, in short. But it must have the atmosphere, it must find itself amidst the order of ideas, in order to work freely; and these it is not so easy to command. This is why great creative epochs in literature are so rare; this is why there is so much that is unsatisfactory in the productions of many men of real genius; because for the creation of a master-work of literature two powers must concur, the power of the man and the power of the moment, and the man is not enough without the moment; the creative power has, for its happy exercise, appointed elements, and those elements are not in its own control.

Nay, they are more within the control of the critical power. It is the business of the critical power, as I said in the words already quoted, 'in all branches of knowledge, theology, philosophy, history, art, science, to see the object as in itself it really is'. Thus it tends, at last, to make an intellectual situation of which the creative power can profitably avail itself. It tends to establish an order of ideas, if not absolutely true, yet true by comparison with that which it displaces; to make the best ideas prevail. Presently these new ideas reach society, the touch of truth is the touch of life, and there is a stir and growth everywhere; out of this stir and growth come the creative epochs of literature.

Or, to narrow our range, and quit these considerations of the general march of genius and of society, considerations which are apt to become too abstract and impalpable,—everyone can see that a poet, for instance, ought to know life and the world before dealing with them in poetry; and life and the world being, in modern times, very complex things, the creation of a modern poet, to be worth much, implies a great critical effort behind it; else it must be a comparatively poor, barren, and short-lived affair. This is why Byron's poetry had so little endurance in it, and Goethe's so much; both Byron and Goethe had a great productive power, but Goethe's was nourished by a great critical effort providing the true materials for it, and Byron's was not; Goethe knew life and the world, the poet's necessary subjects, much more comprehensively and thoroughly than Byron. He knew a great deal more of them, and he knew them much more as they really are.

It has long seemed to me that the burst of creative activity in our literature, through the first quarter of this century, had about it, in fact, something premature; and that from this cause its productions are doomed, most of them, in spite of the sanguine hopes which accompanied and do still accompany them, to prove hardly more lasting than the productions of far less splendid epochs. And this prematureness comes from its having proceeded without having its proper data, without sufficient materials to work with. In other words, the English poetry of the first quarter of this century, with plenty of energy, plenty of creative force, did not know enough. This makes Byron so empty of matter, Shelley so incoherent, Wordsworth even, profound as he is, yet so wanting in completeness and variety. Wordsworth cared little for books, and disparaged Goethe. I admire Wordsworth, as he is, so much that I cannot wish him different; and it is vain, no doubt, to imagine such a man different from what he is, to suppose that he could have been different. But surely the one thing wanting to make Wordsworth an even greater poet than he is,—his thought richer, and his influence of wider application,—was that he should have read more books, among them, no doubt, those of that Goethe whom he disparaged without reading him.

But to speak of books and reading may easily lead to a misunderstanding here. It was not really books and reading that lacked to our poetry at this epoch; Shelley had plenty of reading, Coleridge had immense reading. Pindar and Sophocles—as we all say so glibly, and often with so little discernment of the real import of what we are saying—had not many books; Shakespeare was no deep reader. True; but in the Greece of Pindar and Sophocles, in the England of Shakespeare, the poet lived in a current of ideas in the highest degree animating and nourishing to the creative power; society was, in the fullest measure, permeated by fresh thought, intelligent and alive; and this state of things is the true basis for the creative power's exercise,—in this it finds its data, its materials, truly ready for its hand; all the books and reading in the world are only valuable as they are helps to this. Even when this does not actually exist, books and reading may enable a man to construct a kind of semblance of it in his own mind, a world of knowledge and intelligence in which he may live and work: this is by no means an equivalent, to the artist, for the nationally diffused life and thought of the epochs of Sophocles or Shakespeare, but, besides that it may be a means of preparation for such epochs, it does really constitute, if many share in it, a quickening and sustaining atmosphere of great value. Such an atmosphere the many-sided learning and the long and widely combined critical effort of Germany formed for Goethe, when he lived and worked. There was no national glow of life and thought there as in the Athens of Pericles, or the England of Elizabeth. That was the poet's weakness. But there was a sort of equivalent for it in the complete culture and unfettered thinking of a large body of Germans. That was his strength. In the England of the first quarter of this century, there was neither a national glow of life and thought, such as we had in the age of Elizabeth, nor yet a culture and a force of learning and criticism, such as were to be found in Germany. Therefore the creative power of poetry wanted, for success in the highest sense, materials and a basis; a thorough interpretation of the world was necessarily denied to it.

At first sight it seems strange that out of the immense stir of the French Revolution and its age should not have come a crop of works of genius equal to that which came out of the stir of the great productive time of Greece, or out of that of the Renascence, with its powerful episode the Reformation. But the truth is that the stir of the French Revolution took a character which essentially distinguished it from such movements as these. These were, in the main, disinterestedly intellectual and spiritual movements; movements in which the human spirit looked for its satisfaction in itself and in the increased play of its own activity: the French Revolution took a political, practical character. The movement which went on in France under the old régime, from 1700 to 1789, was far more really akin than that of the Revolution itself to the movement of the Renascence; the France of Voltaire and Rousseau told far more powerfully upon the mind of Europe than the France of the Revolution. Goethe reproached this last expressly with having 'thrown quiet culture back'. Nay, and the true key to how much in our Byron, even in our Wordsworth, is this!—that they had their source in a great movement of feeling, not in a great movement of mind. The French Revolution, however,—that object of so much blind love and so much blind hatred,—found undoubtedly its motive-power in the intelligence of men and not in their practical sense;—this is what distinguishes it from the English Revolution of Charles the First's time; this is what makes it a more spiritual event than our Revolution, an event of much more powerful and world-wide interest, though practically less successful;—it appeals to an order of ideas which are universal, certain, permanent. 1789 asked of a thing, Is it rational? 1642 asked of a thing, Is it legal? or, when it went furthest, Is it according to conscience? This is the English fashion; a fashion to be treated, within its own sphere, with the highest respect; for its success, within its own sphere, has been prodigious. But what is law in one place, is not law in another; what is law here today, is not law even here to-morrow; and as for conscience, what is binding on one man's conscience is not binding on another's; the old woman who threw her stool at the head of the surpliced minister in St Giles's Church at Edinburgh obeyed an impulse to which millions of the human race may be permitted to remain strangers. But the prescriptions of reason are absolute, unchanging, of universal validity; *to count by tens is the easiest way of counting,*—that is a proposition of which every one, from here to the Antipodes, feels the force; at least, I should say so, if we did not live in a country where it is not impossible that any morning we may find a letter in *The Times* declaring that a decimal coinage is an absurdity. That a whole nation should have been penetrated with an enthusiasm for pure reason, and with an ardent zeal for making its prescriptions triumph, is a very remarkable thing, when we consider how little of mind, or anything so worthy and quickening as mind, comes into the natives which alone, in general, impel great masses of men. In spite of the extravagant direction given to this enthusiasm, in spite of the crimes and follies in which it lost itself, the French Revolution derives from the force, truth, and universality of the ideas which it took for its law, and from the passion with which it could inspire a multitude for these ideas, a unique and still living power; it is—it will probably long remain—the greatest, the most animating event in history. And, as no sincere passion for the things of the mind, even though it turns out in many respects an unfortunate passion, is ever quite thrown away and quite barren of good, France has reaped from hers one fruit—the natural and legitimate fruit, though not precisely the grand fruit she expected: she is the country in Europe where *the people* is most alive.

But the mania for giving an immediate political and practical

application to all these fine ideas of the reason was fatal. Here an
Englishman is in his element: on this theme we can all go on for
hours. And all we are in the habit of saying on it has undoubtedly
a great deal of truth. Ideas cannot be too much prized in and for
themselves, cannot be too much lived with; but to transport
them abruptly into the world of politics and practice, violently
to revolutionize this world to their bidding,—that is quite
another thing. There is the world of ideas and there is the world
of practice; the French are often for suppressing the one and the
English the other; but neither is to be suppressed. A member
of the House of Commons said to me the other day: 'That a
thing is an anomaly, I consider to be no objection to it whatever.'
I venture to think he was wrong; that a thing is an anomaly *is*
an objection to it, but absolutely and in the sphere of ideas: it
is not necessarily, under such and such circumstances, or at
such and such a moment, an objection to it in the sphere of
politics and practice. Joubert has said beautifully: 'C'est la
force et la droit qui règlent toutes choses dans le monde; la force
en attendant le droit.' (Force and right are the governors of this
world; force till right is ready.) *Force till right is ready*; and till
right is ready, force, the existing order of things, is justified,
is the legitimate ruler. But right is something moral, and implies
inward recognition, free assent of the will; we are not ready for
right,—*right*, so far as we are concerned, *is not ready*,—until we
have attained this sense of seeing it and willing it. The way in
which for us it may change and transform force, the existing
order of things, and become, in its turn, the legitimate ruler of
the world, should depend on the way in which, when our time
comes, we see it and will it. Therefore for other people enamoured
of their own newly discerned right, to attempt to impose it upon
us as ours, and violently to substitute their right for our force,
is an act of tyranny, and to be resisted. It sets at nought the
second great half of our maxim, *force till right is ready*. This was
the grand error of the French Revolution; and its movement of
ideas, by quitting the intellectual sphere and rushing furiously
into the political sphere, ran, indeed, a prodigious and memorable course, but produced no such intellectual fruit as the movement of ideas of the Renascence, and created, in opposition to
itself, what I may call an *epoch of concentration*. The great force
of that epoch of concentration was England; and the great voice

of that epoch of concentration was Burke. It is the fashion to treat Burke's writings on the French Revolution as superannuated and conquered by the event; as the eloquent but unphilosophical tirades of bigotry and prejudice. I will not deny that they are often disfigured by the violence and passion of the moment, and that in some directions Burke's view was bounded, and his observation therefore at fault; but on the whole, and for those who can make the needful corrections, what distinguishes these writings is their profound, permanent, fruitful, philosophical truth; they contain the true philosophy of an epoch of concentration, dissipate the heavy atmosphere which its own nature is apt to engender round it, and make its resistance rational instead of mechanical.

But Burke is so great because, almost alone in England, he brings thought to bear upon politics, he saturates politics with thought; it is his accident that his ideas were at the service of an epoch of concentration, not of an epoch of expansion; it is his characteristic that he so lived by ideas, and had such a source of them welling up within him, that he could float even an epoch of concentration and English Tory politics with them. It does not hurt him that Dr Price and the Liberals were enraged with him; it does not even hurt him that George the Third and the Tories were enchanted with him. His greatness is that he lived in a world which neither English Liberalism nor English Toryism is apt to enter;—the world of ideas, not the world of catchwords and party habits. So far is it from being really true of him that he 'to party gave up what was meant for mankind', that at the very end of his fierce struggle with the French Revolution, after all his invectives against its false pretensions, hollowness, and madness, with his sincere conviction of its mischievousness, he can close a memorandum on the best means of combating it, some of the last pages he ever wrote,—the *Thoughts on French Affairs*, in December 1791,—with these striking words:

The evil is stated, in my opinion, as it exists. The remedy must be where power, wisdom, and information, I hope, are more united with good intentions than they can be with me. I have done with this subject, I believe, for ever. It has given me many anxious moments for the last two years. *If a great change is to be made in human affairs, the minds of men will be*

fitted to it; the general opinions and feelings will draw that way.
Every fear, every hope will forward it; and then they who persist
in opposing this mighty current in human affairs, will appear
rather to resist the decrees of Providence itself, than the mere
designs of men. They will not be resolute and firm, but perverse
and obstinate.'

That return of Burke upon himself has always seemed to me
one of the finest things in English literature, or indeed in any
literature. That is what I call living by ideas; when one side of a
question has long had your earnest support, when all your feelings are engaged, when you hear all round you no language but
one, when your party talks this language like a steam-engine and
can imagine no other,—still to be able to think, still to be irresistibly carried, if so it be, by the current of thought to the opposite
side of the question, and, like Balaam, to be unable to speak
anything *but what the Lord has put in your mouth.* I know nothing
more striking, and I must add that I know nothing more un-
English.

For the Englishman in general is like my friend the Member
of Parliament, and believes, point-blank, that for a thing to be
an anomaly is absolutely no objection to it whatever. He is like
the Lord Auckland of Burke's day, who, in a memorandum on
the French Revolution, talks of 'certain miscreants, assuming
the name of philosophers, who have presumed themselves
capable of establishing a new system of society'. The Englishman has been called a political animal, and he values what is
political and practical so much that ideas easily become objects
of dislike in his eyes, and thinkers 'miscreants', because ideas
and thinkers have rashly meddled with politics and practice.
This would be all very well if the dislike and neglect confined
themselves to ideas transported out of their own sphere, and
meddling rashly with practice; but they are inevitably extended
to ideas as such, and to the whole life of intelligence; practice is
everything, a free play of the mind is nothing. The notion of the
free play of the mind upon all subjects being a pleasure in itself,
being an object of desire, being an essential provider of elements
without which a nation's spirit, whatever compensations it may
have for them, must, in the long run, die of inanition, hardly
enters into an Englishman's thoughts. It is noticeable that the

word *curiosity*, which in other languages is used in a good sense, to mean, as a high and fine quality of man's nature, just this disinterested love of a free play of the mind on all subjects, for its own sake,—it is noticeable, I say, that this word has in our language no sense of the kind, no sense but a rather bad and disparaging one. But criticism, real criticism, is essentially the exercise of this very quality; it obeys an instinct prompting it to know the best that is known and thought in the world, irrespectively of practice, politics, and everything of the kind; and to value knowledge and thought as they approach this best, without the intrusion of any other considerations whatever. This is an instinct for which there is, I think, little original sympathy in the practical English nature, and what there was of it has undergone a long benumbing period of blight and suppression in the epoch of concentration which followed the French Revolution.

But epochs of concentration cannot well endure for ever; epochs of expansion, in the due course of things, follow them. Such an epoch of expansion seems to be opening in this country. In the first place all danger of a hostile forcible pressure of foreign ideas upon our practice has long disappeared; like the traveller in the fable, therefore, we begin to wear our cloak a little more loosely. Then, with a long peace, the ideas of Europe steal gradually and amicably in, and mingle, though in infinitesimally small quantities at a time, with our own notions. Then, too, in spite of all that is said about the absorbing and brutalizing influence of our passionate material progress, it seems to me indisputable that this progress is likely, though not certain, to lead in the end to an apparition of intellectual life; and that man, after he has made himself perfectly comfortable and has now to determine what to do with himself next, may begin to remember that he has a mind, and that the mind may be made the source of great pleasure. I grant it is mainly the privilege of faith, at present, to discern this end to our railways, our business, and our fortune-making; but we shall see if, here as elsewhere, faith is not in the end the true prophet. Our ease, our travelling, and our unbounded liberty to hold just as hard and securely as we please to the practice to which our notions have given birth, all tend to beget an inclination to deal a little more freely with these notions themselves, to canvass them a little, to penetrate a little into their real nature. Flutterings of curiosity, in the foreign sense of the word, appear amongst us, and it is in these that criticism must look to find its account. Criticism first; a time of true creative activity, perhaps,—which, as I have said, must inevitably be preceded amongst us by a time of criticism,—hereafter, when criticism has done its work.

It is of the last importance that English criticism should clearly discern what rule for its course, in order to avail itself of the field now opening to it, and to produce fruit for the future, it ought to take. The rule may be summed up in one word,— *disinterestedness*. And how is criticism to show disinterestedness? By keeping aloof from practice; by resolutely following the law of its own nature, which is to be a free play of the mind on all subjects which it touches; by steadily refusing to lend itself to any of those ulterior, political, practical considerations about ideas which plenty of people will be sure to attach to them, which perhaps ought often to be attached to them, which in this country at any rate are certain to be attached to them quite sufficiently, but which criticism has really nothing to do with. Its business is, as I have said, simply to know the best that is known and thought in the world, and by in its turn making this known, to create a current of true and fresh ideas. Its business is to do this with inflexible honesty, with due ability; but its business is to do no more, and to leave alone all questions of practical consequences and applications, questions which will never fail to have due prominence given to them. Else criticism, besides being really false to its own nature, merely continues in the old rut which it has hitherto followed in this country, and will certainly miss the chance now given to it. For what is at present the bane of criticism in this country? It is that practical considerations cling to it and stifle it; it subserves interests not its own; our organs of criticism are organs of men and parties having practical ends to serve, and with them those practical ends are the first thing and the play of mind the second; so much play of mind as is compatible with the prosecution of those practical ends is all that is wanted. An organ like the *Revue des Deux Mondes*, having for its main function to understand and utter the best that is known and thought in the world, existing, it may be said, as just an organ for a free play of the mind, we have not; but we have the *Edinburgh Review*, existing as an organ of the

old Whigs, and for as much play of the mind as may suit its
being that; we have the *Quarterly Review*, existing as an organ
of the Tories, and for as much play of mind as may suit its being
that; we have the *British Quarterly Review*, existing as an organ
of the political Dissenters, and for as much play of mind as may
suit its being that; we have *The Times*, existing as an organ of the
common, satisfied, well-to-do Englishman, and for as much play
of mind as may suit its being that. And so on through all the
various fractions, political and religious, of our society; every
fraction has, as such, its organ of criticism, but the notions of
combining all fractions in the common pleasure of a free disinterested play of mind meets with no favour. Directly this play
of mind wants to have more scope, and to forget the pressure of
practical considerations a little, it is checked, it is made to feel
the chain; we saw this the other day in the extinction, so much
to be regretted, of the *Home and Foreign Review*; perhaps in no
organ of criticism in this country was there so much knowledge,
so much play of mind; but these could not save it: the *Dublin
Review* subordinates play of mind to the practical business of
English and Irish Catholicism, and lives. It must needs be that
men should act in sects and parties, that each of these sects and
parties should have its organ, and should make this organ sub-
serve the interests of its action; but it would be well, too, that
there should be a criticism, not the minister of these interests,
not their enemy, but absolutely and entirely independent of
them. No other criticism will ever attain any real authority or
make any real way towards its end,—the creating a current of
true and fresh ideas.

It is because criticism has so little kept in the pure intellectual
sphere, has so little detached itself from practice, has been so
directly polemical and controversial, that it has so ill accomplished, in this country, its best spiritual work; which is to keep
man from a self-satisfaction which is retarding and vulgarizing,
to lead him towards perfection, by making his mind dwell upon
what is excellent in itself, and the absolute beauty and fitness of
things. A polemical practical criticism makes men blind even
to the ideal imperfection of their practice, makes them willingly
assert its ideal perfection, in order the better to secure it against
attack; and clearly this is narrowing and baneful for them. If they
were reassured on the practical side, speculative considerations

of ideal perfection they might be brought to entertain, and their spiritual horizon would thus gradually widen. Mr Adderley says to the Warwickshire farmers:

> Talk of the improvement of breed! Why, the race we ourselves represent, the men and women, the old Anglo-Saxon race, are the best breed in the whole world. . . . The absence of a too enervating climate, too unclouded skies, and a too luxurious nature, has produced so vigorous a race of people, and has rendered us so superior to all the world.

Mr Roebuck says to the Sheffield cutlers:

> I look around me and ask what is the state of England? Is not property safe? Is not every man able to say what he likes? Can you not walk from one end of England to the other in perfect security? I ask you whether, the world over or in past history, there is anything like it? Nothing. I pray that our unrivalled happiness may last.

Now obviously there is a peril for poor human nature in words and thoughts of such exuberant self-satisfaction, until we find ourselves safe in the streets of the Celestial City.

> Das wenige verschwindet leicht dem Blicke
> Der vorwärts sieht, wie viel noch übrig bleibt—

says Goethe; the little that is done seems nothing when we look forward and see how much we have yet to do. Clearly this is a better line of reflection for weak humanity, so long as it remains on this earthly field of labour and trial.

But neither Mr Adderley nor Mr Roebuck is by nature inaccessible to considerations of this sort. They only lose sight of them owing to the controversial life we all lead, and the practical form which all speculation takes with us. They have in view opponents whose aim is not ideal, but practical; and in their zeal to uphold their own practice against these innovators, they go so far as even to attribute to this practice an ideal perfection. Somebody has been wanting to introduce a six-pound franchise, or to abolish church-rates, or to collect agricultural statistics by force, or to diminish local self-government. How natural, in reply to such proposals, very likely improper or ill-timed, to go a little beyond the mark and to say stoutly: 'Such a race of people as we stand, so superior to all the world! The old Anglo-Saxon race, the best breed in the whole world! I pray that our unrivalled happiness may last! I ask you whether, the world over or in past history, there is anything like it?' And so long as criticism answers this dithyramb by insisting that the old Anglo-Saxon race would be still more superior to all others if it had no church-rates, or that our unrivalled happiness would last yet longer with a six-pound franchise, so long will the strain, 'The best breed in the whole world!' swell louder and louder, everything ideal and refining will be lost out of sight, and both the assailed and their critics will remain in a sphere, to say the truth, perfectly unvital, a sphere in which spiritual progression is impossible. But let criticism leave church-rates and the franchise alone, and in the most candid spirit, without a single lurking thought of practical innovation, confront with our dithyramb this paragraph on which I stumbled in a newspaper immediately after reading Mr Roebuck:

A shocking child murder has just been committed at Nottingham. A girl named Wragg left the workhouse there on Saturday morning with her young illegitimate child. The child was soon afterwards found dead on Mapperly Hills, having been strangled. Wragg is in custody.

Nothing but that; but, in juxtaposition with the absolute eulogies of Mr Adderley and Mr Roebuck, how eloquent, how suggestive are those few lines! 'Our old Anglo-Saxon breed, the best in the whole world!'—how much that is harsh and ill-favoured there is in this best! *Wragg!* If we are to talk of ideal perfection, of 'the best in the whole world', has anyone reflected what a touch of grossness in our race, what an original shortcoming in the more delicate spiritual perceptions, is shown by the natural growth amongst us of such hideous names,—Higginbottom, Stiggins, Bugg! In Ionia and Attica they were luckier in this respect than 'the best race in the world'; by the Ilissus there was no Wragg, poor thing! And 'our unrivalled happiness';— what an element of grimness, bareness, and hideousness mixes with it and blurs it; the workhouse, the dismal Mapperly Hills,— how dismal those who have seen them will remember;—the gloom, the smoke, the cold, the strangled illegitimate child! 'I ask you whether, the world over or in past history, there is any-thing like it?' Perhaps not, one is inclined to answer; but at any

rate, in that case, the world is very much to be pitied. And the
final touch,—short, bleak, and inhuman: *Wragg is in custody.*
The sex lost in the confusion of our unrivalled happiness; or
(shall I say?) the superfluous Christian name lopped off by the
straightforward vigour of our old Anglo-Saxon breed! There is
profit for the spirit in such contrasts as this; criticism serves the
cause of perfection by establishing them. By eluding sterile
conflict, by refusing to remain in the sphere where alone narrow
and relative conceptions have any worth and validity, criticism
may diminish its momentary importance, but only in this way
has it a chance of gaining admittance for those wider and more
perfect conceptions to which all its duty is really owed. Mr
Roebuck will have a poor opinion of an adversary who replies
to his defiant songs of triumph only by murmuring under his
breath, *Wragg is in custody*; but in no other way will these songs
of triumph be induced gradually to moderate themselves, to
get rid of what in them is excessive and offensive, and to fall
into a softer and truer key.

It will be said that it is a very subtle and indirect action which
I am thus prescribing for criticism, and that, by embracing in
this manner the Indian virtue of detachment and abandoning
the sphere of practical life, it condemns itself to a slow and
obscure work. Slow and obscure it may be, but it is the only
proper work of criticism. The mass of mankind will never have
any ardent zeal for seeing things as they are; very inadequate
ideas will always satisfy them. On these inadequate ideas reposes,
and must repose, the general practice of the world. That is as
much as saying that whoever sets himself to see things as they
are will find himself one of a very small circle; but it is only by
this small circle resolutely doing its own work that adequate
ideas will ever get current at all. The rush and roar of practical
life will always have a dizzying and attracting effect upon the
most collected spectator, and tend to draw him into its vortex;
most of all will this be the case where that life is so powerful as
it is in England. But it is only by remaining collected, and refusing to lend himself to the point of view of the practical man,
that the critic can do the practical man any service; and it is
only by the greatest sincerity in pursuing his own course, and
by at last convincing even the practical man of his sincerity, that
he can escape misunderstandings which perpetually threaten him.

For the practical man is not apt for fine distinctions, and yet in these distinctions truth and the highest culture greatly find their account. But it is not easy to lead a practical man—unless you reassure him as to your practical intentions, you have no chance of leading him—to see that a thing which he has always been used to look at from one side only, which he greatly values, and which, looked at from that side, quite deserves, perhaps, all the prizing and admiring which he bestows upon it,—that this thing, looked at from another side, may appear much less beneficent and beautiful, and yet retain all its claims to our practical allegiance. Where shall we find language innocent enough, how shall we make the spotless purity of our intentions evident enough, to enable us to say to the political Englishman that the British Constitution itself, which, seen from the practical side, looks such a magnificent organ of progress and virtue, seen from the speculative side,—with its compromises, its love of facts, its horror of theory, its studied avoidance of clear thoughts,—that, seen from this side, our august Constitution sometimes looks,—forgive me, shade of Lord Somers!—a colossal machine for the manufacture of Philistines? How is Cobbett to say this and not be misunderstood, blackened as he is with the smoke of a lifelong conflict in the field of political practice? how is Mr Carlyle to say it and not be misunderstood, after his furious raid into this field with his *Latter-day Pamphlets*? how is Mr Ruskin, after his pugnacious political economy? I say, the critic must keep out of the region of immediate practice in the political, social, humanitarian sphere, if he wants to make a beginning for that more free speculative treatment of things, which may perhaps one day make its benefits felt even in this sphere, but in a natural and thence irresistible manner.

Do what he will, however, the critic will still remain exposed to frequent misunderstandings, and nowhere so much as in this country. For here people are particularly indisposed even to comprehend that without this free disinterested treatment of things, truth and the highest culture are out of the question. So immersed are they in practical life, so accustomed to take all their notions from this life and its processes, that they are apt to think that truth and culture themselves can be reached by the processes of this life, and that it is an impertinent singularity to think of reaching them in any other. 'We are all *terrae filii*,' cries their eloquent advocate; 'all Philistines together. Away with the notion of proceeding by any other course than the course dear to the Philistines; let us have a social movement, let us organize and combine a party to pursue truth and new thought, let us call it *the liberal party*, and let us all stick to each other, and back each other up. Let us have no nonsense about independent criticism, and intellectual delicacy, and the few and the many. Don't let us trouble ourselves about foreign thought; we shall invent the whole thing for ourselves as we go along: if one of us speaks well, applaud him; if one of us speaks ill, applaud him too; we are all in the same movement, we are all liberals, we are all in pursuit of truth.' In this way the pursuit of truth becomes really a social, practical, pleasurable affair, almost requiring a chairman, a secretary, and advertisements; with the excitement of an occasional scandal, with a little resistance to give the happy sense of difficulty overcome; but, in general, plenty of bustle and very little thought. To act is so easy, as Goethe says; to think is so hard! It is true that the critic has many temptations to go with the stream, to make one of the party movement, one of these *terrae filii*; it seems ungracious to refuse to be a *terrae filius*, when so many excellent people are; but the critic's duty is to refuse, or, if resistance is vain, at least to cry with Obermann: *Périssons en résistant*.

How serious a matter it is to try and resist, I had ample opportunity of experiencing when I ventured some time ago to criticize the celebrated first volume of Bishop Colenso.[1] The echoes of the storm which was then raised I still, from time to time, hear grumbling round me. That storm arose out of a misunderstanding almost inevitable. It is a result of no little culture to attain to a clear perception that science and religion are two wholly different things; the multitude will for ever confuse them; but happily that is of no great real importance, for while the

---

[1] So sincere is my dislike to all personal attack and controversy, that I abstain from reprinting, at this distance of time from the occasion which called them forth, the essays in which I criticized Dr Colenso's book; I feel bound, however, after all that has passed, to make here a final declaration of my sincere impenitence for having published them. Nay, I cannot forbear repeating yet once more, for his benefit and that of his readers, this sentence from my original remarks upon him: *There is truth of science and truth of religion; truth of science does not become truth of religion till it is made religious.* And I will add: Let us have all the science there is from the men of science; from the men of religion let us have religion.

multitude imagines itself to live by its false science, it does really live by its true religion. Dr Colenso, however, in his first volume did all he could to strengthen the confusion,[1] and to make it dangerous. He did this with the best intentions, I freely admit, and with the most candid ignorance that this was the natural effect of what he was doing; but, says Joubert, 'Ignorance, which in matters of morals extenuates the crime, is itself, in intellectual matters, a crime of the first order.' I criticized Bishop Colenso's speculative confusion. Immediately there was a cry raised: 'What is this? here is a liberal attacking a liberal. Do not you belong to the movement? are not you a friend of truth? Is not Bishop Colenso in pursuit of truth? then speak with proper respect of his book. Dr Stanley is another friend of truth, and you speak with proper respect of his book; why make these invidious differences? both books are excellent, admirable, liberal; Bishop Colenso's perhaps the most so, because it is the boldest, and will have the best practical consequences for the liberal cause. Do you want to encourage to the attack of a brother liberal his, and your, and our implacable enemies, the *Church and State Review* or the *Record*,—the High Church rhinoceros and the Evangelical hyaena? Be silent, therefore; or rather speak, speak as loud as ever you can, and go into ecstasies over the eighty and odd pigeons.'

But criticism cannot follow this coarse and indiscriminate method. It is unfortunately possible for a man in pursuit of truth to write a book which reposes upon a false conception. Even the practical consequences of a book are to genuine criticism no recommendation of it, if the book is, in the highest sense, blundering. I see that a lady who herself, too, is in pursuit of truth, and who writes with great ability, but a little too much, perhaps, under the influence of the practical spirit of the English liberal movement, classes Bishop Colenso's book and M. Renan's together, in her survey of the religious state of Europe, as facts of the same order, works, both of them, of 'great importance'; 'great ability, power, and skill'; Bishop Colenso's, perhaps, the most powerful; at least, Miss Cobbe gives special expression to her gratitude that to Bishop Colenso 'has been given the

---

[1] It has been said I make it 'a crime against literary criticism and the higher culture to attempt to inform the ignorant'. Need I point out that the ignorant are not informed by being confirmed in a confusion?

strength to grasp, and the courage to teach, truths of such deep
import'. In the same way, more than one popular writer has
compared him to Luther. Now it is just this kind of false estimate
which the critical spirit is, it seems to me, bound to resist. It is
really the strongest possible proof of the low ebb at which, in
England, the critical spirit is, that while the critical hit in the
religious literature of Germany is Dr Strauss's book, in that of
France M. Renan's book, the book of Bishop Colenso is the
critical hit in the religious literature of England. Bishop Colenso's
book reposes on a total misconception of the essential elements
of the religious problem, as that problem is now presented for
solution. To criticism, therefore, which seeks to have the best
that is known and thought on this problem, it is, however well
meant, of no importance whatever. M. Renan's book attempts a
new synthesis of the elements furnished to us by the Four
Gospels. It attempts, in my opinion, a synthesis, perhaps premature, perhaps impossible, certainly not successful. Up to the
present time, at any rate, we must acquiesce in Fleury's sentence
on such recastings of the Gospel story: *Quiconque s'imagine la
pouvoir mieux écrire, ne l'entend pas.* M. Renan had himself passed
by anticipation a like sentence on his own work, when he said:
'If a new presentation of the character of Jesus were offered to
me, I would not have it; its very clearness would be, in my
opinion, the best proof of its insufficiency.' His friends may with
perfect justice rejoin that at the sight of the Holy Land, and of
the actual scene of the Gospel story, all the current of M.
Renan's thoughts may have naturally changed, and a new casting
of that story irresistibly suggested itself to him; and that this
is just a case for applying Cicero's maxim: Change of mind
is not inconsistency—*nemo doctus unquam mutationem consilii
inconstantiam dixit esse.* Nevertheless, for criticism, M. Renan's
first thought must still be the truer one, as long as his new
casting so fails more fully to commend itself, more fully (to
use Coleridge's happy phrase about the Bible) to *find* us. Still
M. Renan's attempt is, for criticism, of the most real interest
and importance, since, with all its difficulty, a fresh synthesis
of the New Testament *data,*—not a making war on them, in
Voltaire's fashion, not a leaving them out of mind, in the world's
fashion, but the putting a new construction upon them, the
taking them from under the old, adoptive, traditional, unspiritual

point of view and placing them under a new one,—is the very essence of the religious problem, as now presented; and only by efforts in this direction can it receive a solution.

Again, in the same spirit in which she judges Bishop Colenso, Miss Cobbe, like so many earnest liberals of our practical race, both here and in America, herself sets vigorously about a positive reconstruction of religion, about making a religion of the future out of hand, or at least setting about making it; we must not rest, she and they are always thinking and saying, in negative criticism, we must be creative and constructive; hence we have such works as her recent *Religious Duty*, and works still more considerable, perhaps, by others, which will be in everyone's mind. These works often have much ability; they often spring out of sincere convictions, and a sincere wish to do good; and they sometimes, perhaps, do good. Their fault is (if I may be permitted to say so) one which they have in common with the British College of Health, in the New Road. Everyone knows the British College of Health; it is that building with the lion and the statue of the Goddess Hygeia before it; at least I am sure about the lion, though I am not absolutely certain about the Goddess Hygeia. This building does credit, perhaps, to the resources of Dr Morrison and his disciples; but it falls a good deal short of one's idea of what a British College of Health ought to be. In England, where we hate public interference and love individual enterprise, we have a whole crop of places like the British College of Health; the grand name without the grand thing. Unluckily, creditable to individual enterprise as they are, they tend to impair our taste by making us forget what more grandiose, noble, or beautiful character properly belongs to a public institution. The same may be said of the religions of the future of Miss Cobbe and others. Creditable, like the British College of Health, to the resources of their authors, they yet tend to make us forget what more grandiose, noble, or beautiful character properly belongs to religious constructions. The historic religions, with all their faults, have had this; it certainly belongs to the religious sentiment, when it truly flowers, to have this; and we impoverish our spirit if we allow a religion of the future without it. What then is the duty of criticism here? To take the practical point of view, to applaud the liberal movement and all its works,—its New Road religions of the future into the bargain,—for their general utility's sake? By no means; but to be perpetually dissatisfied with these works, while they perpetually fall short of a high and perfect ideal.

For criticism, these are elementary laws; but they never can be popular, and in this country they have been very little followed, and one meets with immense obstacles in following them. That is a reason for asserting them again and again. Criticism must maintain its independence of the practical spirit and its aims. Even with well-meant efforts of the practical spirit it must express dissatisfaction, if in the sphere of the ideal they seem impoverishing and limiting. It must not hurry on to the goal because of its practical importance. It must be patient, and know how to wait; and flexible, and know how to attach itself to things and how to withdraw from them. It must be apt to study and praise elements that for the fulness of spiritual perfection are wanted, even though they belong to a power which in the practical sphere may be maleficent. It must be apt to discern the spiritual shortcomings or illusions of powers that in the practical sphere may be beneficent. And this without any notion of favouring or injuring, in the practical sphere, one power or the other; without any notion of playing off, in this sphere, one power against the other. When one looks, for instance, at the English Divorce Court,—an institution which perhaps has its practical conveniences, but which in the ideal sphere is so hideous; an institution which neither makes divorce impossible nor makes it decent, which allows a man to get rid of his wife, or a wife of her husband, but makes them drag one another first, for the public edification, through a mire of unutterable infamy,—when one looks at this charming institution, I say, with its crowded benches, its newspaper-reports, and its money-compensations, this institution in which the gross unregenerate British Philistine has indeed stamped an image of himself,—one may be permitted to find the marriage-theory of Catholicism refreshing and elevating. Or when Protestantism, in virtue of its supposed rational and intellectual origin, gives the law to criticism too magisterially, criticism may and must remind it that its pretensions, in this respect, are illusive and do it harm; that the Reformation was a moral rather than an intellectual event; that Luther's theory of grace no more exactly reflects the mind of the spirit than Bossuet's philosophy of history reflects it; and that there is no more antecedent probability of the Bishop of Durham's stock of ideas being agreeable to perfect reason than of Pope Pius the Ninth's. But criticism will not on that account forget the achievements of Protestantism in the practical and moral sphere; nor that, even in the intellectual sphere, Protestantism, though in a blind and stumbling manner, carried forward the Renascence, while Catholicism threw itself violently across its path.

I lately heard a man of thought and energy contrasting the want of ardour and movement which he now found amongst young men in this country with what he remembered in his own youth, twenty years ago. 'What reformers we were then!' he exclaimed; 'what a zeal we had! how we canvassed every institution in Church and State, and were prepared to remodel them all on first principles!' He was inclined to regret, as a spiritual flagging, the lull which he saw. I am disposed rather to regard it as a pause in which the turn to a new mode of spiritual progress is being accomplished; everything was long seen, by the young and ardent amongst us, in inseparable connection with politics and practical life; we have pretty well exhausted the benefits of seeing things in this connection, we have got all that can be got by so seeing them. Let us try a more disinterested mode of seeing them; let us betake ourselves more to the serener life of the mind and spirit. This life, too, may have its excesses and dangers; but they are not for us at present. Let us think of quietly enlarging our stock of true and fresh ideas, and not, as soon as we get an idea or half an idea, be running out with it into the street, and trying to make it rule there. Our ideas will, in the end, shape the world all the better for maturing a little. Perhaps in fifty years' time it will in the English House of Commons be an objection to an institution that it is an anomaly, and my friend the Member of Parliament will shudder in his grave. But let us in the meanwhile rather endeavour that in twenty years' time it may, in English literature, be an objection to a proposition that it is absurd. That will be a change so vast, that the imagination almost fails to grasp it. *Ab integro saeclorum nascitur ordo.*

If I have insisted so much on the course which criticism must take where politics and religion are concerned, it is because, where these burning matters are in question, it is most likely to go astray. I have wished, above all, to insist on the attitude which criticism should adopt towards everything; on its right tone and temper of mind. Then comes the question as to the subject-matter which criticism should most seek. Here, in general, its course is determined for it by the idea which is the law of its being; the idea of a disinterested endeavour to learn and propagate the best that is known and thought in the world, and thus to establish a current of fresh and true ideas. By the very nature of things, as England is not all the world, much of the best that is known and thought in the world cannot be of English growth, must be foreign; by the nature of things, again, it is just this that we are least likely to know, while English thought is streaming in upon us from all sides, and takes excellent care that we shall not be ignorant of its existence; the English critic, there-fore, must dwell much on foreign thought, and with particular heed on any part of it, which, while significant and fruitful in itself, is for any reason specially likely to escape him. Again, judging is often spoken of as the critic's one business, and so in some sense it is; but the judgment which almost insensibly forms itself in a fair and clear mind, along with fresh knowledge, is the valuable one; and thus knowledge, and ever fresh knowledge, must be the critic's great concern for himself; and it is by com-municating fresh knowledge, and letting his own judgment pass along with it,—but insensibly, and in the second place not the first, as a sort of companion and clue, not as an abstract law-giver,—that he will generally do most good to his readers. Sometimes, no doubt, for the sake of establishing an author's place in literature, and his relation to a central standard (and if this is not done, how are we to get at our *best in the world*?) criticism may have to deal with a subject-matter so familiar that fresh knowledge is out of the question, and then it must be all judgment; an enunciation and detailed application of principles. Here the great safeguard is never to let oneself become abstract, always to retain an intimate and lively consciousness of the truth of what one is saying, and, the moment this fails us, to be sure that something is wrong. Still, under all circumstances, this mere judgment and application of principles is, in itself, not the most satisfactory work to the critic; like mathematics, it is tautological, and cannot well give us, like fresh learning, the sense of creative activity.

But stop, someone will say; all this talk is of no practical use to us whatever; this criticism of yours is not what we have in our minds when we speak of criticism; when we speak of critics and criticism, we mean critics and criticism of the current English literature of the day; when you offer to tell criticism its function, it is to this criticism that we expect you to address yourself. I am sorry for it, for I am afraid I must disappoint these expectations. I am bound by my own definition of criticism: *a disinterested endeavour to learn and propagate the best that is known and thought in the world.* How much of current English literature comes into this 'best that is known and thought in the world'? Not very much, I fear; certainly less, at this moment, than of the current literature of France or Germany. Well, then, am I to alter my definition of criticism, in order to meet the requirements of a number of practising English critics, who, after all, are free in their choice of a business? That would be making criticism lend itself just to one of those alien practical considerations, which, I have said, are so fatal to it. One may say, indeed, to those who have to deal with the mass—so much better disregarded—of current English literature, that they may at all events endeavour, in dealing with this, to try it, so far as they can, by the standard of the best that is known and thought in the world; one may say, that to get anywhere near this standard, every critic should try and possess one great literature, at least, besides his own; and the more unlike his own, the better. But, after all, the criticism I am really concerned with,—the criticism which alone can much help us for the future, the criticism which, throughout Europe, is at the present day meant, when so much stress is laid on the importance of criticism and the critical spirit,—is a criticism which regards Europe as being, for intellectual and spiritual purposes, one great confederation, bound to a joint action and working to a common result; and whose members have, for their proper outfit, a knowledge of Greek, Roman, and Eastern antiquity, and of one another. Special, local, and temporary advantages being put out of account, that modern nation will in the intellectual and spiritual sphere make most progress, which most thoroughly carries out this programme. And what is that but saying that we too, all of us, as individuals, the more thoroughly we carry it out, shall make the more progress?

There is so much inviting us!—what are we to take? what will nourish us in growth towards perfection? That is the question which, with the immense field of life and of literature lying before him, the critic has to answer; for himself first, and afterwards for others. In this idea of the critic's business the essays brought together in the following pages have had their origin; in this idea, widely different as are their subjects, they have, perhaps, their unity.

I conclude with what I said at the beginning: to have the sense of creative activity is the great happiness and the great proof of being alive, and it is not denied to criticism to have it; but then criticism must be sincere, simple, flexible, ardent, ever widening its knowledge. Then it may have, in no contemptible measure, a joyful sense of creative activity; a sense which a man of insight and conscience will prefer to what he might derive from a poor, starved, fragmentary, inadequate creation. And at some epochs no other creation is possible.

Still, in full measure, the sense of creative activity belongs only to genuine creation; in literature we must never forget that. But what true man of letters ever can forget it? It is no such common matter for a gifted nature to come into possession of a current of true and living ideas, and to produce amidst the inspiration of them, that we are likely to underrate it. The epochs of Aeschylus and Shakespeare make us feel their pre-eminence. In an epoch like those is, no doubt, the true life of a literature; there is the promised land, towards which criticism can only beckon. That promised land it will not be ours to enter, and we shall die in the wilderness: but to have desired to enter it, to have saluted it from afar, is already, perhaps, the best distinction among contemporaries; it will certainly be the best title to esteem with posterity.

II

THE LITERARY INFLUENCE OF ACADEMIES

IT IS impossible to put down a book like the history of the French Academy, by Pellisson and D'Olivet, which M. Charles Livet has lately re-edited, without being led to reflect upon the absence, in our own country, of any institution like the French Academy, upon the probable causes of this absence, and upon its results. A thousand voices will be ready to tell us that this absence is a signal mark of our national superiority; that it is in great part owing to this absence that the exhilarating words of Lord Macaulay, lately given to the world by his clever nephew, Mr Trevelyan, are so profoundly true: 'It may safely be said that the literature now extant in the English language is of far greater value than all the literature which three hundred years ago was extant in all the languages of the world together.' I daresay this is so, only, remembering Spinoza's maxim that the two great banes of humanity are self-conceit and the laziness coming from self-conceit, I think it may do us good, instead of resting in our pre-eminence with perfect security, to look a little more closely why this is so, and whether it is so without any limitations.

But first of all I must give a very few words to the outward history of the French Academy. About the year 1629, seven or eight persons in Paris, fond of literature, formed themselves into a sort of little club to meet at one another's houses and discuss literary matters. Their meetings got talked of, and Cardinal Richelieu, then minister and all-powerful, heard of them. He himself had a noble passion for letters, and for all fine culture; he was interested by what he heard of the nascent society. Himself a man in the grand style, if ever man was, he had the insight to perceive what a potent instrument of the grand style was here to his hand. It was the beginning of a great century for France, the seventeenth; men's minds were working, the

French language was forming. Richelieu sent to ask the members of the new society whether they would be willing to become a body with a public character, holding regular meetings. Not without a little hesitation,—for apparently they found themselves very well as they were, and these seven or eight gentlemen of a social and literary turn were not perfectly at their ease as to what the great and terrible minister could want with them,—they consented. The favours of a man like Richelieu are not easily refused, whether they are honestly meant or no; but this favour of Richelieu's was meant quite honestly. The Parliament, however, had its doubts of this. The Parliament had none of Richelieu's enthusiasm about letters and culture; it was jealous of the apparition of a new public body in the State; above all, of a body called into existence by Richelieu. The King's letters patent, establishing and authorizing the new society, were granted early in 1635; but, by the old constitution of France, these letters patent required the verification of the Parliament. It was two years and a half,—towards the autumn of 1637,—before the Parliament would give it; and it then gave it only after pressing solicitations, and earnest assurances of the innocent intentions of the young Academy. Jocose people said that this society, with its mission to purify and embellish the language, filled with terror a body of lawyers like the French Parliament, the stronghold of barbarous jargon and of chicane.

This improvement of the language was in truth the declared grand aim for the operations of the Academy. Its statutes of foundation, approved by Richelieu before the royal edict establishing it was issued, say expressly: 'The Academy's principal function shall be to work with all the care and all the diligence possible at giving sure rules to our language, and rendering it pure, eloquent, and capable of treating the arts and sciences.' This zeal for making a nation's great instrument of thought,—its language,—correct and worthy, is undoubtedly a sign full of promise, a weighty earnest of future power. It is said that Richelieu had it in his mind that French should succeed Latin in its general ascendency, as Latin had succeeded Greek; if it was so, even this wish has to some extent been fulfilled. But, at any rate, the *ethical* influences of style in language,—its close relations, so often pointed out, with character,—are most important. Richelieu, a man of high culture, and, at the same time, of great character, felt them profoundly; and that he should have sought to regularize, strengthen, and perpetuate them by an institution for perfecting language, is alone a striking proof of his governing spirit and of his genius.

This was not all he had in his mind, however. The new Academy, now enlarged to a body of forty members, and meant to contain all the chief literary men of France, was to be a *literary tribunal*. The works of its members were to be brought before it previous to publication, were to be criticized by it, and finally, if it saw fit, to be published with its declared approbation. The works of other writers, not members of the Academy, might also, at the request of these writers themselves, be passed under the Academy's review. Besides this, in essays and discussions the Academy examined and judged works already published, whether by living or dead authors, and literary matters in general. The celebrated opinion on Corneille's *Cid*, delivered in 1637 by the Academy at Richelieu's urgent request, when this poem, which strongly occupied public attention, had been attacked by M. de Scudéry, shows how fully Richelieu designed his new creation to do duty as a supreme court of literature, and how early it in fact began to exercise this function. One [1] who had known Richelieu declared, after the Cardinal's death, that he had projected a yet greater institution than the Academy, a sort of grand European college of art, science, and literature, a Prytaneum, where the chief authors of all Europe should be gathered together in one central home, there to live in security, leisure, and honour; —that was a dream which will not bear to be pulled about too roughly. But the project of forming a high court of letters for France was no dream; Richelieu in great measure fulfilled it. This is what the Academy, by its idea, really is; this is what it has always tended to become; this is what it has, from time to time, really been; by being, or tending to be this, far more than even by what it has done for the language, it is of such importance in France. To give the law, the tone to literature, and that tone a high one, is its business. 'Richelieu meant it', says M. Sainte-Beuve, 'to be a *haut jury*',—a jury the most choice and authoritative that could be found on all important literary matters in question before the public; to be, as it in fact became in the latter half of the eighteenth century, 'a sovereign organ of

[1] La Mesnardière.

opinion'. 'The duty of the Academy is', says M. Renan, '*maintenir la délicatesse de l'esprit français*'—to keep the fine quality of the French spirit unimpaired; it represents a kind of '*maîtrise en fait de bon ton*'—the authority of a recognized master in matters of tone and taste. 'All ages', says M. Renan again, 'have had their inferior literature; but the great danger of our time is that this inferior literature tends more and more to get the upper place. No one has the same advantage as the Academy for fighting against this mischief'; the Academy, which, as he says elsewhere, has even special facilities for 'creating a form of intellectual culture *which shall impose itself on all around*'. M. Sainte-Beuve and M. Renan are, both of them, very keen-sighted critics; and they show it signally by seizing and putting so prominently forward this character of the French Academy.

Such an effort to set up a recognized authority, imposing on us a high standard in matters of intellect and taste, has many enemies in human nature. We all of us like to go our own way, and not to be forced out of the atmosphere of commonplace habitual to most of us;—'*was uns alle bändigt*,' says Goethe, '*das Gemeine*'. We like to be suffered to lie comfortably in the old straw of our habits, especially of our intellectual habits, even though this straw may not be very clean and fine. But if the effort to limit this freedom of our lower nature finds, as it does and must find, enemies in human nature, it finds also auxiliaries in it. Out of the four great parts, says Cicero, of the *honestum*, or good, which forms the matter on which *officium*, or human duty, finds employment, one is the fixing of a *modus* and an *ordo*, a measure and an order, to fashion, and wholesomely constrain our action, in order to lift it above the level it keeps if left to itself, and to bring it nearer to perfection. Man alone of living creatures, he says, goes feeling after '*quid sit* ordo, *quid sit quod* deceat, *in factis dictisque qui* modus'—the discovery of an *order*, a law of *good taste*, a *measure* for his words and actions. Other creatures submissively follow the law of their nature; man alone has an impulse leading him to set up some other law to control the bent of his nature.

This holds good, of course, as to moral matters, as well as intellectual matters; and it is of moral matters that we are generally thinking when we affirm it. But it holds good as to intellectual matters too. Now, probably, M. Sainte-Beuve had not these words of Cicero in his mind when he made, about the French nation, the assertion I am going to quote; but, for all that, the assertion leans for support, one may say, upon the truth conveyed in those words of Cicero, and wonderfully illustrates and confirms them. 'In France', says M. Sainte-Beuve, 'the first consideration for us is not whether we are amused and pleased by a work of art or mind, nor is it whether we are touched by it. What we seek above all to learn is, whether *we were right* in being amused with it, and in applauding it, and in being moved by it.' Those are very remarkable words, and they are, I believe, in the main quite true. A Frenchman has, to a considerable degree, what one may call a conscience in intellectual matters; he has an active belief that there is a right and a wrong in them, that he is bound to honour and obey the right, that he is disgraced by cleaving to the wrong. All the world has, or professes to have, this conscience in moral matters. The word *conscience* has become almost confined, in popular use, to the moral sphere, because this lively susceptibility of feeling is, in the moral sphere, so far more common than in the intellectual sphere; the livelier, in the moral sphere, this susceptibility is, the greater becomes a man's readiness to admit a high standard of action, an ideal authoritatively correcting his everyday moral habits; here, such willing admission of authority is due to sensitiveness of conscience. And a like deference to a standard higher than one's own habitual standard in intellectual matters, a like respectful recognition of a superior ideal, is caused, in the intellectual sphere, by sensitiveness of intelligence. Those whose intelligence is quickest, openest, most sensitive, are readiest with this deference; those whose intelligence is less delicate and sensitive are less disposed to it. Well, now we are on the road to see why the French have their Academy and we have nothing of the kind.

What are the essential characteristics of the spirit of our nation? Not, certainly, an open and clear mind, not a quick and flexible intelligence. Our greatest admirers would not claim for us that we have these in a pre-eminent degree; they might say that we had more of them than our detractors gave us credit for; but they would not assert them to be our essential characteristics. They would rather allege, as our chief spiritual characteristics, energy and honesty; and, if we are judged favourably and positively, not invidiously and negatively, our chief characteristics are, no doubt, these:—energy and honesty, not an open and clear mind, not a quick and flexible intelligence. Openness of mind and flexibility of intelligence were very signal characteristics of the Athenian people in ancient times; everybody will feel that. Openness of mind and flexibility of intelligence are remarkable characteristics of the French people in modern times; at any rate, they strikingly characterize them as compared with us; I think everybody, or almost everybody, will feel that. I will not now ask what more the Athenian or the French spirit has than this, nor what shortcomings either of them may have as a set-off against this; all I want now to point out is that they have this, and that we have it in a much lesser degree.

Let me remark, however, that not only in the moral sphere, but also in the intellectual and spiritual sphere, energy and honesty are most important and fruitful qualities; that, for instance, of what we call genius, energy is the most essential part. So, by assigning to a nation energy and honesty as its chief spiritual characteristics,—by refusing to it, as at all eminent characteristics, openness of mind and flexibility of intelligence,—we do not by any means, as some people might at first suppose, relegate its importance and its power of manifesting itself with effect from the intellectual to the moral sphere. We only indicate its probable special line of successful activity in the intellectual sphere, and, it is true, certain imperfections and failings to which, in this sphere, it will always be subject. Genius is mainly an affair of energy, and poetry is mainly an affair of genius; therefore, a nation whose spirit is characterized by energy may well be eminent in poetry;—and we have Shakespeare. Again, the highest reach of science is, one may say, an inventive power, a faculty of divination, akin to the highest power exercised in poetry; therefore, a nation whose spirit is characterized by energy may well be eminent in science;—and we have Newton. Shakespeare and Newton: in the intellectual sphere there can be no higher names. And what that energy, which is the life of genius, above everything demands and insists upon, is freedom, entire independence of all authority, prescription, and routine,—the fullest room to expand as it will. Therefore, a nation whose chief spiritual characteristic is energy, will not be very apt to set up, in intellectual matters, a fixed standard, an authority, like an academy. By this it certainly escapes certain real inconveniences and dangers, and it can, at the same time, as we have seen, reach undeniably splendid heights in poetry and science. On the other hand, some of the requisites of intellectual work are specially the affair of quickness of mind and flexibility of intelligence. The form, the method of evolution, the precision, the proportions, the relations of the parts to the whole, in an intellectual work, depend mainly upon them. And these are the elements of an intellectual work which are really most communicable from it, which can most be learned and adopted from it, which have, therefore, the greatest effect upon the intellectual performance of others. Even in poetry, these requisites are very important; and the poetry of a nation, not eminent for the gifts on which they depend, will, more or less, suffer by this shortcoming. In poetry, however, they are, after all, secondary, and energy is the first thing; but in prose they are of first-rate importance. In its prose literature, therefore, and in the routine of intellectual work generally, a nation with no particular gifts for these will not be so successful. These are what, as I have said, can to a certain degree be learned and appropriated, while the free activity of genius cannot. Academies consecrate and maintain them, and, therefore, a nation with an eminent turn for them naturally establishes academies. So far as routine and authority tend to embarrass energy and inventive genius, academies may be said to be obstructive to energy and inventive genius, and, to this extent, to the human spirit's general advance. But then this evil is so much compensated by the propagation, on a large scale, of the mental aptitudes and demands which an open mind and a flexible intelligence naturally engender, genius itself, in the long run, so greatly finds its account in this propagation, and bodies like the French Academy have such power for promoting it, that the general advance of the human spirit is perhaps, on the whole, rather furthered than impeded by their existence.

How much greater is our nation in poetry than prose! how much better, in general, do the productions of its spirit show in the qualities of genius than in the qualities of intelligence! One may constantly remark this in the work of individuals; how much more striking, in general, does any Englishman,—of some vigour of mind, but by no means a poet,—seem in his verse than in his prose! No doubt his verse suffers from the same defects which impair his prose, and he cannot express himself with thorough success in it; but how much more powerful a personage does he appear in it, by dint of feeling, and of originality and movement of ideas, than when he is writing prose! With a Frenchman of like stamp, it is just the reverse: set him to write poetry, he is limited, artificial, and impotent; set him to write prose, he is free, natural, and effective. The power of French literature is in its prose-writers, the power of English literature is in its poets. Nay, many of the celebrated French poets depend wholly for their fame upon the qualities of intelligence which they exhibit,—qualities which are the distinctive support of prose; many of the celebrated English prose-writers depend wholly for their fame upon the qualities of genius and imagination which they exhibit,—qualities which are the distinctive support of poetry. But, as I have said, the qualities of genius are less transferable than the qualities of intelligence; less can be immediately learned and appropriated from their product; they are less direct and stringent intellectual agencies, though they may be more beautiful and divine. Shakespeare and our great Elizabethan group were certainly more gifted writers than Corneille and his group; but what was the sequel to this great literature, this literature of genius, as we may call it, stretching from Marlowe to Milton? What did it lead up to in English literature? To our provincial and second-rate literature of the eighteenth century. What, on the other hand, was the sequel to the literature of the French 'great century', to this literature of intelligence, as, by comparison with our Elizabethan literature, we may call it; what did it lead up to? To the French literature of the eighteenth century, one of the most powerful and pervasive intellectual agencies that have ever existed,— the greatest European force of the eighteenth century. In science, again, we had Newton, a genius of the very highest order, a type of genius in science, if ever there was one. On the continent, as a sort of counterpart to Newton, there was Leibnitz; a man, it seems to me (though on these matters I speak under correction), of much less creative energy of genius, much less power of divination than Newton, but rather a man of admirable intelligence, a type of intelligence in science, if ever there was one. Well, and what did they each directly lead up to in science? What was the intellectual generation that sprang from each of them? I only repeat what the men of science have themselves pointed out. The man of genius was continued by the English analysts of the eighteenth century, comparatively powerless and obscure followers of the renowned master; the man of intelligence was continued by successors like Bernouilli, Euler, Lagrange, and Laplace, the greatest names in modern mathematics.

What I want the reader to see is, that the question as to the utility of academies to the intellectual life of a nation is not settled when we say, for instance: 'Oh, we have never had an academy, and yet we have, confessedly, a very great literature.' It still remains to be asked: 'What sort of a great literature? a literature great in the special qualities of genius, or great in the special qualities of intelligence?' If in the former, it is by no means sure that either our literature, or the general intellectual life of our nation, has got already, without academies, all that academies can give. Both the one and the other may very well be somewhat wanting in those qualities of intelligence out of a lively sense for which a body like the French Academy, as I have said, springs, and which such a body does a great deal to spread and confirm. Our literature, in spite of the genius manifested in it, may fall short in form, method, precision, proportions, arrangement,—all of them, I have said, things where intelligence proper comes in. It may be comparatively weak in prose, that branch of literature where intelligence proper is, so to speak, all in all. In this branch it may show many grave faults to which the want of a quick, flexible intelligence, and of the strict standard which such an intelligence tends to impose, makes it liable; it may be full of haphazard, crudeness, provincialism, eccentricity, violence, blundering. It may be a less stringent and effective intellectual agency, both upon our own nation and upon the world at large, than other literatures which show less genius, perhaps, but more intelligence.

The right conclusion certainly is that we should try, so far as we can, to make up our shortcomings; and that to this end, instead of always fixing our thoughts upon the points in which our literature, and our intellectual life generally, are strong, we should, from time to time, fix them upon those in which they are weak, and so learn to perceive clearly what we have to amend. What is our second great spiritual characteristic,—our honesty,

—good for, if it is not good for this? But it will,—I am sure it will,—more and more, as time goes on, be found good for this.

Well, then, an institution like the French Academy,—an institution owing its existence to a national bent towards the things of the mind, towards culture, towards clearness, correctness, and propriety in thinking and speaking, and, in its turn, promoting this bent,—sets standards in a number of directions, and creates, in all these directions, a force of educated opinion, checking and rebuking those who fall below these standards, or who set them at nought. Educated opinion exists here as in France; but in France the Academy serves as a sort of centre and rallying-point to it, and gives it a force which it has not got here. Why is all the *journeyman work* of literature, as I may call it, so much worse done here than it is in France? I do not wish to hurt anyone's feelings; but surely this is so. Think of the difference between our books of reference and those of the French, between our biographical dictionaries (to take a striking instance) and theirs; think of the difference between the translations of the classics turned out for Mr Bohn's library and those turned out for M. Nisard's collection! As a general rule, hardly any one amongst us, who knows French and German well, would use an English book of reference when he could get a French or German one; or would look at an English prose translation of an ancient author when he could get a French or German one. It is not that there do not exist in England, as in France, a number of people perfectly well able to discern what is good, in these things, from what is bad, and preferring what is good; but they are isolated, they form no powerful body of opinion, they are not strong enough to set a standard, up to which even the journeyman work of literature must be brought, if it is to be vendible. Ignorance and charlatanism in work of this kind are always trying to pass off their wares as excellent, and to cry down criticism as the voice of an insignificant, over-fastidious minority; they easily persuade the multitude that this is so when the minority is scattered about as it is here; not so easily when it is banded together as in the French Academy. So, again, with freaks in dealing with language; certainly all such freaks tend to impair the power and beauty of language; and how far more common they are with us than with the French! To take a very familiar instance. Everyone has noticed the way in which *The Times* chooses to spell the word 'diocese'; it always spells it diocess,[1] deriving it, I suppose, from *Zeus* and *census*. The *Journal des Débats* might just as well write 'diocess' instead of 'diocèse', but imagine the *Journal des Débats* doing so! Imagine an educated Frenchman indulging himself in an orthographical antic of this sort, in face of the grave respect with which the Academy and its dictionary invest the French language! Some people will say these are little things; they are not; they are of bad example. They tend to spread the baneful notion that there is no such thing as a high, correct standard in intellectual matters; that everyone may as well take his own way; they are at variance with the severe discipline necessary for all real culture; they confirm us in habits of wilfulness and eccentricity, which hurt our minds, and damage our credit with serious people. The late Mr Donaldson was certainly a man of great ability, and I, who am not an Orientalist, do not pretend to judge his *Jashar*; but let the reader observe the form which a foreign Orientalist's judgment of it naturally takes. M. Renan calls it a *tentative malheureuse*, a failure, in short; this it may be, or it may not be; I am no judge. But he goes on: 'It is astonishing that a recent article' (in a French periodical, he means) 'should have brought forward as the last word of German exegesis a work like this, composed by a doctor of the University of Cambridge, and universally condemned by German critics.' You see what he means to imply: an extravagance of this sort could never have come from Germany, where there is a great force of critical opinion controlling a learned man's vagaries, and keeping him straight; it comes from the native home of intellectual eccentricity of all kinds,[2]—from England, from a doctor of the University of Cambridge;—and I daresay he would not expect much better things from a doctor of the University of Oxford. Again, after speaking of what Germany and France have done for the history of Mahomet: 'America and England', M. Renan goes on, 'have also occupied themselves with Mahomet.' He mentions Washington Irving's *Life of Mahomet*, which does not, he says,

---

[1] *The Times* has now (1868) abandoned this spelling and adopted the ordinary one.

[2] A critic declares I am wrong in saying that M. Renan's language implies this. I still think that there is a shade, a *nuance* of expression, in M. Renan's language, which does imply this; but, I confess, the only person who can really settle such a question is M. Renan himself.

evince much of an historical sense, a *sentiment historique fort élevé*; 'but', he proceeds, 'this book shows a real progress, when one thinks that in 1829 Mr Charles Forster published two thick volumes, which enchanted the English *révérends*, to make out that Mahomet was the little horn of the he-goat that figures in the eighth chapter of Daniel, and that the Pope was the great horn. Mr Forster founded on this ingenious parallel a whole philosophy of history, according to which the Pope represented the Western corruption of Christianity, and Mahomet the Eastern; thence the striking resemblances between Mahometanism and Popery'. And in a note M. Renan adds: 'This is the same Mr Charles Forster who is the author of a mystification about the Sinaitic inscriptions, in which he declares he finds the primitive language.' As much as to say: 'It is an Englishman, be surprised at no extravagance.' If these innuendoes had no ground, and were made in hatred and malice, they would not be worth a moment's attention; but they come from a grave Orientalist, on his own subject, and they point to a real fact;—the absence, in this country, of any force of educated literary and scientific opinion, making aberrations like those of the author of *The One Primeval Language* out of the question. Not only the author of such aberrations, often a very clever man, suffers by the want of check, by the not being kept straight, and spends force in vain on a false road, which, under better discipline, he might have used with profit on a true one; but all his adherents, both 'reverends' and others, suffer too, and the general rate of information and judgment is in this way kept low.

In a production which we have all been reading lately, a production stamped throughout with a literary quality very rare in this country, and of which I shall have a word to say presently,—*urbanity*; in this production, the work of a man never to be named by any son of Oxford without sympathy, a man who alone in Oxford of his generation, alone of many generations, conveyed to us in his genius that same charm, that same ineffable sentiment which this exquisite place itself conveys,—I mean Dr Newman,—an expression is frequently used which is more common in theological than in literary language, but which seems to me fitted to be of general service; the *note* of so and so, the note of catholicity, the note of antiquity, the note of sanctity, and so on. Adopting this expressive word, I say that in the bulk of the intellectual work of a nation which has no centre, no intellectual metropolis like an academy, like M. Sainte-Beuve's 'sovereign organ of opinion', like M. Renan's 'recognized authority in matters of tone and taste',— there is observable a *note of provinciality*. Now to get rid of provinciality is a certain stage of culture; a stage the positive result of which we must not make of too much importance, but which is, nevertheless, indispensable; for it brings us on to the platform where alone the best and highest intellectual work can be said fairly to begin. Work done after men have reached this platform is *classical*; and that is the only work which, in the long run, can stand. All the *scoriae* in the work of men of great genius who have not lived on this platform are due to their not having lived on it. Genius raises them to it by moments, and the portions of their work which are immortal are done at these moments; but more of it would have been immortal if they had not reached this platform at moments only, if they had had the culture which makes men live there.

The less a literature has felt the influence of a supposed centre of correct information, correct judgment, correct taste, the more we shall find in it this note of provinciality. I have shown the note of provinciality as caused by remoteness from a centre of correct information. Of course the note of provinciality from the want of a centre of correct taste is still more visible, and it is also still more common. For here great—even the greatest— powers of mind most fail a man. Great powers of mind will make him inform himself thoroughly, great powers of mind will make him think profoundly, even with ignorance and platitude all round him; but not even great powers of mind will keep his taste and style perfectly sound and sure, if he is left too much to himself, with no 'sovereign organ of opinion', in these matters, near him. Even men like Jeremy Taylor and Burke suffer here. Take this passage from Taylor's funeral sermon on Lady Carbery:

So have I seen a river, deep and smooth, passing with a still foot and a sober face, and paying to the *fiscus*, the great exchequer of the sea, a tribute large and full; and hard by it a little brook, skipping and making a noise upon its unequal and neighbour bottom; and after all its talking and bragged motion, it paid to its common audit no more than the revenues of a little cloud or a contemptible vessel: so have I sometimes compared the issues of her religion to the solemnities and famed outsides of another's piety.

That passage has been much admired, and, indeed, the genius in it is undeniable. I should say, for my part, that genius, the ruling divinity of poetry, had been too busy in it, and intelligence, the ruling divinity of prose, not busy enough. But can anyone, with the best models of style in his head, help feeling the note of provinciality there, the want of simplicity, the want of measure, the want of just the qualities that make prose classical? If he does not feel what I mean, let him place beside the passage of Taylor this passage from the Panegyric of St Paul, by Taylor's contemporary, Bossuet:

> Il ira, cet ignorant dans l'art de bien dire, avec cette locution rude, avec cette phrase qui sent l'étranger, il ira en cette Grèce polie, la mère des philosophes et des orateurs; et malgré la résistance du monde, il y établira plus d'Eglises que Platon n'y a gagné de disciples par cette éloquence qu'on a crue divine.

There we have prose without the note of provinciality—classical prose, prose of the centre.

Or take Burke, our greatest English prose-writer, as I think; take expressions like this:

> Blindfold themselves, like bulls that shut their eyes when they push, they drive, by the point of their bayonets, their slaves, blindfolded, indeed, no worse than their lords, to take their fictions for currencies, and to swallow down paper pills by thirty-four millions sterling at a dose.

Or this:

> They used it [the royal name] as a sort of navel-string, to nourish their unnatural offspring from the bowels of royalty itself. Now that the monster can purvey for its own subsistence, it will only carry the mark about it, as a token of its having torn the womb it came from.

Or this:

> Without one natural pang, he [Rousseau] casts away, as a

sort of offal and excrement, the spawn of his disgustful amours, and sends his children to the hospital of foundlings.

Or this:

I confess I never liked this continual talk of resistance and revolution, or the practice of making the extreme medicine of the constitution its daily bread. It renders the habit of society dangerously valetudinary; it is taking periodical doses of mercury sublimate, and swallowing down repeated provocatives of cantharides to our love of liberty.

I say that is extravagant prose; prose too much suffered to indulge its caprices; prose at too great a distance from the centre of good taste; prose, in short, with the note of provinciality. People may reply, it is rich and imaginative; yes, that is just it, it is *Asiatic* prose, as the ancient critics would have said; prose somewhat barbarously rich and overloaded. But the true prose is Attic prose.

Well, but Addison's prose is Attic prose. Where, then, it may be asked, is the note of provinciality in Addison? I answer, in the commonplace of his ideas.[1] This is a matter worth remarking. Addison claims to take leading rank as a moralist. To do that, you must have ideas of the first order on your subject—the best ideas, at any rate, attainable in your time—as well as be able to express them in a perfectly sound and sure style. Else you show your distance from the centre of ideas by your matter; you are provincial by your matter, though you may not be provincial by your style. It is comparatively a small matter to express oneself well, if one will be content with not expressing much, with expressing only trite ideas; the problem is to express new and profound ideas in a perfectly sound and classical style. He is the true classic, in every age, who does that. Now Addison has

---

[1] A critic says this is paradoxical, and urges that many second-rate French academicians have uttered the most common-place ideas possible. I agree that many second-rate French academicians have uttered the most commonplace ideas possible; but Addison is not a second-rate man. He is a man of the order, I will not say of Pascal, but at any rate of La Bruyère and Vauvenargues; why does he not equal them? I say, because of the medium in which he finds himself, the atmosphere in which he lives and works; an atmosphere which tells unfavourably, or rather *tends* to tell unfavourably (for that is the truer way of putting it) either upon style or else upon ideas; tends to make even a man of great ability either a Mr Carlyle or else a Lord Macaulay.

It is to be observed, however, that Lord Macaulay's style has in its turn suffered by his failure in ideas, and this cannot be said of Addison's.

not, on his subject of morals, the force of ideas of the moralists of the first class,—the classical moralists; he has not the best ideas attainable in or about his time, and which were, so to speak, in the air then, to be seized by the finest spirits; he is not to be compared for power, searchingness, or delicacy of thought to Pascal or La Bruyère or Vauvenargues; he is rather on a level, in this respect, with a man like Marmontel; therefore, I say, he has the note of provinciality as a moralist; he is provincial by his matter, though not by his style.

To illustrate what I mean by an example. Addison, writing as a moralist on fixedness in religious faith, says:

> Those who delight in reading books of controversy do very seldom arrive at a fixed and settled habit of faith. The doubt which was laid revives again, and shows itself in new difficulties; and that generally for this reason,—because the mind, which is perpetually tossed in controversies and disputes, is apt to forget the reasons which had once set it at rest, and to be disquieted with any former perplexity when it appears in a new shape, or is started by a different hand.

It may be said, that is classical English, perfect in lucidity, measure, and propriety. I made no objection; but, in my turn, I say that the idea expressed is perfectly trite and barren, and that it is a note of provinciality in Addison, in a man whom a nation puts forward as one of its great moralists, to have no profounder and more striking idea to produce on this great subject. Compare, on the same subject, these words of a moralist really of the first order, really at the centre by his ideas,—Joubert:

> L'expérience de beaucoup d'opinions donne à l'esprit beaucoup de flexibilité et l'affermit dans celles qu'il croit les meilleures.

With what a flash of light that touches the subject! how it sets us thinking! what a genuine contribution to moral science it is!

In short, where there is no centre like an academy, if you have genius and powerful ideas, you are apt not to have the best style going; if you have precision of style and not genius, you are apt not to have the best ideas going.

The provincial spirit, again, exaggerates the value of its ideas for want of a high standard at hand by which to try them. Or

rather, for want of such a standard, it gives one idea too much
prominence at the expense of others; it orders its ideas amiss;
it is hurried away by fancies; it likes and dislikes too passionately, too exclusively. Its admiration weeps hysterical tears, and
its disapprobation foams at the mouth. So we get the *eruptive*
and the *aggressive* manner in literature; the former prevails most
in our criticism, the latter in our newspapers. For, not having
the lucidity of a large and centrally placed intelligence, the
provincial spirit has not its graciousness; it does not persuade,
it makes war; it has not urbanity, the tone of the city, of the
centre, the tone which always aims at a spiritual and intellectual
effect, and not excluding the use of banter, never disjoins banter
itself from politeness, from felicity. But the provincial tone is
more violent, and seems to aim rather at an effect upon the blood
and senses than upon the spirit and intellect; it loves hard-hitting
rather than persuading. The newspaper, with its party spirit, its
thorough-goingness, its resolute avoidance of shades and distinctions, its short, highly charged, heavy-shotted articles, its
style so unlike that style *lenis minimèque pertinax*—easy and not
too violently insisting—which the ancients so much admired,
is its true literature; the provincial spirit likes in the newspaper
just what makes the newspaper such bad food for it,—just what
made Goethe say, when he was pressed hard about the immor-
ality of Byron's poems, that, after all, they were not so immoral
as the newspapers. The French talk of the *brutalité des journaux
anglais*. What strikes them comes from the necessary inherent
tendencies of newspaper-writing not being checked in England
by any centre of intelligent and urbane spirit, but rather stimulated by coming in contact with a provincial spirit. Even a
newspaper like the *Saturday Review*, that old friend of all of us,
a newspaper expressly aiming at an immunity from the common
newspaper-spirit, aiming at being a sort of organ of reason,—
and, by thus aiming, it merits great gratitude and has done great
good,—even the *Saturday Review*, replying to some foreign
criticism on our precautions against invasion, falls into a strain
of this kind:

To do this [to take these precautions] seems to us eminently
worthy of a great nation, and to talk of it as unworthy of a
great nation, seems to us eminently worthy of a great fool.

There is what the French mean when they talk of the *brutalité des journaux anglais*; there is a style certainly as far removed from urbanity as possible,—a style with what I call the note of provinciality. And the same note may not unfrequently be observed even in the ideas of this newspaper, full as it is of thought and cleverness: certain ideas allowed to become fixed ideas, to prevail too absolutely. I will not speak of the immediate present, but, to go a little while back, it had the critic who so disliked the Emperor of the French; it had the critic who so disliked the subject of my present remarks—academies; it had the critic who was so fond of the German element in our nation, and, indeed, everywhere; who ground his teeth if one said *Charlemagne*, instead of *Charles the Great*, and, in short, saw all things in Teutonism, as Malebranche saw all things in God. Certainly anyone may fairly find faults in the Emperor Napoleon or in academies, and merit in the German element; but it is a note of the provincial spirit not to hold ideas of this kind a little more easily, to be so devoured by them, to suffer them to become crotchets.

In England there needs a miracle of genius like Shakespeare's to produce balance of mind, and a miracle of intellectual delicacy like Dr Newman's to produce urbanity of style. How prevalent all round us in the want of balance of mind and urbanity of style! How much, doubtless, it is to be found in ourselves,— in each of us! but, as human nature is constituted, everyone can see it clearest in his contemporaries. There, above all, we should consider it, because they and we are exposed to the same influences; and it is in the best of one's contemporaries that it is most worth considering, because one then most feels the harm it does, when one sees what they would be without it. Think of the difference between Mr Ruskin exercising his genius, and Mr Ruskin exercising his intelligence; consider the truth and beauty of this:

Go out, in the spring-time, among the meadows that slope from the shores of the Swiss lakes to the roots of their lower mountains. There, mingled with the taller gentians and the white narcissus, the grass grows deep and free; and as you follow the winding mountain paths, beneath arching boughs all veiled and dim with blossom,—paths that for ever droop and rise over the green banks and mounds sweeping down in scented undulation, steep to the blue water studded here and there with new-mown heaps, filling all the air with fainter sweetness,—look up towards the higher hills, where the waves of everlasting green roll silently into their long inlets among the shadows of the pines. . . .

There is what the genius, the feeling, the temperament in Mr Ruskin, the original and incommunicable part, has to do with; and how exquisite it is! All the critic could possibly suggest, in the way of objection, would be, perhaps, that Mr Ruskin is there trying to make prose do more than it can perfectly do; that what he is there attempting he will never, except in poetry, be able to accomplish to his own entire satisfaction: but he accomplishes so much that the critic may well hesitate to suggest even this. Place beside this charming passage another,—a passage about Shakespeare's names, where the intelligence and judgment of Mr Ruskin, the acquired, trained, communicable part in him, are brought into play,—and see the difference:

Of Shakespeare's names I will afterwards speak at more length; they are curiously—often barbarously—mixed out of various traditions and languages. Three of the clearest in meaning have been already noticed. Desdemona—'δυσδαι-μονία', *miserable fortune*—is also plain enough. Othello is, I believe, 'the careful'; all the calamity of the tragedy arising from the single flaw and error in his magnificently collected strength. Ophelia, 'serviceableness', the true, lost wife of Hamlet, is marked as having a Greek name by that of her brother, Laertes; and its signification is once exquisitely alluded to in that brother's last word of her, where her gentle preciousness is opposed to the uselessness of the churlish clergy:—'A *ministering* angel shall my sister be, when thou liest howling.' Hamlet is, I believe, connected in some way with 'homely', the entire event of the tragedy turning on betrayal of home duty. Hermione (ἔρμα), 'pillar-like' (ἡ εἶδος ἔχε χρυσῆς 'Αφροδίτης); Titania (τιτήνη), 'the queen'; Benedict and Beatrice, 'blessed and blessing'; Valentine and Proteus, 'enduring or strong' (*valens*), and 'changeful'. Iago and Iach-imo have evidently the same root—probably the Spanish Iago, Jacob, 'the supplanter'.

Now, really, what a piece of extravagance all that is! I will not say that the meaning of Shakespeare's names (I put aside the question as to the correctness of Mr Ruskin's etymologies) has no effect at all, may be entirely lost sight of; but to give it that degree of prominence is to throw the reins to one's whim, to forget all moderation and proportion, to lose the balance of one's mind altogether. It is to show in one's criticism, to the highest excess, the note of provinciality.

Again, there is Mr Palgrave, certainly endowed with a very fine critical tact; his *Golden Treasury* abundantly proves it. The plan of arrangement which he devised for that work, the mode in which he followed his plan out, nay, one might even say, merely the juxtaposition, in pursuance of it, of two such pieces as those of Wordsworth and Shelley which form the 285th and 286th in his collection, show a delicacy of feeling in these matters which is quite indisputable and very rare. And his notes are full of remarks which show it too. All the more striking, conjoined with so much justness of perception, are certain freaks and violences in Mr Palgrave's criticism, mainly imputable, I think, to the critic's isolated position in this country, to his feeling himself too much left to take his own way, too much without any central authority representing high culture and sound judgment, by which he may be, on the one hand, confirmed as against the ignorant, on the other, held in respect when he himself is inclined to take liberties. I mean such things as this note on Milton's line,

The great Emathian conqueror bade spare . . .

When Thebes was destroyed, Alexander ordered the house of Pindar to be spared. *He was as incapable of appreciating the poet as Louis XIV of appreciating Racine; but even the narrow and barbarian mind of Alexander could understand the advantage of a showy act of homage to poetry.*

A note like that I call a freak or a violence; if this disparaging view of Alexander and Louis XIV, so unlike the current view, is wrong,—if the current view is, after all, the truer one of them, —the note is a freak. But, even if its disparaging view is right, the note is a violence; for, abandoning the true mode of intellectual action—persuasion, the instilment of conviction,—it simply astounds and irritates the hearer by contradicting without a word of proof or preparation, his fixed and family notions; and this is mere violence. In either case, the fitness, the measure, the centrality, which is the soul of all good criticism, is lost, and the note of provinciality shows itself.

Thus, in the famous *Handbook*, marks of a fine power of perception are everywhere discernible, but so, too, are marks of the want of sure balance, of the check and support afforded by knowing one speaks before good and severe judges. When Mr Palgrave dislikes a thing, he feels no pressure constraining him either to try his dislike closely or to express it moderately; he does not mince matters, he gives his dislike all its own way; both his judgment and his style would gain if he were under more restraint. 'The style which has filled London with the dead monotony of Gower or Harley Streets, or the pale commonplace of Belgravia, Tyburnia, and Kensington; which has pierced Paris and Madrid with the feeble frivolities of the Rue Rivoli and the Strada de Toledo.' He dislikes the architecture of the Rue Rivoli, and he puts it on a level with the architecture of Belgravia and Gower Street; he lumps them all together in one condemnation, he loses sight of the shade, the distinction, which is everything here; the distinction, namely, that the architecture of the Rue Rivoli expresses show, splendour, pleasure,—unworthy things, perhaps, to express alone and for their own sakes, but it expresses them; whereas the architecture of Gower Street and Belgravia merely expresses the impotence of the architect to express anything. Then, as to style: 'sculpture which stands in a contrast with Woolner hardly more shameful than diverting' ... 'passing from Davy or Faraday to the art of the mountebank or the science of the spirit-rapper' ... 'it is the old, old story with Marochetti, the frog trying to blow himself out to bull dimensions. He may puff and be puffed, but he will never do it'. We all remember that shower of amenities on poor M. Marochetti. Now, here Mr Palgrave himself enables us to form a contrast which lets us see just what the presence of an academy does for style; for he quotes a criticism by M. Gustave Planche on this very M. Marochetti. M. Gustave Planche was a critic of the very first order, a man of strong opinions, which he expressed with severity; he, too, condemns M. Marochetti's work, and Mr Palgrave calls him a witness to back what he has himself said; certainly Mr Palgrave's translation will not exaggerate

M. Planche's urbanity in dealing with M. Marochetti, but, even in this translation, see the difference in sobriety, in measure, between the critic writing in Paris and the critic writing in London:

> These conditions are so elementary, that I am at a perfect loss to comprehend how M. Marochetti has neglected them. There are soldiers here like the leaden playthings of the nursery: it is almost impossible to guess whether there is a body beneath the dress. We have here no question of style, not even of grammar; it is nothing beyond mere matter of the alphabet of art. To break these conditions is the same as to be ignorant of spelling.

That is really more formidable criticism than Mr Palgrave's, and yet in how perfectly temperate a style! M. Planche's advantage is, that he feels himself to be speaking before competent judges, that there is a force of cultivated opinion for him to appeal to. Therefore, he must not be extravagant, and he need not storm; he must satisfy the reason and taste,—that is his business. Mr Palgrave, on the other hand, feels himself to be speaking before a promiscuous multitude, with the few good judges so scattered through it as to be powerless; therefore, he has no calm confidence and no self-control; he relies on the strength of his lungs; he knows that big words impose on the mob, and that, even if he is outrageous, most of his audience are apt to be a great deal more so.[1]

Again, the first two volumes of Mr Kinglake's *Invasion of the Crimea* were certainly among the most successful and renowned English books of our time. Their style was one of the most renowned things about them, and yet how conspicuous a fault in Mr Kinglake's style is this over-charge of which I have been speaking! Mr James Gordon Bennett, of the *New York Herald*, says, I believe, that the highest achievement of the human intellect is what he calls 'a good editorial'. This is not quite so; but, if it were so, on what a height would these two volumes by Mr Kinglake stand! I have already spoken of the Attic and the Asiatic styles; besides these, there is the Corinthian style. That is the style for 'a good editorial', and Mr Kinglake has really

---

[1] When I wrote this I had before me the first edition of Mr Palgrave's *Handbook*. I am bound to say that in the second edition much strong language has been expunged, and what remains, softened.

reached perfection in it. It has not the warm glow, blithe movement, and soft pliancy of life, as the Attic style has; it has not
the over-heavy richness and encumbered gait of the Asiatic
style; it has glitter without warmth, rapidity without ease,
effectiveness without charm. Its characteristic is, that it has no
soul; all it exists for, is to get its ends, to make its points, to
damage its adversaries, to be admired, to triumph. A style so
bent on effect at the expense of soul, simplicity, and delicacy; a
style so little studious of the charm of the great models; so far
from classic truth and grace, must surely be said to have the
note of provinciality. Yet Mr Kinglake's talent is a really eminent one, and so in harmony with our intellectual habits and
tendencies, that, to the great bulk of English people, the faults
of his style seem its merits; all the more needful that criticism
should not be dazzled by them, but should try closely this, the
form of his work. The matter of the work is a separate thing;
and, indeed, this has been, I believe, withdrawn from discussion,
Mr Kinglake declaring that this must and shall stay as it is, and
that he is resolved, like Pontius Pilate, to stand by what he has
written. And here, I must say, he seems to me to be quite right.
On the breast of the huge Mississippi of falsehood called *history*,
a foam-bell more or less is of no consequence. But he may, at
any rate, ease and soften his style.

We must not compare a man of Mr Kinglake's literary talent
with French writers like M. de Bazancourt. We must compare
him with M. Thiers. And what a superiority in style has M.
Thiers from being formed in a good school, with severe traditions, wholesome restraining influences! Even in this age of Mr
James Gordon Bennett, his style has nothing Corinthian about
it, its lightness and brightness make it almost Attic. It is not
quite Attic, however; it has not the infallible sureness of Attic
taste. Sometimes his head gets a little hot with the fumes of
patriotism, and then he crosses the line, he loses perfect measure,
he declaims, he raises a momentary smile. France condemned
'à être l'effroi du monde *dont elle pourrait être l'amour*',—Caesar,
whose exquisite simplicity M. Thiers so much admires, would
not have written like that. There is, if I may be allowed to say
so, the slightest possible touch of fatuity in such language,—of
that failure in good sense which comes from too warm a self-
satisfaction. But compare this language with Mr Kinglake's

Marshal St Arnaud—'dismissed from the presence' of Lord Raglan or Lord Stratford, 'cowed and pressed down' under their 'stern reproofs', or under 'the majesty of the great Elchi's Canning brow and tight, merciless lips'! The failure in good sense and good taste there reaches far beyond what the French mean by *fatuity*; they would call it by another word, a word expressing blank defect of intelligence, a word for which we have no exact equivalent in English,—*bête*. It is the difference between a venial, momentary, good-tempered excess, in a man of the world, of an amiable and social weakness,—vanity; and a serious, settled, fierce, narrow, provincial misconception of the whole relative value of one's own things and the things of others. So baneful to the style of even the cleverest man may be the total want of checks.

In all I have said, I do not pretend that the examples given prove my rule as to the influence of academies; they only illustrate it. Examples in plenty might very likely be found to set against them; the truth of the rule depends, no doubt, on whether the balance of all the examples is in its favour or not; but actually to strike this balance is always out of the question. Here, as everywhere else, the rule, the idea, if true, commends itself to the judicious, and then the examples make it clearer still to them. This is the real use of examples, and this alone is the purpose which I have meant mine to serve. There is also another side to the whole question,—as to the limiting and prejudicial operation which academies may have; but this side of the question it rather behoves the French, not us, to study.

The reader will ask for some practical conclusion about the establishment of an Academy in this country, and perhaps I shall hardly give him the one he expects. But nations have their own modes of acting, and these modes are not easily changed; they are even consecrated, when great things have been done in them. When a literature has produced Shakespeare and Milton, when it has even produced Barrow and Burke, it cannot well abandon its traditions; it can hardly begin, at this late time of day, with an institution like the French Academy. I think academies with a limited, special, scientific scope, in the various lines of intellectual work,—academies like that of Berlin, for instance,—we with time may, and probably shall, establish. And no doubt they will do good; no doubt the presence of such influential centres of correct information will tend to raise the standard amongst us for what I have called the *journeyman work* of literature, and to free us from the scandal of such biographical dictionaries as Chalmers's, or such translations as a recent one of Spinoza, or perhaps, such philological freaks as Mr Forster's about the one primeval language. But an academy quite like the French Academy, a sovereign organ of the highest literary opinion, a recognized authority in matters of intellectual tone and taste, we shall hardly have, and perhaps we ought not to wish to have it. But then every one amongst us with any turn for literature will do well to remember to what shortcomings and excesses, which such an academy tends to correct, we are liable; and the more liable, of course, for not having it. He will do well constantly to try himself in respect of these, steadily to widen his culture, severely to check in himself the provincial spirit; and he will do this the better the more he keeps in mind that all mere glorification by ourselves of ourselves or our literature, in the strain of what, at the beginning of these remarks, I quoted from Lord Macaulay, is both vulgar, and, besides being vulgar, retarding.

III

MAURICE DE GUÉRIN

I WILL not presume to say that I now know the French language well; but at a time when I knew it even less well than at present, —some fifteen years ago,—I remember pestering those about me with this sentence, the rhythm of which had lodged itself in my head, and which, with the strangest pronunciation possible, I kept perpetually declaiming: '*Les dieux jaloux ont enfoui quelque part les témoignages de la descendance des choses; mais au bord de quel Océan ont-ils roulé la pierre qui les couvre, ô Macarée!*'

These words come from a short composition called the *Centaur*, of which the author, Georges-Maurice de Guérin, died in the year 1839, at the age of twenty-eight, without having published anything. In 1840, Madame Sand brought out the *Centaur* in the *Revue des Deux Mondes*, with a short notice of its author, and a few extracts from his letters. A year or two afterwards she reprinted these at the end of a volume of her novels; and there it was that I fell in with them. I was so much struck with the *Centaur* that I waited anxiously to hear something more of its author, and of what he had left; but it was not till the other day —twenty years after the first publication of the *Centaur* in the *Revue des Deux Mondes*, that my anxiety was satisfied. At the end of 1860 appeared two volumes with the title *Maurice de Guérin, Reliquiae*, containing the *Centaur*, several poems of Guérin, his journals, and a number of his letters, collected and edited by a devoted friend, M. Trebutien, and preceded by a notice of Guérin by the first of living critics, M. Sainte-Beuve.

The grand power of poetry is its interpretative power; by which I mean, not a power of drawing out in black and white an explanation of the mystery of the universe, but the power of so dealing with things as to awaken in us a wonderfully full, new, and intimate sense of them, and of our relations with them. When this sense is awakened in us, as to objects without us, we feel ourselves to be in contact with the essential nature of those objects, to be no longer bewildered and oppressed by them, but to have their secret, and to be in harmony with them; and this feeling calms and satisfies us as no other can. Poetry, indeed, interprets in another way besides this; but one of its two ways of interpreting, of exercising its highest power, is by awakening this sense in us. I will not now inquire whether this sense is illusive, whether it can be proved not to be illusive, whether it does absolutely make us possess the real nature of things; all I say is, that poetry can awaken it in us, and that to awaken it is one of the highest powers of poetry. The interpretations of science do not give us this intimate sense of objects as the inter- pretations of poetry give it; they appeal to a limited faculty, and not to the whole man. It is not Linnaeus, or Cavendish, or Cuvier who gives us the true sense of animals, or water, or plants, who seizes their secret for us, who makes us participate in their life; it is Shakespeare, with his

> daffodils
> that come before the swallow dares, and take
> The winds of March with beauty;

it is Wordsworth, with his

> voice . . . . heard
> In spring-time from the cuckoo-bird,
> Breaking the silence of the seas
> Among the farthest Hebrides;

it is Keats, with his

> moving waters at their priest-like task
> Of pure ablution round earth's human shores;

it is Chateaubriand, with his, 'cîme indéterminee des forêts'; it is Senancour, with his mountain birch tree: 'Cette écorce blanche, lisse et crevassée; cette tige agreste; ces branches qui s'inclinent vers la terre; la mobilité des feuilles, et tout cet abandon, simplicité de la nature, attitude des déserts.'

Eminent manifestations of this magical power of poetry are very rare and very precious; the compositions of Guérin mani- fest it, I think, in singular eminence. Not his poems, strictly so called,—his verse,—so much as his prose; his poems in general take for their vehicle that favourite metre of French poetry, the Alexandrine; and, in my judgment, I confess they have thus, as compared with his prose, a great disadvantage to start with. In prose, the character of the vehicle for the composer's thoughts is not determined beforehand; every composer has to make his own vehicle; and who has ever done this more admirably than the great prose-writers of France,—Pascal, Bossuet, Fénelon, Voltaire? But in verse the composer has (with comparatively narrow liberty of modification) to accept his vehicle ready-made; it is therefore of vital importance to him that he should find at his disposal a vehicle adequate to convey the highest matters of poetry. We may even get a decisive test of the poetical power of a language and nation by ascertaining how far the principal poetical vehicle which they have employed, how far (in plainer words) the established national metre for high poetry, is adequate or inadequate. It seems to me that the established metre of this kind in France,—the Alexandrine,—is inadequate; that as a vehicle for high poetry it is greatly inferior to the hexameter or to the iambics of Greece (for example), or to the blank verse of England. Therefore the man of genius who uses it is at a disadvantage as compared with the man of genius who has for conveying his thoughts a more adequate vehicle, metrical or not. Racine is at a disadvantage as compared with Sophocles or Shakespeare, and he is likewise at a disadvantage as compared with Bossuet.

The same may be said of our own poets of the eighteenth century, a century which gave them as the main vehicle for their high poetry a metre inadequate (as much as the French Alexandrine, and nearly in the same way) for this poetry,—the ten-syllable couplet. It is worth remarking, that the English poet of the eighteenth century whose compositions wear best and give one the most entire satisfaction,—Gray,—hardly uses that couplet at all: this abstinence, however, limits Gray's productions to a few short compositions, and (exquisite as these are) he is a poetical nature repressed and without free issue. For English poetical production on a great scale, for an English poet deploying all the forces of his genius, the ten-syllable couplet was, in the eighteenth century, the established, one may almost say the inevitable, channel. Now this couplet, admirable (as Chaucer uses it) for story-telling not of the epic pitch, and often admirable for a few lines even in poetry of a very high pitch, is for continuous use in poetry of this latter kind inadequate. Pope, in his *Essay on Man*, is thus at a disadvantage compared with Lucretius in his poem on Nature: Lucretius has an adequate vehicle, Pope has not. Nay, though Pope's genius for didactic poetry was not less than that of Horace, while his satirical power was certainly greater, still one's taste receives, I cannot but think, a certain satisfaction when one reads the Epistles and Satires of Horace, which it fails to receive when one reads the Satires and Epistles of Pope. Of such avail is the superior adequacy of the vehicle used to compensate even an inferiority of genius in the user! In the same way Pope is at a disadvantage as compared with Addison. The best of Addison's composition (the 'Coverley Papers' in the *Spectator*, for instance) wears better than the best of Pope's, because Addison has in his prose an intrinsically better vehicle for his genius than Pope in his couplet. But Bacon has no such advantage over Shakespeare; nor has Milton, writing prose (for no contemporary English prose-writer must be matched with Milton except Milton himself), any such advantage over Milton writing verse: indeed, the advantage here is all the other way.

It is in the prose remains of Guérin,—his journals, his letters, and the striking composition which I have already mentioned, the *Centaur*,—that his extraordinary gift manifests itself. He has a truly interpretative faculty; the most profound and delicate sense of the life of Nature, and the most exquisite felicity in finding expressions to render that sense. To all who love poetry, Guérin deserves to be something more than a name; and I shall try, in spite of the impossibility of doing justice to such a master of expression by translations, to make English readers see for themselves how gifted an organization his was, and how few artists have received from Nature a more magical faculty of interpreting her.

In the winter of the year 1832 there was collected in Brittany, around the well-known Abbé Lamennais, a singular gathering. At a lonely place, La Chênaie, he had founded a religious retreat, to which disciples, attracted by his powers or by his reputation, repaired. Some came with the intention of preparing themselves for the ecclesiastical profession; others merely to profit by the society and discourse of so distinguished a master. Among the inmates were men whose names have since become known to all Europe,—Lacordaire and M. de Montalembert; there were others, who have acquired a reputation, not European, indeed, but considerable,—the Abbé Gerbet, the Abbé Rohrbacher; others, who have never quitted the shade of private life. The winter of 1832 was a period of crisis in the religious world of France: Lamennais's rupture with Rome, the condemnation of his opinions by the Pope, and his revolt against that condemnation, were imminent. Some of his followers, like Lacordaire, had already resolved not to cross the Rubicon with their leader, not to go into rebellion against Rome; they were preparing to separate from him. The society of La Chênaie was soon to dissolve; but, such as it is shown to us for a moment, with its voluntary character, its simple and severe life in common, its mixture of lay and clerical members, the genius of its chiefs, the sincerity of its disciples,—above all, its paramount fervent interest in matters of spiritual and religious concernment,—it offers a most instructive spectacle. It is not the spectacle we most of us think to find in France, the France we have imagined from common English notions, from the streets of Paris, from novels; it shows us how, wherever there is greatness like that of France, there are, as its foundation, treasures of fervour, pure-mindedness, and spirituality somewhere, whether we know of them or not;—a store of that which Goethe calls *Halt*;—since greatness can never be founded upon frivolity and corruption.

On the evening of the 18th of December in this year 1832, M. de Lamennais was talking to those assembled in the sitting-room of La Chênaie of his recent journey to Italy. He talked with all his usual animation; 'but', writes one of his hearers, a Breton gentleman, M. de Marzan, 'I soon became inattentive and absent, being struck with the reserved attitude of a young stranger some twenty-two years old, pale in face, his black hair already thin over his temples, with a southern eye, in which brightness and melancholy were mingled. He kept himself somewhat aloof, seeming to avoid notice rather than to court it. All the old faces of friends which I found about me at this my re-entry into the circle of La Chênaie failed to occupy me so much as the sight of this stranger, looking on, listening, observing, and saying nothing'.

The unknown was Maurice de Guérin. Of a noble but poor family, having lost his mother at six years old, he had been brought up by his father, a man saddened by his wife's death, and austerely religious, at the château of Le Cayla, in Languedoc. His childhood was not gay; he had not the society of other boys; and solitude, the sight of his father's gloom, and the habit of accompanying the curé of the parish on his rounds among the sick and dying, made him prematurely grave and familiar with sorrow. He went to school first at Toulouse, then at the Collège Stanislas at Paris, with a temperament almost as unfit as Shelley's for common school life. His youth was ardent, sensitive, agitated, and unhappy. In 1832 he procured admission to La Chênaie to brace his spirit by the teaching of Lamennais, and to decide whether his religious feelings would determine themselves into a distinct religious vocation. Strong and deep religious feelings he had, implanted in him by nature, developed in him by the circumstances of his childhood; but he had also (and here is the key to his character) that temperament which opposes itself to the fixedness of a religious vocation, or of any vocation of which fixedness is an essential attribute; a temperament mobile, inconstant, eager, thirsting for new impressions, abhorring rules, aspiring to a 'renovation without end'; a temperament common enough among artists, but with which few artists, who have it to the same degree as Guérin, unite a seriousness and a sad intensity like his. After leaving school, and before going to La Chênaie, he had been at home at Le Cayla with his sister Eugénie (a wonderfully gifted person, whose genius so competent a judge as M. Sainte-Beuve is inclined to pronounce even superior to her brother's) and his sister Eugénie's friends. With one of these friends he had fallen in love,—a slight and transient fancy, but which had already called his poetical powers into exercise; and his poems and fragments, in a certain green notebook (*le Cahier Vert*) which he long continued to make the depository of his thoughts, and which became famous among his friends, he brought with him to La Chênaie. There he found among the younger members of the Society several who, like himself, had a secret passion for poetry and literature; with these he became intimate, and in his letters and journal we find him occupied, now with a literary commerce established with these friends, now with the fortunes, fast coming to a crisis, of the Society,

and now with that for the sake of which he came to La Chênaie,
—his religious progress and the state of his soul.

On Christmas Day, 1832, having been then three weeks at
La Chênaie, he writes thus of it to a friend of his family, M. de
Bayne:

> La Chênaie is a sort of oasis in the midst of the steppes of
> Brittany. In front of the château stretches a very large garden
> cut in two by a terrace with a lime avenue, at the end of which
> is a tiny chapel. I am extremely fond of this little oratory,
> where one breathes a twofold peace,—the peace of solitude
> and the peace of the Lord. When spring comes we shall walk
> to prayers between two borders of flowers. On the east side,
> and only a few yards from the château, sleeps a small mere
> between two woods, where the birds in warm weather sing all
> day long; and then,—right, left, on all sides,—woods, woods,
> everywhere woods. It looks desolate just now that all is bare
> and the woods are rust-colour, and under this Brittany sky,
> which is always clouded and so low that it seems as if it were
> going to fall on your head; but as soon as spring comes the
> sky raises itself up, the woods come to life again, and every-
> thing will be full of charm.

Of what La Chênaie will be when spring comes he has a fore-
taste on the 3rd of March.

> Today [he writes in his journal] has enchanted me. For the
> first time for a long while the sun has shown himself in all his
> beauty. He has made the buds of the leaves and flowers swell,
> and he has waked up in me a thousand happy thoughts. The
> clouds assume more and more their light and graceful shapes,
> and are sketching, over the blue sky, the most charming
> fancies. The woods have not yet got their leaves, but they are
> taking an indescribable air of life and gaiety, which gives them
> quite a new physiognomy. Everything is getting ready for the
> great festival of Nature.

Storm and snow adjourn this festival a little longer. On the
11th of March he writes:

> It has snowed all night. I have been to look at our primroses;
> each of them has its small load of snow, and was bowing its
> head under its burden. These pretty flowers, with their rich

yellow colour, had a charming effect under their white hoods. I saw whole tufts of them roofed over by a single block of snow; all these laughing flowers thus shrouded and leaning one upon another, made one think of a group of young girls surprised by a shower, and sheltering under a white apron.'

The burst of spring comes at last, though late. On the 5th of April we find Guérin 'sitting in the sun to penetrate himself to the very marrow with the divine spring'. On the 3d of May, one can actually *see* the progress of the green; it has made a start from the garden to the shrubberies, it is getting the upper hand all along the mere; it leaps, one may say, from tree to tree, from thicket to thicket, in the fields and on the hill-sides; and I can see it already arrived at the forest edge and beginning to spread itself over the broad back of the forest. Soon it will have overrun everything as far as the eye can reach, and all those wide spaces between here and the horizon will be moving and sounding like one vast sea, a sea of emerald.'

Finally, on the 16th of May, he writes to M. de Bayne that 'the gloomy and bad days,—bad because they bring temptation by their gloom,—are, thanks to God and the spring, over; and I see approaching a long file of shining and happy days, to do me all the good in the world. This Brittany of ours', he continues, 'gives one the idea of the grayest and most wrinkled old woman possible suddenly changed back by the touch of a fairy's wand into a girl of twenty, and one of the loveliest in the world; the fine weather has so decked and beautified the dear old country.' He felt, however, the cloudiness and cold of the 'dear old country' with all the sensitiveness of a child of the South. 'What a difference', he cries, 'between the sky of Brittany, even on the finest day, and the sky of our South! Here the summer has, even on its highdays and holidays, something mournful, overcast, and stinted about it. It is like a miser who is making a show; there is a niggardliness in his magnificence. Give me our Languedoc sky, so bountiful of life, so blue, so largely vaulted!' And somewhat later, complaining of the short and dim sunlight of a February day in Paris, 'What a sunshine', he exclaims, 'to gladden eyes accustomed to all the wealth of light of the South! —*aux larges et libérales effusions de lumière du ciel du Midi.*'

In the long winter of La Chênaie his great resource was

literature. One has often heard that an educated Frenchman's reading seldom goes much beyond French and Latin, and that he makes the authors in these two languages his sole literary standard. This may or may not be true of Frenchmen in general, but there can be no question as to the width of the reading of Guérin and his friends, and as to the range of their literary sympathies. One of the circle, Hippolyte la Morvonnais,—a poet who published a volume of verse, and died in the prime of life,—had a passionate admiration for Wordsworth, and had even, it is said, made a pilgrimage to Rydal Mount to visit him; and in Guérin's own reading I find, besides the French names of Bernardin de St Pierre, Chateaubriand, Lamartine, and Victor Hugo, the names of Homer, Dante, Shakespeare, Milton, and Goethe; and he quotes both from Greek and from English authors in the original. His literary tact is beautifully fine and true. 'Every poet', he writes to his sister, 'has his own art of poetry written on the ground of his own soul; there is no other. Be constantly observing Nature in her smallest details, and then write as the current of your thoughts guides you;—that is all.' But with all this freedom from the bondage of forms and rules, Guérin marks with perfect precision the faults of the *free* French literature of his time,—the *littérature facile*,—and judges the romantic school and its prospects like a master: 'that youthful literature which has put forth all its blossom prematurely, and has left itself a helpless prey to the returning frost, stimulated as it has been by the burning sun of our century, by this atmosphere charged with a perilous heat, which has over-hastened every sort of development, and will most likely reduce to a handful of grains the harvest of our age'. And the popular authors,—those 'whose name appears once and disappears for ever, whose books, unwelcome to all serious people, welcome to the rest of the world, to novelty-hunters and novel-readers, fill with vanity these vain souls, and then, falling from hands heavy with the languor of satiety, drop for ever into the gulf of oblivion'; and those, more noteworthy, 'the writers of books celebrated, and, as works of art, deserving celebrity, but which have in them not one grain of that hidden manna, not one of those sweet and wholesome thoughts which nourish the human soul and refresh it when it is weary',—these he treats with such severity that he may in some sense be described, as he describes himself, as 'invoking with his whole heart a classical restoration'. He is best described, however, not as a partisan of any school, but as an ardent seeker for that mode of expression which is the most natural, happy, and true. He writes to his sister Eugénie:

> I want you to reform your system of composition; it is too loose, too vague, too Lamartinian. Your verse is too sing-song; it does not *talk* enough. Form for yourself a style of your own, which shall be your real expression. Study the French language by attentive reading, making it your care to remark constructions, turns of expression, delicacies of style, but without ever adopting the manner of any master. In the works of these masters we must learn our language, but we must use it each in our own fashion.[1]

It was not, however, to perfect his literary judgment that Guérin came to La Chênaie. The religious feeling, which was as much a part of his essence as the passion for Nature and the literary instinct, shows itself at moments jealous of these its rivals, and alarmed at their predominance. Like all powerful feelings, it wants to exclude every other feeling and to be absolute. One Friday in April, after he has been delighting himself with the shapes of the clouds and the progress of the spring, he suddenly bethinks himself that the day is Good Friday, and exclaims in his diary:

> My God, what is my soul about that it can thus go running after such fugitive delights on Good Friday on this day all filled with thy death and our redemption? There is in me I know not what damnable spirit, that awakens in me strong discontents, and is for ever prompting me to rebel against the holy exercises and the devout collectedness of soul which are the meet preparation for these great solemnities of our faith. Oh how well can I trace here the old leaven, from which I have not yet perfectly cleared my soul!

And again, in a letter to M. de Marzan: 'Of what, my God, are we made', he cries, 'that a little verdure and a few trees should be enough to rob us of our tranquillity and to distract

[1] Part of these extracts date from a time a little after Guérin's residence at La Chênaie; but already, amidst the readings and conversations of La Chênaie, his literary judgment was perfectly formed.

us from thy love?' And writing, three days after Easter Sunday, in his journal, he records the reception at La Chênaie of a fervent neophyte, in words which seem to convey a covert blame of his own want of fervency:

Three days have passed over our heads since the great festival. One anniversary the less for us yet to spend of the death and resurrection of our Saviour! Every year thus bears away with it its solemn festivals; when will the everlasting festival be here? I have been witness of a most touching sight; François has brought us one of his friends whom he has gained to the faith. This neophyte joined us in our exercises during the Holy week, and on Easter day he received the communion with us. François was in raptures. It is a truly good work which he has thus done. François is quite young, hardly twenty years old; M. de la M. is thirty, and is married. There is something most touching and beautifully simple in M. de la M. letting himself thus be brought to God by quite a young man; and to see friendship, on François's side, thus doing the work of an Apostle, is not less beautiful and touching.

Admiration for Lamennais worked in the same direction with this feeling. Lamennais never appreciated Guérin; his combative, rigid, despotic nature, of which the characteristic was energy, had no affinity with Guérin's elusive, undulating, impalpable nature, of which the characteristic was delicacy. He set little store by his new disciple, and could hardly bring himself to understand what others found so remarkable in him, his own genuine feeling towards him being one of indulgent compassion. But the intuition of Guérin, more discerning than the logic of his master, instinctively felt what there was commanding and tragic in Lamennais's character, different as this was from his own; and some of his notes are among the most interesting records of Lamennais which remain.

'Do you know what it is', M. Féli [1] said to us on the evening of the day before yesterday, 'which makes man the most suffering of all creatures? It is that he has one foot in the finite and the other in the infinite, and that he is torn asunder, not by four horses, as in the horrible old times, but between two

---

[1] The familiar name given to M. de Lamennais by his followers at La Chênaie.

worlds.' Again he said to us as we heard the clock strike: 'If that clock knew that it was to be destroyed the next instant, it would still keep striking its hour until that instant arrived. My children, be as the clock; whatever may be going to happen to you, strike always your hour.'

Another time Guérin writes:

'Today M. Féli startled us. He was sitting behind the chapel, under the two Scotch firs; he took his stick and marked out a grave on the turf, and said to Elie, 'It is there I wish to be buried, but no tombstone! only a simple hillock of grass. Oh, how well I shall be there!' Elie thought he had a presentiment that his end was near. This is not the first time he has been visited by such a presentiment; when he was setting out for Rome, he said to those here: 'I do not expect ever to come back to you; you must do the good which I have failed to do.' He is impatient for death.

Overpowered by the ascendancy of Lamennais, Guérin, in spite of his hesitations, in spite of his confession to himself that, 'after a three weeks' close scrutiny of his soul, in the hope of finding the pearl of a religious vocation hidden in some corner of it', he had failed to find what he sought, took, at the end of August 1833, a decisive step. He joined the religious order which Lamennais had founded. But at this very moment the deepening displeasure of Rome with Lamennais determined the Bishop of Rennes to break up, in so far as it was a religious congregation, the Society of La Chênaie, to transfer the novices to Ploërmel, and to place them under other superintendence. In September, Lamennais, 'who had not yet ceased', writes M. de Marzan, a fervent Catholic, 'to be a Christian and a priest, took leave of his beloved colony of La Chênaie, with the anguish of a general who disbands his army down to the last recruit, and withdraws annihilated from the field of battle'. Guérin went to Ploërmel. But here, in the seclusion of a real religious house, he instantly perceived how alien to a spirit like his,—a spirit which, as he himself says somewhere, 'had need of the open air, wanted to see the sun and the flowers',—was the constraint and monotony of a monastic life, when Lamennais's genius was no longer present to enliven this life for him. On the 7th of October he renounced the novitiate, believing himself a partisan of Lamennais in his

quarrel with Rome, reproaching the life he had left with demand-
ing passive obedience instead of trying 'to put in practice the
admirable alliance of order with liberty, and of variety with
unity', and declaring that, for his part, he preferred taking the
chances of a life of adventure to submitting himself to be '*garotté
par un règlement*,—tied hand and foot by a set of rules'. In real
truth, a life of adventure, or rather a life free to wander at its
own will, was that to which his nature irresistibly impelled him.

For a career of adventure, the inevitable field was Paris. But
before this career began, there came a stage, the smoothest, the
smoothest,
perhaps, and the most happy in the short life of Guérin. M. la
Morvonnais, one of his La Chênaie friends,—some years older
than Guérin, and married to a wife of singular sweetness and
charm,—had a house by the seaside at the mouth of one of the
beautiful rivers of Brittany, the Arguenon. He asked Guérin,
when he left Ploërmel, to come and stay with him at this place,
called Le Val de l'Arguenon, and Guérin spent the winter of
1833–4 there. I grudge every word about Le Val and its inmates
which is not Guérin's own, so charming is the picture he draws
of them, so truly does his talent find itself in its best vein as he
draws it.

'How full of goodness [he writes in his journal of the 7th
of December] is Providence to me! For fear the sudden passage from the mild and temperate air of a religious life to the
torrid clime of the world should be too trying for my soul, it
has conducted me, after I have left my sacred shelter, to a
house planted on the frontier between the two regions, where,
without being in solitude, one is not yet in the world; a house
whose windows look on the one side towards the plain where
the tumult of men is rocking, on the other towards the wilderness where the servants of God are chanting. I intend to write
down the record of my sojourn here, for the days here spent
are full of happiness, and I know that in the time to come I
shall often turn back to the story of these past felicities. A
man, pious, and a poet; a woman, whose spirit is in such
perfect sympathy with his that you would say they had but
one being between them: a child, called Marie like her mother,
and who sends, like a star, the first rays of her love and thought
through the white cloud of infancy; a simple life in an

old-fashioned house; the ocean, which comes morning and evening to bring us its harmonies; and lastly, a wanderer who descends from Carmel and is going on to Babylon, and who has laid down at this threshold his staff and his sandals, to take his seat at the hospitable table;—here is matter to make a biblical poem of, if I could only describe things as I can feel them!

Every line written by Guérin during this stay at Le Val is worth quoting, but I have only room for one extract more:

Never [he writes, a fortnight later, on the 20th of December], never have I tasted so inwardly and deeply the happiness of home-life. All the little details of this life, which in their succession make up the day, are to me so many stages of a continuous charm carried from one end of the day to the other. The morning greeting, which in some sort renews the pleasure of the first arrival, for the words with which one meets are almost the same, and the separation at night, through the hours of darkness and uncertainty, does not ill represent longer separations; then breakfast, during which you have the fresh enjoyment of having met together again; the stroll afterwards, when we go out and bid Nature good-morning; the return and setting to work in an old panelled chamber looking out on the sea, inaccessible to all the stir of the house, a perfect sanctuary of labour; dinner, to which we are called, not by a bell, which reminds one too much of school or a great house, but by a pleasant voice; the gaiety, the merriment, the talk flitting from one subject to another and never dropping so long as the meal lasts; the cracking fire of dry branches to which we draw our chairs directly afterwards, the kind words that are spoken round the warm flame which sings while we talk; and then, if it is fine, the walk by the seaside, when the sea has for its visitors a mother with her child in her arms, this child's father and a stranger, each of these two last with a stick in his hand; the rosy lips of the little girl, which keep talking at the same time with the waves,—now and then tears shed by her and cries of childish fright at the edge of the sea; our thoughts, the father's and mine, as we stand and look at the mother and child smiling at one another, or at the child in tears and the mother trying to comfort it by her caresses and exhortations; the Ocean, going on all the while rolling up his waves and noises; the dead boughs which we go and cut, here and there, out of the copse-wood, to make a quick and bright fire when we get home,—this little taste of the woodman's calling which brings us closer to Nature and makes us think of M. Féli's eager fondness for the same work; the hours of study and poetical flow which carry us to supper-time; this meal, which summons us by the same gentle voice as its predecessor, and which is passed amid the same joys, only less loud, because evening sobers everything, tones everything down; then our evening, ushered in by the blaze of a cheerful fire, and which with its alternations of reading and talking brings us at last to bed-time:—to all the charms of a day so spent add the dreams which follow it, and your imagination will still fall far short of these home-joys in their delightful reality.

I said the foregoing should be my last extract, but who could resist this picture of a January evening on the coast of Brittany?

All the sky is covered over with gray clouds just silvered at the edges. The sun, who departed a few minutes ago, has left behind him enough light to temper for a while the black shadows, and to soften down, as it were, the approach of night. The winds are hushed, and the tranquil ocean sends up to me, when I go out on the doorstep to listen, only a melodious murmur, which dies away in the soul like a beautiful wave on the beach. The birds, the first to obey the nocturnal influence, make their way towards the woods, and you hear the rustle of their wings in the clouds. The copses which cover the whole hill-side of Le Val, which all the day-time are alive with the chirp of the wren, the laughing whistle of the woodpecker,[1] and the different notes of a multitude of birds, have no longer any sound in their paths and thickets, unless it be the prolonged high call of the blackbirds at play with one another and chasing one another, after all the other birds have their heads safe under their wings. The noise of man, always the last to be silent, dies gradually out over the face of the fields. The general murmur fades away, and one hears hardly

---

[1] 'The woodpecker *laughs*,' says White of Selborne; and here is Guérin in Brittany, confirming his testimony.

a sound except what comes from the villages and hamlets, in which, up till far into the night, there are cries of children and barking of dogs. Silence wraps me round; everything seeks repose except this pen of mine, which perhaps disturbs the rest of some living atom asleep in a crease of my notebook, for it makes its light scratching as it puts down these idle thoughts. Let it stop, then! for all I write, have written, or shall write, will never be worth setting against the sleep of an atom.

On the 1st of February we find him in a lodging at Paris. 'I enter the world' (such are the last words written in his journal at Le Val) 'with a secret horror.' His outward history for the next five years is soon told. He found himself in Paris, poor, fastidious, and with health which already, no doubt, felt the obscure presence of the malady of which he died,—consumption. One of his Brittany acquaintances introduced him to editors, tried to engage him in the periodical literature of Paris; and so unmistakable was Guérin's talent, that even his first essays were immediately accepted. But Guérin's genius was of a kind which unfitted him to get his bread in this manner. At first he was pleased with the notion of living by his pen; '*je n'ai qu'à écrire,*' he says to his sister,—'I have only got to write'. But to a nature like his, endued with the passion for perfection, the necessity to produce, to produce constantly, to produce whether in the vein or out of the vein, to produce something good or bad or middling, as it may happen, but at all events *something*,—is the most intolerable of tortures. To escape from it he betook himself to that common but most perfidious refuge of men of letters, that refuge to which Goldsmith and poor Hartley Coleridge had betaken themselves before him,—the profession of teaching. In September 1834 he procured an engagement at the Collège Stanislas, where he had himself been educated. It was vacation-time, and all he had to do was to teach a small class composed of boys who did not go home for the holidays,—in his own words, 'scholars left like sick sheep in the fold, while the rest of the flock are frisking in the fields'. After the vacation he was kept on at the college as a supernumerary.

The master of the fifth class has asked for a month's leave of absence; I am taking his place, and by this work I get one hundred francs [£4]. I have been looking about for pupils to give private lessons to, and I have found three or four. School-work and private lessons together fill my day from half past seven in the morning till half past nine at night. The college dinner serves me for breakfast, and I go and dine in the evening at twenty-four *sous*, as a young man beginning life should.

To better his position in the hierarchy of public teachers it was necessary that he should take the degree of *agrégé ès-lettres*, corresponding to our degree of Master of Arts; and to his heavy work in teaching there was thus added that of preparing for a severe examination. The drudgery of this life was very irksome to him, although less insupportable than the drudgery of the profession of letters; inasmuch as to a sensitive man like Guérin, to silence his genius is more tolerable than to hackney it. Still the yoke wore him deeply, and he had moments of bitter revolt: he continued, however, to bear it with resolution, and on the whole with patience, for four years. On the 15th of November 1838 he married a young Creole lady of some fortune, Made-moiselle Caroline de Gervain, 'whom', to use his own words, 'Destiny, who loves these surprises, has wafted from the farthest Indies into my arms'. The marriage was happy, and it ensured to Guérin liberty and leisure; but now 'the blind Fury with the abhorred shears' was hard at hand. Consumption declared itself in him: 'I pass my life', he writes, with his old playfulness and calm, to his sister on the 8th of April 1839, 'within my bed-curtains, and wait patiently enough, thanks to Caro's [1] goodness, books, and dreams, for the recovery which the sunshine is to bring with it.' In search of this sunshine he was taken to his native country, Languedoc, but in vain. He died at Le Cayla on the 19th of July 1839.

The vicissitudes of his inward life during these five years were more considerable. His opinions and tastes underwent great, or what seem to be great, changes. He came to Paris the ardent partisan of Lamennais: even in April 1834, after Rome had finally condemned Lamennais,—'Tonight there will go forth from Paris,' he writes, 'with his face set to the west, a man whose every step I would fain follow, and who returns to the desert for which I sigh. M. Féli departs this evening for La

---

[1] His wife.

Chênaie.' But in October 1835,—'I assure you', he writes to his sister, 'I am at last weaned from M. de Lamennais; one does not remain a babe and suckling for ever; I am perfectly freed from his influence.' There was a greater change than this. In 1834 the main cause of Guérin's aversion to the literature of the French romantic school, was that this literature, having had a religious origin, had ceased to be religious: 'it has forgotten', he says, 'the house and the admonitions of its Father'. But his friend, M. de Marzan, tells us of a 'deplorable revolution' which, by 1836, had taken place in him. Guérin had become intimate with the chiefs of this very literature; he no longer went to church; 'the bond of a common faith, in which our friendship had its birth, existed between us no longer'. Then, again, 'this interregnum was not destined to last'. Reconverted to his old faith by suffering and by the pious efforts of his sister Eugénie, Guérin died a Catholic. His feelings about society underwent a like change. After 'entering the world with a secret horror', after congratulating himself when he had been some months at Paris on being 'disengaged from the social tumult, out of the reach of those blows which, when I live in the thick of the world, bruise me, irritate me, or utterly crush me', M. Sainte-Beuve tells us of him, two years afterwards, appearing in society 'a man of the world, elegant, even fashionable; a talker who could hold his own against the most brilliant talkers of Paris'.

In few natures, however, is there really such essential consistency as in Guérin's. He says of himself, in the very beginning of his journal: 'I owe everything to poetry, for there is no other name to give to the sum total of my thoughts; I owe to it whatever I now have pure, lofty, and solid in my soul; I owe to it all my consolations in the past; I shall probably owe to it my future.' Poetry, the poetical instinct, was indeed the basis of his nature; but to say so thus absolutely is not quite enough. One aspect of poetry fascinated Guérin's imagination and held it prisoner. Poetry is the interpretress of the natural world, and she is the interpretress of the moral world; it was as the interpretress of the natural world that she had Guérin for her mouthpiece. To make magically near and real the life of Nature, and man's life only so far as it is a part of that Nature, was his faculty; a faculty of naturalistic, not of moral interpretation. This faculty always has for its basis a peculiar temperament, an extraordinary delicacy

of organization and susceptibility to impressions; in exercising
it the poet is in a great degree passive (Wordsworth thus speaks
of a *wise passiveness*); he aspires to be a sort of human Aeolian
harp, catching and rendering every rustle of Nature. To assist
at the evolution of the whole life of the world is his craving, and
intimately to feel it all:

> . . . the glow, the thrill of life,
> Where, where do these abound?

is what he asks: he resists being riveted and held stationary by
any single impression, but would be borne on for ever down an
enchanted stream. He goes into religion and out of religion, into
society and out of society, not from the motives which impel
men in general, but to feel what it is all like; he is thus hardly a
moral agent, and, like the passive and ineffectual Uranus of
Keats's poem, he may say:

> . . . I am but a voice;
> My life is but the life of winds and tides;
> No more than winds and tides can I avail.

He hovers over the tumult of life, but does not really put his
hand to it.

No one has expressed the aspirations of this temperament
better than Guérin himself. In the last year of his life he writes:

> I return, as you see, to my old brooding over the world of
> Nature, that line which my thoughts irresistibly take; a sort
> of passion which gives me enthusiasm, tears, bursts of joy,
> and an eternal food for musing; and yet I am neither philo-
> sopher nor naturalist, nor anything learned whatsoever. There
> is one word which is the God of my imagination, the tyrant, I
> ought rather to say, that fascinates it, lures it onward, gives it
> work to do without ceasing, and will finally carry it I know not
> where; the word *life*.

And in one place in his journal he says:

> My imagination welcomes every dream, every impression,
> without attaching itself to any, and goes on for ever seeking
> something new.

And again in another:

> The longer I live, and the clearer I discern between true
> and false in society, the more does the inclination to live, not

as a savage or a misanthrope, but as a solitary man on the frontiers of society, on the outskirts of the world, gain strength and grow in me. The birds come and go and make nests around our habitations, they are fellow citizens of our farms and hamlets with us; but they take their flight in a heaven which is boundless, but the hand of God alone gives and measures to them their daily food, but they build their nests in the heart of the thick bushes, or hang them in the height of the trees. So would I, too, live, hovering round society, and having always at my back a field of liberty vast as the sky.

In the same spirit he longed for travel. 'When one is a wanderer', he writes to his sister, 'one feels that one fulfils the true condition of humanity.' And the last entry in his journal is,— 'The stream of travel is full of delight. Oh, who will set me adrift on this Nile!'

Assuredly it is not in this temperament that the active virtues have their rise. On the contrary, this temperament, considered in itself alone, indisposes for the discharge of them. Something morbid and excessive, as manifested in Guérin, it undoubtedly has. In him, as in Keats, and as in another youth of genius, whose name, but the other day unheard of, Lord Houghton has so gratefully written in the history of English poetry,—David Gray,—the temperament, the talent itself, is deeply influenced by their mysterious malady; the temperament is *devouring*; it uses vital power too hard and too fast, paying the penalty in long hours of unutterable exhaustion and in premature death. The intensity of Guérin's depression is described to us by Guérin himself with the same incomparable touch with which he describes happier feelings; far oftener than any pleasurable sense of his gift he has 'the sense profound, near, immense, of my misery, of my inward poverty'. And again: 'My inward misery gains upon me; I no longer dare look within.' And on another day of gloom he does look within, and here is the terrible analysis:

Craving, unquiet, seeing only by glimpses, my spirit is stricken by all those ills which are the sure fruit of a youth doomed never to ripen into manhood. I grow old and wear myself out in the most futile mental straining, and make no progress. My head seems dying, and when the wind blows I fancy I feel it, as if I were a tree, blowing through a number of withered branches in my top. Study is intolerable to me, or rather it is quite out of my power. Mental work brings on, not drowsiness, but an irritable and nervous disgust which drives me out, I know not where, into the streets and public places. The Spring, whose delights used to come every year stealthily and mysteriously to charm me in my retreat, crushes me this year under a weight of sudden hotness. I should be glad of any event which delivered me from the situation in which I am. If I were free I would embark for some distant country where I could begin life anew.

Such is this temperament in the frequent hours when the sense of its own weakness and isolation crushes it to the ground. Certainly it was not for Guérin's happiness, or for Keats's, as men count happiness, to be as they were. Still the very excess and predominance of their temperament has given to the fruits of their genius a unique brilliancy and flavour. I have said that poetry interprets in two ways; it interprets by expressing with magical felicity the physiognomy and movement of the outward world, and it interprets by expressing, with inspired conviction, the ideas and laws of the inward world of man's moral and spiritual nature. In other words, poetry is interpretative both by having *natural magic* in it, and by having *moral profundity*. In both ways it illuminates man; it gives him a satisfying sense of reality; it reconciles him with himself and the universe. Thus Aeschylus's '$\delta\rho\acute{\alpha}\sigma\alpha\nu\tau\iota$ $\pi\alpha\theta\epsilon\hat{\iota}\nu$' and his '$\grave{\alpha}\nu\acute{\eta}\rho\iota\theta\mu\sigma\nu$ $\gamma\acute{\epsilon}\lambda\alpha\sigma\mu\alpha$' are alike interpretative. Shakespeare interprets both when he says,

> Full many a glorious morning have I seen
> Flatter the mountain-tops with sovereign eye;

and when he says,

> There's a divinity that shapes our ends,
> Rough-hew them how we will.

These great poets unite in themselves the faculty of both kinds of interpretation, the naturalistic and the moral. But it is observable that in the poets who unite both kinds, the latter (the moral) usually ends by making itself the master. In Shakespeare the two kinds seem wonderfully to balance one another; but even in him the balance leans; his expression tends to become too little sensuous and simple, too much intellectualized. The same thing may be yet more strongly affirmed of Lucretius and of Wordsworth. In Shelley there is not a balance of the two gifts, nor even a co-existence of them, but there is a passionate straining after them both, and this is what makes Shelley, as a man, so interesting: I will not now inquire how much Shelley achieves as a poet, but whatever he achieves, he in general fails to achieve natural magic in his expression; in Mr Palgrave's charming *Treasury* may be seen a gallery of his failures.[1] But in Keats and Guérin, in whom the faculty of naturalistic interpretation is overpoweringly predominant, the natural magic is perfect; when they speak of the world they speak like Adam naming by divine inspiration the creatures; their expression corresponds with the thing's essential reality. Even between Keats and Guérin, however, there is a distinction to be drawn. Keats has, above all, a sense of what is pleasurable and open in the life of nature; for him she is the *Alma Parens*: his expression has, therefore, more than Guérin's, something genial, outward, and sensuous. Guérin has, above all, a sense of what there is adorable and secret in the life of Nature; for him she is the *Magna Parens*; his expression has, therefore, more than Keats's, something mystic, inward, and profound.

So he lived like a man possessed; with his eye not on his own career, not on the public, not on fame, but on the Isis whose veil he had uplifted. He published nothing. 'There is more power and beauty', he writes, 'in the well-kept secret of one's-self and one's thoughts, than in the display of a whole heaven that one may have inside one.' 'My spirit', he answers the friends who urge him to write, 'is of the home-keeping order, and has no fancy for adventure; literary adventure is above all distasteful to it; for this, indeed (let me say so without the least self-sufficiency), it has a contempt. The literary career seems to me unreal, both in its own essence and in the rewards which one seeks from it, and therefore fatally marred by a secret absurdity.' His acquaintances, and among them distinguished men of letters, full of admiration for the originality and delicacy of his

---

[1] Compare, for example, his 'Lines Written in the Euganean Hills', with Keats's 'Ode to Autumn' (*Golden Treasury*, pp. 256, 284). The latter piece *renders* Nature; the former *tries to render* her. I will not deny, however, that Shelley has natural magic in his rhythm; what I deny is, that he has it in his language. It always seems to me that the right sphere for Shelley's genius was the sphere of music, not of poetry; the medium of sounds he can master, but to master the more difficult medium of words he has neither intellectual force enough nor sanity enough.

talent, laughed at his self-depreciation, warmly assured him of
his powers. He received their assurances with a mournful
incredulity, which contrasts with the self-assertion of poor
David Gray, whom I just now mentioned. 'It seems to me
intolerable', he writes, 'to appear to men other than one appears
to God. My worst torture at this moment is the over-estimate
which generous friends form of me. We are told that at the last
judgment the secret of all consciences will be laid bare to the
universe; would that mine were so this day, and that every passer-
by could see me as I am!' 'High above my head,' he says at
another time, 'far, far away, I seem to hear the murmur of that
world of thought and feeling to which I aspire so often, but
where I can never attain. I think of those of my own age who
have wings strong enough to reach it, but I think of them without
jealousy, and as men on earth contemplate the elect and their
felicity.' And, criticizing his own composition, 'When I begin a
subject, my self-conceit' (says this exquisite artist) 'imagines I
am doing wonders; and when I have finished, I see nothing but
a wretched made-up imitation, composed of odds and ends of
colour stolen from other people's palettes, and tastelessly mixed
together on mine.' Such was his *passion for perfection*, his disdain
for all poetical work not perfectly adequate and felicitous. The
magic of expression, to which by the force of this passion he won
his way, will make the name of Maurice de Guérin remembered
in literature.

I have already mentioned the *Centaur*, a sort of prose poem
by Guérin, which Madame Sand published after his death. The
idea of this composition came to him, M. Sainte-Beuve says, in
the course of some visits which he made with his friend, M.
Trebutien, a learned antiquarian, to the Museum of Antiquities
in the Louvre. The free and wild life which the Greeks expressed
by such creations as the Centaur had, as we might well expect,
a strong charm for him; under the same inspiration he composed
a *Bacchante*, which was meant by him to form part of a prose
poem on the adventures of Bacchus in India. Real as was the
affinity which Guérin's nature had for these subjects, I doubt
whether, in treating them, he would have found the full and
final employment of his talent. But the beauty of his *Centaur* is
extraordinary; in its whole conception and expression this piece
has in a wonderful degree that natural magic of which I have

said so much, and the rhythm has a charm which bewitches even a foreigner. An old Centaur on his mountain is supposed to relate to Melampus, a human questioner, the life of his youth. Untranslatable as the piece is, I shall conclude with some extracts from it:

THE CENTAUR

I had my birth in the caves of these mountains. Like the stream of this valley, whose first drops trickle from some weeping rock in a deep cavern, the first moment of my life fell in the darkness of a remote abode, and without breaking the silence. When our mothers draw near to the time of their delivery, they withdraw to the caverns, and in the depth of the loneliest of them, in the thickest of its gloom, bring forth, without uttering a plaint, a fruit silent as themselves. Their puissant milk makes us surmount, without weakness or dubious struggle, the first difficulties of life; and yet we leave our caverns later than you your cradles. The reason is that we have a doctrine that the early days of existence should be kept apart and enshrouded, as days filled with the presence of the gods. Nearly the whole term of my growth was passed in the darkness where I was born. The recesses of my dwelling ran so far under the mountain that I should not have known on which side was the exit, had not the winds, when they sometimes made their way through the opening, sent fresh airs in, and a sudden trouble. Sometimes, too, my mother came back to me, having about her the odours of the valleys, or streaming from the waters which were her haunt. Her returning thus, without a word said of the valleys or the rivers, but with the emanations from them hanging about her, troubled my spirit, and I moved up and down restlessly in my darkness. 'What is it,' I cried, 'this outside world whither my mother is borne, and what reigns there in it so potent as to attract her so often?' At these moments my own force began to make me unquiet. I felt in it a power which could not remain idle; and betaking myself either to toss my arms or to gallop backwards and forwards in the spacious darkness of the cavern, I tried to make out from the blows which I dealt in the empty space or from the transport of my course through it, in what direction my arms were meant to reach, or my feet to bear me. Since that day, I have wound my arms round the bust of Centaurs, and round the body of heroes, and round the trunk of oaks; my hands have assayed the rocks, the waters, plants without number, and the subtlest impressions of the air,— for I uplift them in the dark and still nights to catch the breaths of wind, and to draw signs whereby I may augur my road; my feet,—look, O Melampus, how worn they are! And yet all benumbed as I am in this extremity of age, there are days when, in broad sunlight, on the mountain-tops, I renew these gallopings of my youth in the cavern, and with the same object, brandishing my arms and employing all the fleetness which yet is left to me.

O Melampus, thou who wouldst know the life of the Centaurs, wherefore have the gods willed that thy steps should lead thee to me, the oldest and most forlorn of them all? It is long since I have ceased to practise any part of their life. I quit no more this mountain summit, to which age has confined me. The point of my arrows now serves me only to uproot some tough-fibred plant; the tranquil lakes know me still, but the rivers have forgotten me. I will tell thee a little of my youth; but these recollections, issuing from a worn memory, come like the drops of a niggardly libation poured from a damaged urn.

The course of my youth was rapid and full of agitation. Movement was my life, and my steps knew no bound. One day when I was following the course of a valley seldom entered by the Centaurs, I discovered a man making his way up the stream-side on the opposite bank. He was the first whom my eyes had lighted on: I despised him. 'Behold,' I cried, 'at the utmost but the half of what I am! How short are his steps! and his movement how full of labour! Doubtless he is a Centaur overthrown by the gods, and reduced by them to drag himself along thus.'

Wandering along at my own will like the rivers, feeling wherever I went the presence of Cybele, whether in the bed of the valleys, or on the height of the mountains, I bounded whither I would, like a blind and chainless life. But when

Night, filled with the charm of the gods, overtook me on the slopes of the mountain, she guided me to the mouth of the caverns, and there tranquillized me as she tranquillizes the billows of the sea. Stretched across the threshold of my retreat, my flanks hidden within the cave, and my head under the open sky, I watched the spectacle of the dark. The sea-gods, it is said, quit during the hours of darkness their palaces under the deep; they seat themselves on the promontories, and their eyes wander over the expanse of the waves. Even so I kept watch, having at my feet an expanse of life like the hushed sea. My regards had free range, and travelled to the most distant points. Like sea-beaches which never lose their wetness, the line of mountains to the west retained the imprint of gleams not perfectly wiped out by the shadows. In that quarter still survived, in pale clearness, mountain-summits naked and pure. There I beheld at one time the god Pan descend, ever solitary; at another the choir of the mystic divinities; or I saw pass some mountain nymph charm-struck by the night. Sometimes the eagles of Mount Olympus traversed the upper sky, and were lost to view among the far-off constellations, or in the shade of the dreaming forests.

Thou pursuest after wisdom, O Melampus, which is the science of the will of the gods; and thou roamest from people to people like a mortal driven by the destinies. In the times when I kept my night-watches before the caverns, I have sometimes believed that I was about to surprise the thought of the sleeping Cybele, and that the mother of the gods, betrayed by her dreams, would let fall some of her secrets; but I have never made out more than sounds which faded away in the murmur of night, or words inarticulate as the bubbling of the rivers.

'O Macareus,' one day said the great Chiron to me, whose old age I tended; 'we are, both of us, Centaurs of the mountain; but how different are our lives! Of my days all the study is (thou seest it) the search for plants; thou, thou art like those mortals who have picked up on the waters or in the woods, and carried to their lips, some pieces of the reed-pipe thrown away by the god Pan. From that hour these mortals, having caught from their relics of the god a passion for wild life, or perhaps smitten with some secret madness, enter into the wilderness, plunge among the forests, follow the course of the streams, bury themselves in the heart of the mountains, restless, and haunted by an unknown purpose. The mares beloved of the winds in the farthest Scythia are not wilder than thou, nor more cast down at nightfall, when the North Wind has departed. Seekest thou to know the gods, O Macareus, and from what source men, animals, and the elements of the universal fire have their origin? But the aged Ocean, the father of all things, keeps locked within his own breast these secrets; and the nymphs, who stand around, sing as they weave their eternal dance before him, to cover any sound which might escape from his lips half-opened by slumber. The mortals, dear to the gods for their virtue, have received from their hands lyres to give delight to man, or the seeds of new plants to make him rich; but from their inexorable lips, nothing!'

Such were the lessons which the old Chiron gave me. Waned to the very extremity of life, the Centaur yet nourished in his spirit the most lofty discourse.

For me, O Melampus, I decline into my last days, calm as the setting of the constellations. I still retain enterprise enough to climb to the top of the rocks, and there I linger late, either gazing on the wild and restless clouds, or to see come up from the horizon the rainy Hyades, the Pleiades, or the great Orion; but I feel myself perishing and passing quickly away, like a snow-wreath floating on the stream; and soon shall I be mingled with the waters which flow in the vast bosom of Earth.

IV

EUGÉNIE DE GUÉRIN

WHO that had spoken of Maurice de Guérin could refrain from speaking of his sister Eugénie, the most devoted of sisters, one of the rarest and most beautiful of souls? 'There is nothing fixed, no duration, no vitality in the sentiments of women towards one another; their attachments are mere pretty knots of ribbon, and no more. In all the friendships of women I observe this slightness of the tie. I know no instance to the contrary, even in history. Orestes and Pylades have no sisters.' So she herself speaks of the friendships of her own sex. But Electra can attach herself to Orestes, if not to Chrysothemis. And to her brother Maurice, Eugénie de Guérin was Pylades and Electra in one.

The name of Maurice de Guérin,—that young man so gifted, so attractive, so careless of fame, and so early snatched away; who died at twenty-nine; who, says his sister, 'let what he did be lost with a carelessness so unjust to himself, set no value on any of his own productions, and departed hence without reaping the rich harvest which seemed his due'; who, in spite of his immaturity, in spite of his fragility, exercised such a charm, 'furnished to others so much of that which all live by', that some years after his death his sister found in a country-house where he used to stay, in the journal of a young girl who had not known him, but who heard her family speak of him, his name, the date of his death, and these words, '*il était leur vie*' (he was their life); whose talent, exquisite as that of Keats, with much less of sunlight, abundance, inventiveness, and facility in it than that of Keats, but with more of distinction and power, had 'that winning, delicate, and beautifully happy turn of expression' which is the stamp of the master,—is beginning to be well known to all lovers of literature. This establishment of Maurice's name was an object for which his sister Eugénie passionately laboured. While he was alive, she placed her whole joy in the flowering of this gifted nature; when he was dead, she had no other thought than to make the world know him as she knew him. She outlived him nine years, and her cherished task for those years was to rescue the fragments of her brother's composition, to collect them, to get them published. In pursuing this task she had at first cheering hopes of success; she had at last baffling and bitter disappointment. Her earthly business was at an end; she died. Ten years afterwards, it was permitted to the love of a friend, M. Trebutien, to effect for Maurice's memory what the love of a sister had failed to accomplish. But those who read, with delight and admiration, the journal and letters of Maurice de Guérin, could not but be attracted and touched by this sister Eugénie, who met them at every page. She seemed hardly less gifted, hardly less interesting, than Maurice himself. And presently M. Trebutien did for the sister what he had done for the brother. He published the journal of Mdlle Eugénie de Guérin, and a few (too few, alas!) of her letters.[1] The book has made a profound impression in France; and the fame which she sought only for her brother now crowns the sister also.

Parts of Mdlle de Guérin's journal were several years ago printed for private circulation, and a writer in the *National Review* had the good fortune to fall in with them. The bees of our English criticism do not often roam so far afield for their honey, and this critic deserved thanks for having flitted in his quest of blossom to foreign parts, and for having settled upon a beautiful flower there. He had the discernment to see that Mdlle de Guérin was well worth speaking of, and he spoke of her with feeling and appreciation. But that, as I have said, was several years ago; even a true and feeling homage needs to be from time to time renewed, if the memory of its object is to endure; and criticism must not lose the occasion offered by Mdlle de Guérin's journal being for the first time published to the world, of directing notice once more to this religious and beautiful character.

Eugénie de Guérin was born in 1805, at the château of Le Cayla, in Languedoc. Her family, though reduced in circumstances, was noble; and even when one is a saint one cannot quite forget that one comes of the stock of the Guarini of Italy, or that one counts among one's ancestors a Bishop of Senlis, who had the

[1] A volume of these, also, has just been brought out by M. Trebutien. One good book, at least, in the literature of the year 1865!

marshalling of the French order of battle on the day of Bouvines.
Le Cayla was a solitary place, with its terrace looking down upon
a stream-bed and valley; 'one may pass days there without seeing
any living thing but the sheep, without hearing any living thing
but the birds'. M. de Guérin, Eugénie's father, lost his wife
when Eugénie was thirteen years old, and Maurice seven; he
was left with four children,—Eugénie, Marie, Erembert, and
Maurice,—of whom Eugénie was the eldest, and Maurice was
the youngest. This youngest child, whose beauty and delicacy
had made him the object of his mother's most anxious fondness,
was commended by her in dying to the care of his sister Eugénie.
Maurice at eleven years old went to school at Toulouse; then
he went to the Collège Stanislas at Paris; then he became a
member of the religious society which M. de Lamennais had
formed at La Chênaie in Brittany; afterwards he lived chiefly
at Paris, returning to Le Cayla, at the age of twenty-nine, to die.
Distance, in those days, was a great obstacle to frequent meetings
of the separated members of a French family of narrow means.
Maurice de Guérin was seldom at Le Cayla after he had once
quitted it, though his few visits to his home were long ones; but
he passed five years,—the period of his sojourn in Brittany,
and of his first settlement in Paris,—without coming home at all.
In spite of the check from these absences, in spite of the more
serious check from a temporary alteration in Maurice's religious
feelings, the union between the brother and sister was wonderfully close and firm. For they were knit together, not only by
the tie of blood and early attachment, but also by the tie of a
common genius. 'We were', says Eugénie, 'two eyes looking
out of one head.' She, on her part, brought to her love for her
brother the devotedness of a woman, the intensity of a recluse,
almost the solicitude of a mother. Her home duties prevented
her from following the wish, which often arose in her, to join a
religious sisterhood. There is a trace,—just a trace,—of an early
attachment to a cousin; but he died when she was twenty-four.
After that, she lived for Maurice. It was for Maurice that, in
addition to her constant correspondence with him by letter, she
began in 1834 her journal, which was sent to him by portions as
it was finished. After his death she tried to continue it, addressing
it to 'Maurice in heaven'. But the effort was beyond her strength;
gradually the entries become rarer and rarer; and on the last

day of December, 1840, the pen dropped from her hand: the journal ends.

Other sisters have loved their brothers, and it is not her affection for Maurice, admirable as this was, which alone could have made Eugénie de Guérin celebrated. I have said that both brother and sister had genius: M. Sainte-Beuve goes so far as to say that the sister's genius was equal, if not superior, to her brother's. No one has a more profound respect for M. Sainte-Beuve's critical judgments than I have; but it seems to me that this particular judgment needs to be a little explained and guarded. In Maurice's special talent, which was a talent for interpreting nature, for finding words which incomparably render the subtlest impressions which nature makes upon us, which bring the intimate life of nature wonderfully near to us, it seems to me that his sister was by no means his equal. She never, indeed, expresses herself without grace and intelligence; but her words, when she speaks of the life and appearance of nature, are in general but intellectual signs; they are not like her brother's—symbols equivalent with the thing symbolized. They bring the notion of the thing described to the mind, they do not bring the feeling of it to the imagination. Writing from the Nivernais, that region of vast woodlands in the centre of France: 'It does one good', says Eugénie, 'to be going about in the midst of this enchanting nature, with flowers, birds, and verdure all round one, under this large and blue sky of the Nivernais. How I love the gracious form of it, and those little white clouds here and there, like cushions of cotton, hung aloft to rest the eye in this immensity!' It is pretty and graceful, but how different from the grave and pregnant strokes of Maurice's pencil! 'I have been along the Loire, and seen on its banks the plains where nature is puissant and gay; I have seen royal and antique dwellings, all marked by memories which have their place in the mournful legend of humanity,—Chambord, Blois, Amboise, Chenonceaux; then the towns on the two banks of the river,—Orleans, Tours, Saumur, Nantes; and at the end of it all, the Ocean rumbling. From these I passed back into the interior of the country, as far as Bourges and Nevers, a region of vast woodlands, in which murmurs of an immense range and fulness' (*ce beau torrent de rumeurs*, as, with an expression worthy of Wordsworth, he elsewhere calls them) 'prevail and never cease.' Words whose charm is like that of the sounds of the murmuring forest itself, and whose reverberations, like theirs, die away in the infinite distance of the soul.

Maurice's life was in the life of nature, and the passion for it consumed him; it would have been strange if his accent had not caught more of the soul of nature than Eugénie's accent, whose life was elsewhere. 'You will find in him,' Maurice says to his sister of a friend whom he was recommending to her, 'you will find in him that which you love, and which suits you better than anything else,—*l'onction, l'effusion, la mysticité*.' Unction, the pouring out of the soul, the rapture of the mystic, were dear to Maurice also; but in him the bent of his genius gave even to those a special direction of its own. In Eugénie they took the direction most native and familiar to them; their object was the religious life.

And yet, if one analyses this beautiful and most interesting character quite to the bottom, it is not exactly as a saint that Eugénie de Guérin is remarkable. The ideal saint is a nature like Saint François de Sales or Fénelon; a nature of ineffable sweetness and serenity, a nature in which struggle and revolt is over, and the whole man (so far as is possible to human infirmity) swallowed up in love. Saint Theresa (it is Mdlle de Guérin herself who reminds us of it) endured twenty years of unacceptance and of repulse in her prayers; yes, but the Saint Theresa whom Christendom knows is Saint Theresa repulsed no longer! it is Saint Theresa accepted, rejoicing in love, radiant with ecstasy. Mdlle de Guérin is not one of these saints arrived at perfect sweetness and calm, steeped in ecstasy; there is something primitive, indomitable in her, which she governs, indeed, but which chafes, which revolts; somewhere in the depths of that strong nature there is a struggle, an impatience, an inquietude, an ennui, which endures to the end, and which leaves one, when one finally closes her journal, with an impression of profound melancholy. 'There are days', she writes to her brother, 'when one's nature rolls itself up, and becomes a hedgehog. If I had you here at this moment, here close by me, how I should prick you! how sharp and hard!' 'Poor soul, poor soul,' she cries out to herself another day, 'what is the matter, what would you have? Where is that which will do you good? Everything is green, everything is in bloom, all the air has a breath of flowers. How beautiful it is!

well, I will go out. No, I should be alone, and all this beauty, when one is alone, is worth nothing. What shall I do then? Read, write, pray, take a basket of sand on my head like that hermit-saint, and walk with it? Yes, work, work! keep busy the body which does mischief to the soul! I have been too little occupied today, and that is bad for one, and it gives a certain ennui which I have in me time to ferment.'

A certain ennui which I have in me: her wound is there. In vain she follows the counsel of Fénelon: 'If God tires you, *tell him that he tires you.*' No doubt she obtained great and frequent solace and restoration from prayer: 'This morning I was suffering; well, at present I am calm, and this I owe to faith, simply to faith, to an act of faith. I can think of death and eternity without trouble, without alarm. Over a deep of sorrow there floats a divine calm, a suavity which is the work of God only. In vain have I tried over things at a time like this: nothing human comforts the soul, nothing human upholds it:

> A l'enfant il faut sa mère,
> A mon âme il faut mon Dieu.'

Still the ennui reappears, bringing with it hours of unutterable forlornness, and making her cling to her one great earthly happiness,—her affection for her brother,—with an intenseness, an anxiety, a desperation in which there is something morbid, and by which she is occasionally carried into an irritability, a jealousy which she herself is the first, indeed, to censure, which she severely represses, but which nevertheless leaves a sense of pain.

Mdlle de Guérin's admirers have compared her to Pascal, and in some respects the comparison is just. But she cannot exactly be classed with Pascal, any more than with Saint François de Sales. Pascal is a man, and the inexhaustible power and activity of his mind leave him no leisure for ennui. He had not the sweetness and serenity of the perfect saint; he is, perhaps, 'der strenge, kranke Pascal—*the severe, morbid Pascal*',—as Goethe (and, strange to say, Goethe at twenty-three, an age which usually feels Pascal's charm most profoundly) calls him. But the stress and movement of the lifelong conflict waged in him between his soul and his reason keep him full of fire, full of agitation, and keep his reader, who witnesses this conflict, animated and excited;

the sense of forlornness and dejected weariness which clings to
Eugénie de Guérin does not belong to Pascal. Eugénie de Guérin
is a woman, and longs for a state of firm happiness, for an affection in which she may repose; the inward bliss of Saint Theresa
or Fénelon would have satisfied her; denied this, she cannot
rest satisfied with the triumphs of self-abasement, with the
sombre joy of trampling the pride of life and of reason under-
foot, of reducing all human hope and joy to insignificance; she
repeats the magnificent words of Bossuet, words which both
Catholicism and Protestantism have uttered with indefatigable
iteration: 'On trouve au fond de tout le vide et le néant—*at the
bottom of everything one finds emptiness and nothingness,*'—but
she feels, as every one but the true mystic must ever feel, their
incurable sterility.

She resembles Pascal, however, by the clearness and firmness
of her intelligence, going straight and instinctively to the bottom
of any matter she is dealing with, and expressing herself about
it with incomparable precision; never fumbling with what she
has to say, never imperfectly seizing or imperfectly presenting
her thought. And to this admirable precision she joins a lightness
of touch, a feminine ease and grace, a flowing facility which are
her own. 'I do not say', writes her brother Maurice, an excellent
judge, 'that I find in myself a dearth of expression; but I have
not this abundance of yours, this productiveness of soul which
streams forth, which courses along without ever failing, and
always with an infinite charm.' And writing to her of some composition of hers, produced after her religious scruples had for a
long time kept her from the exercise of her talent: 'You see, my
dear Tortoise,' he writes, 'that your talent is no illusion, since
after a period, I know not how long, of poetical inaction,—a trial
to which any half-talent would have succumbed,—it rears its
head again more vigorous than ever. It is really heart-breaking
to see you repress and bind down, with I know not what scruples,
your spirit, which tends with all the force of its nature to develop
itself in this direction. Others have made it a case of conscience
for you to resist this impulse, and I make it one for you to follow
it.' And she says of herself, on one of her freer days: 'It is the
instinct of my life to write, as it is the instinct of the fountain to
flow.' The charm of her expression is not a sensuous and imaginative charm like that of Maurice, but rather an intellectual

charm; it comes from the texture of the style rather than from its elements; it is not so much in the words as in the turn of the phrase, in the happy cast and flow of the sentence. Recluse as she was, she had a great correspondence: everyone wished to have letters from her; and no wonder.

To this strength of intelligence and talent of expression she joined a great force of character. Religion had early possessed itself of this force of character, and reinforced it: in the shadow of the Cevennes, in the sharp and tonic nature of this region of Southern France, which has seen the Albigensians, which has seen the Camisards, Catholicism too is fervent and intense. Eugénie de Guérin was brought up amidst strong religious influences, and they found in her a nature on which they could lay firm hold. I have said that she was not a saint of the order of Saint François de Sales or Fénelon; perhaps she had too keen an intelligence to suffer her to be this, too forcible and impetuous a character. But I did not mean to imply the least doubt of the reality, the profoundness, of her religious life. She was penetrated by the power of religion; religion was the master-influence of her life; she derived immense consolations from religion, she earnestly strove to conform her whole nature to it; if there was an element in her which religion could not perfectly reach, perfectly transmute, she groaned over this element in her, she chid it, she made it bow. Almost every thought in her was brought into harmony with religion; and what few thoughts were not thus brought into harmony were brought into subjection.

Then she had her affection for her brother; and this, too, though perhaps there might be in it something a little over-eager a little too absolute, a little too susceptible, was a pure, a devoted affection. It was not only passionate, it was tender. It was tender, pliant, and self-sacrificing to a degree that not in one nature out of a thousand,—of natures with a mind and will like hers,—is found attainable. She thus united extraordinary power of intelligence, extraordinary force of character, and extraordinary strength of affection; and all these under the control of a deep religious feeling.

This is what makes her so remarkable, so interesting. I shall try and make her speak for herself, that she may show us the characteristic sides of her rare nature with her own inimitable touch.

It must be remembered that her journal is written for Maurice only; in her lifetime no eye but his ever saw it. '*Ceci n'est pas pour le public*,' she writes; '*c'est de l'intime, c'est de l'âme, c'est pour un.*' 'This is not for the public; it contains my inmost thoughts, my very soul; it is for *one*.' And Maurice, this *one*, was a kind of second self to her. 'We see things with the same eyes; what you find beautiful, I find beautiful; God has made our souls of one piece.' And this genuine confidence in her brother's sympathy gives to the entries in her journal a naturalness and simple freedom rare in such compositions. She felt that he would understand her, and be interested in all that she wrote.

One of the first pages of her journal relates an incident of the home-life of Le Cayla, the smallest detail of which Maurice liked to hear; and in relating it she brings this simple life before us. She is writing in November, 1834:

I am furious with the gray cat. The mischievous beast has made away with a little half-frozen pigeon, which I was trying to thaw by the side of the fire. The poor little thing was just beginning to come round; I meant to tame him; he would have grown fond of me; and there is my whole scheme eaten up by a cat! This event, and all the rest of today's history, has passed in the kitchen. Here I take up my abode all the morning and a part of the evening, ever since I am without Mimi.[1] I have to superintend the cook; sometimes papa comes down, and I read to him by the oven, or by the fireside, some bits out of the *Antiquities of the Anglo-Saxon Church*. This book struck Pierril[2] with astonishment. '*Que de mouts aqui dédins!* What a lot of words there are inside it!' This boy is a real original. One evening he asked me if the soul was immortal; then afterwards, what a philosopher was? We had got upon great questions, as you see. When I told him that a philosopher was a person who was wise and learned: 'Then, mademoiselle, you are a philosopher.' This was said with an air of simplicity and sincerity which might have made even Socrates take it as a compliment; but it made me laugh so much that my gravity as catechist was gone for that evening. A day or two ago Pierril left us, to his great sorrow: his time with us was up on Saint Brice's day. Now he goes about with his little dog,

---

[1] The familiar name of her sister Marie.
[2] A servant-boy at Le Cayla.

truffle-hunting. If he comes this way I shall go and ask him
if he still thinks I look like a philosopher.

Her good sense and spirit made her discharge with alacrity
her household tasks in this patriarchal life of Le Cayla, and
treat them as the most natural thing in the world. She sometimes
complains, to be sure, of burning her fingers at the kitchen-fire.
But when a literary friend of her brother expresses enthusiasm
about her and her poetical nature: 'The poetess,' she says,
'whom this gentleman believes me to be, is an ideal being, infinitely removed from the life which is actually mine—a life of
occupations, a life of household-business, which takes up all
my time. How could I make it otherwise? I am sure I do not
know; and, besides, my duty is in this sort of life, and I have
no wish to escape from it.'

Among these occupations of the patriarchal life of the châtelaine of Le Cayla intercourse with the poor fills a prominent
place:

Today [she writes on the 9th of December 1834] I have
been warming myself at every fireside in the village. It is a
round which Mimi and I often make, and in which I take
pleasure. Today we have been seeing sick people, and holding
forth on doses and sick-room drinks. 'Take this, do that';
and they attend to us just as if we were the doctor. We prescribed shoes for a little thing who was amiss from having
gone barefoot; to the brother, who, with a bad headache, was
lying quite flat, we prescribed a pillow; the pillow did him
good, but I am afraid it will hardly cure him. He is at the
beginning of a bad feverish cold: and these poor people live
in the filth of their hovels like animals in their stable; the bad
air poisons them. When I come home to Le Cayla I seem to
be in a palace.

She had books, too; not in abundance, not for the fancying
them; the list of her library is small, and it is enlarged slowly and
with difficulty. The *Letters of Saint Theresa*, which she had long
wished to get, she sees in the hands of a poor servant girl before
she can procure them for herself. 'What then?' is her comment;
'very likely she makes a better use of them than I could.' But
she has the *Imitation*, the *Spiritual Works* of Bossuet and Fénelon,
the *Lives of the Saints*, Corneille, Racine, André Chénier, and

Lamartine; Madame de Staël's book on Germany, and French translations of Shakespeare's plays, Ossian, the *Vicar of Wakefield*, Scott's *Old Mortality* and *Redgauntlet*, and the *Promessi Sposi* of Manzoni. Above all, she has her own mind; her meditations in the lonely fields, on the oak-grown hill-side of 'The Seven Springs'; her meditations and writing in her own room, her *chambrette*, her *délicieux chez moi*, where every night, before she goes to bed, she opens the window to look out upon the sky, —the balmy moonlit sky of Languedoc. This life of reading, thinking, and writing was the life she liked best, the life that most truly suited her.

I find writing has become almost a necessity to me. Whence does it arise, this impulse to give utterance to the voice of one's spirit, to pour out my thoughts before God and one human being? I say one human being, because I always imagine that you are present, that you see what I write. In the stillness of a life like this my spirit is happy, and, as it were, dead to all that goes on upstairs or downstairs, in the house or out of the house. But this does not last long. 'Come, my poor spirit,' I then say to myself, 'we must go back to the things of this world.' And I take my spinning, or a book, or a saucepan, or I play with Wolf or Trilby. Such a life as this I call heaven upon earth.

Tastes like these, joined with a talent like Mdlle de Guérin's, naturally inspire thoughts of literary composition. Such thoughts she had, and perhaps she would have been happier if she had followed them; but she never could satisfy herself that to follow them was quite consistent with the religious life, and her projects of composition were gradually relinquished:

Would to God that my thoughts, my spirit, had never taken their flight beyond the narrow round in which it is my lot to live! In spite of all that people say to the contrary, I feel that I cannot go beyond my needlework and my spinning without going too far: I feel it, I believe it: well, then, I will keep in my proper sphere; however much I am tempted, my spirit shall not be allowed to occupy itself with great matters until it occupies itself with them in Heaven.

And again:

My journal has been untouched for a long while. Do you

want to know why? It is because the time seems to me mis-
spent which I spend in writing it. We owe God an account of
every minute; and is it not a wrong use of our minutes to
employ them in writing a history of our transitory days?

She overcomes her scruples, and goes on writing the journal;
but again and again they return to her. Her brother tells her of
the pleasure and comfort something she has written gives to a
friend of his in affliction. She answers:

It is from the Cross that those thoughts come, which your
friend finds so soothing, so unspeakably tender. None of them
come from me. I feel my own aridity; but I feel, too, that God,
when he will, can make an ocean flow upon this bed of sand.
It is the same with so many simple souls, from which proceed
the most admirable things; because they are in direct relation
with God, without false science and without pride. And thus
I am gradually losing my taste for books; I say to myself:
'What can they teach me which I shall not one day know in
Heaven? let God be my master and my study here!' I try to
make him so, and I find myself the better for it. I read little;
I go out little; I plunge myself in the inward life. How infinite
are the saying, doings, feelings, events of that life! Oh, if you
could but see them! But what avails it to make them known?
God alone should be admitted to the sanctuary of the soul.

Beautifully as she says all this, one cannot, I think, read it
without a sense of disquietude, without a presentiment that this
ardent spirit is forcing itself from its natural bent, that the beatitude of the true mystic will never be its earthly portion. And
yet how simple and charming is her picture of the life of religion
which she chose as her ark of refuge, and in which she desired
to place all her happiness:

Cloaks, clogs, umbrellas, all the apparatus of winter, went
with us this morning to Andillac, where we have passed the
whole day; some of it at the curé's house, the rest in church.
How I like this life of a country Sunday, with its activity, its
journeys to church, its liveliness! You find all your neighbours
on the road; you have a curtsey from every woman you meet,
and then, as you go along, such a talk about the poultry, the
sheep and cows, the good man and the children! My great

delight is to give a kiss to these children, and see them run away and hide their blushing faces in their mother's gown. They are alarmed at *las doumaïsélos*,[1] as at a being of another world. One of these little things said the other day to its grandmother, who was talking of coming to see us: '*Minino*, you mustn't go to that castle; there is a black hole there.' What is the reason that in all ages the noble's château has been an object of terror? Is it because of the horrors that were committed there in old times? I suppose so.

This vague horror of the château, still lingering in the mind of the French peasant fifty years after he has stormed it, is indeed curious, and is one of the thousand indications how unlike aristocracy on the Continent has been to aristocracy in England. But this is one of the great matters with which Mdlle de Guérin would not have us occupied; let us pass to the subject of Christmas in Languedoc:

Christmas is come; the beautiful festival, the one I love most, and which gives me the same joy as it gave the shepherds of Bethlehem. In real truth, one's whole soul sings with joy at this beautiful coming of God upon earth,—a coming which here is announced on all sides of us by music and by our charming *nadalet*.[2] Nothing at Paris can give you a notion of what Christmas is with us. You have not even the midnight-mass. We all of us went to it, papa at our head, on the most perfect night possible. Never was there a finer sky than ours was that midnight;—so fine that papa kept perpetually throwing back the hood of his cloak, that he might look up at the sky. The ground was white with hoar-frost, but we were not cold; besides, the air, as we met it, was warmed by the bundles of blazing torchwood which our servants carried in front of us to light us on our way. It was delightful, I do assure you; and I should like you to have seen us there on our road to church, in those lanes with the bushes along their banks as white as if they were in flower. The hoar-frost makes the most lovely flowers. We saw a long spray so beautiful that we wanted to take it with us as a garland for the communion-table, but it melted in our hands: all flowers fade so soon! I was very sorry

[1] The young lady.
[2] A peculiar peal rung at Christmas-time by the church bells of Languedoc.

about my garland; it was mournful to see it drip away, and get smaller and smaller every minute.

The religious life is at bottom everywhere alike; but it is curious to note the variousness of its setting and outward circumstance. Catholicism has these so different from Protestantism! and in Catholicism these accessories have, it cannot be denied, a nobleness and amplitude which in Protestantism are often wanting to them. In Catholicism they have, from the antiquity of this form of religion, from its pretensions to universality, from its really widespread prevalence, from its sensuousness, something European, august, and imaginative: in Protestantism they often have, from its inferiority in all these respects, something provincial, mean, and prosaic. In revenge, Protestantism has a future before it, a prospect of growth in alliance with the vital movement of modern society; while Catholicism appears to be bent on widening the breach between itself and the modern spirit, to be fatally losing itself in the multiplication of dogmas, Mariolatry, and miracle-mongering. But the style and circumstance of actual Catholicism is grander than its present tendency, and the style and circumstance of Protestantism is meaner than its tendency. While I was reading the journal of Mdlle de Guérin there came into my hands the memoir and poems of a young Englishwoman, Miss Emma Tatham; and one could not but be struck with the singular contrast which the two lives,—in their setting rather than in their inherent quality,—present. Miss Tatham had not, certainly, Mdlle de Guérin's talent, but she had a sincere vein of poetic feeling, a genuine aptitude for composition. Both were fervent Christians, and, so far, the two lives have a real resemblance; but, in the setting of them, what a difference! The Frenchwoman is a Catholic in Languedoc; the Englishwoman is a Protestant at Margate; Margate, that brick-and-mortar image of English Protestantism, representing it in all its prose, all its uncomeliness,—let me add, all its salubrity. Between the external form and fashion of these two lives, between the Catholic Mdlle de Guérin *nadalet* at the Languedoc Christmas, her chapel of moss at Easter-time, her daily reading of the life of a saint, carrying her to the most diverse times, places, and peoples,—her quoting, when she wants to fix her mind upon the staunchness which the religious aspirant needs, the words of

Saint Macedonius to a hunter whom he met in the mountains, 'I pursue after God, as you pursue after game',—her quoting, when she wants to break a village girl of disobedience to her mother, the story of the ten disobedient children whom at Hippo Saint Augustine saw palsied;—between all this and the bare, blank, narrowly English setting of Miss Tatham's Protestantism, her 'union in church-fellowship with the worshippers at Hawley Square Chapel, Margate'; her 'singing with soft, sweet voice, the animating lines—

> My Jesus to know, and feel His blood flow,
> 'Tis life everlasting, 'tis heaven below';

her 'young female teachers belongings to the Sunday-school', and her 'Mr Thomas Rowe, a venerable class-leader',—what a dissimilarity! In the ground of the two lives, a likeness; in all their circumstance, what unlikeness! An unlikeness, it will be said, in that which is non-essential and indifferent. Non-essential, —yes; indifferent,—no. The signal want of grace and charm in English Protestantism's setting of its religious life is not an indifferent matter; it is a real weakness. *This ought ye to have done, and not to have left the other undone.*

I have said that the present tendency of Catholicism,—the Catholicism of the main body of the Catholic clergy and laity,— seems likely to exaggerate rather than to remove all that in this form of religion is most repugnant to reason; but this Catholicism was not that of Mdlle de Guérin. The insufficiency of her Catholicism comes from a doctrine which Protestantism, too, has adopted, although Protestantism, from its inherent element of freedom, may find it easier to escape from it; a doctrine with a certain attraction for all noble natures, but, in the modern world at any rate, incurably sterile,—the doctrine of the emptiness and nothingness of human life, of the superiority of renouncement to activity, of quietism to energy; the doctrine which makes effort for things on this side of the grave a folly, and joy in things on this side of the grave a sin. But her Catholicism is remarkably free from the faults which Protestants commonly think inseparable from Catholicism; the relation to the priest, the practice of confession, assume, when she speaks of them, an aspect which is not that under which Exeter Hall knows them, but which,— unless one is of the number of those who prefer regarding that by which men and nations die to regarding that by which they live,—one is glad to study. '*La confession*', she says twice in her journal, '*n'est qu'une expansion du repentir dans l'amour;*' and her weekly journey to the confessional in the little church of Cahuzac is her '*cher pèlerinage*'; the little church is the place where she has '*laissé tant de misères*'.

> This morning [she writes one 28th of November] I was up before daylight, dressed quickly, said my prayers, and started with Marie for Cahuzac. When we got there, the chapel was occupied, which I was not sorry for. I like not to be hurried, and to have time, before I go in, to lay bare my soul before God. This often takes me a long time, because my thoughts are apt to be flying about like these autumn leaves. At ten o'clock I was on my knees, listening to words the most salutary that were ever spoken; and I went away, feeling myself a better being. Every burden thrown off leaves us with a sense of brightness; and when the soul has laid down the load of its sins at God's feet, it feels as if it had wings. What an admirable thing is confession! What comfort, what light, what strength is given me every time after I have said, *I have sinned*.

This blessing of confession is the greater, she says, 'the more the heart of the priest to whom we confide our repentance is like that divine heart which "has so loved us". This is what attaches me to M. Bories.' M. Bories was the curé of her parish, a man no longer young, and of whose loss, when he was about to leave them, she thus speaks:

> What a grief for me! how much I lose in losing this faithful guide of my conscience, heart, and mind, of my whole self, which God has appointed to be in his charge, and which let itself be in his charge so gladly! He knew the resolves which God had put in my heart, and I had need of his help to follow them. Our new curé cannot supply his place: he is so young! and then he seems so inexperienced, so undecided! It needs firmness to pluck a soul out of the midst of the world, and to uphold it against the assaults of flesh and blood. It is Saturday, my day for going to Cahuzac; I am just going there, perhaps I shall come back more tranquil. God has always given me some good thing there, in that chapel where I have left behind me so many miseries.

Such is confession for her when the priest is worthy; and, when he is not worthy, she knows how to separate the man from the office:

Today I am going to do something which I dislike; but I will do it, with God's help. Do not think I am on my way to the stake; it is only that I am going to confess to a priest in whom I have not confidence, but who is the only one here. In this act of religion the man must always be separated from the priest, and sometimes the man must be annihilated.

The same clear sense, the same freedom from superstition, shows itself in all her religious life. She tells us, to be sure, how once, when she was a little girl, she stained a new frock, and on praying, in her alarm, to an image of the Virgin which hung in her room, saw the stains vanish: even the austerest Protestant will not judge such Mariolatry as this very harshly. But, in general, the Virgin Mary fills in the religious parts of her journal no prominent place; it is Jesus, not Mary. 'Oh, how well has Jesus said; "Come unto me, all ye that labour and are heavy laden." It is only there, only in the bosom of God, that we can rightly weep, rightly rid ourselves of our burden.' And again: 'The mystery of suffering makes one grasp the belief of something to be expiated, something to be won. I see it in Jesus Christ, the Man of Sorrow. *It was necessary that the Son of Man should suffer*. That is all we know in the troubles and calamities of life.'

And who has ever spoken of justification more impressively and piously than Mdlle de Guérin speaks of it, when, after reckoning the number of minutes she has lived she, exclaims:

My God, what have we done with all these minutes of ours, which thou, too, wilt one day reckon? Will there be any of them to count for eternal life? will there be many of them? will there be one of them? 'If thou, O Lord, wilt be extreme to mark what is done amiss, O Lord, who may abide it?' This close scrutiny of our time may well make us tremble, all of us who have advanced more than a few steps in life; for God will judge us otherwise than as he judges the lilies of the field. I have never been able to understand the security of those who placed their whole reliance, in presenting themselves before God, upon a good conduct in the ordinary relations of human life. As if all our duties were confined within the narrow sphere of this world! To be a good parent, a good child, a good citizen, a good brother or sister, is not enough to procure entrance into the kingdom of heaven. God demands other things besides these kindly social virtues of him whom he means to crown with an eternity of glory.

And, with this zeal for the spirit and power of religion, what prudence in her counsels of religious practice; what discernment, what measure! She has been speaking of the charm of the *Lives of the Saints*, and she goes on:

> Notwithstanding this, the *Lives of the Saints* seem to me, for a great many people, dangerous reading. I would not recommend them to a young girl, or even to some women who are no longer young. What one reads has such power over one's feelings; and these, even in seeking God, sometimes go astray. Alas, we have seen it in poor C.'s case. What care one ought to take with a young person; with what she reads, what she writes, her society, her prayers,—all of them matters which demand a mother's tender watchfulness! I remember many things I did at fourteen, which my mother, had she lived, would not have let me do. I would have done anything for God's sake; I would have cast myself into an oven, and assuredly things like that are not God's will; he is not pleased by the hurt one does to one's health through that ardent but ill-regulated piety which, while it impairs the body, often leaves many a fault flourishing. And, therefore, Saint François de Sales used to say to the nuns who asked his leave to go bare-foot: 'Change your brains and keep your shoes.'

Meanwhile Maurice, in a five years' absence, and amid the distractions of Paris, lost, or seemed to his sister to lose, something of his fondness for his home and its inmates: he certainly lost his early religious habits and feelings. It is on this latter loss that Mdlle de Guérin's journal oftenest touches,—with infinite delicacy, but with infinite anguish:

> Oh, the agony of being in fear for a soul's salvation, who can describe it! That which caused our Saviour the keenest suffering, in the agony of his Passion, was not so much the thought of the torments he was to endure, as the thought that these torments would be of no avail for a multitude of sinners; for all those who set themselves against their redemption, or

who do not care for it. The mere anticipation of this obstinacy and this heedlessness had power to make sorrowful, even unto death, the divine Son of Man. And this feeling all Christian souls, according to the measure of faith and love granted them, more or less share.

Maurice returned to Le Cayla in the summer of 1837, and passed six months there. This meeting entirely restored the union between him and his family. 'These six months with us,' writes his sister, 'he ill, and finding himself so loved by us all, had entirely reattached him to us. Five years without seeing us, had perhaps made him a little lose sight of our affection for him; having found it again, he met it with all the strength of his own. He had so firmly renewed, before he left us, all family-ties, that nothing but death could have broken them.' The separation in religious matters between the brother and sister gradually diminished, and before Maurice died it had ceased. I have elsewhere spoken of Maurice's religious feeling and his character. It is probable that his divergence from his sister in this sphere of religion was never so wide as she feared, and that his reunion with her was never so complete as she hoped. 'His errors were passed,' she says, 'his illusions were cleared away; by the call of his nature, by original disposition, he had come back to sentiments of order. I knew all, I followed each of his steps; out of the fiery sphere of the passions (which held him but a little moment) I saw him pass into the sphere of the Christian life. It was a beautiful soul, the soul of Maurice.' But the illness which had caused his return to Le Cayla reappeared after he got back to Paris in the winter of 1837–8. Again he seemed to recover; and his marriage with a young Creole lady, Mdlle Caroline de Gervain, took place in the autumn of 1838. At the end of September in that year Mdlle de Guérin had joined her brother in Paris; she was present at his marriage, and stayed with him and his wife for some months afterwards. Her journal recommences in April 1839. Zealously as she had promoted her brother's marriage, cordial as were her relations with her sister-in-law, it is evident that a sense of loss, of loneliness, invades her, and sometimes weighs her down. She writes in her journal on the 4th of May:

God knows when we shall see one another again! My own

Maurice, must it be our lot to live apart, to find that this
marriage which I had so much share in bringing about, which
I hoped would keep us so much together, leaves us more
asunder than ever? For the present and for the future, this
troubles me more than I can say. My sympathies, my inclina-
tions, carry me more towards you than towards any other
member of our family. I have the misfortune to be fonder of
you than of anything else in the world, and my heart had from
of old built in you its happiness. Youth gone and life declining, I looked forward to quitting the scene with Maurice. At
any time of life a great affection is a great happiness; the spirit
comes to take refuge in it entirely. O delight and joy which
will never be your sister's portion! Only in the direction of
God shall I find an issue for my heart to love as it has the
notion of loving, as it has the power of loving.

From such complainings, in which there is undoubtedly
something morbid,—complainings which she herself blamed,
to which she seldom gave way, but which, in presenting her
character, it is not just to put wholly out of sight,—she was called
by the news of an alarming return of her brother's illness. For
some days the entries in the journal show her agony of apprehension. 'He coughs, he coughs still! Those words keep echo-
ing for ever in my ears and, pursue me wherever I go; I cannot
look at the leaves on the trees without thinking that the winter
will come, and then the consumptive die.' She went to him, and
brought him back by slow stages to Le Cayla, dying. He died
on the 19th of July, 1839.

Thenceforward the energy of life ebbed in her; but the main
chords of her being, the chord of affection, the chord of religious
longing, the chord of intelligence, the chord of sorrow, gave,
so long as they answered to the touch at all, a deeper and finer
sound than ever. Always she saw before her, 'that beloved pale
face'; 'that beautiful head, with all its different expressions,
smiling, speaking, suffering, dying', regarded her always:

I have seen his coffin in the same room, in the same spot
where I remember seeing, when I was a very little girl, his
cradle, when I was brought home from Gaillac, where I was
then staying, for his christening. This christening was a grand
one, full of rejoicing, more than that of any of the rest of us;

specially marked. I enjoyed myself greatly, and went back to Gaillac next day, charmed with my new little brother. Two years afterwards I came home, and brought with me a frock for him of my own making. I dressed him in the frock, and took him out with me along by the warren at the north of the house, and there he walked a few steps alone,—his first walking alone,—and I ran with delight to tell my mother the news: 'Maurice, Maurice, has begun to walk by himself!'—recollections which, coming back today, break one's heart.

The shortness and suffering of her brother's life filled her with an agony of pity.

Poor beloved soul, you have had hardly any happiness here below; your life has been so short, your repose so rare. O God, uphold me, establish my heart in thy faith! Alas, I have too little of this supporting me! How we have gazed at him and loved him, and kissed him,—his wife, and we, his sisters; he lying lifeless in his bed, his head on the pillow as if he were asleep! Then we followed him to the churchyard, to the grave, to his last resting-place, and prayed over him, and wept over him; and we are here again, and I am writing to him again, as if he were staying away from home, as if he were in Paris. My beloved one, can it be, shall we never see one another again on earth?

But in heaven?—and here, though love and hope finally prevailed, the very passion of the sister's longing sometimes inspired torturing inquietudes:

I am broken down with misery. I want to see him. Every moment I pray to God to grant me this grace. Heaven, the world of spirits, is it so far from us? O depth, O mystery of the other life which separates us! I, who was so eagerly anxious about him, who wanted so to know all that happened to him, —wherever he may be now, it is over! I follow him into the three abodes; I stop wistfully before the place of bliss, I pass on to the place of suffering,—to the gulf of fire. My God, my God, no! Not there let my brother be! not there! And he is not: his soul, the soul of Maurice, among the lost . . . horrible fear, no! But in purgatory, where the soul is cleansed by suffering, where the failings of the heart are expiated, the doubtings of the spirit, the half-yieldings to evil? Perhaps my brother is there and suffers, and calls to us amidst his anguish of repentance, as he used to call to us amidst his bodily suffering: 'Help me, you who love me.' Yes, beloved one, by prayer. I will go and pray; prayer has been such a power to me, and I will pray to the end. Prayer! Oh! and prayer for the dead; it is the dew of purgatory.

Often, alas, the gracious dew would not fall; the air of her soul was parched; the arid wind, which was somewhere in the depths of her being, blew. She marks in her journal the 1st of May, 'this return of the loveliest month in the year', only to keep up the old habit; even the month of May can no longer give her any pleasure: '*Tout est changé*—all is changed.' She is crushed by 'the misery which has nothing good in it, the tear-less, dry misery, which bruises the heart like a hammer'.

I am dying to everything. I am dying of a slow moral agony, a condition of unutterable suffering. Lie there, my poor journal! be forgotten with all this world which is fading away from me. I will write here no more until I come to life again, until God re-awakens me out of this tomb in which my soul lies buried. Maurice, my beloved! it was not thus with me when I had *you*! The thought of Maurice could revive me from the most profound depression: to have him in the world was enough for me. With Maurice, to be buried alive would have not seemed dull to me.

And, as a burden to this funeral strain, the old *vide et néant* of Bossuet, profound, solemn, sterile:

So beautiful in the morning, and in the evening, *that*! how the thought disenchants one, and turns one from the world! I can understand that Spanish grandee who, after lifting up the winding-sheet of a beautiful queen, threw himself into the cloister and became a great saint. I would have all my friends at La Trappe, in the interest of their eternal welfare. Not that in the world one cannot be saved, not that there are not in the world duties to be discharged as sacred and as beautiful as there are in the cloister, but . . .

And there she stops, and a day or two afterwards her journal comes to an end. A few fragments, a few letters carry us on a little later, but after the 22d of August, 1845, there is nothing. To make known her brother's genius to the world was the one task she set herself after his death; in 1840 came Madame Sand's noble tribute to him in the *Revue des Deux Mondes*; then followed projects of raising a yet more enduring monument to his fame by collecting and publishing his scattered compositions; these projects I have already said, were baffled;—Mdlle de Guérin's letter of the 22d of August, 1845, relates to this disappointment. In silence, during nearly three years more, she faded away at Le Cayla. She died on the 31st of May, 1848.

M. Trebutien has accomplished the pious task in which Mdlle de Guérin was baffled, and has established Maurice's fame; by publishing this journal he has established Eugénie's also. She was very different from her brother; but she too, like him, had that in her which preserves a reputation. Her soul had the same characteristic quality as his talent,—*distinction*. Of this quality the world is impatient; it chafes against it, rails at it, insults it, hates it;—it ends by receiving its influence, and by undergoing its law. This quality at last inexorably corrects the world's blunders, and fixes the world's ideals. It procures that the popular poet shall not finally pass for a Pindar, nor the popular historian for a Tacitus, nor the popular preacher for a Bossuet. To the circle of spirits marked by this rare quality, Maurice and Eugénie de Guérin belong; they will take their place in the sky which these inhabit, and shine close to one another, *lucida sidera.*

V

HEINRICH HEINE

I KNOW not if I deserve that a laurel-wreath should one day be laid on my coffin. Poetry, dearly as I have loved it, has always been to me but a divine plaything. I have never attached any great value to poetical fame; and I trouble myself very little whether people praise my verses or blame them. But lay on my coffin a *sword*; for I was a brave soldier in the war of liberation of humanity.

Heine had his full share of love of fame, and cared quite as much as his brethren of the *genus irritabile* whether people praised his verses or blamed them. And he was very little of a hero. Posterity will certainly decorate his tomb with the emblem of the laurel rather than with the emblem of the sword. Still, for his contemporaries, for us, for the Europe of the present century, he is significant chiefly for the reason which he himself in the words just quoted assigns. He is significant because he was, if not pre-eminently a brave, yet a brilliant, a most effective soldier in the war of liberation of humanity.

To ascertain the master-current in the literature of an epoch, and to distinguish this from all minor currents, is one of the critic's highest functions; in discharging it he shows how far he possesses the most indispensable quality of his office,—justness of spirit. The living writer who has done most to make England acquainted with German authors, a man of genius, but to whom precisely this one quality of justness of spirit is perhaps wanting, —I mean Mr Carlyle,—seems to me in the result of his labours on German literature to afford a proof how very necessary to the critic this quality is. Mr Carlyle has spoken admirably of Goethe; but then Goethe stands before all men's eyes, the manifest centre of German literature; and from this central source many rivers flow. Which of these rivers is the main stream? which of the courses of spirit which we see active in Goethe is the course which will most influence the future, and attract and

be continued by the most powerful of Goethe's successors?—
that is the question. Mr Carlyle attaches, it seems to me, far too
much importance to the romantic school of Germany,—Tieck,
Novalis, Jean Paul Richter,—and gives to these writers, really
gifted as two, at any rate, of them are, an undue prominence.
These writers, and others with aims and a general tendency the
same as theirs, are not the real inheritors and continuators of
Goethe's power; the current of their activity is not the main
current of German literature after Goethe. Far more in Heine's
works flows this main current; Heine, far more than Tieck or
Jean Paul Richter, is the continuator of that which, in Goethe's
varied activity, is the most powerful and vital; on Heine, of all
German authors who survived Goethe, incomparably the largest
portion of Goethe's mantle fell. I do not forget that when Mr
Carlyle was dealing with German literature, Heine, though he
was clearly risen above the horizon, had not shone forth with all
his strength; I do not forget, too, that after ten or twenty years
many things may come out plain before the critic which before
were hard to be discerned by him; and assuredly no one would
dream of imputing it as a fault to Mr Carlyle that twenty years
ago he mistook the central current in German literature, over-
looked the rising Heine, and attached undue importance to that
romantic school which Heine was to destroy; one may rather
note it as a misfortune, sent perhaps as a delicate chastisement
to a critic, who,—man of genius as he is, and no one recognizes
his genius more admirably than I do,—has, for the functions of
the critic, a little too much of the self-will and eccentricity of a
genuine son of Great Britain.

Heine is noteworthy, because he is the most important German successor and continuator of Goethe in Goethe's most
important line of activity. And which of Goethe's lines of activity
is this?—his line of activity as 'a soldier in the war of liberation
of humanity'.

Heine himself would hardly have admitted this affiliation,
though he was far too powerful-minded a man to decry, with
some of the vulgar German liberals, Goethe's genius.

The wind of the Paris Revolution [he writes after the three
days of 1830] blew about the candles a little in the dark night
of Germany, so that the red curtains of a German throne or

two caught fire; but the old watchmen, who do the police of the German kingdoms, are already bringing out the fire-engines, and will keep the candles closer snuffed for the future. Poor, fast-bound German people, lose not all heart in thy bonds! The fashionable coating of ice melts off from my heart, my soul quivers and my eyes burn, and that is a dis-advantageous state of things for a writer, who should control his subject matter and keep himself beautifully objective, as the artistic school would have us, and as Goethe has done; he has come to be eighty years old doing this, and minister, and in good condition:—poor German people! that is thy greatest man!

But here Goethe himself: 'If I were to say what I had really been to the Germans in general, and to the young German poets in particular, I should say I had been their *liberator*.'

Modern times find themselves with an immense system of institutions, established facts, accredited dogmas, customs, rules, which have come to them from times not modern. In this system their life has to be carried forward; yet they have a sense that this system is not of their own creation, that it by no means corresponds exactly with the wants of their actual life, that, for them, it is customary, not rational. The awakening of this sense is the awakening of the modern spirit. The modern spirit is now awake almost everywhere; the sense of want of correspondence between the forms of modern Europe and its spirit, between the new wine of the eighteenth and nineteenth centuries, and the old bottles of the eleventh and twelfth centuries, or even of the sixteenth and seventeenth, almost everyone now perceives; it is no longer dangerous to affirm that this want of correspondence exists; people are even begin-ning to be shy of denying it. To remove this want of correspon-dence is beginning to be the settled endeavour of most persons of good sense. Dissolvents of the old European system of domin-ant ideas and facts we must all be, all of us who have any power of working; what we have to study is that we may not be acrid dissolvents of it.

And how did Goethe, that grand dissolvent in an age when there were fewer of them than at present, proceed in his task of dissolution, of liberation of the modern European from the old routine? He shall tell us himself:

Through me the German poets have become aware that, as man must live from within outwards, so the artist must work from within outwards, seeing that, make what contortions he will, he can only bring to light his own individuality. I can clearly mark where this influence of mine has made itself felt; there arises out of it a kind of poetry of nature, and only in this way it is possible to be original.

My voice shall never be joined to those which decry Goethe, and if it is said that the foregoing is a lame and impotent conclusion to Goethe's declaration that he had been the liberator of the Germans in general, and of the young German poets in particular, I say it is not. Goethe's profound, imperturbable naturalism is absolutely fatal to all routine thinking; he puts the standard, once for all, inside every man instead of outside him; when he is told such a thing must be so, there is immense authority and custom in favour of its being so, it has been held to be so for a thousand years, he answers with Olympian politeness, 'But *is* it so? is it so to *me*?' Nothing could be more really subversive of the foundations on which the old European order rested; and it may be remarked that no persons are so radically detached from this order, no persons so thoroughly modern, as those who have felt Goethe's influence most deeply. If it is said that Goethe professes to have in this way deeply influenced but a few persons, and those persons poets, one may answer that he could have taken no better way to secure, in the end, the ear of the world; for poetry is simply the most beautiful, impressive, and widely effective mode of saying things, and hence its importance. Nevertheless the process of liberation, as Goethe worked it, though sure, is undoubtedly slow; he came, as Heine says, to be eighty years old in thus working it, and at the end of that time the old Middle-Age machine was still creaking on, the thirty German courts and their chamberlains subsisted in all their glory; Goethe himself was a minister, and the visible triumph of the modern spirit over prescription and routine seemed as far off as ever. It was the year 1830; the German sovereigns had passed the preceding fifteen years in breaking the promises of freedom they had made to their subjects when they wanted their help in the final struggle with Napoleon. Great events were happening in France; the revolution, defeated in 1815, had arisen from its defeat, and was wresting from its adversaries the power. Heinrich Heine, a young man of genius, born at Hamburg, and with all the culture of Germany, but by race a Jew; with warm sympathies for France, whose revolution had given to his race the rights of citizenship, and whose rule had been, as is well known, popular in the Rhine provinces, where he passed his youth; with a passionate admiration for the great French Emperor, with a passionate contempt for the sovereigns who had overthrown him, for their agents, and for their policy,—Heinrich Heine was in 1830 in no humour for any such gradual process of liberation from the old order of things as that which Goethe had followed. His counsel was for open war. With that terrible modern weapon, the pen, in his hand, he passed the remainder of his life in one fierce battle. What was that battle? the reader will ask. It was a life and death battle with Philistinism.

Philistinism!—we have not the expression in English. Perhaps we have not the word because we have so much of the thing. At Soli, I imagine, they did not talk of solecisms; and here, at the very headquarters of Goliath, nobody talks of Philistinism. The French have adopted the term *épicier* (grocer), to designate the sort of being whom the Germans designate by the term Philistine; but the French term,—besides that it casts a slur upon a respectable class, composed of living and susceptible members, while the original Philistines are dead and buried long ago,—is really, I think, in itself much less apt and expressive than the German term. Efforts have been made to obtain in English some term equivalent to *Philister* or *épicier*; Mr Carlyle has made several such efforts: 'respectability with its thousand gigs', he says;—well, the occupant of every one of these gigs is, Mr Carlyle means, a Philistine. However, the word *respectable* is far too valuable a word to be thus perverted from its proper meaning; if the English are ever to have a word for the thing we are speaking of,—and so prodigious are the changes which the modern spirit is introducing, that even we English shall perhaps one day come to want such a word,—I think we had much better take the term *Philistine* itself.

Philistine must have originally meant, in the mind of those who invented the nickname, a strong, dogged, unenlightened opponent of the chosen people, of the children of the light. The party of change, the would-be remodellers of the old traditional European order, the invokers of reason against custom, the representatives of the modern spirit in every sphere where it is applicable, regarded themselves, with the robust self-confidence natural to reformers as a chosen people, as children of the light. They regarded their adversaries as humdrum people, slaves to routine, enemies to light; stupid and oppressive, but at the same time very strong. This explains the love which Heine, that Paladin of the modern spirit, has for France; it explains the preference which he gives to France over Germany: 'the French', he says, 'are the chosen people of the new religion, its first gospels and dogmas have been drawn up in their language; Paris is the new Jerusalem, and the Rhine is the Jordan which divides the consecrated land of freedom from the land of the Philistines'. He means that the French, as a people, have shown more accessibility to ideas than any other people; that prescription and routine have had less hold upon them than upon any other people; that they have shown most readiness to move and to alter at the bidding (real or supposed) of reason. This explains, too, the detestation which Heine had for the English: 'I might settle in England', he says, in his exile, 'if it were not that I should find there two things, coal-smoke and Englishmen; I cannot abide either.' What he hated in the English was the 'ächtbrittische Beschränktheit', as he called it,—the *genuine British narrowness*. In truth, the English, profoundly as they have modified the old Middle-Age order, great as is the liberty which they have secured for themselves, have in all their changes proceeded, to use a familiar expression, by the rule of thumb; what was intolerably inconvenient to them they have suppressed, and as they have suppressed it, not because it was irrational, but because it was practically inconvenient, they have seldom in suppressing it appealed to reason, but always, if possible, to some precedent, or form, or letter, which served as a convenient instrument for their purpose, and which saved them from the necessity of recurring to general principles. They have thus become, in a certain sense, of all people the most inaccessible to ideas and the most impatient of them; inaccessible to them, because of their want of familiarity with them; and impatient

of them because they have got on so well without them, that
they despise those who, not having got on as well as themselves,
still make a fuss for what they themselves have done so well
without. But there has certainly followed from hence, in this
country, somewhat of a general depression of pure intelligence:
Philistia has come to be thought by us the true Land of Promise,
and it is anything but that; the born lover of ideas, the born
hater of commonplaces, must feel in this country that the sky
over his head is of brass and iron. The enthusiast for the idea,
for reason, values reason, the idea, in and for themselves; he
values them, irrespectively of the practical conveniences which
their triumph may obtain for him; and the man who regards
the possession of these practical conveniences as something
sufficient in itself, something which compensates for the absence
or surrender of the idea, of reason, is, in his eyes, a Philistine.
This is why Heine so often and so mercilessly attacks the liberals;
much as he hates conservatism he hates Philistinism even more,
and whoever attacks conservatism itself ignobly, not as a child
of light, not in the name of the idea, is a Philistine. Our Cobbett
is thus for him, much as he disliked our clergy and aristocracy
whom Cobbett attacked, a Philistine with six fingers on every
hand and on every foot six toes, four-and-twenty in number: a
Philistine, the staff of whose spear is like a weaver's beam. Thus
he speaks of him:

While I translate Cobbett's words, the man himself comes
bodily before my mind's eye, as I saw him at that uproarious
dinner at the Crown and Anchor Tavern, with his scolding
red face and his radical laugh, in which venomous hate
mingles with a mocking exultation at his enemies' surely
approaching downfall. He is a chained cur, who falls with
equal fury on everyone whom he does not know, often bites the
best friend of the house in his calves, barks incessantly, and
just because of this incessantness of his barking cannot get
listened to, even when he barks at a real thief. Therefore the
distinguished thieves who plunder England do not think it
necessary to throw the growling Cobbett a bone to stop his
mouth. This makes the dog furiously savage, and he shows all
his hungry teeth. Poor old Cobbett! England's dog! I have
no love for thee, for every vulgar nature my soul abhors; but

thou touchest me to the inmost soul with pity, as I see how thou strainest in vain to break loose and to get at those thieves, who make off with their booty before thy very eyes, and mock at thy fruitless springs and thine impotent howling.

There is balm in Philistia as well as in Gilead. A chosen circle of children of the modern spirit, perfectly emancipated from prejudice and commonplace, regarding the ideal side of things in all its efforts for change, passionately despising half-measures and condescension to human folly and obstinacy,—with a bewildered, timid, torpid multitude behind,—conducts a country to the government of Herr von Bismarck. A nation regarding the practical side of things in its efforts for change, attacking not what is irrational, but what is pressingly inconvenient, and attacking this as one body, 'moving altogether if it move at all' and treating children of light like the very harshest of step-mothers, comes to the prosperity and liberty of modern England. For all that, however, Philistia (let me say it again) is not the true promised land, as we English commonly imagine it to be; and our excessive neglect of the idea, and consequent inaptitude for it, threatens us, at a moment when the idea is beginning to exercise a real power in human society, with serious future inconvenience, and, in the meanwhile, cuts us off from the sympathy of other nations, which feel its power more than we do.

But, in 1830, Heine very soon found that the fire-engines of the German governments were too much for his direct efforts at incendiarism.

What demon drove me [he cries] to write my *Reisebilder*, to edit a newspaper, to plague myself with our time and its interests, to try and shake the poor German Hodge out of his thousand years' sleep in his hole? What good did I get by it? Hodge opened his eyes, only to shut them again immediately; he yawned, only to begin snoring again the next minute louder than ever; he stretched his stiff ungainly limbs, only to sink down again directly afterwards, and lie like a dead man in the old bed of his accustomed habits. I must have rest; but where am I to find a resting-place? In Germany I can no longer stay.'

This is Heine's jesting account of his own efforts to rouse Germany: now for his pathetic account of them; it is because he unites so much wit with so much pathos that he is so effective a writer:

> The Emperor Charles the Fifth sate in sore straits, in the Tyrol encompassed by his enemies. All his knights and courtiers had forsaken him; not one came to his help. I know not if he had at that time the cheese face with which Holbein has painted him for us. But I am sure that under-lip of his, with its contempt for mankind, stuck out even more than it does in his portraits. How could he but contemn the tribe which in the sunshine of his prosperity had fawned on him so devotedly, and now, in his dark distress, left him all alone? Then suddenly his door opened, and there came in a man in disguise, and, as he threw back his cloak, the Kaiser recognized in him his faithful Conrad von der Rosen, the court jester. This man brought him comfort and counsel, and he was the court jester!
>
> O German fatherland! dear German people! I am thy Conrad von der Rosen. The man whose proper business was to amuse thee, and who in good times should have catered only for thy mirth, makes his way into thy prison in time of need; here, under my cloak, I bring thee thy sceptre and crown; dost thou not recognize me, my Kaiser? If I cannot free thee, I will at least comfort thee, and thou shalt at least have one with thee who will prattle with thee about thy sorest affliction, and whisper courage to thee, and love thee, and whose best joke and best blood shall be at thy service. For thou, my people, art the true Kaiser, the true lord of the land; thy will is sovereign, and more legitimate far than that purple *Tel est notre plaisir*, which invokes a divine right with no better warrant than the anointings of shaven and shorn jugglers; thy will, my people, is the sole rightful source of power. Though now thou liest down in thy bonds, yet in the end will thy rightful cause prevail; the day of deliverance is at hand, a new time is beginning. My Kaiser, the night is over, and out there glows the ruddy dawn.
>
> 'Conrad von der Rosen, my fool, thou art mistaken; perhaps thou takest a headsman's gleaming axe for the sun, and the red of dawn is only blood.'
>
> 'No, my Kaiser, it is the sun, though it is rising in the west;

these six thousand years it has always risen in the east; it is high time there should come a change.'

'Conrad von der Rosen, my fool, thou hast lost the bells out of thy red cap, and it has now such an odd look, that red cap of thine!'

'Ah, my Kaiser, thy distress has made me shake my head so hard and fierce, that the fool's bells have dropped off my cap; the cap is none the worse for that.'

'Conrad von der Rosen, my fool, what is that noise of breaking and cracking outside there?'

'Hush! that is the saw and the carpenter's axe, and soon the doors of thy prison will be burst open, and thou wilt be free, my Kaiser!'

'Am I then really Kaiser? Ah, I forgot, it is the fool who tells me so!'

'Oh, sigh not, my dear master, the air of thy prison makes thee so desponding! when once thou has got thy rights again, thou wilt feel once more the bold imperial blood in thy veins, and thou wilt be proud like a Kaiser, and violent, and gracious, and unjust, and smiling, and ungrateful, as princes are.'

'Conrad von der Rosen, my fool, when I am free, what wilt thou do then?'

'I will then sew new bells on to my cap.'

'And how shall I recompense thy fidelity?'

'Ah, dear master, by not leaving me to die in a ditch!'

I wish to mark Heine's place in modern European literature, the scope of his activity, and his value. I cannot attempt to give here a detailed account of his life, or a description of his separate works. In May 1831 he went over his Jordan, the Rhine, and fixed himself in his new Jerusalem, Paris. There, henceforward, he lived, going in general to some French wateringplace in the summer, but making only one or two short visits to Germany during the rest of his life. His works, in verse and prose, succeeded each other without stopping; a collected edition of them, filling seven closely printed octavo volumes, has been published in America;[1] in the collected editions of few people's works is there so little to skip. Those who wish for a single good specimen of him should read his first important

[1] A complete edition has at last appeared in Germany.

work, the work which made his reputation, the *Reisebilder*, or 'Travelling Sketches': prose and verse, wit and seriousness, are mingled in it, and the mingling of these is characteristic of Heine, and is nowhere to be seen practised more naturally and happily than in his *Reisebilder*. In 1847 his health, which till then had always been perfectly good, gave way. He had a kind of paralytic stroke. His malady proved to be a softening of the spinal marrow: it was incurable; it made rapid progress. In May, 1848, not a year after his first attack, he went out of doors for the last time; but his disease took more than eight years to kill him. For nearly eight years he lay helpless on a couch, with the use of his limbs gone, wasted almost to the proportions of a child, wasted so that a woman could carry him about; the sight of one eye lost, that of the other greatly dimmed, and requiring, that it might be exercised, to have the palsied eyelid lifted and held up by the finger; all this, and, besides this, suffering at short intervals paroxysms of nervous agony. I have said he was not pre-eminently brave; but in the astonishing force of spirit with which he retained his activity of mind, even his gaiety, amid all his suffering, and went on composing with undiminished fire to the last, he was truly brave. Nothing could clog that aërial lightness. 'Pouvez-vous siffler?' his doctor asked him one day, when he was almost at his last gasp;—'siffler,' as everyone knows, has the double meaning of *to whistle* and *to hiss*:—'Hélas! non,' was his whispered answer; 'pas même une comédie de M. Scribe!' M. Scribe is, or was, the favourite dramatist of the French Philistine. 'My nerves,' he said to someone who asked him about them in 1855, the year of the great Exhibition in Paris, 'my nerves are of that quite singularly remarkable miserableness of nature, that I am convinced they would get at the Exhibition the grand medal for pain and misery.' He read all the medical books which treated of his complaint. 'But', said he to someone who found him thus engaged, 'what good this reading is to do me I don't know, except that it will qualify me to give lectures in heaven on the ignorance of doctors on earth about diseases of the spinal marrow.' What a matter of grim seriousness are our own ailments to most of us! yet with this gaiety Heine treated his to the end. That end, so long in coming, came at last. Heine died on the 17th of February, 1856, at the age of fifty-eight. By his will he forbade that his remains should be transported to

Germany. He lies buried in the cemetery of Montmartre, at Paris.

His direct political action was null, and this is neither to be wondered at nor regretted; direct political action is not the true function of literature, and Heine was a born man of letters. Even in his favourite France the turn taken by public affairs was not at all what he wished, though he read French politics by no means as we in England, most of us, read them. He thought things were tending there to the triumph of communism; and to a champion of the idea like Heine, what there is gross and narrow in communism was very repulsive. 'It is all of no use,' he cried on his death-bed, 'the future belongs to our enemies, the Communists, and Louis Napoleon is their John the Baptist.' 'And yet',—he added with all his old love for that remarkable entity, so full of attraction for him, so profoundly unknown in England, the French people,—'do not believe that God lets all this go forward merely as a grand comedy. Even though the Communists deny him today, he knows better than they do that a time will come when they will learn to believe in him.' After 1831 his hopes of soon upsetting the German Governments had died away, and his propagandism took another, a more truly literary, character. It took the character of an intrepid application of the modern spirit to literature. To the ideas with which the burning questions of modern life filled him, he made all his subject matter minister. He touched all the great points in the career of the human race, and here he but followed the tendency of the wide culture of Germany; but he touched them with a wand which brought them all under a light where the modern eye cares most to see them, and here he gave a lesson to the culture of Germany,—so wide, so impartial, that it is apt to become slack and powerless, and to lose itself in its material (for want of a strong central idea round which to group all its other ideas. So the mystic and romantic school of Germany lost itself in the Middle Ages, was overpowered by their influence, came to ruin by its vain dreams of renewing them. Heine, with a far profounder sense of the mystic and romantic charm of the Middle Age than Goerres, or Brentano, or Arnim, Heine the chief romantic poet of Germany, is yet also much more than a romantic poet; he is a great modern poet, he is not conquered by the Middle Age, he has a talisman by which he can feel,—

along with but above the power of the fascinating Middle Age itself,—the power of modern ideas.

A French critic of Heine thinks he has said enough in saying that Heine proclaimed in German countries, with beat of drum, the ideas of 1789, and that at the cheerful noise of his drum the ghosts of the Middle Age took to flight. But this is rather too French an account of the matter. Germany, that vast mine of ideas, had no need to import ideas, as such, from any foreign country; and if Heine had carried ideas, as such, from France into Germany, he would but have been carrying coals to Newcastle. But that for which France, far less meditative than Germany, is eminent, is the prompt, ardent, and practical application of an idea, when she seizes it, in all departments of human activity which admit it. And that in which Germany most fails, and by failing in which she appears so helpless and impotent, is just the practical application of her innumerable ideas. 'When Candide', says Heine himself, 'came to Eldorado, he saw in the streets a number of boys who were playing with gold-nuggets instead of marbles. This degree of luxury made him imagine that they must be the king's children, and he was not a little astonished when he found that in Eldorado gold-nuggets are of no more value than marbles are with us, and that the schoolboys play with them. A similar thing happened to a friend of mine, a foreigner, when he came to Germany and first read German books. He was perfectly astounded at the wealth of ideas which he found in them; but he soon remarked that ideas in Germany are as plentiful as gold-nuggets in Eldorado, and that those writers whom he had taken for intellectual princes were in reality only common schoolboys.' Heine was, as he calls himself, a 'Child of the French Revolution', an 'Initiator', because he vigorously assured the Germans that ideas were not counters or marbles, to be played with for their own sake; because he exhibited in literature modern ideas applied with the utmost freedom, clearness, and originality. And therefore he declared that the great task of his life had been the endeavour to establish a cordial relation between France and Germany. It is because he thus operates a junction between the French spirit, and German ideas and German culture, that he founds something new, opens a fresh period, and deserves the attention of criticism far more than the German poets his contemporaries, who merely continue an old period till it expires. It may be predicted that in the literature of other countries, too, the French spirit is destined to make its influence felt,—as an element, in alliance with the native spirit, of novelty and movement,—as it has made its influence felt in German literature; fifty years hence a critic will be demonstrating to our grandchildren how this phenomenon has come to pass.

We in England, in our great burst of literature during the first thirty years of the present century, had no manifestation of the modern spirit, as this spirit manifests itself in Goethe's works or Heine's. And the reason is not far to seek. We had neither the German wealth of ideas, nor the French enthusiasm for applying ideas. There reigned in the mass of the nation that inveterate inaccessiblity to ideas, that Philistinism,—to use the German nickname,—which reacts even on the individual genius that is exempt from it. In our greatest literary epoch, that of the Elizabethan age, English society at large was accessible to ideas, was permeated by them, was vivified by them, to a degree which has never been reached in England since. Hence the unique greatness in English literature of Shakespeare and his contemporaries; they were powerfully upheld by the intellectual life of their nation; they applied freely in literature the then modern ideas,—the ideas of the Renascence and the Reformation. A few years afterwards the great English middle class, the kernel of the nation, the class whose intelligent sympathy had upheld a Shakespeare, entered the prison of Puritanism, and had the key turned on its spirit there for two hundred years. *He enlargeth a nation*, says Job, *and straiteneth it again.* In the literary movement of the beginning of the nineteenth century the signal attempt to apply freely the modern spirit was made in England by two members of the aristocratic class, Byron and Shelley. Aristocracies are, as such, naturally impenetrable by ideas; but their individual members have a high courage and a turn for breaking bounds; and a man of genius, who is the born child of the idea, happening to be born in the aristocratic ranks, chafes against the obstacles which prevent him from freely developing it. But Byron and Shelley did not succeed in their attempt freely to apply the modern spirit in English literature; they could not succeed in it; the resistance to baffle them, the want of intelligent sympathy to guide and uphold them, were too great. Their literary creation, compared with the literary creation of Shakespeare and Spenser, compared with the literary creation of Goethe and Heine, is a failure. The best literary creation of that time in England proceeded from men who did not make the same bold attempt as Byron and Shelley. What, in fact was the career of the chief English men of letters, their contemporaries? The greatest of them, Wordsworth, retired (in Middle-Age phrase) into a monastery. I mean, he plunged himself in the inward life, he voluntarily cut himself off from the modern spirit. Coleridge took to opium. Scott became the historiographer royal of feudalism. Keats passionately gave himself up to a sensuous genius, to his faculty for interpreting nature; and he died of consumption at twenty-five. Wordsworth, Scott, and Keats have left admirable works; far more solid and complete works than those which Byron and Shelley have left. But their works have this defect,—they do not belong to that which is the main current of the literature of modern epochs, they do not apply modern ideas to life; they constitute, therefore, *minor currents*, and all other literary work of our day, however popular, which has the same defect, also constitutes but a minor current. Byron and Shelley will long be remembered, long after the inadequacy of their actual work is clearly recognized for their passionate, their Titanic effort to flow in the main stream of modern literature; their names will be greater than their writings; *stat magni nominis umbra.*

Heine's literary good fortune was superior to that of Byron and Shelley. His theatre of operations was Germany, whose Philistinism does not consist in her want of ideas, or in her inaccessibility to ideas, for she teems with them and loves them, but, as I have said, in her feeble and hesitating application of modern ideas to life. Heine's intense modernism, his absolute freedom, his utter rejection of stock classicism and stock romanticism, his bringing all things under the point of view of the nineteenth century, were understood and laid to heart by Germany, through virtue of her immense, tolerant intellectualism, much as there was in all Heine said to affront and wound Germany. The wit and ardent modern spirit of France Heine joined to the culture, the sentiment, the thought of Germany. This is what makes him so remarkable; his wonderful clearness, lightness, and freedom, united with such power of feeling, and width of range. Is there anywhere keener wit than in his story of the French abbé who was his tutor, and who wanted to get from him that *la religion* is French for *der Glaube*: ' Six times did he ask me the question: "Henry, what is *der Glaube* in French?" and six times, and each time with a greater burst of tears, did I answer him—"It is *le crédit*." And at the seventh time, his face purple with rage, the infuriated questioner screamed out: "It is *la religion*"; and a rain of cuffs descended upon me, and all the other boys burst out laughing. Since that day I have never been able to hear *la religion* mentioned without feeling a tremor run through my back, and my cheeks grow red with shame.' Or in that comment on the fate of Professor Saalfeld, who had been addicted to writing furious pamphlets against Napoleon, and who was a professor at Göttingen, a great seat, according to Heine, of pedantry and Philistinism: ' It is curious ', says Heine, ' the three greatest adversaries of Napoleon have all of them ended miserably. Castlereagh cut his own throat; Louis the Eighteenth rotted upon his throne; and Professor Saalfeld is still a professor at Göttingen.' It is impossible to go beyond that.

What wit, again, in that saying which everyone has heard: ' The Englishman loves liberty like his lawful wife, the Frenchman loves her like his mistress, the German loves her like his old grandmother.' But the turn Heine gives to this incomparable saying is not so well known; and it is by that turn he shows himself the born poet he is,—full of delicacy and tenderness, of inexhaustible resource, infinitely new and striking:

> And yet, after all, no one can ever tell how things may turn out. The grumpy Englishman, in an ill-temper with his wife, is capable of some day putting a rope round her neck, and taking her to be sold at Smithfield. The inconstant Frenchman may become unfaithful to his adored mistress, and be seen fluttering about the Palais Royal after another. *But the German will never quite abandon his old grandmother*; he will always keep for her a nook by the chimney-corner, where she can tell her fairy stories to the listening children.

Is it possible to touch more delicately and happily both the weakness and the strength of Germany;—pedantic, simple, enslaved, free, ridiculous, admirable Germany?

And Heine's verse,—his *Lieder*? Oh, the comfort, after

dealing with French people of genius, irresistibly impelled to try and express themselves in verse, launching out into a deep which destiny has sown with so many rocks for them,—the comfort of coming to a man of genius, who finds in verse his freest and most perfect expression, whose voyage over the deep of poetry destiny makes smooth! After the rhythm, to us, at any rate, with the German paste in our composition, so deeply unsatisfying, of

> Ah! que me dites-vous, et que vous dit mon âme?
> Que dit le ciel à l'aube et la flamme à la flamme?

what a blessing to arrive at rhythms like

> Take, oh, take those lips away,
> That so sweetly were forsworn—

or—

> Siehst sehr sterbeblässlich aus,
> Doch getrost! du bist zu Haus—

in which one's soul can take pleasure! The magic of Heine's poetical form is incomparable; he chiefly uses a form of old German popular poetry, a ballad-form which has more rapidity and grace than any ballad-form of ours; he employs this form with the most exquisite lightness and ease, and yet it has at the same time the inborn fulness, pathos, and old-world charm of all true forms of popular poetry. Thus in Heine's poetry, too, one perpetually blends the impression of French modernism and clearness with that of German sentiment and fulness; and to give this blended impression is, as I have said, Heine's great characteristic. To feel it, one must read him; he gives it in his form as well as in his contents, and by translation I can only reproduce it so far as his contents give it. But even the contents of many of his poems are capable of giving a certain sense of it. Here, for instance, is a poem in which he makes his profession of faith to an innocent beautiful soul, a sort of Gretchen, the child of some simple mining people having their hut among the pines at the foot of the Hartz Mountains, who reproaches him with not holding the old articles of the Christian creed:

> Ah, my child, while I was yet a little boy, while I yet sate upon my mother's knee, I believed in God the Father, who rules up there in Heaven, good and great;
>
> Who created the beautiful earth, and the beautiful men and

women thereon; who ordained for sun, moon, and stars their courses.

When I got bigger, my child, I comprehended yet a great deal more than this, and comprehended, and grew intelligent; and I believe on the Son also;

On the beloved Son, who loved us, and revealed love to us; and, for his reward, as always happens, was crucified by the people.

Now, when I am grown up, have read much, have travelled much, my heart swells within me, and with my whole heart I believe on the Holy Ghost.

The greatest miracles were of his working, and still greater miracles doth he even now work; he burst in sunder the oppressor's stronghold, and he burst in sunder the bondman's yoke.

He heals old death-wounds, and renews the old right; all mankind are one race of noble equals before him.

He chases away the evil clouds and the dark cobwebs of the brain, which have spoilt love and joy for us, which day and night have loured on us.

A thousand knights, well harnessed, has the Holy Ghost chosen out to fulfil his will, and he has put courage into their souls.

Their good swords flash, their bright banners wave; what, thou wouldst give much, my child, to look upon such gallant knights?

Well, on me, my child, look! kiss me, and look boldly upon me! one of those knights of the Holy Ghost am I.

One has only to turn over the pages of his *Romancero*,—a collection of poems written in the first years of his illness, with his whole power and charm still in them, and not, like his latest poems of all, painfully touched by the air of his *Matrazzen-gruft*, his 'mattress-grave'—to see Heine's width of range; the most varied figures succeed one another,—Rhampsinitus, Edith with the Swan Neck, Charles the First, Marie Antoinette, King David, a heroine of *Mabille*, Melisanda of Tripoli, Richard Cœur de Lion, Pedro the Cruel, Firdusi, Cortes, Dr Döllinger;—but never does Heine attempt to be *hübsch objectiv*, 'beautifully objective', to become in spirit an old Egyptian, or an old Hebrew, or a Middle-Age knight, or a Spanish adventurer, or an English royalist; he always remains Heinrich Heine, a son of a the nineteenth century. To give a notion of his tone, I will quote a few stanzas at the end of the *Spanish Atridae*, in which he describes, in the character of a visitor at the court of Henry of Transtamare at Segovia, Henry's treatment of the children of his brother, Pedro the Cruel. Don Diego Albuquerque, his neighbour, strolls after dinner through the castle with him:

In the cloister-passage, which leads to the kennels where are kept the king's hounds, that with their growling and yelping let you know a long way off where they are,

There I saw, built into the wall, and with a strong iron grating for its outer face, a cell like a cage.

Two human figures sate therein, two young boys; chained by the leg, they crouched in the dirty straw.

Hardly twelve years old seemed the one, the other not much older; their faces fair and noble, but pale and wan with sickness.

They were all in rags, almost naked; and their lean bodies showed wounds, the marks of ill-usage; both of them shivered with fever.

They looked up at me out of the depth of their misery; 'who', I cried in horror to Don Diego, 'are these pictures of wretchedness?'

Don Diego seemed embarrassed; he looked round to see that no one was listening; then he gave a deep sigh; and at last, putting on the easy tone of a man of the world, he said:

'These are a pair of king's sons, who were early left orphans; the name of their father was King Pedro, the name of their mother, Maria de Padilla.

'After the great battle of Navarette, when Henry of Transtamare had relieved his brother, King Pedro, of the troublesome burden of the crown,

'And likewise of that still more troublesome burden, which is called life, then Don Henry's victorious magnanimity had to deal with his brother's children.

'He has adopted them, as an uncle should; and he has given them free quarters in his own castle.

'The room which he has assigned to them is certainly rather small, but then it is cool in summer, and not intolerably cold in winter.

'Their fare is rye-bread, which tastes as sweet as if the goddess Ceres had baked it express for her beloved Proserpine.

'Not unfrequently, too, he sends a scullion to them with garbanzos, and then the young gentlemen know that it is Sunday in Spain.

'But it is not Sunday every day, and garbanzos do not come every day; and the master of the hounds gives them the treat of the whip.

'For the master of the hounds, who has under his superintendence the kennels and the pack, and the nephews' cage also,

'Is the unfortunate husband of that lemon-faced woman with the white ruff, whom we remarked today at dinner.

'And she scolds so sharp, that often her husband snatches his whip, and rushes down here, and gives it to the dogs and to the poor little boys.

'But his majesty has expressed his disapproval of such proceedings, and has given orders that for the future his nephews are to be treated differently from the dogs.

'He has determined no longer to entrust the disciplining of his nephews to a mercenary stranger, but to carry it out with his own hands.'

Don Diego stopped abruptly; for the seneschal of the castle joined us, and politely expressed his hope that we had dined to our satisfaction.

Observe how the irony of the whole of that, finishing with the grim innuendo of the last stanza but one, is at once truly masterly and truly modern.

No account of Heine is complete which does not notice the Jewish element in him. His race he treated with the same freedom with which he treated everything else, but he derived a great force from it, and no one knew this better than he himself. He has excellently pointed out how in the sixteenth century there was a double renascence,—a Hellenic renascence and a Hebrew renascence,—and how both have been great powers ever since. He himself had in him both the spirit of Greece and the spirit of Judaea; both these spirits reach the infinite, which is the true goal of all poetry and all art,—the Greek spirit by beauty, the Hebrew spirit by sublimity. By his perfection of literary form, by his love of clearness, by his love of beauty, Heine is Greek; by his intensity, by his untamableness, by his 'longing which cannot be uttered', he is Hebrew. Yet what Hebrew ever treated the things of the Hebrews like this?

There lives at Hamburg, in a one-roomed lodging in the Baker's Broad Walk, a man whose name is Moses Lump; all the week he goes about in wind and rain, with his pack on his back to earn his few shillings; but when on Friday evening he comes home, he finds the candlestick with seven candles lighted, and the table covered with a fair white cloth, and he puts away from him his pack and his cares, and he sits down to table with his squinting wife and yet more squinting daughter, and eats fish with them, fish which has been dressed in beautiful white garlic sauce, sings therewith the grandest psalms of King David, rejoices with his whole heart over the deliverance of the children of Israel out of Egypt, rejoices, too, that all the wicked ones who have done the children of Israel hurt, have ended by taking themselves off; that King Pharaoh, Nebuchadnezzar, Haman, Antiochus, Titus, and all such people, are well dead, while he, Moses Lump, is yet alive, and eating fish with wife and daughter; and I can tell you, Doctor, the fish is delicate and the man is happy, he has no call to torment himself about culture, he sits contented in his religion and in his green bed-gown, like Diogenes in his tub, he contemplates with satisfaction his candles, which he on no account will snuff for himself; and I can tell you, if the candles burn a little dim, and the snuffers-woman, whose business it is to snuff them, is not at hand, and Rothschild the Great were at that moment to come in, with all his brokers, bill discounters, agents, and chief clerks, with whom he conquers the world, and Rothschild were to say: 'Moses Lump, ask of me what favour you will, and it shall be granted you';— Doctor, I am convinced, Moses Lump would quietly answer: 'Snuff me those candles!' and Rothschild the Great would exclaim with admiration: 'If I were not Rothschild, I would be Moses Lump.'

There Heine shows us his own people by its comic side; in the poem of the *Princess Sabbath* he shows it to us by a more serious side. The Princess Sabbath, 'the *tranquil Princess*, pearl and flower of all beauty, fair as the Queen of Sheba, Solomon's bosom friend, that blue stocking from Ethiopia, who wanted to shine by her *esprit*, and with her wise riddles made herself in the long run a bore' (with Heine the sarcastic turn is never far off), this princess has for her betrothed a prince whom sorcery has transformed into an animal of lower race, the Prince Israel.

A dog with the desires of a dog, he wallows all the week long in the filth and refuse of life, amidst the jeers of the boys in the street.

But every Friday evening, at the twilight hour, suddenly the magic passes off, and the dog becomes once more a human being.

A man with the feelings of a man, with head and heart raised aloft, in festal garb, in almost clean garb, he enters the halls of his Father.

Hail, beloved halls of my royal Father! Ye tents of Jacob, I kiss with my lips your holy door-posts!

Still more he shows us this serious side in his beautiful poem on Jehuda ben Halevy, a poet belonging to 'the great golden age of the Arabian, Old-Spanish, Jewish school of poets', a contemporary of the troubadours:

He, too,—the hero whom we sing,—Jehuda ben Halevy, too, had his lady-love; but she was of a special sort.

She was no Laura, whose eyes, mortal stars, in the cathedral on Good Friday kindled that world-renowned flame.

She was no châtelaine, who in the blooming glory of her youth presided at tourneys, and awarded the victor's crown.

No casuistess in the Gay Science was she, no lady *doctrinaire*, who delivered her oracles in the judgment-chamber of a Court of Love.

She, whom the Rabbi loved, was a woe-begone poor darling, a mourning picture of desolation . . . and her name was Jerusalem.

Jehuda ben Halevy, like the Crusaders, makes his pilgrimage to Jerusalem; and there, amid the ruins, sings a song of Sion which has become famous among his people:

That lay of pearled tears is the wide-famed Lament, which is sung in all the scattered tents of Jacob throughout the world,

On the ninth day of the month which is called Ab, on the anniversary of Jerusalem's destruction by Titus Vespasianus.

Yes, that is the song of Sion, which Jehuda ben Halevy sang with his dying breath amid the holy ruins of Jerusalem.

Barefoot, and in penitential weeds, he sate there upon the fragment of a fallen column; down to his breast fell,

Like a gray forest, his hair; and cast a weird shadow on the face which looked out through it,—his troubled pale face, with the spiritual eyes.

So he sate and sang, like unto a seer out of the foretime to look upon; Jeremiah, the Ancient, seemed to have risen out of his grave.

But a bold Saracen came riding that way, aloft on his barb, lolling in his saddle, and brandishing a naked javelin;

Into the breast of the poor singer he plunged his deadly shaft, and shot away like a winged shadow.

Quietly flowed the Rabbi's life-blood, quietly he sang his song to an end; and his last dying sigh was Jerusalem!

But, most of all, Heine shows us this side in a strange poem describing a public dispute, before King Pedro and his Court, between a Jewish and a Christian champion, on the merits of their respective faiths. In the strain of the Jew all the fierceness of the old Hebrew genius, all its rigid defiant Monotheism, appear:

Our God has not died like a poor innocent lamb for mankind; he is no gushing philanthropist, no declaimer.

Our God is not love, caressing is not his line; but he is a God of thunder, and he is a God of revenge.

The lightnings of his wrath strike inexorably every sinner, and the sins of the fathers are often visited upon their remote posterity.

Our God, he is alive, and in his hall of heaven he goes on existing away, throughout all the eternities.

Our God, too, is a God in robust health, no myth, pale and thin as sacrificial wafers, or as shadows by Cocytus.

Our God is strong. In his hand he upholds sun, moon, and stars; thrones break, nations reel to and fro, when he knits his forehead.

Our God loves music, the voice of the harp and the song of feasting; but the sound of church-bells he hates, as he hates the grunting of pigs.

Nor must Heine's sweetest note be unheard,—his plaintive note, his note of melancholy. Here is a strain which came from him as he lay, in the winter night, on his 'mattress-grave' at Paris, and let his thoughts wander home to Germany, 'the great child, entertaining herself with her Christmas-tree.' 'Thou tookest',—he cries to the German exile—

Thou tookest thy flight towards sunshine and happiness; naked and poor returnest thou back. German truth, German shirts,—one gets them worn to tatters in foreign parts.

Deadly pale are thy looks, but take comfort, thou art at home! one lies warm in German earth, warm as by the old pleasant fireside.

Many a one, alas, became crippled, and could get home no more! longingly he stretches out his arms; God have mercy upon him!

God have mercy upon him! for what remain of the days of the years of his life are few and evil.

Can it be that I still actually exist? My body is so shrunk that there is hardly anything of me left but my voice, and my bed makes me think of the melodious grave of the enchanter Merlin, which is in the forest of Broceliand in Brittany, under high oaks whose tops shine like green flames to heaven. Ah, I envy thee those trees, brother Merlin, and their fresh waving! for over my mattress-grave here in Paris no green leaves rustle; and early and late I hear nothing but the rattle of carriages, hammering, scolding, and the jingle of the piano. A grave without rest, death without the privileges of the departed, who have no longer any need to spend money, or to write letters, or to compose books. What a melancholy situation!

He died, and has left a blemished name; with his crying faults,
—his intemperate susceptibility, his unscrupulousness in passion,
his inconceivable attacks on his enemies, his still more inconceivable attacks on his friends, his want of generosity, his sensuality, his incessant mocking,—how could it be otherwise? Not
only was he not one of Mr Carlyle's 'respectable' people, he
was profoundly *dis*respectable; and not even the merit of not
being a Philistine can make up for a man's being that. To his
intellectual deliverance there was an addition of something else
wanting, and that something else was something immense; the
old-fashioned, laborious, eternally needful moral deliverance.
Goethe says that he was deficient in *love*; to me his weakness
seems to be not so much a deficiency in love as a deficiency in
self-respect, in true dignity of character. But on this negative
side of one's criticism of a man of great genius, I for my part,
when I have once clearly marked that this negative side is and
must be there, have no pleasure in dwelling. I prefer to say of
Heine something positive. He is not an adequate interpreter of
the modern world. He is only a brilliant soldier in the war of
liberation of humanity. But, such as he is, he is (and posterity
too, I am quite sure, will say this), in the European poetry of that
quarter of a century which follows the death of Goethe, incomparably the most important figure.

What a spendthrift, one is tempted to cry, is Nature! With
what prodigality, in the march of generations, she employs
human power, content to gather almost always little result from
it, sometimes none! Look at Byron, that Byron whom the present
generation of Englishmen are forgetting; Byron, the greatest
natural force, the greatest elementary power, I cannot but think,
which has appeared in our literature since Shakespeare. And
what became of this wonderful production of nature? He shattered himself, he inevitably shattered himself to pieces against
the huge, black, cloud-topped, interminable precipice of British
Philistinism. But Byron, it may be said, was eminent only by
his genius, only by his inborn force and fire; he had not the
intellectual equipment of a supreme modern poet; except for
his genius he was an ordinary nineteenth-century English gentleman, with little culture and with no ideas. Well, then, look at
Heine. Heine had all the culture of Germany; in his head fer-
mented all the ideas of modern Europe. And what have we got

from Heine? A half-result, for want of moral balance, and of nobleness of soul and character. That is what I say; there is so much power, so many seem able to run well, so many give promise of running well;—so few reach the goal, so few are chosen. *Many are called, few chosen.*

VI

PAGAN AND MEDIAEVAL
RELIGIOUS SENTIMENT

I READ the other day in the *Dublin Review*:

> We Catholics are apt to be cowed and scared by the lordly
> oppression of public opinion, and not to bear ourselves as
> men in the face of the anti-Catholic society of England. It is
> good to have an habitual consciousness that the public opinion
> of Catholic Europe looks upon Protestant England with a
> mixture of impatience and compassion, which more than
> balances the arrogance of the English poeple towards the
> Catholic Church in these countries.

The Holy Catholic Church, Apostolic and Roman, can take
very good care of herself, and I am not going to defend her
against the scorns of Exeter Hall. Catholicism is not a great
visible force in this country, and the mass of mankind will always
treat lightly even things the most venerable, if they do not present themselves as visible forces before its eyes. In Catholic
countries, as the *Dublin Review* itself says with triumph, they
make very little account of the greatness of Exeter Hall. The
majority has eyes only for the things of the majority, and in
England the immense majority is Protestant. And yet, in spite
of all the shocks which the feeling of a good Catholic, like the
writer in the *Dublin Review*, has in this Protestant country
inevitably to undergo, in spite of the contemptuous insensibility
to the grandeur of Rome which he finds so general and so hard
to bear, how much has he to console him, how many acts of
homage to the greatness of his religion may he see if he has his
eyes open! I will tell him of one of them. Let him go in London
to that delightful spot, that Happy Island in Bloomsbury, the
reading-room of the British Museum. Let him visit its sacred
quarter, the region where its theological books are placed. I am
almost afraid to say what he will find there, for fear Mr Spurgeon,

like a second Caliph Omar, should give the library to the flames.
He will find an immense Catholic work, the collection of the
Abbé Migne, lording it over that whole region, reducing to
insignificance the feeble Protestant forces which hang upon its
skirts. Protestantism is duly represented, indeed: the librarian
knows his business too well to suffer it to be otherwise; all the
varieties of Protestantism are there; there is the Library of
Anglo-Catholic Theology, learned, decorous, exemplary, but a
little uninteresting; there are the works of Calvin, rigid, militant,
menacing; there are the works of Dr Chalmers, the Scotch
thistle valiantly doing duty as the rose of Sharon, but keeping
something very Scotch about it all the time; there are the works
of Dr Channing, the last word of religious philosophy in a land
where everyone has some culture, and where superiorities are
discountenanced,—the flower of moral and intelligent mediocrity. But how are all these divided against one another, and how,
though they were all united, are they dwarfed by the Catholic
Leviathan, their neighbour! Majestic in its blue and gold unity,
this fills shelf after shelf and compartment after compartment,
its right mounting up into heaven among the white folios of the
Acta Sanctorum, its left plunging down into hell among the
yellow octavos of the *Law Digest*. Everything is there, in that
immense *Patrologae Cursus Completus*, in that *Encyclopédie
Théologique*, that *Nouvelle Encyclopédie Théologique*, that *Troi-
sième Encyclopédie Théologique*; religion, philosophy, history,
biography, arts, sciences, bibliography, gossip. The work
embraces the whole range of human interest; like one of the
great Middle-Age Cathedrals, it is in itself a study for a life.
Like the net in Scripture, it drags everything to land, bad and
good, lay and ecclesiastical, sacred and profane, so that it be but
matter of human concern. Wide-embracing as the power whose
product it is! a power, for history at any rate, eminently *the
Church*; not, perhaps, the Church of the future, but indisputably
the Church of the past and, in the past, the Church of the multitude.

This is why the man of imagination—nay, and the philosopher
too, in spite of her propensity to burn him—will always have a
weakness for the Catholic Church; because of the rich treasures
of human life which have been stored within her pale. The
mention of other religious bodies, or of their leaders, at once calls

up in our mind the thought of men of a definite type as their adherents; the mention of Catholicism suggests no such special following. Anglicanism suggests the English episcopate; Calvin's name suggests Dr Candlish; Chalmers's, the Duke of Argyll; Channing's, Boston society; but Catholicism suggests,—what shall I say?—all the pell-mell of the men and women of Shakespeare's plays. This abundance the Abbé Migne's collection faithfully reflects. People talk of this or that work which they would choose, if they were to pass their life with only one; for my part I think I would choose the Abbé Migne's collection. *Quicquid agunt homines*,—everything, as I have said, is there. Do not seek in it splendour of form, perfection of editing; its paper is common, its type ugly, its editing indifferent, its printing careless. The greatest and most baffling crowd of misprints I ever met with in my life occurs in a very important page of the introduction to the *Dictionnaire des Apocryphes*. But this is just what you have in the world,—quantity rather than quality. Do not seek in it impartiality, the critical spirit; in reading it you must do the criticism for yourself; it loves criticism as little as the world loves it. Like the world, it chooses to have things all its own way, to abuse its adversary, to back its own notion through thick and thin, to put forward all the *pros* for its own notion, to suppress all the *contras*; it does just all that the world does, and all that the critical shrinks from. Open the *Dictionnaire des Erreurs Sociales*: 'The religious persecutions of Henry the Eighth's and Edward the Sixth's time abated a little in the reign of Mary, to break out again with new fury in the reign of Elizabeth.' There is a summary of the history of religious persecution under the Tudors! But how unreasonable to reproach the Abbé Migne's work with wanting a criticism, which, by the very nature of things, it cannot have, and not rather to be grateful to it for its abundance, its variety, its infinite suggestiveness, its happy adoption, in many a delicate circumstance, of the urbane tone and temper of the man of the world, instead of the acrid tone and temper of the fanatic!

Still, in spite of their fascinations, the contents of this collection sometimes rouse the critical spirit within one. It happened that lately, after I had been thinking much of Marcus Aurelius and his times, I took down the *Dictionnaire des Origines du Christianisme*, to see what it had to say about paganism and pagans. I found much what I expected. I read the article, *Révélation Évangélique, sa Nécessité*. There I found what a sink of iniquity was the whole pagan world; how one Roman fed his oysters on his slaves, how another put a slave to death that a curious friend might see what dying was like; how Galen's mother tore and bit her waiting-women when she was in a passion with them. I found this account of the religion of paganism: 'Paganism invented a mob of divinities with the most hateful character, and attributed to them the most monstrous and abominable crimes. It personified in them drunkenness, incest, kidnapping, adultery, sensuality, knavery, cruelty, and rage.' And I found that from this religion there followed such practice as was to be expected: 'What must naturally have been the state of morals under the influence of such a religion, which penetrated with its own spirit the public life, the family life, and the individual life of antiquity?'

The colours in this picture are laid on very thick, and I for my part cannot believe that any human societies, with a religion and practice such as those just described, could ever have endured as the societies of Greece and Rome endured, still less have done what the societies of Greece and Rome did. We are not brought far by descriptions of the vices of great cities, or even of individuals driven mad by unbounded means of self-indulgence. Feudal and aristocratic life in Christendom has produced horrors of selfishness and cruelty not surpassed by the grandee of pagan Rome; and then, again, in antiquity there is Marcus Aurelius's mother to set against Galen's. Eminent examples of vice and virtue in individuals prove little as to the state of societies. What, under the first emperors, was the condition of the Roman poor upon the Aventine compared with that of our poor in Spitalfields and Bethnal Green? What, in comfort, morals, and happiness, were the rural population of the Sabine country under Augustus's rule, compared with the rural population of Hertfordshire and Buckinghamshire under the rule of Queen Victoria?

But these great questions are not now for me. Without trying to answer them, I ask myself, when I read such declamation as the foregoing, if I can find anything that will give me a near, distinct sense of the real difference in spirit and sentiment between paganism and Christianity, and of the natural effect of this difference upon people in general. I take a representative religious poem of paganism,—of the paganism which all the world has in its mind when it speaks of paganism. To be a representative poem, it must be one for popular use, one that the multitude listens to. Such a religious poem may be found at the end of one of the best and happiness of Theocritus's idylls, the fifteenth. In order that the reader may the better go along with me in the line of thought I am following, I will translate it; and, that he may see the medium in which religious poetry of this sort is found existing, the society out of which it grows, the people who form it and are formed by it, I will translate the whole, or nearly the whole, of the idyll (it is not long) in which the poem occurs.

The idyll is dramatic. Somewhere about two hundred and eighty years before the Christian era, a couple of Syracusan women, staying at Alexandria, agreed on the occasion of a great religious solemnity,—the feast of Adonis,—to go together to the palace of King Ptolemy Philadelphus, to see the image of Adonis, which the queen Arsinoe, Ptolemy's wife, had had decorated with peculiar magnificence. A hymn, by a celebrated performer, was to be recited over the image. The names of the two women are Gorgo and Praxinoe; their maids, who are mentioned in the poem, are called Eunoe and Eutychis. Gorgo comes by appointment to Praxinoe's house to fetch her, and there the dialogue begins:

Gorgo. Is Praxinoe at home?

Praxinoe. My dear Gorgo, at last! Yes, here I am. Eunoe, find a chair,—get a cushion for it.

Gorgo. It will do beautifully as it is.

Praxinoe. Do sit down.

Gorgo. Oh, this gad-about spirit! I could hardly get to you, Praxinoe, through all the crowd and all the carriages. Nothing but heavy boots, nothing but men in uniform. And what a journey it is! My dear child, you really live *too* far off.

Praxinoe. It is all that insane husband of mine. He has chosen to come out here to the end of the world, and take a hole of a place,—for a house it is not,—on purpose that you and I might not be neighbours. He is always just the same;—anything to quarrel with one! anything for spite!

Gorgo. My dear, don't talk so of your husband before the

little fellow. Just see how astonished he looks at you. Never mind, Zopyrio, my pet, she is not talking about papa.

Praxinoe. Good heavens! the child does really understand.

Gorgo. Pretty papa!

Praxinoe. That pretty papa of his the other day (though I told him beforehand to mind what he was about), when I sent him to a shop to buy soap and rouge, brought me home salt instead;—stupid, great, big, interminable animal!

Gorgo. Mine is just the fellow to him. . . . But never mind now, get on your things and let us be off to the palace to see the Adonis. I hear the Queen's decorations are something splendid.

Praxinoe. In grand people's houses everything is grand. What things you have seen in Alexandria! What a deal you will have to tell to anybody who has never been here!

Gorgo. Come, we ought to be going.

Praxinoe. Every day is holiday to people who have nothing to do. Eunoe, pick up your work; and take care, lazy girl, how you leave it lying about again; the cats find it just the bed they like. Come, stir yourself, fetch me some water, quick! I wanted the water first, and the girl brings me the soap. Never mind; give it me. Not all that, extravagant! Now pour out the water;—stupid! why don't you take care of my dress? That will do. I have got my hands washed as it pleased God. Where is the key of the large wardrobe? Bring it here;—quick!

Gorgo. Praxinoe, you can't think how well that dress, made full, as you have got it, suits you. Tell me, how much did it cost?—the dress by itself, I mean.

Praxinoe. Don't talk of it, Gorgo: more than eight guineas of good hard money. And about the work on it I have almost worn my life out.

Gorgo. Well, you couldn't have done better.

Praxinoe. Thank you. Bring me my shawl, and put my hat properly on my head;—properly. No, child (*to her little boy*), I am not going to take you; there's a bogy on horseback, who bites. Cry as much as you like; I'm not going to have you lamed for life. Now we'll start. Nurse, take the little one and amuse him; call the dog in, and shut the street-door. (*They go out.*) Good heavens! what a crowd of people! How on earth are we ever to get through all this? They are like ants: you can't count them. My dearest Gorgo, what will become of us? here are the royal Horse Guards. My good man, don't ride over me! Look at that bay horse rearing bolt upright; what a vicious one! Eunoe, you mad girl, do take care!—that horse will certainly be the death of the man on his back. How glad I am now, that I left the child safe at home!

Gorgo. All right, Praxinoe, we are safe behind them; and they have gone on to where they are stationed.

Praxinoe. Well, yes, I begin to revive again. From the time I was a little girl I have had more horror of horses and snakes than of anything in the world. Let us get on; here's a great crowd coming this way upon us.

Gorgo (*to an old woman*). Mother, are you from the palace?

Old Woman. Yes, my dears.

Gorgo. Has one a tolerable chance of getting there?

Old Woman. My pretty young lady, the Greeks got to Troy by dint of trying hard; trying will do anything in this world.

Gorgo. The old creature has delivered herself of an oracle and departed.

Praxinoe. Women can tell you everything about everything, Jupiter's marriage with Juno not excepted.

Gorgo. Look, Praxinoe, what a squeeze at the palace gates!

Praxinoe. Tremendous! Take hold of me, Gorgo; and you, Eunoe, take hold of Eutychis!—tight hold, or you'll be lost. Here we go in all together. Hold tight to us, Eunoe! Oh, dear! oh, dear! Gorgo, there's my scarf torn right in two. For heaven's sake, my good man, as you hope to be saved, take care of my dress!

Stranger. I'll do what I can, but it doesn't depend upon me.

Praxinoe. What heaps of people! They push like a drove of pigs.

Stranger. Don't be frightened, ma'am, we are all right.

Praxinoe. May you be all right, my dear sir, to the last day you live, for the care you have taken of us! What a kind, considerate man! There is Eunoe jammed in a squeeze. Push, you goose, push! Capital! We are all of us the right side of the door, as the bridegroom said when he had locked himself in with the bride.

Gorgo. Praxinoe, come this way. Do but look at that work, how delicate it is!—how exquisite! Why, they might wear it in heaven.

Praxinoe. Heavenly patroness of needlewomen, what hands were hired to do that work? Who designed those beautiful patterns? They seem to stand up and move about, as if they were real;—as if they were living things, and not needlework. Well, man is a wonderful creature! And look, look, how charming he lies there on his silver couch, with just a soft down on his cheeks, that beloved Adonis,—Adonis, whom one loves even though he is dead!

Another Stranger. You wretched women, do stop your incessant chatter! Like turtles, you go on for ever. They are enough to kill one with their broad lingo,—nothing but *a, a, a.*

Gorgo. Lord, where does the man come from? What is it to you if we *are* chatterboxes? Order about your own servants! Do you give orders to Syracusan women? If you want to know, we came originally from Corinth, as Bellerophon did; we speak Peloponnesian. I suppose Dorian women may be allowed to have a Dorian accent.

Praxinoe. Oh, honey-sweet Proserpine, let us have no more masters than the one we've got! We don't the least care for *you*; pray don't trouble yourself for nothing.

Gorgo. Be quiet, Praxinoe! That first-rate singer, the Argive woman's daughter, is going to sing the *Adonis* hymn. She is the same who was chosen to sing the dirge last year. We are sure to have something first-rate from *her*. She is going through her airs and graces ready to begin.—

So far the dialogue; and, as it stands in the original, it can hardly be praised too highly. It is a page torn fresh out of the book of human life. What freedom! What animation! What gaiety! What naturalness! It is said that Theocritus, in composing this poem, borrowed from a work of Sophron, a poet of an earlier and better time; but, even if this is so, the form is still Theocritus's own, and how excellent is that form, how masterly! And this in a Greek poem of the decadence!—for Theocritus's poetry, after all, is poetry of the decadence. When such is Greek poetry of the decadence, what must be Greek poetry of the prime?

Then the singer begins her hymn:

Mistress, who loveth the haunts of Golgi, and Idalium, and high-peaked Eryx, Aphrodite that playest with gold! how have the delicate-footed Hours, after twelve months, brought thy Adonis back to thee from the ever-flowing Acheron! Tardiest of the immortals are the boon Hours, but all mankind wait their approach with longing, for they ever bring something with them, O Cypris, Dione's child! thou didst change—so is the story among men—Berenice from mortal to immortal, by dropping ambrosia into her fair bosom; and in gratitude to thee for this, O thou of many names and many temples! Berenice's daughter, Arsinoe, lovely Helen's living counterpart, makes much of Adonis with all manner of braveries.

All fruits that the tree bears are laid before him, all treasures of the garden in silver baskets, and alabaster boxes, gold-inlaid, of Syrian ointment; and all confectionery that cunning women make on their kneading-tray, kneading up every sort of flowers with white meal, and all that they make of sweet honey and delicate oil, and all winged and creeping things are here set before him. And there are built for him green bowers with wealth of tender anise, and little boy-loves flutter about over them, like young nightingales trying their new wings on the tree, from bough to bough. Oh, the ebony, the gold, the eagle of white ivory that bears aloft his cup-bearer to Kronos-born Zeus! And up there, see! a second couch strewn for lovely Adonis, scarlet coverlets softer than sleep itself (so Miletus and the Samian wool-grower will say); Cypris has hers, and the rosy-armed Adonis has his, that eighteen or nineteen-year-old bridegroom. His kisses will not wound, the hair on his lip is yet light.

Now, Cypris, goodnight, we leave thee with thy bridegroom; but tomorrow morning, with the earliest dew, we will one and all bear him forth to where the waves splash upon the sea-strand, and letting loose our locks, and letting fall our robes, with bosoms bare, we will set up this, our melodious strain:

'Beloved Adonis, alone of the demigods (so men say) thou art permitted to visit both us and Acheron! This lot had neither Agamemnon, nor the mighty moon-struck hero Ajax, nor Hector the first-born of Hecuba's twenty children, nor

Patroclus, nor Pyrrhus who came home from Troy, nor those yet earlier Lapithae and the sons of Deucalion, nor the Pelasgians, the root of Argos and of Pelops' isle. Be gracious to us now, loved Adonis, and be favourable to us for the year to come! Dear to us hast thou been at this coming, dear to us shalt thou be when thou comest again.'

The poem concludes with a characteristic speech from Gorgo:

'Praxinoe, certainly women are wonderful things. That lucky woman to know all that! and luckier still to have such a splendid voice! And now we must see about getting home. My husband has not had his dinner. That man is all vinegar, and nothing else; and if you keep him waiting for his dinner, he's dangerous to go near. Adieu, precious Adonis, and may you find us all well when you come next year!'

So, with the hymn still in her ears, says the incorrigible Gorgo. But what a hymn that is! Of religious emotion, in our acceptation of the words, and of the comfort springing from religious emotion, not a particle. And yet many elements of religious emotion are contained in the beautiful story of Adonis. Symbolically treated, as the thoughtful man might treat it, as the Greek mysteries undoubtedly treated it, this story was capable of a noble and touching application, and could lead the soul to elevating and consoling thoughts. Adonis was the sun in his summer and in his winter course, in his time of triumph and his time of defeat; but in his time of triumph still moving towards his defeat, in his time of defeat still returning towards his triumph. Thus he became an emblem of the power of life and the bloom of beauty, the power of human life and the bloom of human beauty, hastening inevitably to diminution and decay, yet in that very decay finding

Hope, and a renovation without end.

But nothing of this appears in the story as prepared for popular religious use, as presented to the multitude in a popular religious ceremony. Its treatment is not devoid of a certain grace and beauty, but it has nothing whatever that is elevating, nothing that is consoling, nothing that is in our sense of the word religious. The religious ceremonies of Christendom, even on occasion of the most joyful and mundane matters, present the multitude with strains of profoundly religious character, such as the *Kyrie eleison* and the *Te Deum*. But this Greek hymn to Adonis adapts itself exactly to the tone and temper of a gay and pleasure-loving multitude,—of light-hearted people, like Gorgo and Praxinoe, whose moral nature is much of the same calibre as that of Phillina in Goethe's *Wilhelm Meister*, people who seem never made to be serious, never made to be sick or sorry. And, if they happen to be sick or sorry, what will they do then? But that we have no right to ask. Phillina, within the enchanted bounds of Goethe's novel, Gorgo and Praxinoe, within the enchanted bounds of Theocritus's poem, never will be sick and sorry, never can be sick and sorry. The ideal, cheerful, sensuous, pagan life is not sick or sorry. No; yet its natural end is in the sort of life which Pompeii and Herculaneum bring so vividly before us,—a life which by no means in itself suggests the thought of horror and misery, which even, in many ways, gratifies the senses and the understanding; but by the very intensity and unremittingness of its appeal to the senses and the understanding, by its stimulating a single side of us too absolutely, ends by fatiguing and revolting us; ends by leaving us with a sense of confinement, of oppression,—with a desire for an utter change, for clouds, storms, effusion, and relief.

In the beginning of the thirteenth century, when the clouds and storms had come, when the gay sensuous pagan life was gone, when men were not living by the senses and understanding, when they were looking for the speedy coming of Antichrist, there appeared in Italy, to the north of Rome, in the beautiful Umbrian country at the foot of the Apennines, a figure of the most magical power and charm, St Francis. His century is, I think, the most interesting in the history of Christianity after its primitive age, more interesting than even the century of the reformation; and one of the chief figures, perhaps the very chief, to which this interest attaches itself, is St Francis. And why? Because of the profound popular instinct which enabled him, more than any man since the primitive age, to fit religion for popular use. He brought religion to the people. He founded the most popular body of ministers of religion that has ever existed in the Church. He transformed monachism by uprooting the stationary monk, delivering him from the bondage of property, and sending him, as a mendicant friar, to be a stranger and sojourner, not in the wilderness, but in the most crowded haunts of men, to console them and to do them good. This popular instinct of his is at the bottom of his famous marriage with poverty. Poverty and suffering are the condition of the people, the multitude, the immense majority of mankind; and it was towards this *people* that his soul yearned. 'He listens', it was said of him, 'to those to whom God himself will not listen.'

So in return, as no other man he was listened to. When an Umbrian town or village heard of his approach, the whole population went out in joyful procession to meet him, with green boughs, flags, music, and songs of gladness. The master, who began with two disciples, could in his own lifetime (and he died at forty-four) collect to keep Whitsuntide with him, in presence of an immense multitude, five thousand of his Minorites. And thus he found fulfilment to his prophetic cry: 'I hear in my ears the sound of the tongues of all the nations who shall come unto us; Frenchmen, Spaniards, Germans, Englishmen. The Lord will make of us a great people, even unto the ends of the earth.'

Prose could not satisfy this ardent soul, and he made poetry. Latin was too learned for this simple, popular nature, and he composed in his mother tongue, in Italian. The beginnings of the mundane poetry of the Italians are in Sicily, at the court of kings; the beginnings of their religious poetry are in Umbria, with St Francis. His are the humble upper waters of a mighty stream; at the beginning of the thirteenth century it is St Francis, at the end, Dante. Now it happens that St Francis, too, like the Alexandrian songstress, has his hymn for the sun, for Adonis. *Canticle of the Sun, Canticle of the Creatures,*—the poem goes by both names. Like the Alexandrian hymn, it is designed for popular use, but not for use by King Ptolemy's people; artless in language, irregular in rhythm, it matches with the childlike genius that produced it, and the simple natures that loved and repeated it:

O most high, almighty, good Lord God, to thee belong praise, glory, honour, and all blessing!

Praised be my Lord God with all his creatures; and specially our brother the sun, who brings us the day, and who brings us the light; fair is he, and shining with a very great splendour: O Lord, he signifies to us thee!

Praised be my Lord for our sister the moon, and for the stars, the which he has set clear and lovely in heaven.

Praised be my Lord for our brother the wind, and for air and cloud, calms and all weather, by the which thou upholdest in life all creatures.

Praised be my Lord for our sister water, who is very service-able unto us, and humble, and precious, and clean.

Praised be my Lord for our brother fire, through whom thou givest us light in the darkness; and he is bright, and pleasant, and very mighty, and strong.

Praised be my Lord for our mother the earth, the which doth sustain us and keep us, and bringeth forth divers fruits, and flowers of many colours, and grass.

Praised be my Lord for all those who pardon one another for his love's sake, and who endure weakness and tribulation; blessed are they who peaceably shall endure, for thou, O most Highest, shalt give them a crown!

Praised be my Lord for our sister, the death of the body, from whom no man escapeth. Woe to him who dieth in mortal sin! Blessed are they who are found walking by thy most holy will, for the second death shall have no power to do them harm.

Praise ye, and bless ye the Lord, and give thanks unto him, and serve him with great humility.

It is natural that man should take pleasure in his senses. But it is natural, also, that he should take refuge in his heart and imagination from his misery. And when one thinks what human life is for the vast majority of mankind, how little of a feast for their senses it can possibly be, one understands the charm for them of a refuge offered in the heart and imagination. Above all, when one thinks what human life was in the Middle Ages, one understands the charm of such a refuge.

Now, the poetry of Theocritus's hymn is poetry treating the world according to the demand of the senses; the poetry of St Francis's hymn is poetry treating the world according to the demand of the heart and imagination. The first takes the world by its outward, sensible side; the second by its inward, symbolical side. The first admits as much of the world as is pleasure-giving; the second admits the whole world, rough and smooth, painful and pleasure-giving, all alike, but all transfigured by the power of a spiritual emotion, all brought under a law of supersensual love, having its seat in the soul. It can thus even say: 'Praised by my Lord for *our sister, the death of the body.*'

But these very words are, perhaps, an indication that we are touching upon an extreme. When we see Pompeii, we can put our finger upon the pagan sentiment in its extreme. And when we read of Monte Alverno and the *stigmata*; when we read of the repulsive, because self-caused, sufferings of the end of St Francis's life; when we find him even saying, 'I have sinned against my brother the ass', meaning by these words that he had been too hard upon his own body; when we find him assailed, even himself, by the doubt 'whether he who had destroyed himself by the severity of his penances could find mercy in eternity', we can put our finger on the mediaeval Christian sentiment in its extreme. Human nature is neither all senses and understanding, nor all heart and imagination. Pompeii was a sign that for humanity at large the measure of sensualism had been overpassed; St Francis's doubt was a sign that for humanity at large the measure of spiritualism had been over-passed. Humanity, in its violent rebound from one extreme, had swung from Pompeii to Monte Alverno; but it was sure not to stay there.

The Renascence is, in part, a return towards the pagan spirit, in the special sense in which I have been using the word pagan; a return towards the life of the senses and the understanding. The Reformation, on the other hand, is the very opposite to this; in Luther there is nothing Greek or pagan; vehemently as he attacked the adoration of St Francis, Luther had himself something of St Francis in him; he was a thousand times more akin to St Francis than to Theocritus or to Voltaire. The Reformation—I do not mean the inferior piece given under that name, by Henry the Eighth and a second-rate company, in this island, but the real Reformation, the German Reformation, Luther's Reformation—was a reaction of the moral and spiritual sense against the carnal and pagan sense; it was a religious revival like St Francis's, but this time against the Church of Rome, not within her; for the carnal and pagan sense had now, in the government of the Church of Rome herself, its prime representative. But the grand reaction against the rule of the heart and imagination, the strong return towards the rule of the senses and understanding, is in the eighteenth century. And this re-action has had no more brilliant champion than a man of the nineteenth, of whom I have already spoken; a man who could feel not only the pleasurableness but the poetry of the life of the senses (and the life of the senses has its deep poetry); a man who, in his very last poem, divided the whole world into 'bar-barians and Greeks',—Heinrich Heine. No man has reproached the Monte Alverno extreme in sentiment, the Christian extreme, the heart and imagination subjugating the senses and under-standing, more bitterly than Heine; no man has extolled the Pompeii extreme, the pagan extreme, more rapturously.

All through the Middle Age these sufferings, this fever, this over-tension lasted; and we moderns still feel in all our limbs the pain and weakness from them. Even those of us who are cured have still to live with a hospital atmosphere all around us, and find ourselves as wretched in it as a strong man among the sick. Some day or other, when humanity shall have got quite well again, when the body and soul shall have made their peace together, the fictitious quarrel which Christianity has cooked up between them will appear something hardly comprehensible. The fairer and happier generations, offspring of unfettered unions, that will rise up and bloom in the atmo-sphere of a religion of pleasure, will smile sadly when they think of their poor ancestors, whose life was passed in melan-choly abstinence from the joys of this beautiful earth, and who faded away into spectres, from the mortal compression which they put upon the warm and glowing emotions of sense. Yes, with assurance I say it, our descendants will be fairer and happier than we are; for I am a believer in progress, and I hold God to be a kind being who has intended man to be happy.

That is Heine's sentiment, in the prime of life, in the glow of activity, amid the brilliant whirl of Paris. I will no more blame it than I blamed the sentiment of the Greek hymn to Adonis. I wish to decide nothing as of my own authority; the great art of criticism is to get oneself out of the way and to let humanity decide. Well, the sentiment of the 'religion of pleasure' has much that is natural in it; humanity will gladly accept it if it can live by it; to live by it one must never be sick or sorry, and the old, ideal, limited, pagan world never, I have said, *was* sick or sorry, never at least shows itself to us sick or sorry:

What pipes and timbrels! what wild ecstasy!

For our imagination, Gorgo and Praxinoe cross the human stage chattering in their blithe Doric,—*like turtles*, as the cross stranger said,—and keep gaily chattering on till they disappear. But in the new, real, immense, post-pagan world,—in the barbarian world,—the shock of accident is unceasing, the serenity of existence is perpetually troubled, not even a Greek like Heine can get across the mortal stage without bitter calamity. How does the sentiment of the 'religion of pleasure' serve then? does it help, does it console? Can a man live by it? Heine again shall answer; Heine just twenty years older, stricken with incurable disease, waiting for death:

The great pot stands smoking before me, but I have no spoon to help myself. What does it profit me that my health is drunk at banquets out of gold cups and in most exquisite wines, if I myself, while these ovations are going on, lonely and cut off from the pleasures of the world, can only just wet my lips with barley-water? What good does it do me that all the roses of Shiraz open their leaves and burn for me with passionate tenderness? Alas! Shiraz is some two thousand leagues from the Rue d'Amsterdam, where in the solitude of my sick chamber all the perfume I smell is that of hot towels. Alas! the mockery of God is heavy upon me! The great author of the universe, the Aristophanes of Heaven, has determined to make the petty earthly author, the so-called Aristophanes of Germany, feel to his heart's core what pitiful needle-pricks his cleverest sarcasms have been, compared with the thunderbolts which his divine humour can launch against feeble mortals! . . .

In the year 1340, says the Chronicle of Limburg, all over Germany everybody was strumming and humming certain songs more lovely and delightful than any which had ever yet been known in German countries; and all people, old and young, the women particularly, were perfectly mad about them, so that from morning till night you heard nothing else. Only, the Chronicle adds, the author of these songs happened to be a young clerk, afflicted with leprosy, and living apart from all the world in a desolate place. The excellent reader does not require to be told how horrible a complaint was leprosy in the Middle Ages, and how the poor wretches who had this incurable plague were banished from society, and had to keep at a distance from every human being. Like living corpses, in a gray gown reaching down to the feet, and with the hood brought over their face, they went about, carrying in their hands an enormous rattle, called Saint Lazarus's rattle. With this rattle they gave notice of their approach, that every one might have time to get out of their way. This poor clerk, then, whose poetical gift the Limburg Chronicle extols, was a leper, and he sate moping in the dismal deserts of his misery, whilst all Germany, gay and tuneful, was praising his songs.

Sometimes, in my sombre visions of the night, I imagine that I see before me the poor leprosy-stricken clerk of the Limburg Chronicle, and then from under his gray hood his distressed eyes look out upon me in a fixed and strange fashion; but the next instant he disappears, and I hear dying away in the distance, like the echo of a dream, the dull creak of Saint Lazarus's rattle.

We have come a long way from Theocritus there! the expression of that has nothing of the clear, positive, happy, pagan character; it has much more the character of one of the indeterminate grotesques of the suffering Middle Age. Profoundness and power it has, though at the same time it is not truly poetical; it is not natural enough for that, there is too much waywardness in it, too much bravado. But as a condition of sentiment to be popular,—to be a comfort for the mass of mankind, under the pressure of calamity, to live by,—what a manifest failure is this last word of the religion of pleasure! One man in many millions, a Heine, may console himself, and keep himself erect in suffering, by a colossal irony of this sort, by covering himself and the universe with the red fire of this sinister mockery; but the many millions cannot,—cannot if they would. That is where the sentiment of a religion of sorrow has such a vast advantage over the sentiment of a religion of pleasure; in its power to be a general, popular, religious sentiment, a stay for the mass of mankind, whose lives are full of hardship. It really succeeds in conveying far more joy, far more of what the mass of mankind are so much without, than its rival. I do not mean joy in prospect only, but joy in possession, actual enjoyment of the world. Mediaeval Christianity is reproached with its gloom and austerities; it assigns the material world, says Heine, to the devil. But yet what a fulness of delight does St Francis manage to draw from this material world itself, and from its commonest and most universally enjoyed elements,—sun, air, earth, water, plants! His hymn expresses a far more cordial sense of happiness, even in the material world, than the hymn of Theocritus. It is this which made the fortune of Christianity,—its gladness, not its sorrow; not its assigning the spiritual world to Christ, and the material world to the devil, but its drawing from the spiritual world a source of joy so abundant that it ran over upon the material world and transfigured it.

I have said a great deal of harm of paganism; and, taking paganism to mean a state of things which it is commonly taken to mean, and which did really exist, no more harm than it well deserved. Yet I must not end without reminding the reader that, before this state of things appeared, there was an epoch in Greek life—in pagan life—of the highest possible beauty and value; an epoch which alone goes far towards making Greece the Greece we mean when we speak of Greece,—a country hardly less important to mankind than Judaea. The poetry of later paganism lived by the senses and understanding; the poetry of mediaeval Christianity lived by the heart and imagination. But the main element of the modern spirit's life is neither the senses and understanding, nor the heart and imagination; it is the imaginative reason. And there is a century in Greek life,—the century preceding the Peloponnesian war, from about the year 530 to the year 430 B.C.,—in which poetry made, it seems to me, the noblest, the most successful effort she has ever made as the priestess of the imaginative reason, of the element by which the modern spirit, if it would live right, has chiefly to live. Of this effort, of which the four great names are Simonides, Pindar, Aeschylus, Sophocles, I must not now attempt more than the bare mention; but it is right, it is necessary, after all I have said, to indicate it. No doubt that effort was imperfect. Perhaps everything, take it at what point in its existence you will, carries within itself the fatal law of its own ulterior development. Perhaps, even of the life of Pindar's time, Pompeii was the inevitable bourne. Perhaps the life of their beautiful Greece could not afford to its poets all that fulness of varied experience, all that power of emotion, which

> . . . the heavy and the weary weight
> Of all this unintelligible world

affords the poet of after-times. Perhaps in Sophocles the thinking-power a little overbalances the religious sense, as in Dante the religious sense overbalances the thinking-power. The present has to make its own poetry, and not even Sophocles and his compeers, any more than Dante and Shakespeare, are enough for it. That I will not dispute; nor will I set up the Greek poets, from Pindar to Sophocles, as objects of blind worship. But no other poets so well show to the poetry of the present the way it must take; no other poets have lived so much by the imaginative reason; no other poets have made their work so well balanced; no other poets, who have so well satisfied the thinking-power, have so well satisfied the religious sense:

> Oh! that my lot may lead me in the path of holy innocence of word and deed, the path which august laws ordain, laws that in the highest empyrean had their birth, of which Heaven is the father alone, neither did the race of mortal men beget them, nor shall oblivion ever put them to sleep. The power of God is mighty in them, and groweth not old.

Let St Francis—nay, or Luther either—beat that!

VII

JOUBERT

WHY should we ever treat of any dead authors but the famous ones? Mainly for this reason: because, from these famous personages, home or foreign, whom we all know so well, and of whom so much has been said, the amount of stimulus which they contain for us has been in a great measure disengaged; people have formed their opinion about them, and do not readily change it. One may write of them afresh, combat received opinions about them, even interest one's readers in so doing; but the interest one's readers receive has to do, in general, rather with the treatment than with the subject; they are susceptible of a lively impression rather of the course of the discussion itself,—its turns, vivacity, and novelty,—than of the genius of the author who is the occasion of it. And yet what is really precious and inspiring, in all this we get from literature, except this sense of an immediate contact with genius itself, and the stimulus towards what is true and excellent which we derive from it? Now in literature, besides the eminent men of genius who have had their deserts in the way of fame, besides the eminent men of ability who have often had far more than their deserts in the way of fame, there are a certain number of personages who have been real men of genius,—by which I mean, that they have had a genuine gift for what is true and excellent, and are therefore capable of emitting a life-giving stimulus,—but who, for some reason or other, in most cases for very valid reasons, have remained obscure, nay, beyond a narrow circle in their own country, unknown. It is salutary from time to time to come across a genius of this kind, and to extract his honey. Often he has more of it for us, as I have already said, than greater men; for, though it is by no means true that from what is new to us there is most to be learnt, it is yet indisputably true that from what is new to us we in general learn most.

Of a genius of this kind, Joseph Joubert, I am now going to

speak. His name is, I believe, almost unknown in England; and even in France, his native country, it is not famous. M. Sainte-Beuve has given of him one of his incomparable portraits; but,—besides that even M. Sainte-Beuve's writings are far less known amongst us than they deserve to be,—every country has its own point of view from which a remarkable author may most profitably be seen and studied.

Joseph Joubert was born (and his date should be remarked) in 1754, at Montignac, a little town in Périgord. His father was a doctor with small means and a large family; and Joseph, the eldest, had his own way to make in the world. He was for eight years, as pupil first, and afterwards as an assistant-master, in the public school of Toulouse, then managed by the Jesuits, who seem to have left in him a most favourable opinion, not only of their tact and address, but of their really good qualities as teachers and directors. Compelled by the weakness of his health to give up, at twenty-two, the profession of teaching, he passed two important years of his life in hard study, at home at Montignac; and came in 1778 to try his fortune in the literary world of Paris, then perhaps the most tempting field which has ever yet presented itself to a young man of letters. He knew Diderot, D'Alembert, Marmontel, Laharpe; he became intimate with one of the celebrities of the next literary generation, then, like himself, a young man,—Châteaubriand's friend, the future Grand Master of the University, Fontanes. But, even then, it began to be remarked of him, that M. Joubert *s'inquiétait de perfection bien plus que de gloire*—'cared far more about perfecting himself than about making himself a reputation'. His severity of morals may perhaps have been rendered easier to him by the delicacy of his health; but the delicacy of his health will not by itself account for his changeless preference of being to seeming, knowing to showing, studying to publishing; for what terrible public performers have some invalids been! This preference he retained all through his life, and it is by this that he is characterized. 'He has chosen', Châteaubriand (adopting Epicurus's famous words) said of him, '*to hide his life*.' Of a life which its owner was bent on hiding there can be but little to tell. Yet the only two public incidents of Joubert's life, slight as they are, do all concerned in them so much credit that they deserve mention. In 1790 the Constituent Assembly made the office of

justice of the peace elective throughout France. The people of
Montignac retained such an impression of the character of their
young townsman,—one of Plutarch's men of virtue, as he had
lived amongst them, simple, studious, severe,—that, though he
had left them for years, they elected him in his absence without
his knowing anything about it. The appointment little suited
Joubert's wishes or tastes; but at such a moment he thought it
wrong to decline it. He held it for two years, the legal term, discharging its duties with a firmness and integrity which were
long remembered; and then, when he went out of office, his
fellow-townsmen re-elected him. But Joubert thought that he
had now accomplished his duty towards them, and he went back
to the retirement which he loved. That seems to me a little
episode of the great French Revolution worth remembering.
The sage who was asked by the king, why sages were seen at the
doors of kings, but not kings at the doors of sages, replied, that
it was because sages knew what was good for them, and kings did
not. But at Montignac the king—for in 1790 the people in France
was king with a vengeance—knew what was good for him, and
came to the door of the sage.

The other incident was this. When Napoleon, in 1809, re-
organized the public instruction of France, founded the University, and made M. de Fontanes its Grand Master, Fontanes had
to submit to the Emperor a list of persons to form the council
or governing body of the new University. Third on his list, after
two distinguished names, Fontanes placed the unknown name
of Joubert. 'This name', he said in his accompanying memorandum to the Emperor, 'is not known as the two first are; and yet
this is the nomination to which I attach most importance. I have
known M. Joubert all my life. His character and intelligence are
of the very highest order. I shall rejoice if your Majesty will
accept my guarantee for him.' Napoleon trusted his Grand
Master, and Joubert became a councillor of the University. It
is something that a man, elevated to the highest posts of State,
should not forget his obscure friends; or that, if he remembers
and places them, he should regard in placing them their merit
rather than their obscurity. It is more, in the eyes of those whom
the necessities, real or supposed, of a political system have long
familiarized with such cynical disregard of fitness in the distri-
bution of office, to see a minister and his master alike zealous,

in giving away places, to give them to the best men to be found.

Between 1792 and 1809 Joubert had married. His life was passed between Villeneuve-sur-Yonne, where his wife's family lived,—a pretty little Burgundian town, by which the Lyons railroad now passes,—and Paris. Here, in a house in the Rue St-Honoré, in a room high up, and admitting plenty of the light which he so loved,—a room from which he saw, in his own words, 'a great deal of sky and very little earth',—among the treasures of a library collected with infinite pains, taste, and skill, from which every book he thought ill of was rigidly excluded,—he never would possess either a complete Voltaire or a complete Rousseau,—the happiest hours of his life were passed. In the circle of one of those women who leave a sort of perfume in literary history, and who have the gift of inspiring successive generations of readers with an indescribable regret not to have known them—Pauline de Montmorin, Madame de Beaumont,—he had become intimate with nearly all which at that time, in the Paris world of letters or of society, was most attractive and promising. Amongst his acquaintances one only misses the names of Madame de Staël and Benjamin Constant; neither of them was to his taste, and with Madame de Staël he always refused to become acquainted; he thought she had more vehemence than truth, and more heat than light. Years went on, and his friends became conspicuous authors or statesmen; but Joubert remained in the shade. His constitution was of such fragility that how he lived so long, or accomplished so much as he did, is a wonder; his soul had, for its basis of operations, hardly any body at all: both from his stomach and from his chest he seems to have had constant suffering, though he lived by rule, and was as abstemious as a Hindoo. Often, after over-work in thinking, reading, or talking, he remained for days together in a state of utter prostration,—condemned to absolute silence and inaction; too happy if the agitation of his mind would become quiet also, and let him have the repose of which he stood in so much need. With this weakness of health, these repeated suspensions of energy, he was incapable of the prolonged contention of spirit necessary for the creation of great works; but he read and thought immensely; he was an unwearied note-taker, a charming letter-writer; above all, an excellent and delightful talker. The gaiety and amenity of his natural disposition were inexhaustible; and his spirit, too, was of astonishing elasticity; he seemed to hold on to life by a single thread only, but that single thread was very tenacious. More and more, as his soul and knowledge ripened more and more, his friends pressed to his room in the Rue St-Honoré; often he received them in bed, for he seldom rose before three o'clock in the afternoon; and at his bedroom door, on his bad days, Madame Joubert stood sentry, trying, not always with success, to keep back the thirsty comers from the fountain which was forbidden to flow. Fontanes did nothing in the University without consulting him, and Joubert's ideas and pen were always at his friend's service. When he was in the country, at Villeneuve, the young priests of his neighbourhood used to resort to him, in order to profit by his library and by his conversation. He, like our Coleridge, was particularly qualified to attract men of this kind and to benefit them: retaining perfect independence of mind, he was a religious philosopher. As age came on, his infirmities became more and more overwhelming; some of his friends, too, died; others became so immersed in politics, that Joubert, who hated politics, saw them seldomer than of old; but the moroseness of age and infirmity never touched him, and he never quarrelled with a friend or lost one. From these miseries he was preserved by that quality in him of which I have already spoken; a quality which is best expressed by a word, not of common use in English,— alas, we have too little in our national character of the quality which this word expresses,—his inborn, his constant amenity. He lived till the year 1824. On the 4th of May in that year he died, at the age of seventy. A day or two after his death M. de Châteaubriand inserted in the *Journal des Débats* a short notice of him, perfect for its feeling, grace, and propriety. *On ne vit dans la mémoire du monde*, he says and says truly, *que par des travaux pour le monde*,—'a man can live in the world's memory only by what he has done for the world.' But Châteaubriand used the privilege which this great name gave him to assert, delicately but firmly, Joubert's real and rare merits, and to tell the world what manner of man had just left it.

Joubert's papers were accumulated in boxes and drawers. He had not meant them for publication; it was very difficult to sort them and to prepare them for it. Madame Joubert, his widow, had a scruple about giving them a publicity which her husband, she felt, would never have permitted. But, as her own end approached, the natural desire to leave of so remarkable a spirit some enduring memorial, some memorial to outlast the admiring recollection of the living who were so fast passing away, made her yield to the entreaties of his friends, and allow the printing, but for private circulation only, of a volume of his fragments. Châteaubriand edited it; it appeared in 1838, fourteen years after Joubert's death. The volume attracted the attention of those who were best fitted to appreciate it, and profoundly impressed them. M. Sainte-Beuve gave of it, in the *Revue des Deux Mondes*, the admirable notice of which I have already spoken; and so much curiosity was excited about Joubert, that the collection of his fragments, enlarged by many additions, was at last published for the benefit of the world in general. It has since been twice reprinted. The first or preliminary chapter has some fancifulness and affectation in it; the reader should begin with the second.

I have likened Joubert to Coleridge; and indeed the points of resemblance between the two men are numerous. Both of them great and celebrated talkers, Joubert attracting pilgrims to his upper chamber in the Rue St-Honoré, as Coleridge attracted pilgrims to Mr Gilman's at Highgate; both of them desultory and incomplete writers,—here they had an outward likeness with one another. Both of them passionately devoted to reading in a class of books, and to thinking on a class of subjects, out of the beaten line of the reading and thought of their day; both of them ardent students and critics of old literature, poetry, and the metaphysics of religion; both of them curious explorers of words, and of the latent significance hidden under the popular use of them; both of them, in a certain sense, conservative in religion and politics, by antipathy to the narrow and shallow foolishness of vulgar modern liberalism;—here they had their inward and real likeness. But that in which the essence of their likeness consisted is this,—that they both had from nature an ardent impulse for seeking the genuine truth on all matters they thought about, and a gift for finding it and recognizing it when it was found. To have the impulse for seeking this truth is much rarer than most people think; to have the gift for finding it is, I need not say, very rare indeed. By this they have a spiritual relationship of the closest kind with one another, and they become, each of them, a source of stimulus and progress for all of us.

Coleridge had less delicacy and penetration than Joubert, but more richness and power; his production, though far inferior to what his nature at first seemed to promise, was abundant and varied. Yet in all his production how much is there to dissatisfy us! How many reserves must be made in praising either his poetry, or his criticism, or his philosophy! How little either of his poetry, or of his criticism, or of his philosophy, can we expect permanently to stand! But that which will stand of Coleridge is this: the stimulus of his continual effort,—not a moral effort, for he had no morals,—but of his continual instinctive effort, crowned often with rich success, to get at and to lay bare the real truth of his matter in hand, whether that matter were literary, or philosophical, or political, or religious; and this in a country where at that moment such an effort was almost unknown; where the most powerful minds threw themselves upon poetry, which conveys truth, indeed, but conveys it indirectly; and where ordinary minds were so habituated to do without thinking altogether, to regard considerations of established routine and practical convenience as paramount, that any attempt to introduce within the domain of these the disturbing element of thought, they were prompt to resent as an outrage. Coleridge's great action lay in his supplying in England, for many years and under critical circumstances, by the spectacle of this effort of his, a stimulus to all minds, in the generation which grew up around him, capable of profiting by it. His action will still be felt as long as the need for it continues; when, with the cessation of the need, the action too has ceased, Coleridge's memory, in spite of the disesteem—nay, repugnance—which his character may and must inspire, will yet for ever remain invested with that interest and gratitude which invests the memory of founders.

M. de Rémusat, indeed, reproaches Coleridge with his *jugements saugrenus*; the criticism of a gifted truth-finder ought not to be *saugrenu*; so on this reproach we must pause for a moment. *Saugrenu* is a rather vulgar French word, but, like many other vulgar words, very expressive; used as an epithet for a judgment, it means something like *impudently absurd*. The literary judgments of one nation about another are very apt to be *saugrenus*;

it is certainly true, as M. Sainte-Beuve remarks in answer to Goethe's complaint against the French that they have under-valued Du Bartas, that as to the estimate of its own authors every nation is the best judge; the *positive* estimate of them, be it understood, not, of course, the estimate of them in comparison with the authors of other nations. Therefore a foreigner's judg-ments about the intrinsic merit of a nation's authors will gener-ally, when at complete variance with that nation's own, be wrong; but there is a permissible wrongness in these matters, and to that permissible wrongness there is a limit. When that limit is ex-ceeded, the wrong judgment becomes more than wrong, it becomes *saugrenu*, or impudently absurd. For instance, the high estimate which the French have of Racine is probably in great measure deserved; or, to take a yet stronger case, even the high estimate which Joubert had of the Abbé Delille is probably in great measure deserved; but the common disparaging judgment passed on Racine by English readers is not *saugrenu*, still less is that passed by them on the Abbé Delille *saugrenu*, because the beauty of Racine, and of Delille too, so far as Delille's beauty goes, is eminently in their language, and this is a beauty which a foreigner cannot perfectly seize;—this beauty of diction, *apicibus verborum ligata*, as M. Sainte-Beuve, quoting Quintilian, says of Châteaubriand's. As to Châteaubriand himself, again, the common English judgment, which stamps him as a mere shallow rhetorician, all froth and vanity, is certainly wrong; one may even wonder that we English should judge Château-briand so wrongly, for his power goes far beyond beauty of diction; it is a power, as well, of passion and sentiment, and this sort of power the English can perfectly well appreciate. One production of Châteaubriand's, *René*, is akin to the most popular productions of Byron,—to the *Childe Harold* or *Manfred*,—in spirit, equal to them in power, superior to them in form. But this work, I hardly know why, is almost unread in England. And only consider this criticism of Châteaubriand's on the true pathetic! 'It is a dangerous mistake, sanctioned, like so many other dangerous mistakes, by Voltaire, to suppose that the best works of imagination are those which draw most tears. One could name this or that melodrama, which no one would like to own having written, and which yet harrows the feelings far more than the *Aeneid*. The true tears are those which are called forth by the *beauty* of poetry; there must be as much admiration in them as sorrow. They are the tears which come to our eyes when Priam says to Achilles, ἔτλην δ᾽, οἳ᾽ οὔπω . . .—"And I have endured,—the like whereof no soul upon the earth hath yet endured,—to carry to my lips the hand of him who slew my child"; or when Joseph cries out: "I am Joseph your brother, whom ye sold into Egypt."' Who does not feel that the man who wrote that was no shallow rhetorician, but a born man of genius, with the true instinct of genius for what is really admirable? Nay, take these words of Châteaubriand, an old man of eighty, dying, amidst the noise and bustle of the ignoble revolution of February 1848: 'Mon Dieu, mon Dieu, quand donc, quand donc serai-je délivré de tout ce monde, ce bruit; quand donc, quand donc cela finira-t-il?' Who, with any ear, does not feel that those are not the accents of a trumpery rhetorician, but of a rich and puissant nature,—the cry of the dying lion? I repeat it, Châteaubriand is most ignorantly underrated in England; and we English are capable of rating him far more correctly if we knew him better. Still, Châteaubriand has such real and great faults, he falls so decidedly beneath the rank of the truly greatest authors, that the depreciatory judgment passed on him in England, though ignorant and wrong, can hardly be said to transgress the limits of permissible ignorance; it is not a *jugement saugrenu*. But when a critic denies genius to a literature which has produced Bossuet and Molière, he passes the bounds; and Coleridge's judgments on French literature and the French genius are undoubtedly, as M. de Rémusat calls them, *saugrenus*.

And yet, such is the impetuosity of our poor human nature, such its proneness to rush to a decision with imperfect knowledge, that his having delivered a *saugrenu* judgment or two in his life by no means proves a man not to have had, in comparison with his fellow men in general, a remarkable gift for truth, or disqualifies him for being, by virtue of that gift, a source of vital stimulus for us. Joubert had far less smoke and turbid vehemence in him than Coleridge; he had also a far keener sense of what was absurd. But Joubert can write to M. Molé (the M. Molé who was afterwards Louis Philippe's well-known minister): 'As to your Milton, whom the merit of the Abbé Delille' (the Abbé Delille translated *Paradise Lost*) 'makes me admire, and with whom I have nevertheless still plenty of fault to find, why,

I should like to know, are you scandalized that I have not enabled myself to read him? I don't understand the language in which he writes, and I don't much care to. If he is a poet one cannot put up with, even in the prose of the younger Racine, am I to blame for that? If by force you mean beauty manifesting itself with power, I maintain that the Abbé Delille has more force than Milton.' That, to be sure, is a petulant outburst in a private letter; it is not, like Coleridge's, a deliberate proposition in a printed philosophical essay. But is it possible to imagine a more perfect specimen of a *saugrenu* judgment? It is even worse than Coleridge's, because it is *saugrenu* with reasons. That, however, does not prevent Joubert from having been really a man of extraordinary ardour in the search for truth, and of extraordinary fineness in the perception of it; and so was Coleridge.

Joubert had around him in France an atmosphere of literary, philosophical, and religious opinion as alien to him as that in England was to Coleridge. This is what makes Joubert, too, so remarkable, and it is on this account that I begged the reader to remark his date. He was born in 1754; he died in 1824. He was thus in the fulness of his powers at the beginning of the present century, at the epoch of Napoleon's consulate. The French criticism of that day—the criticism of Laharpe's successors, of Geoffroy and his colleagues in the *Journal des Débats* —had a dryness very unlike the telling vivacity of the early Edinburgh reviewers, their contemporaries, but a fundamental narrowness, a want of genuine insight, much on a par with theirs. Joubert, like Coleridge, has no respect for the dominant oracle; he treats his Geoffroy with about as little deference as Coleridge treats his Jeffrey. 'Geoffroy,' he says in an article in the *Journal des Débats* criticizing Châteaubriand's *Génie du Christianisme*—'Geoffroy in this article begins by holding out his paw prettily enough; but he ends by a volley of kicks, which lets the whole world see but too clearly the four iron shoes of the four-footed animal.' There is, however, in France a sympathy with intellectual activity for its own sake, and for the sake of its inherent pleasurableness and beauty, keener than any which exists in England; and Joubert had more effect in Paris,— though his conversation was his only weapon, and Coleridge wielded besides his conversation his pen,—than Coleridge had or could have in London. I mean, a more immediate, appreciable effect; an effect not only upon the young and enthusiastic, to whom the future belongs, but upon formed and important personages to whom the present belongs, and who are actually moving society. He owed this partly to his real advantages over Coleridge. If he had, as I have already said, less power and richness than his English parallel, he had more tact and penetration. He was more *possible* than Coleridge; his doctrine was more intelligible than Coleridge's, more receivable. And yet with Joubert, the striving after a consummate and attractive clearness of expression came from no mere frivolous dislike of labour and inability for going deep, but was a part of his native love of truth and perfection. The delight of his life he found in truth, and in the satisfaction which the enjoying of truth gives to the spirit; and he thought the truth was never really and worthily said, so long as the least cloud, clumsiness, and repulsiveness hung about the expression of it.

Some of his best passages are those in which he upholds this doctrine. Even metaphysics he would not allow to remain difficult and abstract: so long as they spoke a professional jargon, the language of the schools, he maintained,—and who shall gainsay him?—that metaphysics were imperfect; or, at any rate, had not yet reached their ideal perfection.

> The true science of metaphysics [he says] consists not in rendering abstract that which is sensible, but in rendering sensible that which is abstract; apparent that which is hidden; imaginable, if so it may be, that which is only intelligible; and intelligible, finally, that which an ordinary attention fails to seize.

And therefore:

> Distrust, in books on metaphysics, words which have not been able to get currency in the world, and are only calculated to form a special language.

Nor would he suffer common words to be employed in a special sense by the schools:

> Which is the best, if one wants to be useful and to be really understood, to get one's words in the world, or to get them in the schools? I maintain that the good plan is to employ words in their popular sense rather than in their philosophical sense;

and the better plan still, to employ them in their natural sense
rather than in their popular sense. By their natural sense, I
mean the popular and universal acceptation of them brought
to that which in this is essential and invariable. To prove a
thing by definition proves nothing, if the definition is purely
philosophical; for such definitions only bind him who makes
them. To prove a thing by definition, when the definition
expresses the necessary, inevitable, and clear idea which the
world at large attaches to the object, is, on the contrary, all in
all; because then what one does is simply to show people what
they do really think, in spite of themselves and without knowing it. The rule that one is free to give to words what sense
one will, and that the only thing needful is to be agreed upon
the sense one gives them, is very well for the mere purposes
of argumentation, and may be allowed in the schools where this
sort of fencing is to be practised; but in the sphere of the true-
born and noble science of metaphysics, and in the genuine
world of literature, it is good for nothing. One must never
quit sight of realities, and one must employ one's expressions
simply as media, as—glasses, through which one's thoughts
can be best made evident. I know, by my own experience, how
hard this rule is to follow; but I judge of its importance by the
failure of every system of metaphysics. Not one of them has
succeeded; for the simple reason, that in every one ciphers have
been constantly used instead of values, artificial ideas instead
of native ideas, jargon instead of idiom.

I do not know whether the metaphysician will ever adopt
Joubert's rules; but I am sure that the man of letters, whenever
he has to speak of metaphysics, will do well to adopt them. He,
at any rate, must remember:

It is by means of familiar words that style takes hold of the
reader and gets possession of him. It is by means of these that
great thoughts get currency and pass for true metal, like gold
and silver which have had a recognized stamp put upon them.
They beget confidence in the man who, in order to make his
thoughts more clearly perceived, uses them; for people feel
that such an employment of the language of common human
life betokens a man who knows that life and its concerns, and
who keeps himself in contact with them. Besides, these words

make a style frank and easy. They show that an author has long made the thought or the feeling expressed his mental food; that he has so assimilated them and familiarized them, that the most common expressions suffice him in order to express ideas which have become everyday ideas to him by the length of time they have been in his mind. And lastly, what one says in such words looks more true; for, of all the words in use, none are so clear as those which we call common words; and clearness is so eminently one of the characteristics of truth that often it even passes for truth itself.

These are not, in Joubert, mere counsels of rhetoric; they come from his accurate sense of perfection, from his having clearly seized the fine and just idea that beauty and light are properties of truth, and that truth is incompletely exhibited if it is exhibited without beauty and light:

Be profound with clear terms and not with obscure terms. What is difficult will at last become easy; but as one goes deep into things, one must still keep a charm, and one must carry into these dark depths of thought, into which speculation has only recently penetrated, the pure and antique clearness of centuries less learned than ours, but with more light in them.

And elsewhere he speaks of those

spirits, lovers of light, who, when they have an idea to put forth, brood long over it first, and wait patiently till it *shines*, as Buffon enjoyed, when he defined genius to be the aptitude for patience; spirits who know by experience that the driest matter and the dullest words hide within the germ and spark of some brightness, like those fairy nuts in which were found diamonds if one broke the shell and was the right person; spirits who maintain that, to see and exhibit things in beauty, is to see and show things as in their essence they really are, and now as they exist for the eye of the careless, who do not look beyond the outside; spirits hard to satisfy, because of a keen-sightedness in them, which makes them discern but too clearly both the models to be followed and those to be shunned; spirits active though meditative, who cannot rest except in solid truths, and whom only beauty can make happy; spirits far less concerned for glory than for perfection, who, because their art is long and life is short, often die without leaving a monument, having had their own inward sense of life and fruitfulness for their best reward.

No doubt there is something a little too ethereal in all this, something which reminds one of Joubert's physical want of body and substance; no doubt, if a man wishes to be a great author, it is to consider too curiously, to consider as Jourbet did; it is a mistake to spend so much of one's time in setting up one's ideal standard of perfection, and in contemplating it. Joubert himself knew this very well: 'I cannot build a house for my ideas,' said he; 'I have tried to do without words, and words take their revenge on me by their difficulty.' 'If there is a man upon earth tormented by the cursed desire to get a whole book into a page, a whole page into a phrase, and this phrase into one word,—that man is myself.' 'I can sow, but I cannot build.' Joubert, however, makes no claim to be a great author; by renouncing all ambition to be this, by not trying to fit his ideas into a house, by making no compromise with words in spite of their difficulty, by being quite single-minded in his pursuit of perfection, perhaps he is enabled to get closer to the truth of the objects of his study, and to be of more service to us by setting before us ideals, than if he had composed a celebrated work. I doubt whether, in an elaborate work on the philosophy of religion, he would have got his ideas about religion to *shine*, to use his own expression, as they shine when he utters them in perfect freedom. Penetration in these matters is valueless without soul, and soul is valueless without penetration; both of these are delicate qualities, and, even in those who have them, easily lost; the charm of Joubert is, that he has and keeps both. Let us try and show that he does.

One should be fearful of being wrong in poetry when one thinks differently from the poets, and in religion when one thinks differently from the saints.

There is a great difference between taking for idols Mahomet and Luther, and bowing down before Rousseau and Voltaire. People at any rate imagined they were obeying God when they followed Mahomet, and the Scriptures when they hearkened to Luther. And perhaps one ought not too much to disparage that inclination which leads mankind to put into the hands of those whom it thinks the friends of God the direction and government of its heart and mind. It is the subjection to irreligious spirits which alone is fatal, and, in the fullest sense of the word, depraving.

May I say it? It is not hard to know God, provided one will not force oneself to define him.

Do not bring into the domain of reasoning that which belongs to our innermost feeling. State truths of sentiment, and do not try to prove them. There is a danger in such proofs; for in arguing it is necessary to treat that which is in question as something problematic: now that which we accustom ourselves to treat as problematic ends by appearing to us as really doubtful. In things that are visible and palpable, never prove what is believed already; in things that are certain and mysterious,—mysterious by their greatness and by their nature,—make people believe them, and do not prove them; in things that are matters of practice and duty, command, and do not explain. 'Fear God', has made many men pious; the proofs of the existence of God have made many men atheists. From the defence springs the attack; the advocate begets in his hearer a wish to pick holes; and men are almost always led on, from the desire to contradict the doctor, to the desire to contradict the doctrine. Make truth lovely, and do not try to arm her; mankind will then be far less inclined to contend with her.

Why is even a bad preacher almost always heard by the pious with pleasure? *Because he talks to them about what they love.* But you who have to expound religion to the children of this world, you who have to speak to them of that which they once loved perhaps, or which they would be glad to love, —remember that they do not love it yet, and to make them love it take heed to speak with power.

You may do what you like, mankind will believe no one but God; and he only can persuade mankind who believes that God has spoken to him. No one can give faith unless he has faith; the persuaded persuade, as the indulgent disarm.

The only happy people in the world are the good man, the sage, and the saint; but the saint is happier than either of the others, so much is man by his nature formed for sanctity.

The same delicacy and penetration which he here shows in speaking of the inward essence of religion, Joubert shows also in speaking of its outward form, and of its manifestation in the world:

> Piety is not a religion, though it is the soul of all religions. A man has not a religion simply by having pious inclinations, any more than he has a country simply by having philanthropy. A man has not a country until he is a citizen in a state, until he undertakes to follow and uphold certain laws, to obey certain magistrates, and to adopt certain ways of living and acting.
>
> Religion is neither a theology nor a theosophy; it is more than all this; it is a discipline, a law, a yoke, an indissoluble engagement.

Who, again, has ever shown with more truth and beauty the good and imposing side of the wealth and splendour of the Catholic Church, than Joubert in the following passage:

> The pomps and magnificence with which the Church is reproached are in truth the result and the proof of her incomparable excellence. From whence, let me ask, have come this power of hers and these excessive riches, except from the enchantment into which she threw all the world? Ravished with her beauty, millions of men from age to age kept loading her with gifts, bequests, cessions. She had the talent of making herself loved, and the talent of making men happy. It is that which wrought prodigies for her; it is from thence that she drew her power.

'She had the talent of making herself *feared*',—one should add that too, in order to be perfectly just; but Joubert, because he is a true child of light, can see that the wonderful success of the Catholic Church must have been due really to her good rather than to her bad qualities; to her making herself loved rather than to her making herself feared.

How striking and suggestive, again, is this remark on the Old and New Testaments:

> The Old Testament teaches the knowledge of good and evil; the Gospel, on the other hand, seems written for the predestinated; it is the book of innocence. The one is made for

earth, the other seems made for heaven. According as the one or the other of these books takes hold of a nation, what may be called the *religious humours* of nations differ.

So the British and North American Puritans are the children of the Old Testament, as Joachim of Flora and St Francis are the children of the New. And does not the following maxim exactly fit the Church of England, of which Joubert certainly never thought when he was writing it?—'The austere sects excite the most enthusiasm at first; but the temperate sects have always been the most durable.'

And these remarks on the Jansenists and Jesuits, interesting in themselves, are still more interesting because they touch matters we cannot well know at first-hand, and which Joubert, an impartial observer, had had the means of studying closely. We are apt to think of the Jansenists as having failed by reason of their merits; Joubert shows us how far their failure was due to their defects:

We ought to lay stress upon what is clear in Scripture, and to pass quickly over what is obscure; to light up what in Scripture is troubled, by what is serene in it; what puzzles and checks the reason, by what satisfies the reason. The Jansenists have done just the reverse. They lay stress upon what is uncertain, obscure, afflicting, and they pass lightly over all the rest; they eclipse the luminous and consoling truths of Scripture, by putting between us and them its opaque and dismal truths. For example, 'Many are called'; there is a clear truth. 'Few are chosen'; there is an obscure truth. 'We are children of wrath'; there is a sombre, cloudy, terrifying truth. 'We are all the children of God'; 'I came not to call the righteous, but sinners to repentance'; there are truths which are full of clearness, mildness, serenity, light. The Jansenists trouble our cheerfulness, and shed no cheering ray on our trouble. They are not, however, to be condemned for what they say, because what they say is true; but they are to be condemned for what they fail to say, for that is true too,—truer, even, than the other; that is, its truth is easier for us to seize, fuller, rounder, and more complete. Theology, as the Jansenists exhibit her, has but the half of her disk.

Again:

The Jansenists erect 'grace' into a kind of fourth person of the Trinity. They are, without thinking or intending it, Quaternitarians. St Paul and St Augustine, too exclusively studied, have done all the mischief. Instead of 'grace', say help, succour, a divine influence, a dew of heaven; then one can come to a right understanding. The word 'grace' is a sort of talisman, all the baneful spell of which can be broken by translating it. The trick of personifying words is a fatal source of mischief in theology.

Once more:

The Jansenists tell men to love God; the Jesuits make men love him. The doctrine of these last is full of loose-nesses, or, if you will, of errors; still,—singular as it may seem, it is undeniable,—they are the better directors of souls.

The Jansenists have carried into religion more thought than the Jesuits, and they go deeper; they are faster bound with its sacred bonds. They have in their way of thinking an austerity which incessantly constrains the will to keep the path of duty; all the habits of their understanding, in short, are more Christian. But they seem to love God without affection, and solely from reason, from duty, from justice. The Jesuits, on the other hand, seem to love him from pure inclination; out of admiration, gratitude, tenderness; for the pleasure of loving him, in short. In their books of devotion you find joy, because with the Jesuits nature and religion go hand in hand. In the books of the Jansenists there is a sadness and a moral con-straint, because with the Jansenists religion is for ever trying to put nature in bonds.

The Jesuits have suffered, and deservedly suffered, plenty of discredit from what Joubert gently calls their 'loosenesses'; let them have the merit of their amiability.

The most characteristic thoughts one can quote from any writer are always his thoughts on matters like these; but the maxims of Joubert are purely literary subjects also, have the same purged and subtle delicacy; they show the same sedulousness in him to preserve perfectly true the balance of his soul. Let me begin with this, which contains a truth too many people fail to perceive :

Ignorance, which in matters of morals extenuates the crime, is itself, in matters of literature, a crime of the first order.

And here is another sentence, worthy of Goethe, to clear the air at one's entrance into the region of literature :

With the fever of the senses, the delirium of the passions, the weakness of the spirit; with the storms of the passing time and with the great scourges of human life,—hunger, thirst, dishonour, diseases, and death,—authors may as long as they like go on making novels which shall harrow our hearts; but the soul says all the while, 'You hurt me.'

And again :

Fiction has no business to exist unless it is more beautiful than reality. Certainly the monstrosities of fiction may be found in the booksellers' shops; you buy them there for a certain number of francs, and you talk of them for a certain number of days; but they have no place in literature, because in literature the one aim of art is the beautiful. Once lose sight of that, and you have the mere frightful reality.

That is just the right criticism to pass on these 'monstrosities': *they have no place in literature,* and those who produce them are not really men of letters. One would think that this was enough to deter from such production any man of genuine ambition. But most of us, alas! are what we must be, not what we ought to be,—not even what we know we ought to be.

The following, of which the first part reminds one of Words-worth's sonnet, 'If thou indeed derive thy light from heaven', excellently defines the true salutary function of literature, and the limits of this function :

Whether one is an eagle or an ant, in the intellectual world, seems to me not to matter much; the essential thing is to have one's place marked there, one's station assigned, and to belong decidedly to a regular and wholesome order. A small talent, if it keeps within its limits and rightly fulfils its task, may reach the goal just as well as a greater one. To accustom man-kind to pleasures which depend neither upon the bodily appetites nor upon money, by giving them a taste for the

things of the mind, seems to me, in fact, the one proper fruit
which nature has meant our literary productions to have. When
they have other fruits, it is by accident, and, in general, not for
good. Books which absorb our attention to such a degree that
they rob us of all fancy for other books, are absolutely pernicious. In this way they only bring fresh crotchets and sects into
the world; they multiply the great variety of weights, rules,
and measures already existing; they are morally and politically
a nuisance.

Who can read these words and not think of the limiting effect
exercised by certain works in certain spheres and for certain
periods; exercised even by the works of men of genius or virtue,
—by the works of Rousseau, the works of Wesley, the works of
Swedenborg? And what is it which makes the Bible so admirable
a book, to be the one book of those who can have only one, but
the miscellaneous character of the contents of the Bible?

Joubert was all his life a passionate lover of Plato; I hope other
lovers of Plato will forgive me for saying that their adored object
has never been more truly described than he is here:

> Plato shows us nothing, but he brings brightness with him;
> he puts light into our eyes, and fills us with a clearness by which
> all objects afterwards become illuminated. He teaches us
> nothing; but he prepares us, fashions us, and makes us ready
> to know all. Somehow or other, the habit of reading him aug-
> ments in us the capacity for discerning and entertaining what-
> ever fine truths may afterwards present themselves. Like
> mountain air, it sharpens our organs, and gives us an appetite
> for wholesome food.

'Plato loses himself in the void' (he says again); 'but one sees
the play of his wings, one hears their rustle.' And the conclusion
is: 'It is good to breathe his air, but not to live upon him.'

As a pendant to the criticism on Plato, this on the French
moralist Nicole is excellent:

> Nicole is a Pascal without style. It is not what he says which
> is sublime, but what he thinks; he rises, not by the natural
> elevation of his own spirit, but by that of his doctrines. One
> must not look to the form in him, but to the matter, which is
> exquisite. He ought to be read with a direct view of practice.

English people have hardly ears to hear the praises of Bousset, and the Bossuet of Joubert is Bossuet at his very best; but this is a far truer Bossuet than the 'declaimer' Bossuet of Lord Macaulay, himself a born rhetorician, if ever there was one:

> Bossuet employs all our idioms, as Homer employed all the dialects. The language of kings, of statesmen, and of warriors; the language of the people and of the student, of the country and of the schools, of the sanctuary and of the courts of law; the old and the new, the trivial and the stately, the quiet and the resounding,—he turns all to his use; and out of all this he makes a style, simple, grave, majestic. His ideas are like his words, varied,—common and sublime together. Times and doctrines in all their multitude were ever before his spirit, as things and words in all their multitude were ever before it. He is not so much a man as a human nature, with the temperance of a saint, the justice of a bishop, the prudence of a doctor, and the might of a great spirit.

After this on Bossuet, I must quote a criticism on Racine, to show that Joubert did not indiscriminately worship all the French gods of the grand century:

> Those who find Racine enough for them are poor souls and poor wits; they are souls and wits which have never got beyond the callow and boarding-school stage. Admirable, as no doubt he is, for his skill in having made poetical the most humdrum sentiments and the most middling sort of passions, he can yet stand us in stead of nobody but himself. He is a superior writer; and, in literature, that at once puts a man on a pinnacle. But he is not an inimitable writer.

And again: 'The talent of Racine is in his works, but Racine himself is not there. That is why he himself became disgusted with them.' 'Of Racine, as of his ancients, the genius lay in taste. His elegance is perfect, but it is not supreme, like that of Virgil.' And, indeed, there is something *supreme* in an elegance which exercises such a fascination as Virgil's does; which makes one return to his poems again and again, long after one thinks one has done with them; which makes them one of those books that, to use Joubert's words, 'lure the reader back to them, as the proverb says good wine lures back the wine-bibber'. And the highest praise Joubert can at last find for Racine is this, that he is the Virgil of the ignorant;—'*Racine est le Virgile des ignorants.*'

Of Boileau, too, Joubert says: 'Boileau is a powerful poet, but only in the world of half poetry.' How true is that of Pope also! And he adds: 'Neither Boileau's poetry nor Racine's flows from the fountain-head.' No Englishman, controverting the exaggerated French estimate of these poets, could desire to use fitter words.

I will end with some remarks on Voltaire and Rousseau, remarks in which Joubert eminently shows his prime merit as a critic,—the soundness and completeness of his judgments. I mean that he has the faculty of judging with all the powers of his mind and soul at work together in due combination; and how rare is this faculty! how seldom is it exercised towards writers who so powerfully as Voltaire and Rousseau stimulate and call into activity a single side in us!

Voltaire's wits came to their maturity twenty years sooner than the wits of other men, and remained in full vigour thirty years longer. The charm which our style in general gets from our ideas, his ideas get from his style. Voltaire is sometimes afflicted, sometimes strongly moved; but serious he never is. His very graces have an effrontery about them. He has correctness of judgment, liveliness of imagination, nimble wits, quick taste, and a moral sense in ruins. He is the most debauched of spirits, and the worst of him is that one gets debauched along with him. If he had been a wise man, and had had the self-discipline of wisdom, beyond a doubt half his wit would have been gone; it needed an atmosphere of *licence* in order to play freely. Those people who read him every day, create for themselves, by an invincible law, the necessity of liking him. But those people, who having given up reading him, gaze steadily down upon the influences which his spirit has shed abroad, find themselves in simple justice and duty compelled to detest him. It is impossible to be satisfied with him, and impossible not to be fascinated by him.

The literary sense in us is apt to rebel against so severe a judgment on such a charmer of the literary sense as Voltaire, and perhaps we English are not very liable to catch Voltaire's vices, while of some of his merits we have signal need; still, as the real definitive judgment on Voltaire, Joubert's is undoubtedly the true one. It is nearly identical with that of Goethe. Joubert's sentence on Rousseau is in some respects more favourable:

That weight in the speaker (*auctoritas*) which the ancients talk of, is to be found in Bossuet more than in any other French author; Pascal, too, has it, and La Bruyère; even Rousseau has something of it, but Voltaire not a particle. I can understand how a Rousseau—I mean a Rousseau cured of his faults —might at the present day do much good, and may even come to be greatly wanted; but under no circumstances can a Voltaire be of any use.

The peculiar power of Rousseau's style has never been better hit off than in the following passage:

Rousseau imparted, if I may so speak, *bowels of feeling* to the words he used (*donna des entrailles à tous les mots*), and poured into them such a charm, sweetness so penetrating, energy so puissant, that his writings have an effect upon the soul something like that of those illicit pleasures which steal away our taste and intoxicate our reason.

The final judgment, however, is severe, and justly severe:

Life without actions; life entirely resolved into affections and half-sensual thoughts; do-nothingness setting up for a virtue; cowardliness with voluptuousness; fierce pride with nullity underneath it; the strutting phrase of the most sensual of vagabonds, who has made his system of philosophy and can give it eloquently forth: there is Rousseau! A piety in which there is no religion; a severity which brings corruption with it; a dogmatism which serves to ruin all authority: there is Rousseau's philosophy! To all tender, ardent, and elevated natures, I say: Only Rousseau can detach you from religion, and only true religion can cure you of Rousseau.

I must yet find room, before I end, for one at least of Joubert's sayings on political matters; here, too, the whole man shows himself; and here, too, the affinity with Coleridge is very remarkable. How true, how true in France especially, is this remark on the contrasting direction taken by the aspirations of the community in ancient and in modern states:

> The ancients were attached to their country by three things, —their temples, their tombs, and their forefathers. The two great bonds which united them to their government were the bonds of habits and antiquity. With the moderns, hope and the love of novelty have produced a total change. The ancients said *our forefathers*, we say *posterity*: we do not, like them, love our *patria*, that is to say, the country and the laws of our fathers, rather we love the laws and the country of our children; the charm we are most sensible to is the charm of the future, and not the charm of the past.

And how keen and true is this criticism on the changed sense of the word 'liberty':

> A great many words have changed their meaning. The word *liberty*, for example, had at bottom among the ancients the same meaning as the word *dominion*. *I would be free* meant, in the mouth of the ancient, *I would take part in governing or administering the State*; in the mouth of a modern it means, *I would be independent*. The word *liberty* has with us a moral sense; with them its sense was purely political.

Joubert had lived through the French Revolution, and to the modern cry for liberty he was prone to answer:

> Let your cry be for free souls rather even than for free men. Moral liberty is the one vitally important liberty, the one liberty which is indispensable; the other liberty is good and salutary only so far as it favours this. Subordination is in itself a better thing than independence. The one implies order and arrangement; the other implies only self-sufficiency with isolation. The one means harmony, the other a single tone; the one is the whole, the other is but the part.

'Liberty! liberty!' he cries again; 'in all things let us have *justice*, and then we shall have enough liberty.'

Let us have justice, *and then we shall have enough liberty*. The wise man will never refuse to echo those words; but then, such is the imperfection of human governments, that almost always, in order to get justice, one has first to secure liberty.

I do not hold up Joubert as a very astonishing and powerful genius, but rather as a delightful and edifying genius. I have not cared to exhibit him as a sayer of brilliant epigrammatic things, such things as 'Notre vie est du vent tissu . . . les dettes abrégent le vie . . . celui qui a de l'imagination sans érudition a des ailes et n'a pas de pieds' (*Our life is woven wind . . . debts take from life . . . the man of imagination without learning has wings and no feet*), though for such sayings he is famous. In the first place, the French language is in itself so favourable a vehicle for such sayings, that the making them in it has the less merit; at least half the merit ought to go, not to the maker of the saying, but to the French language. In the second place, the peculiar beauty of Joubert is not there; it is not in what is exclusively intellectual,—it is in the union of *soul* with intellect, and in the delightful, satisfying result which this union produces. 'Vivre, c'est penser et sentir son âme . . . le bonheur est de sentir son âme bonne . . . toute vérité nue et crue n'a pas assez passé par l'âme . . . les hommes ne sont justes qu'envers ceux qu'ils aiment' (*The essence of life lies in thinking and being conscious of one's soul . . . happiness is the sense of one's soul being good . . . if a truth is nude and crude, that is a proof it has not been steeped long enough in the soul; . . . man cannot even be just to his neighbour, unless he loves him*); it is much rather in sayings like these that Joubert's best and innermost nature manifests itself. He is the most prepossessing and convincing of witnesses to the good of loving light. Because he sincerely loved light, and did not prefer to it any little private darkness of his own, he found light; his eye was single, and therefore his whole body was full of light. And because he was full of light, he was also full of happiness. In spite of his infirmities, in spite of his sufferings, in spite of his obscurity, he was the happiest man alive; his life was as charming as his thoughts. For certainly it is natural that the love of light, which is already, in some measure, the possession of light, should irradiate and beatify the whole life of him who has it. There is something unnatural and shocking where, as in the case of Coleridge, it does not. Joubert pains us by no such contradiction; 'the same penetration of spirit which made him such delightful company to his friends, served also to make him perfect in his own personal life, by enabling him always to perceive and do what was right'; he loved and sought light till he became so habituated to it, so accustomed to the joyful testimony of a good conscience, that, to use his own words, 'he could no longer exist without this, and was obliged to live without reproach if he would live without misery'.

Joubert was not famous while he lived, and he will not be famous now that he is dead. But, before we pity him for this, let us be sure what we mean, in literature, by *famous*. There are the famous men of genius in literature,—the Homers, Dantes, Shakespeares: of them we need not speak; their praise is for ever and ever. Then there are the famous men of ability in literature: their praise is in their own generation. And what makes this difference? The work of the two orders of men is at the bottom the same,—*a criticism of life*. The end and aim of all literature, if one considers it attentively, is, in truth, nothing but that. But the criticism which the men of genius pass upon human life is permanently acceptable to mankind; the criticism which the men of ability pass upon human life is transitorily acceptable. Between Shakespeare's criticism of human life and Scribe's the difference is there;—the one is permanently acceptable, the other transitorily. Whence then, I repeat, this difference. It is that the acceptableness of Shakespeare's criticism depends upon its inherent truth: the acceptableness of Scribe's upon its suiting itself, by its subject-matter, ideas, mode of treatment, to the taste of the generation that hears it. But the taste and ideas of one generation are not those of the next. This next generation in its turn arrives;—first its sharpshooters, its quick-witted, audacious light troops; then the elephantine main body. The imposing array of its predecessor it confidently assails, riddles it with bullets, passes over its body. It goes hard then with many once popular reputations, with many authorities once oracular. Only two kinds of authors are safe in the general havoc. The first kind are the great abounding fountains of truth, whose criticism of life is a source of illumination and joy to the whole human race for ever,—the Homers, the Shakespeares. These are the sacred personages, whom all civilized warfare respects. The second are those whom the out-skirmishers of the new generation, its forerunners,—quick-witted soldiers, as I have said, the select of the army,—recognize, though the bulk of their comrades behind might not, as of the same family and character with the sacred personages, exercising like them an immortal function, and like them inspiring a permanent interest. They snatch them up, and set them in a place of shelter, where the oncoming multitude may not overwhelm them. These are the Jouberts. They will never, like the Shakespeares, command the homage of the multitude; but they are safe; the multitude will not trample them down. Except these two kinds, no author is safe. Let us consider, for example, Joubert's famous contemporary, Lord Jeffrey. All his vivacity and accomplishment avail him nothing; of the true critic he had in an eminent degree no quality, except one,—curiosity. Curiosity he had, but he had no gift for truth; he cannot illuminate and rejoice us; no intelligent outskirmisher of the new generation cares about him, cares to put him in safety; at this moment we are all passing over his body. Let us consider a greater than Jeffrey, a critic whose reputation still stands firm,—will stand, many people think, for ever,—the great apostle of the Philistines, Lord Macaulay. Lord Macaulay was, as I have already said, a born rhetorician; a splendid rhetorician doubtless, and, beyond that, an *English* rhetorician also, an *honest* rhetorician; still, beyond the apparent rhetorical truth of things he never could penetrate; for their vital truth, for what the French call the *vraie vérité*, he had absolutely no organ; therefore his reputation, brilliant as it is, is not secure. Rhetoric so good as his excites and gives pleasure; but by pleasure alone you cannot permanently bind men's spirits to you. Truth illuminates and gives joy, and it is by the bond of joy, not of pleasure, that men's spirits are indissolubly held. As Lord Macaulay's own generation dies out, as a new generation arrives, without those ideas and tendencies of its predecessor which Lord Macaulay so deeply shared and so happily satisfied, will he give the same pleasure? and, if he ceases to give this, has he enough of light in him to make him last? Pleasure the new generation will get from its own novel ideas and tendencies; but light is another and a rarer thing, and must be treasured wherever it can be found. Will Macaulay be saved, in the sweep and pressure of time, for his light's sake, as Johnson has already been saved by two generations, Joubert by one? I think it very doubtful. But for a spirit of any delicacy and dignity, what a fate, if he could foresee it! to be an oracle for one generation, and then of little or no account for ever. How far better, to pass with scant notice through one's own generation, but to be singled out and preserved by the very iconoclasts of the next, then in their turn by those of the next, and so, like the lamp of life itself, to be handed on from one generation to another in safety! This is Joubert's lot, and it is a very enviable one. The new men of the new generations, while they let the dust deepen on a thousand Laharpes, will say of him: 'He lived in the Philistine's day, in a place and time when almost every idea current in literature had the mark of Dagon upon it, and not the mark of the children of light. Nay, the children of light were as yet hardly so much as heard of: the Canaanite was then in the land. Still, there were even then a few, who, nourished on some secret tradition, or illumined, perhaps, by a divine inspiration, kept aloof from the reigning superstitions, never bowed the knee to the gods of Canaan; and one of these few was called *Joubert*.'

Let us conclude. . . .

VIII

SPINOZA AND THE BIBLE

By the sentence of the angels, by the decree of the saints, we anathematize, cut off, curse, and execrate Baruch Spinoza, in the presence of these sacred books with the six hundred and thirteen precepts which are written therein, with the anathema wherewith Joshua anathematized Jericho; with the cursing wherewith Elisha cursed the children; and with all the cursings which are written in the Book of Law: cursed be he by day, and cursed by night; cursed when he lieth down, and cursed when he riseth up; cursed when he goeth out, and cursed when he cometh in; the Lord pardon him never; the wrath and fury of the Lord burn upon this man, and bring upon him all the curses which are written in the Book of Law. The Lord blot out his name under heaven. The Lord set him apart for destruction from all the tribes of Israel, with all the curses of the firmament which are written in the Book of this Law. . . . There shall no man speak to him, no man write to him, no man show him any kindness, no man stay under the same roof with him, no man come nigh him.

With these amenities, the current compliments of theological parting, the Jews of the Portuguese synagogue at Amsterdam took in 1656 (and not in 1660, as has till now been commonly supposed) their leave of their erring brother, Baruch or Benedict Spinoza. They remained children of Israel, and he became a child of modern Europe.

That was in 1656, and Spinoza died in 1677, at the early age of forty-four. Glory had not found him out. His short life—a life of unbroken diligence, kindliness, and purity—was passed in seclusion. But in spite of that seclusion, in spite of the shortness of his career, in spite of the hostility of the dispensers of renown in the eighteenth century,—of Voltaire's disparagement and Bayle's detraction,—in spite of the repellent form which he has given to his principal work, in spite of the exterior semblance of a rigid dogmatism alien to the most essential tendencies of modern philosophy, in spite, finally, of the immense weight of disfavour cast upon him by the long-repeated charge of atheism, Spinoza's name has silently risen in importance, the man and his work have attracted a steadily increasing notice, and bid fair to become soon what they deserve to become,—in the history of modern philosophy the central point of interest. An avowed translation of one of his works,—his *Tractatus Theologico-Politicus*,—has at last made its appearance in English. It is the principal work which Spinoza published in his lifetime; his book on ethics, the work on which his fame rests, is posthumous.

The English translator has not done his task well. Of the character of his version there can, I am afraid, be no doubt; one such passage as the following is decisive:

> I confess that, *while with them* (the theologians) *I have never been able sufficiently to admire the unfathomed mysteries of Scripture, I have still found them giving utterance to nothing but Aristotelian and Platonic speculations*, artfully dressed up and cunningly accommodated to Holy Writ, lest the speakers should show themselves too plainly to belong to the sect of the Grecian heathens. *Nor was it enough for these men to discourse with the Greeks; they have further taken to raving with the Hebrew prophets.*

This professes to be a translation of these words of Spinoza: 'Fateor, eos nunquam satis mirari potuisse Scripturae profundissima mysteria; attamen praeter Aristotelicorum vel Platonicorum speculationes nihil docuisse video, atque his, ne gentiles sectari viderentur, Scripturam accommodaverunt. Non satis his fuit cum Graecis insanire, sed prophetas cum iisdem deliravisse voluerunt.' After one such specimen of a translator's force, the experienced reader has a sort of instinct that he may as well close the book at once, with a smile or a sigh, according as he happens to be a follower of the weeping or of the laughing philosopher. If, in spite of this instinct, he persists in going on with the English version of the *Tractatus Theologico-Politicus*, he will find many more such specimens. It is not, however, my intention to fill my space with these, or with strictures upon their author. I prefer to remark that he renders a service to literary history by pointing out, in his preface, how 'to Bayle may be traced the disfavour in which the name of Spinoza was so long held'; that, in his observations on the system of the Church of England, he shows a laudable freedom from the prejudices of ordinary English Liberals of that advanced school to which he clearly belongs; and lastly, that, though he manifests little familiarity with Latin, he seems to have considerable familiarity with philosophy, and to be well able to follow and comprehend speculative reasoning. Let me advise him to unite his forces with those of someone who has that accurate knowledge of Latin which he himself has not, and then, perhaps, of that union a really good translation of Spinoza will be the result. And, having given him this advice, let me again turn, for a little, to the *Tractatus Theologico-Politicus* itself.

This work, as I have already said, is a work on the interpretation of Scripture,—it treats of the Bible. What was it exactly which Spinoza thought about the Bible and its inspiration? That will be, at the present moment, the central point of interest for the English readers of his Treatise. Now, it is to be observed, that just on this very point the Treatise, interesting and remarkable as it is, will fail to satisfy the reader. It is important to seize this notion quite firmly, and not to quit hold of it while one is reading Spinoza's work. The scope of that work is this. Spinoza sees that the life and practice of Christian nations professing the religion of the Bible, are not the due fruits of the religion of the Bible; he sees only hatred, bitterness, and strife, where he might have expected to see love, and joy, peace in believing; and he asks himself the reason of this. The reason is, he says, that these people misunderstand their Bible. Well, then, is his conclusion, I will write a *Tractatus Theologico-Politicus*. I will show these people, that, taking the Bible for granted, taking it to be all which it asserts itself to be, taking it to have all the authority which it claims, it is not what they imagine it to be, it does not say what they imagine it to say. I will show them what it really does say, and I will show them that they will do well to accept this real teaching of the Bible, instead of the phantom with which they have so long been cheated. I will show their governments that they will do well to remodel the national churches, to make of them institutions informed with the spirit of the true Bible, instead of institutions informed with the spirit of this false phantom.

* G ¹¹⁵

The comments of men, Spinoza said, had been foisted into the Christian religion; the pure teaching of God had been lost sight of. He determined, therefore, to go again to the Bible, to read it over and over with a perfectly unprejudiced mind, and to accept nothing as its teaching which it did not clearly teach. He began by constructing a method, or set of conditions indispensable for the adequate interpretation of Scripture. These conditions are such, he points out, that a perfectly adequate interpretation of Scripture is now impossible. For example, to understand any prophet thoroughly, we ought to know the life, character, and pursuits of that prophet, under what circumstances his book was composed, and in what state and through what hands it has come down to us; and, in general, most of this we cannot now know. Still, the main sense of the Books of Scripture may be clearly seized by us. Himself a Jew with all the learning of his nation, and a man of the highest natural powers, Spinoza had in the difficult task of seizing this sense every aid which special knowledge or pre-eminent faculties could supply.

In what then, he asks, does Scripture, interpreted by its own aid, and not by the aid of Rabbinical traditions or Greek philosophy, allege its own divinity to consist? In a revelation given by God to the prophets. Now all knowledge is a divine revelation; but prophecy, as represented in Scripture, is one of which the laws of human nature, considered in themselves alone, cannot be the cause. Therefore nothing must be asserted about it, except what is clearly declared by the prophets themselves: for they are our only source of knowledge on a matter which does not fall within the scope of our ordinary knowing faculties. But ignorant people, not knowing the Hebrew genius and phraseology, and not attending to the circumstances of the speaker, often imagine the prophets to assert things which they do not.

The prophets clearly declare themselves to have received the revelation of God through the means of words and images;— not, as Christ, through immediate communication of the mind with the mind of God. Therefore the prophets excelled other men by the power and vividness of their representing and imagining faculty, not by the perfection of their mind. This is why they perceived almost everything through figures, and express themselves so variously, and so improperly, concerning the nature of God. Moses imagined that God could be seen, and attributed to him the passions of anger and jealousy; Micaiah imagined him sitting on a throne, with the host of heaven on his right and left hand; Daniel as an old man, with a white garment and white hair; Ezekiel as a fire; the disciples of Christ thought they saw the Spirit of God in the form of a dove; the apostles in the form of fiery tongues.

Whence, then, could the prophets be certain of the truth of a revelation which they received through the imagination, and not by a mental process?—for only an idea can carry the sense of its own certainty along with it, not an imagination. To make them certain of the truth of what was revealed to them, a reasoning process came in; they had to rely on the testimony of a sign; and (above all) on the testimony of their own conscience, that they were good men, and spoke for God's sake. Either testimony was incomplete without the other. Even the good prophet needed for his message the confirmation of a sign; but the bad prophet, the utterer of an immoral doctrine, had no certainty for his doctrine, no truth in it, even though he confirmed it by a sign. The testimony of a good conscience was, therefore, the prophet's grand source of certitude. Even this, however, was only a moral certitude, not a mathematical; for no man can be perfectly sure of his own goodness.

The power of imagining, the power of feeling what goodness is, and the habit of practising goodness, were therefore the sole essential qualifications of a true prophet. But for the purpose of the message, the revelation, which God designed him to convey, these qualifications were enough. The sum and substance of this revelation was simply: *Believe in God, and lead a good life.* To be the organ of this revelation did not make a man more learned; it left his scientific knowledge as it found it. This explains the contradictory and speculatively false opinions about God, and the laws of nature, which the patriarchs, the prophets, the apostles entertained. Abraham and the patriarchs knew God only as *El Sadai,* the power which gives to every man that which suffices him; Moses knew him as *Jehovah,* a self-existent being, but imagined him with the passions of a man. Samuel imagined that God could not repent of his sentences; Jeremiah, that he could. Joshua, on a day of great victory, the ground being white with hail, seeing the daylight last longer than usual, and imaginatively seizing this as a special sign of the help divinely promised to him, declared that the sun was standing still. To be obeyers of God themselves, and inspired leaders of others to obedience and good life, did not make Abraham and Moses metaphysicians, or Joshua a natural philosopher. His revelation no more changed the speculative opinions of each prophet than it changed his temperament or style. The wrathful Elisha required the natural sedative of music before he could be the messenger of good fortune to Jehoram. The high-bred Isaiah and Nahum have the style proper to their condition, and the rustic Ezekiel and Amos the style proper to theirs. We are not therefore bound to pay heed to the speculative opinions of this or that prophet, for in uttering these he spoke as a mere man: only in exhorting his hearers to obey God and lead a good life was he the organ of a divine revelation.

To know and love God is the highest blessedness of man, and of all men alike; to this all mankind are called, and not any one nation in particular. The divine law, properly so named, is the method of life for attaining this height of human blessedness: this law is universal, written in the heart, and one for all mankind. Human law is the method of life for attaining and preserving temporal security and prosperity: this law is dictated by a lawgiver, and every nation has its own. In the case of the Jews, this law was dictated, by revelation, through the prophets; its fundamental precept was to obey God and to keep his commandments, and it is therefore, in a secondary sense, called divine; but it was, nevertheless, framed in respect of temporal things only. Even the truly moral and divine precept of this law, to practise for God's sake justice and mercy towards one's neighbour, meant for the Hebrew of the Old Testament his Hebrew neighbour only, and had respect to the concord and stability of the Hebrew commonwealth. The Jews were to obey God and to keep his commandments, that they might continue long in the land given to them, and that it might be well with them there. Their election was a temporal one, and lasted only as long as their State. It is now over; and the only election the Jews now have is that of the *pious*, the *remnant* which takes place, and has always taken place, in every other nation also. Scripture itself teaches that there is a universal divine law, that this is common to all nations alike, and is the law which truly confers eternal blessedness. Solomon, the wisest of the Jews, knew this law, as the few wisest men in all nations have ever known it; but for the mass of the Jews, as for the mass of mankind everywhere, this law was hidden, and they had no notion of its moral action, its *vera vita* which conducts to eternal blessedness, except so far as this action was enjoined upon them by the prescriptions of their temporal law. When the ruin of their State brought with it the ruin of their temporal law, they would have lost altogether their only clue to eternal blessedness.

Christ came when that fabric of the Jewish State, for the sake of which the Jewish law existed, was about to fall; and he proclaimed the universal divine law. A certain moral action is prescribed by this law, as a certain moral action was prescribed by the Jewish law: but he who truly conceives the universal divine law conceives God's decrees adequately as eternal truths, and for him moral action has liberty and self-knowledge; while the prophets of the Jewish law inadequately conceived God's decrees as mere rules and commands, and for them moral action had no liberty and no self-knowledge. Christ, who beheld the decrees of God as God himself beholds them,—as eternal truths,— proclaimed the love of God and the love of our neighbour as *commands*, only because of the ignorance of the multitude: to those to whom it was 'given to know the mysteries of the kingdom of God', he announced them, as he himself perceived them, as eternal truths. And the apostles, like Christ, spoke to many of their hearers 'as unto carnal not spiritual'; presented to them, that is, the love of God and their neighbour as a divine command authenticated by the life and death of Christ, not as an eternal idea of reason carrying its own warrant along with it. The presentation of it as this latter their hearers 'were not able to bear'. The apostles, moreover, though they preached and confirmed their doctrines by signs as prophets, wrote their Epistles, not as prophets, but as doctors and reasoners. The essentials of their doctrine, indeed, they took not from reason, but, like the prophets, from fact and revelation; they preached belief in God and goodness of life as a catholic religion existing by virtue of the passion of Christ, as the prophets had preached belief in God and goodness of life as a national religion existing by virtue of the Mosaic covenant: but while the prophets announced their message in a form purely dogmatical, the apostles developed theirs with the forms of reasoning and argumentation, according to each apostle's ability and way of thinking, and as they might best commend their message to their hearers; and for their reasonings they themselves claim no divine authority, submitting them to the judgment of their hearers. Thus each apostle built essential religion on a non-essential foundation of his own, and, as St Paul says, avoided building on the foundations of another apostle, which might be quite different from his own. Hence the discrepancies between the doctrine of one apostle and another —between that of St Paul, for example, and that of St James; but these discrepancies are in the non-essentials not given to them by revelation, and not in essentials. Human churches, seizing these discrepant non-essentials as essentials, one maintaining one of them, another another, have filled the world with unprofitable disputes, have 'turned the Church into an academy, and religion into a science, or rather a wrangling', and have fallen into endless schism.

What, then, are the essentials of religion according both to the Old and to the New Testament? Very few and very simple. The precept to love God and our neighbour. The precepts of the first chapter of Isaiah: 'Wash you, make you clean; put away the evil of your doings from before mine eyes; cease to do evil; learn to do well; seek judgment, relieve the oppressed, judge the fatherless, plead for the widow.' The precepts of the Sermon on the Mount, which add to the foregoing the injunction that we should cease to do evil and learn to do well, not to our brethren and fellow-citizens only, but to all mankind. It is by following these precepts that belief in God is to be shown: if we believe in him, we shall keep his commandment; and this is his commandment, that we love one another. It is because it contains these precepts that the Bible is properly called the Word of God, in spite of its containing much that is mere history, and, like all history, sometimes true, sometimes false; in spite of its containing much that is mere reasoning, and, like all reasoning, sometimes sound, sometimes hollow. These precepts are also the precepts of the universal divine law written in our hearts; and it is only by this that the divinity of Scripture is established; —by its containing, namely, precepts identical with those of this inly-written and self-proving law. This law was in the world, as St John says, before the doctrine of Moses or the doctrine of Christ. And what need was there, then, for these doctrines?

Because the world at large 'knew not' this original divine law, in which precepts are ideas, and the belief in God the knowledge and contemplation of him. Reason gives us this law, reason tells us that it leads to eternal blessedness, and that those who follow it have no need of any other. But reason could not have told us that the moral action of the universal divine law,—followed not from a sense of its intrinsic goodness, truth, and necessity, but simply in proof of obedience (for both the Old and New Testament are but one long discipline of obedience), simply because it is so commanded by Moses in virtue of the covenant, simply because it is so commanded by Christ in virtue of his life and passion,—can lead to eternal blessedness, which means, for reason, eternal knowledge. Reason could not have told us this, and this is what the Bible tells us. This is that 'thing which had been kept secret since the foundation of the world'. It is thus that by means of the foolishness of the world God confounds the wise, and with things that are not brings to naught things that are. Of the truth of the promise thus made to obedience without knowledge, we can have no mathematical certainty; for we can have a mathematical certainty only of things deduced by reason from elements which she in herself possesses. But we can have a moral certainty of it; a certainty such as the prophets had themselves, arising out of the goodness and pureness of those to whom this revelation has been made, and rendered possible for us by its contradicting no principles of reason. It is a great comfort to believe it; because 'as it is only the very small minority who can pursue a virtuous life by the sole guidance of reason, we should, unless we had this testimony of Scripture, be in doubt respecting the salvation of nearly the whole human race'.

It follows from this that philosophy has her own independent sphere, and theology hers, and that neither has the right to invade and try to subdue the other. Theology demands perfect obedience, philosophy perfect knowledge: the obedience demanded by theology and the knowledge demanded by philosophy are alike saving. As speculative opinions about God, theology requires only such as are indispensable to the reality of this obedience; the belief that God is, that he is a rewarder of them that seek him, and that the proof of seeking him is a good life. These are the fundamentals of faith, and they are so clear and simple that none of the inaccuracies provable in the

Bible narrative the least affect them, and they have indubitably come to us uncorrupted. He who holds them may make, as the patriarchs and prophets did, other speculations about God most erroneous, and yet their faith is complete and saving. Nay, beyond these fundamentals, speculative opinions are pious or impious, not as they are true or false, but as they confirm or shake the believer in the practice of obedience. The truest speculative opinion about the nature of God is impious if it makes its holder rebellious; the falsest speculative opinion is pious if it makes him obedient. Governments should never render themselves the tools of ecclesiastical ambition by promulgating as fundamentals of the national Church's faith more than these, and should concede the fullest liberty of speculation.

But the multitude, which respects only what astonishes, terrifies, and overwhelms it, by no means takes this simple view of its own religion. To the multitude, religion seems imposing only when it is subversive of reason, confirmed by miracles, conveyed in documents materially sacred and infallible, and dooming to damnation all without its pale. But this religion of the multitude is not the religion which a true interpretation of Scripture finds in Scripture. Reason tells us that a miracle,—understanding by a miracle a breach of the laws of nature,—is impossible, and that to think it possible is to dishonour God; for the laws of nature are the laws of God, and to say that God violates the laws of nature is to say that he violates his own nature. Reason sees, too, that miracles can never attain their professed object,—that of bringing us to a higher knowledge of God; since our knowledge of God is raised only by perfecting and clearing our conceptions, and the alleged design of miracles is to baffle them. But neither does Scripture anywhere assert, as a general truth, that miracles are possible. Indeed, it asserts the contrary; for Jeremiah declares that Nature follows an invariable order. Scripture, however, like Nature herself, does not lay down speculative propositions (*Scriptura definitiones non tradit, ut nec etiam natura*). It relates matters in such an order and with such phraseology as a speaker (often not perfectly instructed himself) who wanted to impress his hearers with a lively sense of God's greatness and goodness would naturally employ; as Moses, for instance, relates to the Israelites the passage of the Red Sea without any mention of the east wind which attended it, and which is brought accidentally to our knowledge in another place. So that to know exactly what Scripture means in the relation of each seeming miracle, we ought to know (besides the tropes and phrases of the Hebrew language) the circumstances, and also,—since everyone is swayed in his manner of presenting facts by his own preconceived opinions, and we have seen what those of the prophets were,—the preconceived opinions of each speaker. But this mode of interpreting Scripture is fatal to the vulgar notion of its verbal inspiration, of a sanctity and absolute truth in all the words and sentences of which it is composed. This vulgar notion is, indeed, a palpable error. It is demonstrable from the internal testimony of the Scriptures themselves, that the books from the first of the Pentateuch to the last of Kings were put together, after the first destruction of Jerusalem, by a compiler (probably Ezra) who designed to relate the history of the Jewish people from its origin to that destruction; it is demonstrable, moreover, that the compiler did not put his last hand to the work, but left it with its extracts from various and conflicting sources sometimes unreconciled, left it with errors of text and unsettled readings. The prophetic books are mere fragments of the prophets, collected by the Rabbins where they could find them, and inserted in the Canon according to their discretion. They, at first, proposed to admit neither the Book of Proverbs nor the Book of Ecclesiastes into the Canon, and only admitted them because there were found in them passages which commended the law of Moses. Ezekiel also they had determined to exclude; but one of their number remodelled him, so as to procure his admission. The Books of Ezra, Nehemiah, Esther, and Daniel are the work of a single author, and were not written till after Judas Maccabeus had restored the worship of the Temple. The Book of Psalms was collected and arranged at the same time. Before this time, there was no Canon of the sacred writings, and the great synagogue, by which the Canon was fixed, was first convened after the Macedonian conquest of Asia. Of that synagogue none of the prophets were members; the learned men who composed it were guided by their own fallible judgment. In like manner the uninspired judgment of human councils determined the Canon of the New Testament.

Such, reduced to the briefest and plainest terms possible,

stripped of the developments and proofs with which he delivers it, and divested of the metaphysical language in which much of it is clothed by him, is the doctrine of Spinoza's treatise on the interpretation of Scripture. By the whole scope and drift of its argument, by the spirit in which the subject is throughout treated, his work undeniably is most interesting and stimulating to the general culture of Europe. There are alleged contradictions in Scripture; and the question which the general culture of Europe, informed of this, asks with real interest is: *What then?* Spinoza addresses himself to this question. All secondary points of criticism he touches with the utmost possible brevity. He points out that Moses could never have written: 'And the Canaanite was then in the land,' because the Canaanite was in the land still at the death of Moses. He points out that Moses could never have written: 'There arose not a prophet since in Israel like unto Moses.' He points out how such a passage as, 'These are the kings that reigned in Edom *before there reigned any king over the children of Israel*', clearly indicates an author writing not before the times of the Kings. He points out how the account of Og's iron bedstead: 'Only Og the king of Bashan remained of the remnant of giants; behold, his bedstead was a bedstead of iron; is it not in Rabbath of the children of Ammon?' —probably indicates an author writing after David had taken Rabbath, and found there 'abundance of spoil', amongst it this iron bedstead, the gigantic relic of another age. He points out how the language of this passage, and of such a passage as that in the Book of Samuel: 'Beforetime in Israel, when a man went to inquire of God, thus he spake: Come and let us go to the seer; for he that is now called prophet was aforetime called seer'—is certainly the language of a writer describing the events of a long-past age, and not the language of a contemporary. But he devotes to all this no more space than is absolutely necessary. He apologises for delaying over such matters so long: *non est cur circa haec diu detinear—nolo taediosâ lectione lectorem detinere.* For him the interesting question is, not whether the fanatical devotee of the letter is to continue, for a longer or for a shorter time, to believe that Moses sate in the land of Moab writing the description of his own death, but what he is to believe when he does not believe this. Is he to take for the guidance of his life a great gloss put upon the Bible by theologians, who, 'not content with going mad themselves with Plato and Aristotle, want to make Christ and the prophets go mad with them too',—or the Bible itself? Is he to be presented by his national church with metaphysical formularies for his creed, or with the real fundamentals of Christianity? If with the former, religion will never produce its due fruits. A few elect will still be saved; but the vast majority of mankind will remain without grace and without good works, hateful and hating one another. Therefore he calls urgently upon governments to make the national church what it should be. This is the conclusion of the whole matter for him; a fervent appeal to the State, to save us from the untoward generation of metaphysical Article-makers. And therefore, anticipating Mr Gladstone, he called his book *The Church in its Relations with the State.*

Such is really the scope of Spinoza's work. He pursues a great object, and pursues it with signal ability. But it is important to observe that he nowhere distinctly gives his own opinion about the Bible's fundamental character. He takes the Bible as it stands, as he might take the phenomena of nature, and he discusses it as he finds it. Revelation differs from natural knowledge, he says, not by being more divine or more certain than natural knowledge, but by being conveyed in a different way; it differs from it because it is a knowledge 'of which the laws of human nature considered in themselves alone cannot be the cause'. What is really its cause, he says, we need not here inquire (*verum nec nobis jam opus est propheticae cognitionis causam scire*), for we take Scripture, which contains this revelation, as it stands, and do not ask how it arose (*documentorum causas nihil curamus*).

Proceeding on this principle, Spinoza leaves the attentive reader somewhat baffled and disappointed, clear as is his way of treating his subject, and remarkable as are the conclusions with which he presents us. He starts, we feel, from what is to him a hypothesis, and we want to know what he really thinks about this hypothesis. His greatest novelties are all within limits fixed for him by this hypothesis. He says that the voice which called Samuel was an imaginary voice; he says that the waters of the Red Sea retreated before a strong wind; he says that the Shunammite's son was revived by the natural heat of Elisha's body; he says that the rainbow which was made a sign to Noah appeared in the ordinary course of nature. Scripture itself, rightly interpreted, says, he affirms, all this. But he asserts that the divine voice which uttered the commandments on Mount Sinai was a real voice, *vera vox*. He says, indeed, that this voice could not really give to the Israelites that proof which they imagined it gave to them of the existence of God, and that God on Sinai was dealing with the Israelites only according to their imperfect knowledge. Still he asserts the divine voice to have been a real one; and for this reason, that we do violence to Scripture if we do not admit it to have been a real one (*nisi Scripturae vim inferre velimus, omnino concedendum est, Israëlitas veram vocem audivisse*). The attentive reader wants to know what Spinoza himself thought about this *vera vox* and its possibility; he is much more interested in knowing this than in knowing what Spinoza considered Scripture to affirm about the matter.

The feeling of perplexity thus caused is not diminished by the language of the chapter on miracles. In this chapter Spinoza broadly affirms a miracle to be an impossibility. But he himself contrasts the method of demonstration *à priori*, by which he claims to have established this proposition, with the method which he has pursued in treating of prophetic revelation. 'This revelation', he says, 'is a matter out of human reach, and therefore I was bound to take it as I found it.' *Monere volo, me aliâ prorsus methodo circa miracula processisse, quam circa prophetiam ... quod etiam consulto feci, quia de prophetiâ, quandoquidem ipsa captum humanum superat et queastio mere theologica est, nihil affirmare, neque etiam scire poteram in quo ipsa potissimum constiterit, nisi ex fundamentis revelatis.* The reader feels that Spinoza, proceeding on a hypothesis, has presented him with the assertion of a miracle, and afterwards, proceeding *à priori*, has presented him with the assertion that a miracle is impossible. He feels that Spinoza does not adequately reconcile these two assertions by declaring that any event really miraculous, if found recorded in Scripture, must be 'a spurious addition made to Scripture by sacrilegious men'. Is, then, he asks, the *vera vox* of Mount Sinai in Spinoza's opinion a spurious addition made to Scripture by sacrilegious men; or, if not, how is it not miraculous?

Spinoza, in his own mind, regarded the Bible as a vast collection of miscellaneous documents, many of them quite disparate and not at all to be harmonized with others; documents of un-equal value and of varying applicability, some of them conveying ideas salutary for one time, others for another. But in the *Tractatus Theologico-Politicus* he by no means always deals in this free spirit with the Bible. Sometimes he chooses to deal with it in the spirit of the veriest worshipper of the letter; some-times he chooses to treat the Bible as if all its parts were (so to speak) equipollent; to snatch an isolated text which suits his purpose, without caring whether it is annulled by the context, by the general drift of Scripture, or by other passages of more weight and authority. The great critic thus becomes voluntarily as uncritical as Exeter Hall. The epicurean Solomon, whose *Ecclesiastes* the Hebrew doctors, even after they had received it into the canon, forbade the young and weak-minded among their community to read, Spinoza quotes as of the same authority with the severe Moses; he uses promiscuously, as documents of identical force, without discriminating between their essenti-ally different character, the softened cosmopolitan teaching of the prophets of the captivity and the rigid national teaching of the instructors of Israel's youth. He is capable of extracting, from a chance expression of Jeremiah, the assertion of a specula-tive idea which Jeremiah certainly never entertained, and from which he would have recoiled in dismay,—the idea, namely, that miracles are impossible; just as the ordinary Englishman can extract from God's words to Noah, *Be fruitful and multiply*, an exhortation to himself to have a large family. Spinoza, I repeat, knew perfectly well what this verbal mode of dealing with the Bible was worth: but he sometimes uses it because of the hypo-thesis from which he set out; because of his having agreed 'to take Scripture as it stands, and not to ask how it arose'.

No doubt the sagacity of Spinoza's rules for Biblical interpre-tation, the power of his analysis of the contents of the Bible, the interest of his reflections on Jewish history, are, in spite of this, very great, and have an absolute worth of their own, independent of the silence or ambiguity of their author upon a point of cardinal importance. Few candid people will read his rules of interpretation without exclaiming that they are the very dictates of good sense, that they have always believed in them; and without adding, after a moment's reflection, that they have passed their lives in violating them. And what can be more interesting than to find that perhaps the main cause of the decay of the Jewish polity was one of which from our English Bible, which entirely mistranslates the 26th verse of the 20th chapter of Ezekiel, we hear nothing,—the perpetual reproach of impurity and rejection cast upon the priesthood of the tribe of Levi? What can be more suggestive, after Mr Mill and Dr Stanley have been telling us how great an element of strength to the Hebrew nation was the institution of prophets, than to hear from the ablest of Hebrews how this institution seems to him to have been to his nation one of her main elements of weakness? No intelligent man can read the *Tractatus Theologico-Politicus* without being profoundly instructed by it: but neither can he read it without feeling that, as a speculative work, it is, to use a French military expression, *in the air*; that, in a certain sense, it is in want of a base and in want of supports; that this base and these supports are, at any rate, not to be found in the work itself, and, if they exist, must be sought for in other works of the author.

The genuine speculative opinions of Spinoza, which the *Tractatus Theologico-Politicus* but imperfectly reveals, may in his Ethics and in his Letters be found set forth clearly. It is, however, the business of criticism to deal with every independent work as with an independent whole, and, instead of establishing between the *Tractatus Theologico-Politicus* and the Ethics of Spinoza a relation which Spinoza himself has not established,—to seize, in dealing with the *Tractatus Theologico-Politicus*, the important fact that this work has its source, not in the axioms and definition of the Ethics, but in a hypothesis. The Ethics are not yet translated into English, and I have not here to speak of them. Then will be the right time for criticism to try and seize the special character and tendencies of that remarkable work, when it is dealing with it directly. The criticism of the Ethics is far too serious a task to be undertaken incidentally, and merely as a supplement to the criticism of the *Tractatus Theologico-Politicus*. Nevertheless, on certain governing ideas of Spinoza, which receive their systematic expression, indeed, in the Ethics, and on which the *Tractatus Theologico-Politicus* is not formally based, but which are yet never absent from Spinoza's mind in the composition of any work, which breathe through all his works, and fill them with a peculiar effect and power, I have a word or two to say.

A philosopher's real power over mankind resides not in his metaphysical formulas, but in the spirit and tendencies which have led him to adopt those formulas. Spinoza's critic, therefore, has rather to bring to light that spirit and those tendencies of his author, than to exhibit his metaphysical formulas. Propositions about substance pass by mankind at large like the idle wind, which mankind at large regards not; it will not even listen to a word about these propositions, unless it first learns what their author was driving at with them, and finds that this object of his is one with which it sympathizes, one, at any rate, which commands its attention. And mankind is so far right that this object of the author is really, as has been said, that which is most important, that which sets all his work in motion, that which is the secret of his attraction for other minds, which, by different ways, pursue the same object.

Mr Maurice, seeking for the cause of Goethe's great admiration for Spinoza, thinks that he finds it in Spinoza's Hebrew genius. 'He spoke to God', says Mr Maurice, 'as an actual being, to those who had fancied him a name in a book. The child of the circumcision had a message for Lessing and Goethe which the pagan schools of philosophy could not bring.' This seems to me, I confess, fanciful. An intensity and impressiveness, which came to him from his Hebrew nature, Spinoza no doubt has; but the two things which are most remarkable about him, and by which, as I think, he chiefly impressed Goethe, seem to me not to come to him from his Hebrew nature at all,—I mean his denial of final causes, and his stoicism, a stoicism not passive, but active. For a mind like Goethe's,—a mind profoundly impartial and passionately aspiring after the science, not of men only, but of universal nature,—the popular philosophy which explains all things by reference to man, and regards universal nature as existing for the sake of man, and even of certain classes of men, was utterly repulsive. Unchecked, this philosophy would gladly maintain that the donkey exists in order that the invalid Christian may have donkey's milk before breakfast; and such views of nature as this were exactly what Goethe's whole soul abhorred. Creation, he thought, should be made of sterner stuff; he desired to rest the donkey's existence on larger grounds. More than any philosopher who has ever lived, Spinoza satisfied him here. The full exposition of the counter-doctrine to the popular doctrine of final causes is to be found in the Ethics; but this denial of final causes was so essential an element of all Spinoza's thinking that we shall, as has been said already, find it in the work with which we are here concerned, the *Tractatus Theologico-Politicus*, and, indeed, permeating that work and all his works. From the *Tractatus Theologico-Politicus* one may take as good a general statement of this denial as any which is to be found in the Ethics:

Deus naturam dirigit, prout ejus leges universales, non autem prout humanae naturae particulares leges exigunt, adeoque Deus non solius humani generis, sed totius naturae rationem habet. (*God directs nature, according as the universal laws of nature, but not according as the particular laws of human nature require; and so God has regard, not of the human race only, but of entire nature.*)

And, as a pendant to this denial by Spinoza of final causes, comes his stoicism:

Non studemus, ut natura nobis, sed contra ut nos naturae pareamus. (*Our desire is not that nature may obey us, but, on the contrary, that we may obey nature.*)

Here is the second source of his attractiveness for Goethe; and Goethe is but the eminent representative of a whole order of minds whose admiration has made Spinoza's fame. Spinoza first impresses Goethe and any man like Goethe, and then he composes him; first he fills and satisfies his imagination by the width and grandeur of his view of nature, and then he fortifies and stills his mobile, straining, passionate poetic temperament by the moral lesson he draws from his view of nature. And a moral lesson not of mere resigned acquiescence, not of melancholy quietism, but of joyful activity within the limits of man's true sphere:

Ipsa hominis essentia est conatus quo unusquis que suum esse conservare conatur. . . . Virtus hominis est ipsa hominis essentia, quatenus a solo conatu suum esse conservandi definitur. . . . Felicitas in eo consistit quod homo suum esse conservare potest. . . . Laetitia est hominis transitio ad majorem perfectionem. . . . Tristitia est hominis transitio ad minorem perfectionem. (*Man's very essence is the effort wherewith each man strives to maintain his own being. . . . Man's virtue is this very essence, so far as it is defined by this single effort to maintain his own being. . . . Happiness consists in a man's being able to maintain his own being. . . . Joy is man's passage to a greater perfection. . . . Sorrow is man's passage to a lesser perfection.)*

It seems to me that by neither of these, his grand characteristic doctrines, is Spinoza truly Hebrew or truly Christian. His denial of final causes is essentially alien to the spirit of the Old Testament, and his cheerful and self-sufficing stoicism is essentially alien to the spirit of the New. The doctrine that 'God directs nature, not according as the particular laws of human nature, but according as the universal laws of nature require', is at utter variance with that Hebrew mode of representing God's dealings, which makes the locusts visit Egypt to punish Pharaoh's hardness of heart, and the falling dew avert itself from the fleece of Gideon. The doctrine that 'all sorrow is a passage to a lesser perfection' is at utter variance with the Christian recognition of the blessedness of sorrow, working 'repentance to salvation not to be repented of'; of sorrow, which, in Dante's words, 'remarries us to God'.

Spinoza's repeated and earnest assertions that the love of God is man's *summum bonum* do not remove the fundamental diversity between his doctrine and the Hebrew and Christian doctrine. By the love of God he does not mean the same thing which the Hebrew and Christian religions mean by the love of God. He makes the love of God to consist in the knowledge of God; and, as we know God only through his manifestation of himself in the laws of all nature, it is by knowing these laws that we love God, and the more we know them the more we love him. This may be true, but this is not what the Christian means by the love of God. Spinoza's ideal is the intellectual life; the Christian's ideal is the religious life. Between the two conditions there is all the difference which there is between the being in love, and the following, with delighted comprehension, a reasoning of Plato. For Spinoza, undoubtedly, the crown of the intellectual life is a transport, as for the saint the crown of the religious life is a transport; but the two transports are not the same.

This is true; yet it is true, also, that by thus crowning the intellectual life with a sacred transport, by thus retaining in philosophy, amid the discontented murmurs of all the army of atheism, the name of God, Spinoza maintains a profound affinity with that which is truest in religion, and inspires an indestructible interest. One of his admirers, M. Van Vloten, had recently published at Amsterdam a supplementary volume of Spinoza's works, containing the interesting document of Spinoza's sentence of excommunication, from which I have already quoted, and containing, besides, several lately found works alleged to be Spinoza's, which seem to me to be of doubtful authenitcity, and, even if authentic, of no great importance. M. Van Vloten (who, let me be permitted to say in passing, writes a Latin which would make one think that the art of writing Latin must be now a lost art in the country of Lipsius) is very anxious that Spinoza's unscientific retention of the name of God should not afflict his readers with any doubts as to his perfect scientific orthodoxy:

It is a great mistake [he cries] to disparage Spinoza as merely one of the dogmatists before Kant. By keeping the name of God, while he did away with the person and character, he has done himself an injustice. Those who look to the bottom of things will see, that, long ago as he lived, he had even then reached the point to which the post-Hegelian philosophy and the study of natural science has only just brought our own times. Leibnitz expressed his apprehension lest those who did away with final causes should do away with God at the same time. But it is in his having done away with final causes, *and with God along with them*, that Spinoza's true merit consists.

Now it must be remarked that to use Spinoza's denial of final causes in order to identify him with the Coryphaei of atheism, is to make a false use of Spinoza's denial of final causes, just as to use his assertion of the all-importance of loving God to identify him with the saints would be to make a false use of his assertion of the all-importance of loving God. He is no more to be identified with the post-Hegelian philosophers than he is to be identified with St Augustine. Unction, indeed, Spinoza's writings have not; that name does not precisely fit any quality which they exhibit. And yet, so all-important in the sphere of religious thought is the power of edification, that in this sphere a great fame like Spinoza's can never be founded without it. A court of literature can never be very severe to Voltaire: with that inimitable wit and clear sense of his, he cannot write a page in which the fullest head may not find something suggestive: still, because, handling religious ideas, he yet, with all his wit and clear sense, handles them wholly without the power of edification, his fame as a great man is equivocal. Dr Strauss has treated the question of Scripture miracles with an acuteness and fulness which even to the most informed minds is instructive; but because he treats it almost wholly without the power of edification, his fame as a serious thinker is equivocal. But in Spinoza there is not a trace either of Voltaire's passion for mockery or of Strauss's passion for demolition. His whole soul was filled with desire of the love and knowledge of God, and of that only. Philosophy always proclaims herself on the way to the *summum bonum*; but too often on the road she seems to forget her destination, and suffers her hearers to forget it also. Spinoza never forgets his destination: 'The love of God is man's highest happiness and blessedness, and the final end and aim of all human actions;—The supreme reward for keeping God's Word is that Word itself—namely, to know him and with free will and pure and constant heart love him'; these sentences are the keynote to all he produced, and were the inspiration of all his labours. This is why he turns so sternly upon the worshippers of the letter,—the editors of the *Masora*, the editor of the *Record*,—because their doctrine imperils our love and knowledge of God. 'What!' he cries, 'our knowledge of God to depend upon these perishable things, which Moses can dash to the ground and break to pieces like the first tables of stone, or of which the originals can be lost like the original book of the Covenant, like the original book of the Law of God, like the book of the Wars of God! ... which can come to us confused, imperfect, mis-written by copyists, tampered with by doctors! And you accuse others of impiety! It is you who are impious, to believe that God would commit the treasure of the true record of himself to any substance less enduring than the heart!'

And Spinoza's life was not unworthy of this elevated strain. A philosopher who professed that knowledge was its own reward, a devotee who professed that the love of God was its own reward, this philosopher and this devotee believed in what he said. Spinoza led a life the most spotless, perhaps, to be found among the lives of philosophers; he lived simple, studious, even-tempered, kind; declining honours, declining riches, declining notoriety. He was poor, and his admirer Simon de Vries sent him two thousand florins;—he refused them. The same friend left him his fortune;—he returned it to the heir. He was asked to dedicate one of his works to the magnificent patron of letters in his century, Louis the Fourteenth;—he declined. His great work, his Ethics, published after his death, he gave injunctions to his friends to publish anonymously, for fear he should give his name to a school. Truth, he thought, should bear no man's name. And finally,—'Unless', he said, 'I had known that my writings would in the end advance the cause of true religion, I would have suppressed them,—*tacuissem*.' It was in this spirit that he lived; and this spirit gives to all he writes not exactly unction,—I have already said so,—but a kind of sacred solemnity. Not of the same order as the saints, he yet follows the same service: *Doubtless thou art our Father, though Abraham be ignorant of us, and Israel acknowledge us not.*

Therefore he has been, in a certain sphere, edifying, and has inspired in many powerful minds an interest and an admiration such as no other philosopher has inspired since Plato. The lonely precursor of German philosophy, he still shines when the light of his successors is fading away; they had celebrity, Spinoza has fame. Not because his peculiar system of philosophy has had more adherents than theirs; on the contrary, it has had fewer. But schools of philosophy arise and fall; their bands of adherents inevitably dwindle; no master can long persuade a large body of disciples that they give to themselves just the same account of the world as he does; it is only the very young and the very enthusiastic who can think themselves sure that they possess the whole mind of Plato, or Spinoza, or Hegel, at all. The very mature and the very sober can even hardly believe that these philosophers possessed it themselves enough to put it all into their works, and to let us know entirely how the world seemed to them. What a remarkable philosopher really does for human thought, is to throw into circulation a certain number of new and striking ideas and expressions, and to stimulate with them the thought and imagination of his century or of after-times. So Spinoza has made his distinction between adequate and inadequate ideas a current notion for educated Europe. So Hegel seized a single pregnant sentence of Heracleitus, and cast it, with a thousand striking applications, into the world of modern thought. But to do this is only enough to make a philosopher noteworthy; it is not enough to make him great. To be great, he must have something in him which can influence character, which is edifying; he must, in short, have a noble and lofty character himself, a character,—to recur to that much-criticized expression of mine,—*in the grand style*. This is what Spinoza had; and because he had it, he stands out from the multitude of philosophers, and has been able to inspire in powerful minds a feeling which the most remarkable philosophers, without this grandiose character, could not inspire. 'There is no possible view of life but Spinoza's,' said Lessing. Goethe has told us how he was calmed and edified by him in his youth, and how he again went to him for support in his maturity. Heine, the man (in spite of his faults) of truest genius that Germany has produced since Goethe,—a man with faults, as I have said, immense faults, the greatest of them being that he could reverence so little,—reverenced Spinoza. Hegel's influence ran off him like water: 'I have seen Hegel', he cries, 'seated with his doleful air of a hatching hen upon his unhappy eggs, and I have heard his dismal clucking.—How easily one can cheat oneself into thinking that one understands everything, when one has learnt only how to construct dialectical formulas!' But of Spinoza, Heine said: 'His life was a copy of the life of his divine kinsman, Jesus Christ.'

And therefore, when M. Van Vloten violently presses the parallel with the post-Hegelians, one feels that the parallel with St Augustine is the far truer one. Compared with the soldier of irreligion M. Van Vloten would have him to be, Spinoza is religious. 'It is true', one may say to the wise and devout Christian, 'Spinoza's conception of beatitude is not yours, and cannot satisfy you, but whose conception of beatitude would you accept as satisfying? Not even that of the devoutest of your fellow Christians. Fra Angelico, the sweetest and most inspired of devout souls, has given us, in his great picture of the Last Judgment, his conception of beatitude. The elect are going round in a ring on long grass under laden fruit trees; two of them, more restless than the others, are flying up a battlemented street,—a street blank with all the ennui of the Middle Ages.

Across a gulf is visible, for the delectation of the saints, a blazing caldron in which Beelzebub is sousing the damned. This is hardly more your conception of beatitude than Spinoza's is. But "in my Father's house are many mansions"; only, to reach any one of these mansions, there are needed the wings of a genuine sacred transport, of an "immortal longing." These wings Spinoza had; and, because he had them, his own language about himself, about his aspirations and his course, are true: his foot is in the *vera vita*, his eye on the beatific vision.

IX

MARCUS AURELIUS

MR MILL says, in his book on Liberty, that 'Christian morality is in great part merely a protest against paganism; its ideal is negative rather than positive, passive rather than active'. He says, that, in certain most important respects, 'it falls far below the best morality of the ancients'. Now, the object of systems of morality is to take possession of human life, to save it from being abandoned to passion or allowed to drift at hazard, to give it happiness by establishing it in the practice of virtue; and this object they seek to attain by prescribing to human life fixed principles of action, fixed rules of conduct. In its uninspired as well as in its inspired moments, in its days of languor and gloom as well as in its days of sunshine and energy, human life has thus always a clue to follow, and may always be making way towards its goal. Christian morality has not failed to supply to human life aids of this sort. It has supplied them far more abundantly than many of its critics imagine. The most exquisite document, after those of the New Testament, of all the documents the Christian spirit has ever inspired,—the *Imitation*,— by no means contains the whole of Christian morality; nay, the disparagers of this morality would think themselves sure of triumphing if one agreed to look for it in the *Imitation* only. But even the *Imitation* is full of passages like these: 'Vita sine proposito languida et vaga est';—'Omni die renovare debemus propositum nostrum, dicentes: nunc hodiè perfectè incipiamus, quia nihil est quod hactenus fecimus';—'Secundum propositum nostrum est cursus profectus nostri';—'Raro etiam unum vitium perfectè vincimus, et ad *quotidianum* profectum non accendimur';—'Semper aliquid certi proponendum est';—'Tibi ipsi violentiam frequenter fac': (*A life without a purpose is a languid, drifting thing;—Every day we ought to renew our purpose, saying to ourselves: This day let us make a sound beginning, for*

*what we have hitherto done is naught;—Our improvement is in
proportion to our purpose;—We hardly ever manage to get completely rid even of one fault, and do not set our hearts on daily
improvement;—Always place a definite purpose before thee;—
Get the habit of mastering thine inclination.*) These are moral
precepts, and moral precepts of the best kind. As rules to hold
possession of our conduct, and to keep us in the right course
through outward troubles and inward perplexity, they are equal
to the best ever furnished by the great masters of morals—
Epictetus or Marcus Aurelius.

But moral rules, apprehended as ideas first, and then rigorously
followed as laws, are, and must be, for the sage only. The mass
of mankind have neither force of intellect enough to apprehend
them clearly as ideas, nor force of character enough to follow
them strictly as laws. The mass of mankind can be carried along
a course full of hardship for the natural man, can be borne over
the thousand impediments of the narrow way, only by the tide
of a joyful and bounding emotion. It is impossible to rise from
reading Epictetus or Marcus Aurelius without a sense of constraint and melancholy, without feeling that the burden laid
upon man is wellnigh greater than he can bear. Honour to the
sages who have felt this, and yet have borne it! Yet, even for the
sage, this sense of labour and sorrow in his march towards the
goal constitutes a relative inferiority; the noblest souls of whatever creed, the pagan Empedocles as well as the Christian Paul,
have insisted on the necessity of an inspiration, a joyful emotion,
to make moral action perfect; an obscure indication of this
necessity is the one drop of truth in the ocean of verbiage with
which the controversy on justification by faith has flooded the
world. But, for the ordinary man, this sense of labour and sorrow
constitutes an absolute disqualification; it paralyses him; under
the weight of it, he cannot make way towards the goal at all.
The paramount virtue of religion is, that it has *lighted up*
morality; that it has supplied the emotion and inspiration needful
for carrying the sage along the narrow way perfectly, for carrying
the ordinary man along it at all. Even the religions with most
dross in them have had something of this virtue; but the
Christian religion manifests it with unexampled splendour.
'Lead me, Zeus and Destiny!' says the prayer of Epictetus,
'whithersoever I am appointed to go; I will follow without

wavering; even though I turn coward and shrink, I shall have to follow all the same.' The fortitude of that is for the strong, for the few; even for them the spiritual atmosphere with which it surrounds them is bleak and gray. But, 'Let thy loving spirit lead me forth into the land of righteousness';—'The Lord shall be unto thee an everlasting light, and thy God thy glory';—'Unto you that fear my name shall the sun of righteousness arise with healing in his wings,' says the Old Testament. 'Born, not of blood, nor of the will of the flesh, nor of the will of man, but of God';—'Except a man be born again, he cannot see the kingdom of God';—'Whatsoever is born of God, overcometh the world,' says the New. The ray of sunshine is there, the glow of a divine warmth;—the austerity of the sage melts away under it, the paralysis of the weak is healed; he who is vivified by it renews his strength; 'all things are possible to him'; 'he is a new creature'.

Epictetus says: 'Every matter has two handles, one of which will bear taking hold of, the other not. If thy brother sin against thee, lay not hold of the matter by this, that he sins against thee; for by this handle the matter will not bear taking hold of. But rather lay hold of it by this, that he is thy brother, thy born mate; and thou wilt take hold of it by what will bear handling.' Jesus, being asked whether a man is bound to forgive his brother as often as seven times, answers: 'I say not unto thee, until seven times, but until seventy times seven.' Epictetus here suggests to the reason grounds for forgiveness of injuries which Jesus does not; but it is vain to say that Epictetus is on that account a better moralist than Jesus, if the warmth, the emotion, of Jesus's answer fires his hearer to the practice of forgiveness of injuries, while the thought in Epictetus's leaves him cold. So with Christian morality in general: its distinction is not that it propounds the maxim, 'Thou shalt love God and thy neighbour', with more development, closer reasoning, truer sincerity, than other moral systems; it is that it propounds this maxim with an inspiration which wonderfully catches the hearer and makes him act upon it. It is because Mr Mill has attained to the perception of truths of this nature, that he is,—instead of being, like the school from which he proceeds, doomed to sterility,— a writer of distinguished mark and influence, a writer deserving all attention and respect; it is (I must be pardoned for saying) because he is not sufficiently leavened with them, that he falls just short of being a great writer.

That which gives to the moral writings of the Emperor Marcus Aurelius their peculiar character and charm, is their being suffused and softened by something of this very sentiment whence Christian morality draws its best power. Mr Long has recently published in a convenient form a translation of these writings, and has thus enabled English readers to judge Marcus Aurelius for themselves; he has rendered his countrymen a real service by so doing. Mr Long's reputation as a scholar is a sufficient guarantee of the general fidelity and accuracy of his translation; on these matters, besides, I am hardly entitled to speak, and my praise is of no value. But that for which I and the rest of the unlearned may venture to praise Mr Long is this; that he treats Marcus Aurelius's writings, as he treats all the other remains of Greek and Roman antiquity which he touches, not as a dead and dry matter of learning, but as documents with a side of modern applicability and living interest, and valuable mainly so far as this side in them can be made clear; that as in his notes on Plutarch's Roman Lives he deals with the modern epoch of Caesar and Cicero, not as food for schoolboys, but as food for men, and men engaged in the current of contemporary life and action, so in his remarks and essays on Marcus Aurelius he treats this truly modern striver and thinker not as a Classical Dictionary hero, but as a present source from which to draw 'example of life, and instruction of manners'. Why may not a son of Dr Arnold say, what might naturally here be said by any other critic, that in this lively and fruitful way of considering the men and affairs of ancient Greece and Rome, Mr Long resembles Dr Arnold?

One or two little complaints, however, I have against Mr Long, and I will get them off my mind at once. In the first place, why could he not have found gentler and juster terms to describe the translation of his predecessor, Jeremy Collier,—the redoubtable enemy of stage plays,—than these: 'a most coarse and vulgar copy of the original'? As a matter of taste, a translator should deal leniently with his predecessor; but putting that out of the question, Mr Long's language is a great deal too hard. Most English people who knew Marcus Aurelius before Mr Long appeared as his introducer, knew him through Jeremy Collier.

And the acquaintance of a man like Marcus Aurelius is such an imperishable benefit, that one can never lose a peculiar sense of obligation towards the man who confers it. Apart from this claim upon one's tenderness, however, Jeremy Collier's version deserves respect for its genuine spirit and vigour, the spirit and vigour of the age of Dryden. Jeremy Collier too, like Mr Long, regarded in Marcus Aurelius the living moralist, and not the dead classic; and his warmth of feeling gave to his style an impetuosity and rhythm which from Mr Long's style (I do not blame it on that account) are absent. Let us place the two side by side. The impressive opening of Marcus Aurelius's fifth book, Mr Long translates thus:

> In the morning when thou risest unwillingly, let this thought be present: I am rising to the work of a human being. Why then am I dissatisfied if I am going to do the things for which I exist and for which I was brought into the world? Or have I been made for this, to lie in the bedclothes and keep myself warm?—But this is more pleasant.—Dost thou exist then to take thy pleasure, and not at all for action or exertion?

Jeremy Collier has:

> When you find an unwillingness to rise early in the morning, make this short speech to yourself: 'I am getting up now to do the business of a man; and am I out of humour for going about that which I was made for, and for the sake of which I was sent into the world? Was I then designed for nothing but to doze and batten beneath the counterpane? I thought action had been the end of your being.'

In another striking passage, again, Mr Long has:

> No longer wonder at hazard; for neither wilt thou read thy own memoirs, nor the acts of the ancient Romans and Hellenes, and the selections from books which thou wast reserving for thy old age. Hasten then to the end which thou hast before thee, and, throwing away idle hopes, come to thine own aid, if thou carest at all for thyself, while it is in thy power.

Here his despised predecessor has:

> Don't go too far in your books and overgrasp yourself. Alas, you have no time left to peruse your diary, to read over

the Greek and Roman history: come, don't flatter and deceive yourself; look to the main chance, to the end and design of reading, and mind life more than notion: I say, if you have a kindness for your person, drive at the practice and help yourself, for that is in your own power.

It seems to me that here for style and force Jeremy Collier can (to say the least) perfectly stand comparison with Mr Long. Jeremy Collier's real defect as a translator is not his coarseness and vulgarity, but his imperfect acquaintance with Greek; this is a serious defect, a fatal one; it rendered a translation like Mr Long's necessary. Jeremy Collier's work will now be forgotten, and Mr Long stands master of the field; but he may be content, at any rate, to leave his predecessor's grave unharmed, even if he will not throw upon it, in passing, a handful of kindly earth.

Another complaint I have against Mr Long is, that he is not quite idiomatic and simple enough. It is a little formal, at least, if not pedantic, to say *Ethic* and *Dialectic*, instead of *Ethics* and *Dialectics*, and to say 'Hellenes and Romans' instead of 'Greeks and Romans'. And why, too,—the name of Antoninus being preoccupied by Antoninus Pius,—will Mr Long call his author Marcus *Antoninus* instead of Marcus *Aurelius*? Small as these matters appear, they are important when one has to deal with the general public, and not with a small circle of scholars; and it is the general public that the translator of a short masterpiece on morals, such as is the book of Marcus Aurelius, should have in view; his aim should be to make Marcus Aurelius's work as popular as the *Imitation*, and Marcus Aurelius's name as familiar as Socrates's. In rendering or naming him, therefore, punctilious accuracy of phrase is not so much to be sought as accessibility and currency; everything which may best enable the Emperor and his precepts *volitare per ora virûm*. It is essential to render him in language perfectly plain and unprofessional, and to call him by the name by which he is best and most distinctly known. The translators of the Bible talk of *pence* and not *denarii*, and the admirers of Voltaire do not celebrate him under the name of Arouet.

But, after these trifling complaints are made, one must end, as one began, in unfeigned gratitude to Mr Long for his excellent and substantial reproduction in English of an invaluable work.

In general the substantiality, soundness, and precision of Mr Long's rendering are (I will venture, after all, to give my opinion about them) as conspicuous as the living spirit with which he treats antiquity; and these qualities are particularly desirable in the translator of a work like that of Marcus Aurelius, of which the language is often corrupt, almost always hard and obscure. Anyone who wants to appreciate Mr Long's merits as a translator may read, in the original and in Mr Long's translation, the seventh chapter of the tenth book; he will see how, through all the dubiousness and involved manner of the Greek, Mr Long has firmly seized upon the clear thought which is certainly at the bottom of that troubled wording, and, in distinctly rendering this thought, has at the same time thrown round its expression a characteristic shade of painfulness and difficulty which just suits it. And Marcus Aurelius's book is one which, when it is rendered so accurately as Mr Long renders it, even those who know Greek tolerably well may choose to read rather in the translation than in the original. For not only are the contents here incomparably more valuable than the external form, but this form, the Greek of a Roman, is not exactly one of those styles which have a physiognomy, which are an essential part of their author, which stamp an indelible impression of him on the reader's mind. An old Lyons commentator finds, indeed, in Marcus Aurelius's Greek, something characteristic, something specially firm and imperial; but I think an ordinary mortal will hardly find this: he will find crabbed Greek, without any great charm of distinct physiognomy. The Greek of Thucydides and Plato has this charm, and he who reads them in a translation, however accurate, loses it, and loses much in losing it; but the Greek of Marcus Aurelius, like the Greek of the New Testament, and even more than the Greek of the New Testament, is wanting in it. If one could be assured that the English Testament were made perfectly accurate, one might be almost content never to open a Greek Testament again; and, Mr Long's version of Marcus Aurelius being what it is, an Englishman who reads to live, and does not live to read, may henceforth let the Greek original repose upon its shelf.

The man whose thoughts Mr Long has thus faithfully reproduced is perhaps the most beautiful figure in history. He is one of those consoling and hope-inspiring marks, which stand for ever to remind our weak and easily discouraged race how high human goodness and perseverance have once been carried, and may be carried again. The interest of mankind is peculiarly attracted by examples of signal goodness in high places; for that testimony to the worth of goodness is the most striking which is borne by those to whom all the means of pleasure and self-indulgence lay open, by those who had at their command the kingdoms of the world and the glory of them. Marcus Aurelius was the ruler of the grandest of empires; and he was one of the best of men. Besides him, history presents one or two sovereigns eminent for their goodness, such as Saint Louis or Alfred. But Marcus Aurelius has, for us moderns, this great superiority in interest over Saint Louis or Alfred, that he lived and acted in a state of society modern by its essential characteristics, in an epoch akin to our own, in a brilliant centre of civilization. Trajan talks of 'our enlightened age' just as glibly as *The Times* talks of it. Marcus Aurelius thus becomes for us a man like ourselves, a man in all things tempted as we are. Saint Louis inhabits an atmosphere of mediaeval Catholicism, which the man of the nineteenth century may admire, indeed, may even passionately wish to inhabit, but which, strive as he will, he cannot really inhabit: Alfred belongs to a state of society (I say it with all deference to the *Saturday Review* critic who keeps such jealous watch over the honour of our Saxon ancestors) half barbarous. Neither Alfred nor Saint Louis can be morally and intellectually as near to us as Marcus Aurelius.

The record of the outward life of this admirable man has in it little of striking incident. He was born at Rome on the 26th of April, in the year 121 of the Christian era. He was nephew and son-in-law to his predecessor on the throne, Antoninus Pius. When Antoninus died, he was forty years old, but from the time of his earliest manhood he had assisted in administering public affairs. Then, after his uncle's death in 161, for nineteen years he reigned as emperor. The barbarians were pressing on the Roman frontier, and a great part of Marcus Aurelius's nineteen years of reign was passed in campaigning. His absences from Rome were numerous and long. We hear of him in Asia Minor, Syria, Egypt, Greece; but, above all, in the countries on the Danube, where the war with the barbarians was going on,—in Austria, Moravia, Hungary. In these countries much of his

Journal seems to have been written; parts of it are dated from them; and there, a few weeks before his fifty-ninth birthday, he fell sick and died.[1] The record of him on which his fame chiefly rests is the record of his inward life,—his *Journal*, or *Commentaries*, or *Meditations*, or *Thoughts*, for by all these names has the work been called. Perhaps the most interesting of the records of his outward life is that which the first book of this work supplies, where he gives an account of his education, recites the names of those to whom he is indebted for it, and enumerates his obligations to each of them. It is a refreshing and consoling picture, a priceless treasure for those, who, sick of the 'wild and dreamlike trade of blood and guile', which seems to be nearly the whole of what history has to offer to our view, seek eagerly for that substratum of right thinking and well-doing which in all ages must surely have somewhere existed, for without it the continued life of humanity would have been impossible. 'From my mother I learnt piety and beneficence, and abstinence not only from evil deeds but even from evil thoughts; and further, simplicity in my way of living, far removed from the habits of the rich.' Let us remember that the next time we are reading the sixth satire of Juvenal. 'From my tutor I learnt' (hear it, ye tutors of princes!) 'endurance of labour, and to want little, and to work with my own hands, and not to meddle with other people's affairs, and not to be ready to listen to slander.' The vices and foibles of the Greek sophist or rhetorician—the *Graeculus esuriens*—are in everybody's mind; but he who reads Marcus Aurelius's account of his Greek teachers and masters will understand how it is that, in spite of the vices and foibles of individual *Graeculi*, the education of the human race owes to Greece a debt which can never be overrated. The vague and colourless praise of history leaves on the mind hardly any impression of Antoninus Pius: it is only from the private memoranda of his nephew that we learn what a disciplined, hard-working, gentle, wise, virtuous man he was; a man who, perhaps, interests mankind less than his immortal nephew only because he has left in writing no record of his inner life,— *caret quia vate sacro.*

Of the outward life and circumstances of Marcus Aurelius, beyond these notices which he has himself supplied, there are

[1] He died on the 17th of March, A.D. 180.

few of much interest and importance. There is the fine anecdote of his speech when he heard of the assassination of the revolted Avidius Cassius, against whom he was marching; *he was sorry*, he said, *to be deprived of the pleasure of pardoning him*. And there are one or two more anecdotes of him which show the same spirit. But the great record for the outward life of a man who has left such a record of his lofty inward aspirations as that which Marcus Aurelius has left, is the clear consenting voice of all his contemporaries,—high and low, friend and enemy, pagan and Christian, —in praise of his sincerity, justice, and goodness. The world's charity does not err on the side of excess, and here was a man occupying the most conspicuous station in the world, and professing the highest possible standard of conduct;—yet the world was obliged to declare that he walked worthily of his profession. Long after his death, his bust was to be seen in the houses of private men through the wide Roman empire. It may be the vulgar part of human nature which busies itself with the semblance and doings of living sovereigns, it is its nobler part which busies itself with those of the dead; these busts of Marcus Aurelius, in the homes of Gaul, Britain, and Italy, bear witness, not to the inmates' frivolous curiosity about princes and palaces, but to their reverential memory of the passage of a great man upon the earth.

Two things, however, before one turns from the outward to the inward life of Marcus Aurelius, force themselves upon one's notice, and demand a word of comment; he persucuted the Christians, and he had for his son the vicious and brutal Commodus. The persecution at Lyons, in which Attalus and Pothinus suffered, the persecution at Smyrna, in which Polycarp suffered, took place in his reign. Of his humanity, of his tolerance, of his horror of cruelty and violence, of his wish to refrain from severe measures against the Christians, of his anxiety to temper the severity of these measures when they appeared to him indispensable, there is no doubt: but, on the one hand, it is certain that the letter, attributed to him, directing that no Christian should be punished for being a Christian, is spurious; it is almost certain that his alleged answer to the authorities of Lyons, in which he directs that Christians persisting in their profession shall be dealt with according to law, is genuine. Mr Long seems inclined to try to throw doubt over the persecution at Lyons, by pointing out that the letter of the Lyons Christians, relating it, alleges it to have been attended by miraculous and incredible incidents. 'A man', he says, 'can only act consistently by accepting all this letter or rejecting it all, and we cannot blame him for either.' But it is contrary to all experience to say that because a fact is related with incorrect additions, and embellishments, therefore it probably never happened at all; or that it is not, in general, easy for an impartial mind to distinguish between the fact and the embellishments. I cannot doubt that the Lyons persecution took place, and that the punishment of Christians for being Christians was sanctioned by Marcus Aurelius. But then I must add that nine modern readers out of ten, when they read this, will, I believe, have a perfectly false notion of what the moral action of Marcus Aurelius, in sanctioning that punishment, really was. They imagine Trajan, or Antoninus Pius, or Marcus Aurelius, fresh from the perusal of the Gospel, fully aware of the spirit and holiness of the Christian saints, ordering their extermination because he loved darkness rather than light. Far from this, the Christianity which these emperors aimed at repressing was, in their conception of it, something philosophically contemptible, politically subversive, and morally abominable. As men, they sincerely regarded it much as well-conditioned people, with us, regard Mormonism; as rulers, they regarded it much as Liberal statesmen, with us, regard the Jesuits. A kind of Mormonism, constituted as a vast secret society, with obscure aims of political and social subversion, was what Antoninus Pius and Marcus Aurelius believed themselves to be repressing when they punished Christians. The early Christian apologists again and again declare to us under what odious imputations the Christians lay, how general was the belief that these imputations were well-grounded, how sincere was the horror which the belief inspired. The multitude, convinced that the Christians were atheists who ate human flesh and thought incest no crime, displayed against them a fury so passionate as to embarrass and alarm their rulers. The severe expressions of Tacitus, *exitiabilis superstitio—odio humani generis convicti,* show how deeply the prejudices of the multitude imbued the educated class also. One asks oneself with astonishment how a doctrine so benign as that of Jesus Christ can have incurred misrepresentation so monstrous. The inner and moving cause of the misrepresentation lay, no doubt, in this,—that Christianity was a new spirit in the Roman world, destined to act in that world as its dissolvent; and it was inevitable that Christianity in the Roman world, like democracy in the modern world, like every new spirit with a similar mission assigned to it, should at its first appearance occasion an instinctive shrinking and repugnance in the world which it was to dissolve. The outer and palpable causes of the misrepresentation were, for the Roman public at large, the confounding of the Christians with the Jews, that isolated, fierce, and stubborn race, whose stubbornness, fierceness, and isolation, real as they were, the fancy of a civilized Roman yet further exaggerated; the atmosphere of mystery and novelty which surrounded the Christian rites; the very simplicity of Christian theism;—for the Roman statesman, the character of secret assemblages which the meetings of the Christian community wore, under a State-system as jealous of unauthorized associations as is the State-system of modern France.

A Roman of Marcus Aurelius's time and position could not well see the Christians except through the mist of these prejudices. Seen through such a mist, the Christians appeared with a thousand faults not their own: but it has not been sufficiently remarked that faults, really their own, many of them assuredly appeared with besides, faults especially likely to strike such an observer as Marcus Aurelius, and to confirm him in the prejudices of his race, station, and rearing. We look back upon Christianity after it has proved what a future it bore within it, and for us the sole representatives of its early struggles are the pure and devoted spirits through whom it proved this; Marcus Aurelius saw it with its future yet unshown, and with the tares among its professed progeny not less conspicuous than the wheat. Who can doubt that among the professing Christians of the second century, as among the professing Christians of the nineteenth, there was plenty of folly, plenty of rabid nonsense, plenty of gross fanaticism? Who will even venture to affirm that, separated in great measure from the intellect and civilization of the world for one or two centuries, Christianity, wonderful as have been its fruits, had the development perfectly worthy of its inestimable germ? Who will venture to affirm that, by the alliance of Christianity with the virtue and intelligence of men like the Antonines,—of the best product of Greek and Roman civilization, while Greek and Roman civilization had yet life and power,—Christianity and the world, as well as the Antonines themselves, would not have been gainers? That alliance was not to be. The Antonines lived and died with an utter misconception of Christianity; Christianity grew up in the Catacombs, not on the Palatine. And Marcus Aurelius incurs no moral reproach by having authorized the punishment of the Christians; he does not thereby become in the least what we mean by a *persecutor*. One may concede that it was impossible for him to see Christianity as it really was;—as impossible as for even the moderate and sensible Fleury to see the Antonines as they really were;—one may concede that the point of view from which Christianity appeared something anti-civil and anti-social, which the State had the faculty to judge and the duty to suppress, was inevitably his. Still, however, it remains true that this sage, who made perfection his aim and reason his law, did Christianity an immense injustice and rested in an idea of State-attributes which was illusive. And this is, in truth, characteristic of Marcus Aurelius, that he is blameless, yet, in a certain sense, unfortunate; in his character, beautiful as it is, there is something melancholy, circumscribed, and ineffectual.

For of his having such a son as Commodus, too, one may say that he is not to be blamed on that account, but that he is unfortunate. Disposition and temperament are inexplicable things; there are natures on which the best education and example are thrown away; excellent fathers may have, without any fault of theirs, incurably vicious sons. It is to be remembered, also, that Commodus was left, at the perilous age of nineteen, master of the world; while his father, at that age, was but beginning a twenty years' apprenticeship to wisdom, labour, and self-command, under the sheltering teachership of his uncle Antoninus. Commodus was a prince apt to be led by favourites; and if the story is true which says that he left, all through his reign, the Christians untroubled, and ascribes this lenity to the influence of his mistress Marcia, it shows that he could be led to good as well as to evil. But for such a nature to be left at a critical age with absolute power, and wholly without good counsel and direction, was the more fatal. Still one cannot help wishing that the example of Marcus Aurelius could have availed more with his own only son. One cannot but think that with such virtue as his there should go, too, the ardour which removed mountains, and that the ardour which removes mountains might have even won Commodus. The word *ineffectual* again rises to one's mind; Marcus Aurelius saved his own soul by his righteousness, and he could do no more. Happy they who can do this! but still happier, who can do more!

Yet, when one passes from his outward to his inward life, when one turns over the pages of his *Meditations,*—entries jotted down from day to day, amid the business of the city or the fatigues of the camp, for his own guidance and support, meant for no eye but his own, without the slightest attempt at style, with no care, even, for correct writing, not to be surpassed for naturalness and sincerity,—all disposition to carp and cavil dies away, and one is overpowered by the charm of a character of such purity, delicacy, and virtue. He fails neither in small things nor in great; he keeps watch over himself both that the great springs of action may be right in him, and that the minute details of action may be right also. How admirable in a hard-tasked ruler, and a ruler, too, with a passion for thinking and reading, is such a memorandum as the following:

> Not frequently nor without necessity to say to anyone, or to write in a letter, that I have no leisure; nor continually to excuse the neglect of duties required by our relation to those with whom we live, by alleging urgent occupation.

And, when that ruler is a Roman emperor, what an 'idea' is this to be written down and meditated by him:

> The idea of a polity in which there is the same law for all, a polity administered with regard to equal rights and equal freedom of speech, and the idea of a kingly government which respects most of all the freedom of the governed.

And, for all men who 'drive at practice', what practical rules may not one accumulate out of these *Meditations*:

> The greatest part of what we say or do being unnecessary, if a man takes this away, he will have more leisure and less uneasiness. Accordingly, on every occasion a man should ask himself: 'Is this one of the unnecessary things?' Now a man should take away not only unnecessary acts, but also

unnecessary thoughts, for thus superfluous acts will not follow after.

And again:

We ought to check in the series of our thoughts everything that is without a purpose and useless, but most of all the over curious feeling and the malignant; and a man should use himself to think of those things only about which if one should suddenly ask, 'What hast thou now in thy thoughts?' with perfect openness thou mightest immediately answer, 'This or That'; so that from thy words it should be plain that everything in thee is simple and benevolent, and such as befits a social animal, and one that cares not for thoughts about sensual enjoyments, or any rivalry or envy and suspicion, or anything else for which thou wouldst blush if thou shouldst say thou hadst it in thy mind.

So, with a stringent practicalness worthy of Franklin, he discourses on his favourite text, *Let nothing be done without a purpose*. But it is when he enters the region where Franklin cannot follow him, when he utters his thoughts on the ground-motives of human action, that he is most interesting;—that he becomes the unique, the incomparable Marcus Aurelius. Christianity uses language very liable to be misunderstood when it seems to tell men to do good, not, certainly, from the vulgar motives of worldly interest, or vanity, or love of human praise, but 'that their Father which seeth in secret may reward them openly'. The motives of reward and punishment have come, from the misconception of language of this kind, to be strangely over-pressed by many Christian moralists, to the deterioration and disfigurement of Christianity. Marcus Aurelius says, truly and nobly:

One man, when he has done a service to another, is ready to set it down to his account as a favour conferred. Another is not ready to do this, but still in his own mind he thinks of the man as his debtor, and he knows what he has done. A third in a manner does not even know what he has done, *but he is like a vine which has produced grapes, and seeks for nothing more after it has once produced its proper fruit*. As a horse when he has run, a dog when he has caught the game, a bee when it has made its honey, so a man, when he has done a good act, does not call out for others to come and see, but he goes on to another act, as a vine goes on to produce again the grapes in season. Must a man, then, be one of those, who in a manner acts thus without observing it? Yes.

And again:

What more dost thou want when thou hast done a man a service? Art thou not content that thou hast done something conformable to thy nature, and dost thou seek to be paid for it, *just as if the eye demanded a recompense for seeing, or the feet for walking*?

Christianity, in order to match morality of this strain, has to correct its apparent offers of external reward, and to say: *The kingdom of God is within you.*

I have said that it is by its accent of emotion that the morality of Marcus Aurelius acquires a special character, and reminds one of Christian morality. The sentences of Seneca are stimulating to the intellect; the sentences of Epictetus are fortifying to the character; the sentences of Marcus Aurelius find their way to the soul. I have said that religious emotion has the power to *light up* morality: the emotion of Marcus Aurelius does not quite light up his morality, but it suffuses it; it has not power to melt the clouds of effort and austerity quite away, but it shines through them and glorifies them; it is a spirit, not so much of gladness and elation, as of gentleness and sweetness; a delicate and tender sentiment, which is less than joy and more than resignation. He says that in his youth he learned from Maximus, one of his teachers, 'cheerfulness in all circumstances as well as in illness; *and a just admixture in the moral character of sweetness and dignity*'; and it is this very admixture of sweetness with his dignity which makes him so beautiful a moralist. It enables him to carry even into his observation of nature, a delicate penetration, a sympathetic tenderness, worthy of Wordsworth, the spirit of such a remark as the following has hardly a parallel, so far as my knowledge goes, in the whole range of Greek and Roman literature:

Figs, when they are quite ripe, gape open; and in the ripe olives the very circumstance of their being near to rottenness adds a peculiar beauty to the fruit. And the ears of corn bending down, and the lion's eyebrows, and the foam which flows

from the mouth of wild boars, and many other things,—
though they are far from being beautiful, in a certain sense,—
still, because they come in the course of nature, have a beauty
in them, and they please the mind; so that if a man should
have a feeling and a deeper insight with respect to the things
which are produced in the universe, there is hardly anything
which comes in the course of nature which will not seem to
him to be in a manner disposed so as to give pleasure.

But it is when his strain passes to directly moral subjects that
his delicacy and sweetness lend to it the greatest charm. Let
those who can feel the beauty of spiritual refinement read this,
the reflection of an emperor who prized mental superiority
highly:

Thou sayest, 'Men cannot admire the sharpness of thy wits.'
Be it so; but there are many other things of which thou canst
not say, 'I am not formed for them by nature.' Show those
qualities, then, which are altogether in thy power,—sincerity,
gravity, endurance of labour, aversion to pleasure, contentment with thy portion and with few things, benevolence,
frankness, no love of superfluity, freedom from trifling,
magnanimity. Dost thou not see how many qualities thou art
at once able to exhibit, as to which there is no excuse of natural
incapacity and unfitness, and yet thou still remainest voluntarily below the mark? Or art thou compelled, through being
defectively furnished by nature, to murmur, and to be mean,
and to flatter, and to find fault with thy poor body, and to try
to please men, and to make great display, and to be so restless
in thy mind? No, indeed; but thou mightest have been
delivered from these things long ago. Only, if in truth thou
canst be charged with being rather slow and dull of comprehension, thou must exert thyself about this also, not neglecting nor yet taking pleasure in thy dulness.

The same sweetness enables him to fix his mind, when he sees
the isolation and moral death caused by sin, not on the cheerless
thought of the misery of this condition, but on the inspiriting
thought that man is blest with the power to escape from it:

Suppose that thou hast detached thyself from the natural
unity,—for thou wast made by nature a part, but now thou
hast cut thyself off,—yet here is this beautiful provision, that

it is in thy power again to unite thyself. God has allowed this to no other part,—after it has been separated and cut asunder, to come together again. But consider the goodness with which he has privileged man; for he has put it in his power, when he has been separated, to return and to be united and to resume his place.

It enables him to control even the passion for retreat and solitude, so strong in a soul like his, to which the world could offer no abiding city:

Men seek retreat for themselves, houses in the country, seashores, and mountains; and thou, too, art wont to desire such things very much. But this is altogether a mark of the most common sort of men, for it is in thy power whenever thou shalt choose to retire into thyself. For nowhere either with more quiet or more freedom from trouble does a man retire than into his own soul, particularly when he has within him such thoughts that by looking into them he is immediately in perfect tranquillity. Constantly, then, give to thyself this retreat, and renew thyself; and let thy principles be brief and fundamental, which, as soon as thou shalt recur to them, will be sufficient to cleanse the soul completely, and to send thee back free from all discontent with the things to which thou returnest.'

Against this feeling of discontent and weariness, so natural to the great for whom there seems nothing left to desire or to strive after, but so enfeebling to them, so deteriorating, Marcus Aurelius never ceased to struggle. With resolute thankfulness he kept in remembrance the blessings of his lot; the true blessings of it, not the false:

I have to thank Heaven that I was subjected to a ruler and a father (Antoninus Pius) who was able to take away all pride from me, and to bring me to the knowledge that it is possible for a man to live in a palace without either guards, or embroidered dresses, or any show of this kind; but that it is in such a man's power to bring himself very near to the fashion of a private person, without being for this reason either meaner in thought or more remiss in action with respect to the things which must be done for public interest. . . . I have to be thankful that my children have not been stupid nor deformed in body; that I did not make more proficiency in rhetoric, poetry, and the other studies, by which I should perhaps have been completely engrossed, if I had seen that I was making great progress in them; . . . that I knew Apollonius, Rusticus, Maximus; . . . that I received clear and frequent impressions about living according to nature, and what kind of a life that is, so that, so far as depended on Heaven, and its gifts, help, and inspiration, nothing hindered me from forthwith living according to nature, though I still fall short of it through my own fault, and through not observing the admonitions of Heaven, and, I may almost say, its direct instructions; that my body has held out so long in such a kind of life as mine; that though it was my mother's lot to die young, she spent the last years of her life with me; that whenever I wished to help any man in his need, I was never told that I had not the means of doing it; that, when I had an inclination to philosophy, I did not fall into the hands of a sophist.

And, as he dwelt with gratitude on these helps and blessings vouchsafed to him, his mind (so, at least, it seems to me) would sometimes revert with awe to the perils and temptations of the lonely height where he stood, to the lives of Tiberius, Caligula, Nero, Domitian, in their hideous blackness and ruin; and then he wrote down for himself such a warning entry as this, significant and terrible in its abruptness:

A black character, a womanish character, a stubborn character, bestial, childish, animal, stupid, counterfeit, scurrilous, fraudulent, tyrannical!

Or this:

About what am I now employing my soul? On every occasion I must ask myself this question, and enquire, What have I now in this part of me which they call the ruling principle, and whose soul have I now?—that of a child, or of a young man, or of a weak woman, or of a tyrant, or of one of the lower animals in the service of man, or of a wild beast?

The character he wished to attain he knew well, and beautifully he has marked it, and marked, too his sense of shortcoming:

When thou hast assumed these names,—good, modest, true, rational, equal-minded, magnanimous,—take care that thou dost not change these names; and, if thou shouldst lose them, quickly return to them. If thou maintainest thyself in possession of these names without desiring that others should call thee by them, thou wilt be another being, and wilt enter on another life. For to continue to be such as thou hast hitherto been, and to be torn in pieces and defiled in such a life, is the character of a very stupid man, and one overfond of his life, and like those half-devoured fighters with wild beasts, who though covered with wounds and gore still entreat to be kept to the following day, though they will be exposed in the same state to the same claws and bites. Therefore fix thyself in the possession of these few names: and if thou art able to abide in them, abide as if thou wast removed to the Happy Islands.

For all his sweetness and serenity, however, man's point of life 'between two infinities' (of that expression Marcus Aurelius is the real owner) was to him anything but a Happy Island, and the performances on it he saw through no veils of illusion. Nothing is in general more gloomy and monotonous than declamations on the hollowness and transitoriness of human life and grandeur: but here, too, the great charm of Marcus Aurelius, his emotion, comes in to relive the monotony and to break through the gloom; and even on this eternally used topic he is imaginative, fresh and striking:

Consider, for example, the times of Vespasian. Thou wilt see all these things, people marrying, bringing up children, sick, dying, warring, feasting, trafficking, cultivating the ground, flattering, obstinately arrogant, suspecting, plotting, wishing for somebody to die, grumbling about the present, loving, heaping up treasure, desiring to be consuls or kings. Well then that life of these people no longer exists at all. Again, go to the times of Trajan. All is again the same. Their life too is gone. But chiefly thou shouldst think of those whom thou hast thyself known distracting themselves about idle things, neglecting to do what was in accordance with their proper constitution, and to hold firmly to this and to be content with it.

Again:

The things which are much valued in life are empty, and rotten, and trifling; and people are like little dogs, biting one another, and little children quarrelling, crying, and then straightway laughing. But fidelity, and modesty, and justice, and truth are fled

Up to Olympus from the widespread earth.

What then is there which still detains thee here?

And once more:

Look down from above on the countless herds of men, and their countless solemnities, and the infinitely varied voyagings in storms and calms, and the differences among those who are born, who live together, and die. And consider too the life lived by others in olden time, and the life now lived among barbarous nations, and how many know not even thy name, and how many will soon forget it, and how they who perhaps now are praising thee will very soon blame thee, and that neither a posthumous name is of any value, nor reputation, nor anything else.

He recognized, indeed, that (to use his own words) 'the prime principle in man's constitution is the social'; and he laboured sincerely to make not only his acts towards his fellow men, but his thoughts also, suitable to this conviction:

When thou wishest to delight thyself, think of the virtues of those who live with thee; for instance, the activity of one, and the modesty of another, and the liberality of a third, and some other good quality of a fourth.

Still, it is hard for a pure and thoughtful man to live in a state of rapture at the spectacle afforded to him by his fellow creatures; above all it is hard, when such a man is placed as Marcus Aurelius was placed, and has had the meanness and perversity of his fellow creatures thrust, in no common measure, upon his notice, —has had, time after time, to experience how 'within ten days thou wilt seem a god to those to whom thou art now a beast and an ape'. His true strain of thought as to his relations with his fellow men is rather the following. He has been enumerating the higher consolations which may support a man at the approach of death, and he goes on:

But if thou requirest also a vulgar kind of comfort which shall reach thy heart, thou wilt be made best reconciled to death by observing the objects from which thou art going to be removed, and the morals of those with whom thy soul will no longer be mingled. For it is no way right to be offended with men, but it is thy duty to care for them and to bear with them gently; and yet to remember that thy departure will not be from men who have the same principles as thyself. For this is the only thing, if there be any, which could draw us the contrary way and attach us to life, to be permitted to live with those who have the same principles as ourselves. But now thou seest how great is the distress caused by the difference of those who live together, so that thou mayest say: 'Come quick, O death, lest perchance I too should forget myself.'

O faithless and perverse generation, how long shall I be with you? how long shall I suffer you? Sometimes this strain rises even to passion:

Short is the little which remains to thee of life. Live as on a mountain. Let men see, let them know, a real man, who lives as he was meant to live. If they cannot endure him, let them kill him. For that is better than to live as men do.

It is remarkable how little of a merely local and temporary character, how little of those *scoriae* which a reader has to clear away before he gets to the precious ore, how little that even admits of doubt or question, the morality of Marcus Aurelius exhibits. Perhaps as to one point we must make an exception. Marcus Aurelius is fond of urging as a motive for man's cheerful acquiescence in whatever befalls him, that 'whatever happens to every man *is for the interest of the universal*'; that the whole contains nothing *which is not for its advantage*; that everything which happens to a man is to be accepted, 'even if it seems disagreeable, *because it leads to the health of the universe*'. And the whole course of the universe, he adds, has a providential reference to man's welfare: '*all other things have been made for the sake of rational beings*'. Religion has in all ages freely used this language, and it is not religion which will object to Marcus Aurelius's use of it; but science can hardly accept as severely accurate this employment of the terms *interest* and *advantage*. Even to a sound nature and a clear reason the proposition that things happen 'for the interest of the universal', as men conceive of interest, may seem to have no meaning at all, and the proposition that 'all things have been made for the sake of rational beings' may seem to be false. Yet even to this language, not irresistibly cogent when it is thus absolutely used, Marcus Aurelius gives a turn which makes it true and useful, when he says: 'The ruling part of man can make a material for itself out of that which opposes it, as fire lays hold of what falls into it, and rises higher by means of this very material',—when he says: 'What else are all things except exercises for the reason? Persevere then until thou shalt have made all things thine own, as the stomach which is strengthened makes all things its own, as the blazing fire makes flame and brightness out of everything that is thrown into it';—when he says: 'Thou wilt not cease to be miserable till thy mind is in such a condition, that, what luxury is to those who enjoy pleasure, such shall be to thee, in every matter which presents itself, the doing of the things which are conformable to man's constitution; for a man ought to consider as an enjoyment everything which it is in his power to do according to his own nature,—and it is in his power everywhere.' In this sense it is, indeed, most true that 'all things have been made for the sake of rational beings'; that 'all things work together for good'.

In general, however, the action Marcus Aurelius prescribes is action which every sound nature must recognize as right, and the motives he assigns are motives which every clear reason must recognize as valid. And so he remains the especial friend and comforter of all clear-headed and scrupulous, yet pure-hearted and upward striving men, in those ages most especially that walk by sight, not by faith, but yet have no open vision: he cannot give such souls, perhaps, all they yearn for, but he gives them much; and what he gives them, they can receive.

Yet no, it is not for what he thus gives them that such souls love him most! it is rather because of the emotion which lends to his voice so touching an accent, it is because he too yearns as they do for something unattained by him. What an affinity for Christianity had this persecutor of the Christians! the effusion of Christianity, its relieving tears, its happy self-sacrifice, were the very element, one feels, for which his soul longed: they were near him, they brushed him, he touched them, he passed them by. One feels, too, that the Marcus Aurelius one reads must still have remained, even had Christianity been fully known to him, in a great measure himself; he would have been no Justine: but how would Christianity have affected him? in what measure would it have changed him? Granted that he might have found, like the *Alogi* of modern times, in the most beautiful of the Gospels, the Gospel which has leavened Christendom most powerfully, the Gospel of St John, too much Greek metaphysics, too much *gnosis*; granted that this Gospel might have looked too like what he knew already to be a total surprise to him: what, then, would he have said to the Sermon on the Mount, to the twenty-sixth chapter of St Matthew? what would have become of his notions of the *exitiabilis superstitio*, of the 'obstinacy of the Christians'? Vain question! yet the greatest charm of Marcus Aurelius is that he makes us ask it. We see him wise, just, self-governed, tender, thankful, blameless; yet, with all this, agitated, stretching out his arms for something beyond,—*tendentemque manus ripae ulterioris amore.*

End of First Series

ESSAYS IN CRITICISM

Second Series

PREFATORY NOTE

THE collection of Essays contained in this volume was made by Mr Arnold himself, and they are, therefore, in the opinion of a critic, at once competent and severe, worthy to be collected and preserved. Severe is perhaps hardly an epithet ever properly applicable to Mr Arnold; but his judgment was as serene and unbiased in regard to his own compositions as in regard to those of any author whom from time to time he criticized. But it was further characteristic of him to be content to say one thing at one time; and he has been accused, not perhaps entirely without reason, of repeating the same thing in the same words, sometimes almost to the weariness of the reader. This habit, however, had at least the effect of fixing in the mind the phrases, and therefore the thoughts or ideas which the phrases conveyed, and with which for the moment he was concerned. But in order to gather the mind of Mr Arnold on the whole of any subject, literary, political, or religious, it is often necessary to read more than one paper, because in each paper he frequently deals with one aspect of a subject only, which requires, for sound and complete judgment, to be supplemented or completed by another. It is especially necessary to bear this in mind in reading what has become his last utterance on Shelley. In Shelley's case he is known to have intended to write something more; not, indeed, to alter or to qualify what he said, but to say something else which he thought also true, and which needed saying.

This is not the place to attempt a character of Mr Arnold, even as a critic or an essayist. A preface would expand into a volume if it attempted to indicate even the materials for thought on such subjects, handled by Mr Arnold, as Poetry, Gray, Keats, Shelley, Byron, Wordsworth (to name no others), which are the subjects of some of the Essays here collected. This is the last volume he ever put together, and it contains some of the ripest, best, most interesting writing.

Perhaps it is well to add that these few words are contributed at the request of others. *Inane munus* indeed, but all that a friend can do!

C.   (John Duke Coleridge).

I

THE STUDY OF POETRY

THE future of poetry is immense, because in poetry, where it is worthy of its high destinies, our race, as time goes on, will find an ever surer and surer stay. There is not a creed which is not shaken, not an accredited dogma which is not shown to be questionable, not a received tradition which does not threaten to dissolve. Our religion has materialized itself in the fact, in the supposed fact; it has attached its emotion to the fact, and now the fact is failing it. But for poetry the idea is everything; the rest is a world of illusion, of divine illusion. Poetry attaches its emotion to the idea; the idea *is* the fact. The strongest part of our religion today is its unconscious poetry.

Let me be permitted to quote these words of my own, as uttering the thought which should, in my opinion, go with us and govern us in all our study of poetry. In the present work it is the course of one great contributory stream to the world-river of poetry that we are invited to follow. We are here invited to trace the stream of English poetry. But whether we set ourselves, as here, to follow only one of the several streams that make the mighty river of poetry, or whether we seek to know them all, our governing thought should be the same. We should conceive of poetry worthily, and more highly than it has been the custom to conceive of it. We should conceive of it as capable of higher uses, and called to higher destinies, than those which in general men have assigned to it hitherto. More and more mankind will discover that we have to turn to poetry to interpret life for us, to console us, to sustain us. Without poetry, our science will appear incomplete; and most of what now passes with us for religion and philosophy will be replaced by poetry. Science, I say, will appear incomplete without it. For finely and truly does Wordsworth call poetry 'the impassioned expression which is in the

235

countenance of all science'; and what is a countenance without its expression? Again, Wordsworth finely and truly calls poetry 'the breath and finer spirit of all knowledge': our religion, parading evidences such as those on which the popular mind relies now; out philosophy, pluming itself on its reasonings about causation and finite and infinite being; what are they but the shadows and dreams and false shows of knowledge? The day will come when we shall wonder at ourselves for having trusted to them, for having taken them seriously; and the more we perceive their hollowness, the more we shall prize 'the breath and finer spirit of knowledge' offered to us by poetry.

But if we conceive thus highly of the destinies of poetry, we must also set our standard for poetry high, since poetry, to be capable of fulfilling such high destinies, must be poetry of a high order of excellence. We must accustom ourselves to a high standard and to a strict judgment. Sainte-Beuve relates that Napoleon one day said, when somebody was spoken of in his presence as a charlatan: 'Charlatan as much as you please; but where is there *not* charlatanism?'—'Yes,' answers Sainte-Beuve, 'in politics, in the art of governing mankind, that is perhaps true. But in the order of thought, in art, the glory, the eternal honour is that charlatanism shall find no entrance; herein lies the inviolableness of that noble portion of man's being.' It is admirably said, and let us hold fast to it. In poetry, which is thought and art in one, it is the glory, the eternal honour, that charlatanism shall find no entrance; that this noble sphere be kept inviolate and inviolable. Charlatanism is for confusing or obliterating the distinctions between excellent and inferior, sound and unsound or only half-sound, true and untrue or only half-true. It is charlatanism, conscious or unconscious, whenever we confuse or obliterate these. And in poetry, more than anywhere else, it is unpermissible to confuse or obliterate them. For in poetry the distinction between excellent and inferior, sound and unsound or only half-sound, true and untrue or only half-true, is of paramount importance. It is of paramount importance because of the high destinies of poetry. In poetry, as a criticism of life under the conditions fixed for such a criticism by the laws of poetic truth and poetic beauty, the spirit of our race will find, we have said, as time goes on and as other helps fail, its consolation and stay. But the consolation and stay will be of power in proportion to the power of the criticism of life. And the criticism of life will be of power in proportion as the poetry conveying it is excellent rather than inferior, sound rather than unsound or half-sound, true rather than untrue or half-true.

The best poetry is what we want; the best poetry will be found to have a power of forming, sustaining, and delighting us, as nothing else can. A clearer, deeper sense of the best in poetry, and of the strength and joy to be drawn from it, is the most precious benefit which we can gather from a poetical collection such as the present. And yet in the very nature and conduct of such a collection there is inevitably something which tends to obscure in us the consciousness of what our benefit should be, and to distract us from the pursuit of it. We should therefore steadily set it before our minds at the outset, and should compel ourselves to revert constantly to the thought of it as we proceed.

Yes; constantly, in reading poetry, a sense for the best, the really excellent, and of the strength and joy to be drawn from it, should be present in our minds and should govern our estimate of what we read. But this real estimate, the only true one, is liable to be superseded, if we are not watchful, by two other kinds of estimate, the historic estimate and the personal estimate, both of which are fallacious. A poet or a poem may count to us historically, they may count to us on grounds personal to ourselves, and they may count to us really. They may count to us historically. The course of development of a nation's language, thought, and poetry, is profoundly interesting; and by regarding a poet's work as a stage in this course of development we may easily bring ourselves to make it of more importance as poetry than in itself it really is, we may come to use a language of quite exaggerated praise in criticizing it; in short, to overrate it. So arises in our poetic judgments the fallacy caused by the estimate which we may call historic. Then, again, a poet or a poem may count to us on grounds personal to ourselves. Our personal affinities, likings, and circumstances have great power to sway our estimates of this or that poet's work, and to make us attach more importance to it as poetry than in itself it really possesses, because to us it is, or has been, of high importance. Here also we overrate the object of our interest, and apply to it a language of praise which is quite exaggerated. And thus we get the source of a second fallacy in our poetic judgments—the fallacy caused by an estimate which we may call personal.

Both fallacies are natural. It is evident how naturally the study of the history and development of a poetry may incline a man to pause over reputations and works once conspicuous but now obscure, and to quarrel with a careless public for skipping, in obedience to mere tradition and habit, from one famous name or work in its natural poetry to another, ignorant of what it misses, and of the reason for keeping what it keeps, and of the whole process of growth in its poetry. The French have become diligent students of their own early poetry, which they long neglected; the study makes many of them dissatisfied with their so-called classical poetry, the court-tragedy of the seventeenth century, a poetry which Pellisson long ago reproached with its want of the true poetic stamp, with its *politesse stérile et rampante*, but which nevertheless has reigned in France as absolutely as if it had been the perfection of classical poetry indeed. The dissatisfaction is natural; yet a lively and accomplished critic, M. Charles d'Héricault, the editor of Clément Marot, goes too far when he says that 'the cloud of glory playing round a classic is a mist as dangerous to the future of a literature as it is intolerable for the purposes of history'. 'It hinders,' he goes on, 'it hinders us from seeing more than one single point, the culminating and exceptional point; the summary, fictitious and arbitrary, of a thought and of a work. It substitutes a halo for a physiognomy, it puts a statue where there was once a man, and, hiding from us all trace of the labour, the attempts, the weaknesses, the failures, it claims not study but veneration; it does not show us how the thing is done, it imposes upon us a model. Above all, for the historian this creation of classic personages is inadmissible; for it withdraws the poet from his time, from his proper life, it breaks historical relationships, it blinds criticism by conventional admiration, and renders the investigation of literary origins unacceptable. It gives us a human personage no longer, but a God seated immovable amidst His perfect work, like Jupiter on Olympus; and hardly will it be possible for the young student, to whom such work is exhibited at such a distance from him, to believe that it did not issue ready made from that divine head.'

All this is brilliantly and tellingly said, but we must plead for a distinction. Everything depends on the reality of a poet's classic character. If he is a dubious classic, let us sift him; if he is a false classic, let us explode him. But if he is a real classic, if his work belongs to the class of the very best (for this is the true and right meaning of the word *classic, classical*), then the great thing for us is to feel and enjoy his work as deeply as ever we can, and to appreciate the wide difference between it and all work which has not the same high character. This is what is salutary, this is what is formative; this is the great benefit to be got from the study of poetry. Everything which interferes with it, which hinders it, is injurious. True, we must read our classic with open eyes, and not with eyes blinded with superstition; we must perceive when his work comes short, when it drops out of the class of the very best, and we must rate it, in such cases, at its proper value. But the use of this negative criticism is not in itself, it is entirely in its enabling us to have a clearer sense and a deeper enjoyment of what is truly excellent. To trace the labour, the attempts, the weaknesses, the failures of a genuine classic, to acquaint oneself with his time and his life and his historical relationships, is mere literary dilettantism unless it has that clear sense and deeper enjoyment for its end. It may be said that the more we know about a classic the better we shall enjoy him; and, if we lived as long as Methuselah and had all of us heads of perfect clearness and wills of perfect steadfastness, this might be true in fact as it is plausible in theory. But the case here is much the same as the case with the Greek and Latin studies of our schooldays. The elaborate philological ground-work which we require them to lay is in theory an admirable preparation for appreciating the Greek and Latin authors worthily. The more thoroughly we lay the groundwork, the better we shall be able, it may be said, to enjoy the authors. True, if time were not so short, and schoolboys' wits not so soon tired and their power of attention exhausted; only, as it is, the elaborate philological preparation goes on, but the authors are little known and less enjoyed. So with the investigator of 'historic origins' in poetry. He ought to enjoy the true classic all the better for his investigations; he often is distracted from the enjoyment of the best, and with the less good he overbusies himself, and is prone to overrate it in proportion to the trouble which it has cost him.

The idea of tracing historic origins and historical relationships cannot be absent from a compilation like the present. And naturally the poets to be exhibited in it will be assigned to those persons for exhibition who are known to prize them highly, rather than to those who have no special inclination towards them. Moreover, the very occupation with an author, and the business of exhibiting him, disposes us to affirm and amplify his importance. In the present work, therefore, we are sure of frequent temptation to adopt the historic estimate, or the personal estimate, and to forget the real estimate; which latter, nevertheless, we must employ if we are to make poetry yield us its full benefit. So high is that benefit, the benefit of clearly feeling and of deeply enjoying the really excellent, the truly classic in poetry, that we do well, I say, to set it fixedly before our minds as our object in studying poets and poetry, and to make the desire of attaining it the one principle to which, as the *Imitation* says, whatever we may read or come to know, we always return. *Cum multa legeris et cognoveris, ad unum semper oportet redire principium.*

The historic estimate is likely in especial to affect our judgment and our language when we are dealing with ancient poets; the personal estimate when we are dealing with poets our contemporaries, or at any rate modern. The exaggerations due to the historic estimate are not in themselves, perhaps, of very much gravity. Their report hardly enters the general ear; probably they do not always impose even on the literary men who adopt them. But they lead to a dangerous abuse of language. So we hear Caedmon, amongst our own poets, compared to Milton. I have already noticed the enthusiasm of one accomplished French critic for 'historic origins'. Another eminent French critic, M. Vitet, comments upon that famous document of the early poetry of his nation, the *Chanson de Roland*. It is indeed a most interesting document. The *joculator* or *jongleur* Taillefer, who was with William the Conqueror's army at Hastings, marched before the Norman troops, so said the tradition, singing 'of Charlemagne and of Roland and of Oliver, and of the vassals who died at Roncevaux'; and it is suggested that in the *Chanson de Roland* by one Turoldus or Théroulde, a poem preserved in a manuscript of the twelfth century in the Bodleian Library at Oxford, we have certainly the matter,

perhaps even some of the words, of the chant which Taillefer
sang. The poem has vigour and freshness; it is not without
pathos. But M. Vitet is not satisfied with seeing in it a document
of some poetic value, and of very high historic and linguistic
value; he sees in it a grand and beautiful work, a monument of
epic genius. In its general design he finds the grandiose conception, in its details he finds the constant union of simplicity
with greatness, which are the marks, he truly says, of the genuine
epic, and distinguish it from the artificial epic of literary ages.
One thinks of Homer; this is the sort of praise which is given to
Homer, and justly given. Higher praise there cannot well be,
and it is the praise due to epic poetry of the highest order only
and to no other. Let us try, then, the *Chanson de Roland* at its
best. Roland, mortally wounded, lays himself down under a
pine-tree, with his face turned towards Spain and the enemy—

> De plusurs choses a remembrer li prist,
> De tantes teres cume li bers cunquist,
> De dulce France, des humes de sun lign,
> De Carlemagne sun seignor ki l'nurrit.[1]

That is primitive work, I repeat, with an undeniable poetic
quality of its own. It deserves such praise, and such praise is
sufficient for it. But now turn to Homer—

> Ὣς φάτο· τοὺς δ' ἤδη κατέχεν φυσίζοος αἶα
> ἐν Λακεδαίμονι αὖθι, φίλη ἐν πατρίδι γαίη.[2]

We are here in another world, another order of poetry altogether;
here is rightly due such supreme praise as that which M. Vitet
gives to the *Chanson de Roland*. If our words are to have any
meaning, if our judgments are to have any solidity, we must not
heap that supreme praise upon poetry of an order immeasurably
inferior.

Indeed there can be no more useful help for discovering what
poetry belongs to the class of the truly excellent, and can therefore do us most good, than to have always in one's mind lines

---

[1] 'Then began he to call many things to remembrance,—all the lands
which his valour conquered, and pleasant France, and the men of his
lineage, and Charlemagne his liege lord who nourished him.'—*Chanson
de Roland*, iii. 939–42.

[2] 'So said she; they long since in Earth's soft arms were reposing,
There, in their own dear land, their fatherland, Lacedaemon.'
  Iliad, iii. 243, 244 (translated by Dr Hawtrey).

and expressions of the great masters, and to apply them as a touchstone to other poetry. Of course we are not to require this other poetry to resemble them; it may be very dissimilar. But if we have any tact we shall find them, when we have lodged them well in our minds, an infallible touchstone for detecting the presence or absence of high poetic quality, and also the degree of this quality, in all other poetry which we may place beside them. Short passages, even single lines, will serve our turn quite sufficiently. Take the two lines which I have just quoted from Homer, the poet's comment on Helen's mention of her brothers;—or take his

> Ἀ δειλώ, τί σφῶϊ δόμεν Πηλῆϊ ἄνακτι
> θνητῷ; ὑμεῖς δ' ἐστὸν ἀγήρω τ' ἀθανάτω τε.
> ἦ ἵνα δυστήνοισι μετ' ἀνδράσιν ἄλγε' ἔχητον; [1]

the address of Zeus to the horses of Peleus;—or take finally his

> Καὶ σέ, γέρον, τὸ πρὶν μὲν ἀκούομεν ὄλβιον εἶναι· [2]

the words of Achilles to Priam, a suppliant before him. Take that incomparable line and a half of Dante, Ugolino's tremendous words—

> Io no piangeva; sì dentro impietrai.
> Piangevan elli . . . [3]

take the lovely words of Beatrice to Virgil—

> Io son fatta da Dio, sua mercè, tale,
> Che la vostra miseria non mi tange,
> Nè fiamma d' esto incendio non m' assale . . . [4]

take the simple, but perfect, single line—

> In la sua volontade è nostra pace. [5]

---

[1] 'Ah, unhappy pair, why gave we you to King Peleus, to a mortal? but ye are without old age, and immortal. Was it that with men born in misery ye might have sorrow?'—*Iliad*, xvii. 443–5.

[2] 'Nay, and thou too, old man, in former days wast, as we hear, happy.'—*Iliad*, xxiv. 543.

[3] 'I wailed not, so of stone grew I within;—*they* wailed.'—*Inferno*, xxxiii. 39, 40.

[4] 'Of such sort hath God, thanked be His mercy, made me, that your misery toucheth me not, neither doth the flame of this fire strike me.'—*Inferno*, ii. 91–3.

[5] 'In His will is our peace.'—*Paradiso*, iii. 85.

Take of Shakespeare a line or two of Henry the Fourth's expostulation with sleep—

> Wilt thou upon the high and giddy mast
> Seal up the ship-boy's eyes, and rock his brains
> In cradle of the rude imperious surge . . .

and take, as well, Hamlet's dying request to Horatio—

> If thou didst ever hold me in thy heart,
> Absent thee from felicity awhile,
> And in this harsh world draw thy breath in pain
> To tell my story . . .

Take of Milton that Miltonic passage—

> Darken'd so, yet shone
> Above them all the archangel; but his face
> Deep scars of thunder had intrench'd, and care
> Sat on his faded cheek . . .

add two such lines as—

> And courage never to submit or yield
> And what is else not to be overcome . . .

and finish with the exquisite close to the loss of Proserpine, the loss

> . . . which cost Ceres all that pain
> To seek her through the world.

These few lines, if we have tact and can use them, are enough even of themselves to keep clear and sound our judgments about poetry, to save us from fallacious estimates of it, to conduct us to a real estimate.

The specimens I have quoted differ widely from one another, but they have in common this: the possession of the very highest poetical quality. If we are thoroughly penetrated by their power, we shall find that we have acquired a sense enabling us, whatever poetry may be laid before us, to feel the degree in which a high poetical quality is present or wanting there. Critics give themselves great labour to draw out what in the abstract constitutes the characters of a high quality of poetry. It is much better simply to have recourse to concrete examples;—to take specimens of poetry of the high, the very highest quality, and to say: The characters of a high quality of poetry are what is expressed *there*. They are far better recognized by being felt in the verse of the master, than by being perused in the prose of the critic. Nevertheless if we are urgently pressed to give some critical account of them, we may safely, perhaps, venture on laying down, not indeed how and why the characters arise, but where and in what they arise. They are in the matter and substance of the poetry, and they are in its manner and style. Both of these, the substance and matter on the one hand, the style and manner on the other, have a mark, an accent, of high beauty, worth, and power. But if we are asked to define this mark and accent in the abstract, our answer must be: No, for we should thereby be darkening the question, not clearing it. The mark and accent are as given by the substance and matter of that poetry, by the style and manner of that poetry, and of all other poetry which is akin to it in quality.

Only one thing we may add as to the substance and matter of poetry, guiding ourselves by Aristotle's profound observation that the superiority of poetry over history consists in its possessing a higher truth and a higher seriousness (φιλοσοφώτερον καὶ σπουδαιότερον). Let us add, therefore, to what we have said, this: that the substance and matter of the best poetry acquire their special character from possessing, in an eminent degree, truth and seriousness. We may add yet further, what is in itself evident, that to the style and manner of the best poetry their special character, their accent, is given by their diction, and, even yet more, by their movement. And though we distinguish between the two characters, the two accents, of superiority, yet they are nevertheless vitally connected one with the other. The superior character of truth and seriousness, in the matter and substance of the best poetry, is inseparable from the superiority of diction and movement marking its style and manner. The two superiorities are closely related, and are in steadfast proportion one to the other. So far as high poetic truth and seriousness are wanting to a poet's matter and substance, so far also, we may be sure, will a high poetic stamp of diction and movement be wanting to his style and manner. In proportion as this high stamp of diction and movement, again, is absent from a poet's style and manner, we shall find, also, that high poetic truth and seriousness are absent from his substance and matter.

So stated, these are but dry generalities; their whole force lies in their application. And I could wish every student of poetry to make the application of them for himself. Made by himself, the application would impress itself upon his mind far more deeply than if made by me. Neither will my limits allow me to make any full application of the generalities above propounded; but in the hope of bringing out, at any rate, some significance in them, and of establishing an important principle more firmly by their means, I will, in the space which remains to me, follow rapidly from the commencement the course of our English poetry with them in my view.

Once more I return to the early poetry of France, with which our own poetry, in its origins, is indissolubly connected. In the twelfth and thirteenth centuries, that seed-time of all modern language and literature, the poetry of France had a clear predominance in Europe. Of the two divisions of that poetry, its productions in the *langue d'oïl* and its productions in the *langue d'oc*, the poetry of the *langue d'oc*, of southern France, of the troubadours, is of importance because of its effect on Italian literature;—the first literature of modern Europe to strike the true and grand note, and to bring forth, as in Dante and Petrarch it brought forth, classics. But the predominance of French poetry in Europe, during the twelfth and thirteenth centuries, is due to its poetry of the *langue d'oïl*, the poetry of northern France and of the tongue which is now the French language. In the twelfth century the bloom of this romance-poetry was earlier and stronger in England, at the court of our Anglo-Norman kings, than in France itself. But it was a bloom of French poetry; and as our native poetry formed itself, it formed itself out of this. The romance-poems which took possession of the heart and imagination of Europe in the twelfth and thirteenth centuries are French; 'they are', as Southey justly says, 'the pride of French literature, nor have we anything which can be placed in competition with them'. Themes were supplied from all quarters; but the romance-setting which was common to them all, and which gained the ear of Europe, was French. This constituted for the French poetry, literature, and language, at the height of the Middle Age, an unchallenged predominance.

The Italian Brunetto Latini, the master of Dante, wrote his *Treasure* in French because, he says, 'la parleure en est plus délitable et plus commune a toutes gens'. In the same century, the thirteenth, the French romance-writer, Christian of Troyes, formulates the claims, in chivalry and letters, of France, his native country, as follows:

> Or vous ert par ce livre apris,
> Que Gresse ot de chevalerie
> Le premier los et de clergie;
> Puis vint chevalerie à Rome,
> Et de la clergie la some,
> Qui ore est en France venue.
> Diex doinst qu'ele i soit retenue,
> Et que li lius li abelisse
> Tant que de France n'isse
> L'onor qui s'i est arestée!

(Now by this book you will learn that first Greece has the renown for chivalry and letters; then chivalry and the primacy in letters passed to Rome, and now it is come to France. God grant it may be kept there; and that the place may please it so well, that the honour which has come to make stay in France may never depart thence!)

Yet it is now all gone, this French romance-poetry, of which the weight of substance and the power of style are not unfairly represented by this extract from Christian of Troyes. Only by means of the historic estimate can we persuade ourselves now to think that any of it is of poetical importance.

But in the fourteenth century there comes an Englishman nourished on this poetry, taught his trade by this poetry, getting words, rhyme, metre from this poetry; for even of that stanza which the Italians used, and which Chaucer derived immediately from the Italians, the basis and suggestion was probably given in France. Chaucer (I have already named him) fascinated his contemporaries, but so too did Christian of Troyes and Wolfram of Eschenbach. Chaucer's power of fascination, however, is enduring; his poetical importance does not need the assistance of the historic estimate; it is real. He is a genuine source of joy and strength, which is flowing still for us and will flow always. He will be read, as time goes on, far more generally than he is read now. His language is a cause of difficulty for us; but so also, and I think in quite as great a degree, is the language of Burns. In Chaucer's case, as in that of Burns, it is a difficulty to be unhesitatingly accepted and overcome.

If we ask ourselves wherein consists the immense superiority of Chaucer's poetry over the romance-poetry—why it is that in passing from this to Chaucer we suddenly feel ourselves to be in another world, we shall find that his superiority is both in the substance of his poetry and in the style of his poetry. His superiority in substance is given by his large, free, simple, clear yet kindly view of human life,—so unlike the total want, in the romance-poets, of all intelligent command of it. Chaucer has not their helplessness; he has gained the power to survey the world from a central, a truly human point of view. We have only to call to mind the Prologue to *The Canterbury Tales*. The right comment upon it is Dryden's: 'It is sufficient to say, according to the proverb, that *here is God's plenty*.' And again: 'He is a perpetual fountain of good sense.' It is by a large, free, sound representation of things, that poetry, this high criticism of life, has truth of substance; and Chaucer's poetry has truth of substance.

Of his style and manner, if we think first of the romance-poetry and then of Chaucer's divine liquidness of diction, his divine fluidity of movement, it is difficult to speak temperately. They are irresistible, and justify all the rapture with which his successors speak of his 'gold dew-drops of speech'. Johnson misses the point entirely when he finds fault with Dryden for ascribing to Chaucer the first refinement of our numbers, and says that Gower also can show smooth numbers and easy rhymes. The refinement of our numbers means something far more than this. A nation may have versifiers with smooth numbers and easy rhymes, and yet may have no real poetry at all. Chaucer is the father of our splendid English poetry; he is our 'well of English undefiled', because by the lovely charm of his diction, the lovely charm of his movement, he makes an epoch and founds a tradition. In Spenser, Shakespeare, Milton, Keats, we can follow the tradition of the liquid diction, the fluid movement, of Chaucer; at one time it is his liquid diction of which in these poets we feel the virtue, and at another time it is his fluid movement. And the virtue is irresistible.

Bounded as is my space, I must yet find room for an example of Chaucer's virtue, as I have given examples to show the virtue of the great classics. I feel disposed to say that a single line is enough to show the charm of Chaucer's verse; that merely one line like this—

> O martyr souded [1] in virginitee!

has a virtue of manner and movement such as we shall not find in all the verse of romance-poetry;—but this is saying nothing. The virtue is such as we shall not find, perhaps, in all English poetry, outside the poets whom I have named as the special inheritors of Chaucer's tradition. A single line, however, is too little if we have not the strain of Chaucer's verse well in our memory; let us take a stanza. It is from *The Prioress's Tale*, the story of the Christian child murdered in a Jewry—

> My throte is cut unto my nekke-bone
> Saidè this child, and as by way of kinde
> I should have deyd, yea, longè time agone;
> But Jesu Christ, as ye in bookès finde,
> Will that his glory last and be in minde,
> And for the worship of his mother dere
> Yet may I sing *O Alma* loud and clere.

Wordsworth has modernized this Tale, and to feel how delicate and evanescent is the charm of verse, we have only to read Wordsworth's first three lines of this stanza after Chaucer's—

> My throat is cut unto the bone, I trow,
> Said this young child, and by the law of kind
> I should have died, yea, many hours ago.

The charm is departed. It is often said that the power of liquidness and fluidity in Chaucer's verse was dependent upon a free, a licentious, dealing with language, such as is now impossible; upon a liberty, such as Burns too enjoyed, of making words like *neck*, *bird*, into a dissyllable by adding to them, and words like *cause*, *rhyme*, into a dissyllable by sounding the *e* mute. It is true that Chaucer's fluidity is conjoined with this liberty, and is admirably served by it; but we ought not to say that it was

---

[1] The French *soudé*; soldered, fixed fast.

dependent upon it. It was dependent upon his talent. Other poets with a like liberty do not attain to the fluidity of Chaucer; Burns himself does not attain to it. Poets, again, who have a talent akin to Chaucer's, such as Shakespeare or Keats, have known how to attain to his fluidity without the like liberty.

And yet Chaucer is not one of the great classics. His poetry transcends and effaces, easily and without effort, all the romance-poetry of Catholic Christendom; it transcends and effaces all the English poetry contemporary with it; it transcends and effaces all the English poetry subsequent to it down to the age of Elizabeth. Of such avail is poetic truth of substance, in its natural and necessary union with poetic truth of style. And yet, I say, Chaucer is not one of the great classics. He has not their accent. What is wanting to him is suggested by the mere mention of the name of the first great classic of Christendom, the immortal poet who died eighty years before Chaucer,—Dante. The accent of such verse as

In la sua volontade è nostra pace . . .

is altogether beyond Chaucer's reach; we praise him, but we feel that this accent is out of the question for him. It may be said that it was necessarily out of the reach of any poet in the England of that stage of growth. Possibly; but we are to adopt a real, not a historic, estimate of poetry. However we may account for its absence, something is wanting, then, to the poetry of Chaucer, which poetry must have before it can be placed in the glorious class of the best. And there is no doubt what that something is. It is the σπουδαιότης, the high and excellent seriousness, which Aristotle assigns as one of the grand virtues of poetry. The substance of Chaucer's poetry, his views of things and his criticism of life, has largeness, freedom, shrewdness, benignity; but it has not this high seriousness. Homer's criticism of life has it, Dante's has it, Shakespeare's has it. It is this chiefly which gives to our spirits what they can rest upon; and with the increasing demands of our modern ages upon poetry, this virtue of giving us what we can rest upon will be more and more highly esteemed. A voice from the slums of Paris, fifty or sixty years after Chaucer, the voice of poor Villon out of his life of riot and crime, has at its happy moments (as, for instance, in the last stanza of *La Belle*

Heaulmière [1]) more of this important poetic virtue of seriousness than all the productions of Chaucer. But its apparition in Villon, and in men like Villon, is fitful; the greatness of the great poets, the power of their criticism of life, is that their virtue is sustained.

To our praise, therefore, of Chaucer as a poet there must be this limitation; he lacks the high seriousness of the great classics, and therewith an important part of their virtue. Still, the main fact for us to bear in mind about Chaucer is his sterling value according to that real estimate which we firmly adopt for all poets. He has poetic truth of substance, though he has not high poetic seriousness, and corresponding to his truth of substance he has an exquisite virtue of style and manner. With him is born our real poetry.

For my present purpose I need not dwell on our Elizabethan poetry, or on the continuation and close of this poetry in Milton. We all of us profess to be agreed in the estimate of this poetry; we all of us recognize it as great poetry, our greatest, and Shakespeare and Milton as our poetical classics. The real estimate, here, has universal currency. With the next age of our poetry divergency and difficulty begin. An historic estimate of that poetry has established itself; and the question is, whether it will be found to coincide with the real estimate.

The age of Dryden, together with our whole eighteenth century which followed it, sincerely believed itself to have produced poetical classics of its own, and even to have made advance, in poetry, beyond all its predecessors. Dryden regards as not seriously disputable the opinion 'that the sweetness of English

[1] The name *Heaulmière* is said to be derived from a head-dress (helm) worn as a mark by courtesans. In Villon's ballad, a poor old creature of this class laments her days of youth and beauty. The last stanza of the ballad runs thus—

> 'Ainsi le bon temps regretons
> Entre nous, pauvres vieilles sottes.
> Assises bas, à croppetons,
> Tout en ung tas comme pelottes;
> A petit feu de chenevottes
> Tost allumées, tost estainctes.
> Et jadis fusmes si mignottes!
> Ainsi en prend à maintz et maintes.'

('Thus amongst ourselves we regret the good time, poor silly old things, low-seated on our heels, all in a heap like so many balls, by a little fire of hemp-stalks, soon lighted, soon spent. And once we were such darlings! So fares it with many and many a one.')

verse was never understood or practised by our fathers'. Cowley could see nothing at all in Chaucer's poetry. Dryden heartily admired, and, as we have seen, praised its matter admirably; but of its exquisite manner and movement all he can find to say is that 'there is the rude sweetness of a Scotch tune in it, which is natural and pleasing, though not perfect'. Addison, wishing to praise Chaucer's numbers, compares them with Dryden's own. And all through the eighteenth century, and down even into our own times, the stereotyped phrase of approbation for good verse found in our early poetry has been that it even approached the verse of Dryden, Addison, Pope, and Johnson.

Are Dryden and Pope poetical classics? Is the historic estimate, which represents them as such, and which has been so long established that it cannot easily give way, the real estimate? Wordsworth and Coleridge, as is well known, denied it; but the authority of Wordsworth and Coleridge does not weigh much with the young generation, and there are many signs to show that the eighteenth century and its judgments are coming into favour again. Are the favourite poets of the eighteenth century classics?

It is impossible within my present limits to discuss the question fully. And what man of letters would not shrink from seeming to dispose dictatorially of the claims of two men who are, at any rate, such masters in letters as Dryden and Pope; two men of such admirable talent, both of them, and one of them, Dryden, a man, on all sides, of such energetic and genial power? And yet, if we are to gain the full benefit from poetry, we must have the real estimate of it. I cast about for some mode of arriving, in the present case, at such an estimate without offence; and perhaps the best way is to begin, as it is easy to begin, with cordial praise.

When we find Chapman, the Elizabethan translator of Homer, expressing himself in his preface thus: 'Though truth in her very nakedness sits in so deep a pit, that from Gades to Aurora and Ganges few eyes can sound her, I hope yet those few here will so discover and confirm that, the date being out of her darkness in this morning of our poet, he shall now gird his temples with the sun',—we pronounce that such a prose is intolerable. When we find Milton writing: 'And long it was not after, when I was confirmed in this opinion, that he, who would not be frustrate of his hope to write well hereafter in laudable things, ought himself to be a true poem',—we pronounce that such a prose has its own grandeur, but that it is obsolete and inconvenient. But when we find Dryden telling us: 'What Virgil wrote in the vigour of his age, in plenty and at ease, I have undertaken to translate in my declining years; struggling with wants, oppressed with sickness, curbed in my genius, liable to be misconstrued in all I write',—then we exclaim that here at last we have the true English prose, a prose such as we would all gladly use if we only knew how. Yet Dryden was Milton's contemporary.

But after the Restoration the time had come when our nation felt the imperious need of a fit prose. So, too, the time had likewise come when our nation felt the imperious need of freeing itself from the absorbing preoccupation which religion in the Puritan age had exercised. It was impossible that this freedom should be brought about without some negative excess, without some neglect and impairment of the religious life of the soul; and the spiritual history of the eighteenth century shows us that the freedom was not achieved without them. Still, the freedom was achieved; the preoccupation, an undoubtedly baneful and retarding one if it had continued, was got rid of. And as with religion amongst us at that period, so it was also with letters. A fit prose was a necessity; but it was impossible that a fit prose should establish itself amongst us without some touch of frost to the imaginative life of the soul. The needful qualities for a fit prose are regularity, uniformity, precision, balance. The men of letters, whose destiny it may be to bring their nation to the attainment of a fit prose, must of necessity, whether they work in prose or in verse, give a predominating and almost exclusive attention to the qualities of regularity, uniformity, precision, balance. But an almost exclusive attention to these qualities involves some repression and silencing of poetry.

We are to regard Dryden as the puissant and glorious founder, Pope as the splendid high priest, of our age of prose and reason, of our excellent and indispensable eighteenth century. For the purposes of their mission and destiny their poetry, like their prose, is admirable. Do you ask me whether Dryden's verse, take it almost where you will, is not good?

A milk-white Hind, immortal and unchanged,
Fed on the lawns and in the forest ranged.

I answer: Admirable for the purposes of the inaugurator of an age of prose and reason. Do you ask me whether Pope's verse, take it almost where you will, is not good?

> To Hounslow Heath I point, and Banstead Down;
> Thence comes your mutton, and these chicks my own.

I answer: Admirable for the purposes of the high priest of an age of prose and reason. But do you ask me whether such verse proceeds from men with an adequate poetic criticism of life, from men whose criticism of life has a high seriousness, or even, without that high seriousness, has poetic largeness, freedom, insight, benignity? Do you ask me whether the application of ideas to life in the verse of these men, often a powerful application, no doubt, is a powerful *poetic* application? Do you ask me whether the poetry of these men has either the matter or the inseparable manner of such an adequate poetic criticism; whether it has the accent of

> Absent thee from felicity awhile . . .

or of

> And what is else not to be overcome . . .

or of

> O martyr souded in virginitee!

I answer: It has not and cannot have them; it is the poetry of the builders of an age of prose and reason. Though they may write in verse, though they may in a certain sense be masters of the art of versification, Dryden and Pope are not classics of our poetry, they are classics of our prose.

Gray is our poetical classic of that literature and age; the position of Gray is singular, and demands a word of notice here. He has not the volume or the power of poets who, coming in times more favourable, have attained to an independent criticism of life. But he lived with the great poets, he lived, above all, with the Greeks, through perpetually studying and enjoying them; and he caught their poetic point of view for regarding life, caught their poetic manner. The point of view and the manner are not self-sprung in him, he caught them of others; and he had not the free and abundant use of them. But whereas Addison and Pope never had the use of them, Gray had the use of them at times. He is the scantiest and frailest of classics in our poetry, but he is a classic.

And now, after Gray, we are met, as we draw towards the end of the eighteenth century, we are met by the great name of Burns. We enter now on times where the personal estimate of poets begins to be rife, and where the real estimate of them is not reached without difficulty. But in spite of the disturbing pressures of personal partiality, of national partiality, let us try to reach a real estimate of the poetry of Burns.

By his English poetry Burns in general belongs to the eighteenth century, and has little importance for us.

> Mark ruffian Violence, distain'd with crimes,
> Rousing elate in these degenerate times;
> View unsuspecting Innocence a prey,
> As guileful Fraud points out the erring way;
> While subtle Litigation's pliant tongue
> The life-blood equal sucks of Right and Wrong!

Evidently this is not the real Burns, or his name and fame would have disappeared long ago. Nor is Clarinda's love-poet, Sylvander, the real Burns either. But he tells us himself: 'These English songs gravel me to death. I have not the command of the language that I have of my native tongue. In fact, I think that my ideas are more barren in English than in Scotch. I have been at *Duncan Gray* to dress it in English, but all I can do is desperately stupid.' We English turn naturally, in Burns, to the poems in our own language, because we can read them easily; but in those poems we have not the real Burns.

The real Burns is of course in his Scotch poems. Let us boldly say that of much of this poetry, a poetry dealing perpetually with Scotch drink, Scotch religion, and Scotch manners, a Scotchman's estimate is apt to be personal. A Scotchman is used to this world of Scotch drink, Scotch religion, and Scotch manners; he has a tenderness for it; he meets its poet half way. In this tender mood he reads pieces like the *Holy Fair* or *Halloween*. But this world of Scotch drink, Scotch religion, and Scotch manners is against a poet, not for him, when it is not a partial countryman who reads him; for in itself it is not a beautiful world, and no one can deny that it is of advantage to a poet to deal with a beautiful world. Burns's world of Scotch drink,

Scotch religion, and Scotch manners, is often a harsh, a sordid, a repulsive world; even the world of his *Cotter's Saturday Night* is not a beautiful world. No doubt a poet's criticism of life may have such truth and power that it triumphs over its world and delights us. Burns may triumph over his world, often he does triumph over his world, but let us observe how and where. Burns is the first case we have had where the bias of the personal estimate tends to mislead; let us look at him closely—he can bear it.

Many of his admirers will tell us that we have Burns, convivial, genuine, delightful, here—

> Leeze me on drink! it gies us mair
>   Than either school or college;
> It kindles wit, it waukens lair,
>   It pangs us fou o' knowledge.
> Be't whisky gill or penny wheep
>   Or ony stronger potion,
> It never fails, on drinking deep,
>   To kittle up our notion
>   By night or day.

There is a great deal of that sort of thing in Burns, and it is unsatisfactory, not because it is bacchanalian poetry, but because it has not that accent of sincerity which bacchanalian poetry, to do it justice, very often has. There is something in it of bravado, something which makes us feel that we have not the man speaking to us with his real voice; something, therefore, poetically unsound.

With still more confidence will his admirers tell us that we have the genuine Burns, the great poet, when his strain asserts the independence, equality, dignity, of men, as in the famous song *For a' that and a' that—*

> A prince can mak' a belted knight,
>   A marquis, duke, and a' that;
> But an honest man's aboon his might,
>   Guid faith he mauna fa' that!
>   For a' that, and a' that,
>   Their dignities, and a' that,
>   The pith o' sense, and pride o' worth,
>   Are higher rank than a' that.

Here they find his grand, genuine touches; and still more, when

this puissant genius, who so often set morality at defiance, falls
moralizing—

> The sacred lowe o' weel-placed love
>   Luxuriantly indulge it;
> But never tempt th' illicit rove,
>   Tho' naething should divulge it.
> I waive the quantum o' the sin,
>   The hazard o' concealing,
> But och! it hardens a' within,
>   And petrifies the feeling.

Or in a higher strain—

> Who made the heart, 'tis He alone
>   Decidedly can try us;
> He knows each chord, its various tone;
>   Each spring, its various bias.
> Then at the balance let's be mute,
>   We never can adjust it;
> What's *done* we partly may compute,
>   But know not what's resisted.

Or in a better strain yet, a strain, his admirers will say, unsur-
passable—

> To make a happy fire-side clime
>   To weans and wife,
> That's the true pathos and sublime
>   Of human life.

There is criticism of life for you, the admirers of Burns will
say to us; there is the application of ideas to life! There is, undoubtedly. The doctrine of the last-quoted lines coincides
almost exactly with what was the aim and end, Xenophon tells
us, of all the teaching of Socrates. And the application is a powerful one; made by a man of vigorous understanding, and (need
I say?) a master of language.

But for supreme poetical success more is required than the
powerful application of ideas to life; it must be an application
under the conditions fixed by the laws of poetic truth and poetic
beauty. Those laws fix as an essential condition, in the poet's
treatment of such matters as are here in question, high seriousness;—the high seriousness which comes from absolute sincerity.

The accent of high seriousness, born of absolute sincerity, is what gives to such verse as

> In la sua volontade è nostra pace . . .

to such criticism of life as Dante's, its power. Is this accent felt in the passages which I have been quoting from Burns? Surely not; surely, if our sense is quick, we must perceive that we have not in those passages a voice from the very inmost soul of the genuine Burns; he is not speaking to us from these depths, he is more or less preaching. And the compensation for admiring such passages less, from missing the perfect poetic accent in them, will be that we shall admire more the poetry where that accent is found.

No; Burns, like Chaucer, comes short of the high seriousness of the great classics, and the virtue of matter and manner which goes with that high seriousness is wanting to his work. At moments he touches it in a profound and passionate melancholy, as in those four immortal lines taken by Byron as a motto for *The Bride of Abydos*, but which have in them a depth of poetic quality such as resides in no verse of Byron's own—

> Had we never loved sae kindly,
> Had we never loved sae blindly,
> Never met, or never parted,
> We had ne'er been broken-hearted.

But a whole poem of that quality Burns cannot make; the rest, in the *Farewell to Nancy*, is verbiage.

We arrive best at the real estimate of Burns, I think, by conceiving his work as having truth of matter and truth of manner, but not the accent or the poetic virtue of the highest masters. His genuine criticism of life, when the sheer poet in him speaks, is ironic; it is not—

> Thou Power Supreme, whose mighty scheme
> These woes of mine fulfil,
> Here firm I rest, they must be best
> Because they are Thy will!

It is far rather: *Whistle owre the lave o't!* Yet we may say of him as of Chaucer, that of life and the world, as they come before him, his view is large, free, shrewd, benignant,—truly poetic, therefore; and his manner of rendering what he sees is to match. But we must note, at the same time, his great difference from Chaucer. The freedom of Chaucer is heightened, in Burns, by a fiery, reckless energy; the benignity of Chaucer deepens, in Burns, into an overwhelming sense of the pathos of things; —of the pathos of human nature, the pathos, also, of non-human nature. Instead of the fluidity of Chaucer's manner, the manner of Burns has spring, bounding swiftness. Burns is by far the greater force, though he has perhaps less charm. The world of Chaucer is fairer, richer, more significant than that of Burns; but when the largeness and freedom of Burns get full sweep, as in *Tam o' Shanter*, or still more in that puissant and splendid production, *The Jolly Beggars*, his world may be what it will, his poetic genuis triumphs over it. In the world of *The Jolly Beggars* there is more than hideousness and squalor, there is bestiality; yet the piece is a superb poetic success. It has a breadth, truth, and power which make the famous scene in Auerbach's Cellar, of Goethe's *Faust*, seem artificial and tame beside it, and which are matched only by Shakespeare and Aristophanes.

Here, where his largeness and freedom serve him so admirably, and also in those poems and songs where to shrewdness he adds infinite archness and wit, and to benignity infinite pathos, where his manner is flawless, and a perfect poetic whole is the result,— in things like the address to the mouse whose home he had ruined, in things like *Duncan Gray, Tam Glen, Whistle and I'll come to you my Lad, Auld Lang Syne* (this list might be made much longer)—here we have the genuine Burns, of whom the real estimate must be high indeed. Not a classic, nor with the excellent σπουδαιότης of the great classics, nor with a verse rising to a criticism of life and a virtue like theirs; but a poet with thorough truth of substance and an answering truth of style, giving us a poetry sound to the core. We all of us have a leaning towards the pathetic, and may be inclined perhaps to prize Burns most for his touches of piercing, sometimes almost intolerable, pathos; for verse like—

> We twa hae paidl't i' the burn
> From mornin' sun till dine;
> But seas between us braid hae roar'd
> Sin auld lang syne . . .

where he is as lovely as he is sound. But perhaps it is by the perfection of soundness of his lighter and archer masterpieces that he is poetically most wholesome for us. For the votary misled by a personal estimate of Shelley, as so many of us have been, are, and will be,—of that beautiful spirit building his many-coloured haze of words and images

Pinnacled dim in the intense inane—

no contact can be wholesomer than the contact with Burns at his archest and soundest. Side by side with the

On the brink of the night and the morning
My coursers are wont to respire,
But the Earth has just whispered a warning
That their flight must be swifter than fire . . .

of *Prometheus Unbound*, how salutary, how very salutary, to place this from *Tam Glen*—

My minnie does constantly deave me
And bids me beware o' young men;
They flatter, she says, to deceive me;
But wha can think sae o' Tam Glen?

But we enter on burning ground as we approach the poetry of times so near to us—poetry like that of Byron, Shelley, and Wordsworth—of which the estimates are so often not only personal, but personal with passion. For my purpose, it is enough to have taken the single case of Burns, the first poet we come to of whose work the estimate formed is evidently apt to be personal, and to have suggested how we may proceed, using the poetry of the great classics as a sort of touchstone, to correct this estimate, as we had previously corrected by the same means the historic estimate where we met with it. A collection like the present, with its succession of celebrated names and celebrated poems, offers a good opportunity to us for resolutely endeavouring to make our estimates of poetry real. I have sought to point out a method which will help us in making them so, and to exhibit it in use so far as to put any one who likes in a way of applying it for himself.

At any rate the end to which the method and the estimate are designed to lead, and from leading to which, if they do lead to it, they get their whole value,—the benefit of being able clearly to feel and deeply to enjoy the best, the truly classic, in poetry,—is an end, let me say it once more at parting, of supreme importance. We are often told that an era is opening in which we are to see multitudes of a common sort of readers, and masses of a common sort of literature; that such readers do not want and could not relish anything better than such literature, and that to provide it is becoming a vast and profitable industry. Even if good literature entirely lost currency with the world, it would still be abundantly worth while to continue to enjoy it by oneself. But it never will lose currency with the world, in spite of momentary appearances; it never will lose supremacy. Currency and supremacy are insured to it, not indeed by the world's deliberate and conscious choice, but by something far deeper,—by the instinct of self-preservation in humanity.

To habituate ourselves, therefore, to approve, as the Bible

II

MILTON

THE most eloquent voice of our century uttered, shortly before
leaving the world, a warning cry against 'the Anglo-Saxon
contagion'. The tendencies and aims, the view of life and the
social economy of the ever-multiplying and spreading Anglo-
Saxon race, would be found congenial, this prophet feared, by
all the prose, all the vulgarity amongst mankind, and would
invade and overpower all nations. The true ideal would be lost,
a general sterility of mind and heart would set in.

The prophet had in view, no doubt, in the warning thus given,
us and our colonies, but the United States still more. There the
Anglo-Saxon race is already most numerous, there it increases
fastest; there material interests are most absorbing and pursued
with most energy; there the ideal, the saving ideal, of a high and
rare excellence, seems perhaps to suffer most danger of being
obscured and lost. Whatever one may think of the general
danger to the world from the Anglo-Saxon contagion, it appears
to me difficult to deny that the growing greatness and influence
of the United States does bring with it some danger to the ideal
of a high and rare excellence. The *average man* is too much a
religion there; his performance is unduly magnified, his shortcomings are not duly seen and admitted. A lady in the State of
Ohio sent to me only the other day a volume on American
authors; the praise given throughout was of such high pitch that
in thanking her I could not forbear saying that for only one or
two of the authors named was such a strain of praise admissible,
and that we lost all real standard of excellence by praising so
uniformly and immoderately. She answered me with charming
good temper, that very likely I was quite right, but it was
pleasant to her to think that excellence was common and abundant. But excellence is not common and abundant; on the contrary, as the Greek poet long ago said, excellence dwells among
rocks hardly accessible, and a man must almost wear his heart

out before he can reach her. Whoever talks of excellence as common and abundant is on the way to lose all right standard of excellence. And when the right standard of excellence is lost, it is not likely that much which is excellent will be produced.

To habituate ourselves, therefore, to approve, as the Bible says, things that are really excellent, is of the highest importance. And some apprehension may justly be caused by a tendency in Americans to take, or, at any rate, attempt to take, profess to take, the average man and his performances too seriously, to overrate and overpraise what is not really superior.

But we have met here today to witness the unveiling of a gift in Milton's honour, and a gift bestowed by an American, Mr Childs of Philadelphia; whose cordial hospitality so many Englishmen, I myself among the number, have experienced in America. It was only last autumn that Stratford-upon-Avon celebrated the reception of a gift from the same generous donor in honour of Shakespeare. Shakespeare and Milton—he who wishes to keep his standard of excellence high cannot choose two better objects of regard and honour. And it is an American who has chosen them, and whose beautiful gift in honour of one of them, Milton, with Mr Whittier's simple and true lines inscribed upon it, is unveiled today. Perhaps this gift in honour of Milton, of which I am asked to speak, is, even more than the gift in honour of Shakespeare, one to suggest edifying reflections to us.

Like Mr Whittier, I treat the gift of Mr Childs as a gift in honour of Milton, although the window given is in memory of his second wife, Catherine Woodcock, the 'late espoused saint' of the famous sonnet, who died in child-bed at the end of the first year of her marriage with Milton, and who lies buried here with her infant. Milton is buried in Cripplegate, but he lived for a good while in this parish of St Margaret's, Westminster, and here he composed part of *Paradise Lost*, and the whole of *Paradise Regained* and *Samson Agonistes*. When death deprived him of the Catherine whom the new window commemorates, Milton had still some eighteen years to live, and Cromwell, his 'chief of men', was yet ruling England. But the Restoration, with its 'Sons of Belial', was not far off; and in the meantime Milton's heavy affliction had laid fast hold upon him, his eyesight had failed totally, he was blind. In what remained to him of life he had the consolation of producing the *Paradise Lost* and the *Samson Agonistes*, and such a consolation we may indeed count as no slight one. But the daily life of happiness in common things and in domestic affections—a life of which, to Milton as to Dante, too small a share was given—he seems to have known most, if not only, in his one married year with the wife who is here buried. Her form 'vested all in white' as in his sonnet he relates that after her death she appeared to him, her face veiled, but with 'love, sweetness, and goodness' shining in her person, —this fair and gentle daughter of the rigid sectarist of Hackney, this lovable companion with whom Milton had rest and happiness one year, is a part of Milton indeed, and in calling up her memory, we call up his.

And in calling up Milton's memory we call up, let me say, a memory upon which, in prospect of the Anglo-Saxon contagion and of its dangers supposed and real, it may be well to lay stress even more than upon Shakespeare's. If to our English race an inadequate sense for perfection of work is a real danger, if the discipline of respect for a high and flawless excellence is peculiarly needed by us, Milton is of all our gifted men the best lesson, the most salutary influence. In the sure and flawless perfection of his rhythm and diction he is as admirable as Virgil or Dante, and in this respect he is unique amongst us. No one else in English literature and art possesses the like distinction.

Thomson, Cowper, Wordsworth, all of them good poets who have studied Milton, followed Milton, adopted his form, fail in their diction and rhythm if we try them by that high standard of excellence maintained by Milton constantly. From style really high and pure Milton never departs; their departures from it are frequent.

Shakespeare is divinely strong, rich, and attractive. But sureness of perfect style Shakespeare himself does not possess. I have heard a politician express wonder at the treasures of political wisdom in a certain celebrated scene of *Troilus and Cressida*; for my part I am at least equally moved to wonder at the fantastic and false diction in which Shakespeare has in that scene clothed them. Milton, from one end of *Paradise Lost* to the other, is in his diction and rhythm constantly a great artist in the great style. Whatever may be said as to the subject of his poem, as to the conditions under which he received his subject and treated it, that praise, at any rate, is assured to him.

For the rest, justice is not at present done, in my opinion, to Milton's management of the inevitable matter of a Puritan epic, a matter full of difficulties for a poet. Justice is not done to the *architectonics*, as Goethe would have called them, of *Paradise Lost*; in these, too, the power of Milton's art is remarkable. But this may be a proposition which requires discussion and development for establishing it, and they are impossible on an occasion like the present.

That Milton, of all our English race, is by his diction and rhythm the one artist of highest rank in the great style whom we have; this I take as requiring no discussion, this I take as certain.

The mighty power of poetry and art is generally admitted. But where the soul of this power, of this power at its best, chiefly resides, very many of us fail to see. It resides chiefly in the refining and elevation wrought in us by the high and rare excellence of the great style. We may feel the effect without being able to give ourselves clear account of its cause, but the thing is so. Now, no race needs the influences mentioned, the influences of refining and elevation, more than ours; and in poetry and art our grand source for them is Milton.

To what does he owe this supreme distinction? To nature first and foremost, to that bent of nature for inequality which to the worshippers of the average man is so unacceptable; to a gift, a divine favour. 'The older one grows', says Goethe, 'the more one prizes natural gifts, because by no possibility can they be procured and stuck on.' Nature formed Milton to be a great poet. But what other poet has shown so sincere a sense of the grandeur of his vocation, and a moral effort so constant and sublime to make and keep himself worthy of it? The Milton of religious and political controversy, and perhaps of domestic life also, is not seldom disfigured by want of amenity, by acerbity. The Milton of poetry, on the other hand, is one of those great men 'who are modest'—to quote a fine remark of Leopardi, that gifted and stricken young Italian, who in his sense for poetic style is worthy to be named with Dante and Milton—'who are modest, because they continually compare themselves, not with other men, but with that idea of the perfect which they have before their minds'. The Milton of poetry is the man, in his own magnificent phrase, of 'devout prayer to that Eternal Spirit that can enrich with all utterance and knowledge, and sends out his Seraphim with the hallowed fire of his altar, to touch and purify the lips of whom he pleases'. And finally, the Milton of poetry is, in his own words again, the man of 'industrious and select reading'. Continually he lived in companionship with high and rare excellence, with the great Hebrew poets and prophets, with the great poets of Greece and Rome. The Hebrew compositions were not in verse, and can be not inadequately represented by the grand, measured prose of our English Bible. The verse of the poets of Greece and Rome no translation can adequately reproduce. Prose cannot have the power of verse; verse-translation may give whatever of charm is in the soul and talent of the translator himself, but never the specific charm of the verse and poet translated. In our race are thousands of readers, presently there will be millions, who know not a word of Greek and Latin, and will never learn those languages. If this host of readers are ever to gain any sense of the power and charm of the great poets of antiquity, their way to gain it is not through translations of the ancients, but through the original poetry of Milton, who has the like power and charm, because he has the like great style.

Through Milton they may gain it, for, in conclusion, Milton is English; this master in the great style of the ancients is English. Virgil, whom Milton loved and honoured, has at the end of the *Aeneid* a noble passage, where Juno, seeing the defeat of Turnus and the Italians imminent, the victory of the Trojan invaders assured, entreats Jupiter that Italy may nevertheless survive and be herself still, may retain her own mind, manners, and language, and not adopt those of the conqueror.

Sit Latium, sint Albani per secula reges!

Jupiter grants the prayer; he promises perpetuity and the future to Italy—Italy reinforced by whatever virtue the Trojan race has, but Italy, not Troy. This we may take as a sort of parable suiting ourselves. All the Anglo-Saxon contagion, all the flood of Anglo-Saxon commonness, beats vainly against the great style but cannot shake it, and has to accept its triumph. But it triumphs in Milton, in one of our own race, tongue, faith, and morals. Milton has made the great style no longer an exotic here; he has made it an inmate amongst us, a leaven, and a power.

Nevertheless he, and his hearers on both sides of the Atlantic, are English, and will remain English—

Sermonem Ausonii patrium moresque tenebunt.

The English race overspreads the world, and at the same time the ideal of an excellence the most high and the most rare abides a possession with it for ever.

III

THOMAS GRAY

JAMES BROWN, Master of Pembroke Hall at Cambridge, Gray's friend and executor, in a letter written a fortnight after Gray's death to another of his friends, Dr Wharton of Old Park, Durham, has the following passage:

> Everything is now dark and melancholy in Mr Gray's room, not a trace of him remains there; it looks as if it had been for some time uninhabited, and the room bespoke for another inhabitant. The thoughts I have of him will last, and will be useful to me the few years I can expect to live. He never spoke out, but I believe from some little expressions I now remember to have dropped from him, that for some time past he thought himself nearer his end than those about him apprehended.

He never spoke out. In these four words is contained the whole history of Gray, both as a man and as a poet. The words fell naturally, and as it were by chance, from their writer's pen; but let us dwell upon them, and press into their meaning, for in following it we shall come to understand Gray.

He was in his fifty-fifth year when he died, and he lived in ease and leisure, yet a few pages hold all his poetry; *he never spoke out* in poetry. Still, the reputation which he has achieved by his few pages is extremely high. True, Johnson speaks of him with coldness and disparagement. Gray disliked Johnson, and refused to make his acquaintance; one might fancy that Johnson wrote with some irritation from this cause. But Johnson was not by nature fitted to do justice to Gray and to his poetry; this by itself is a sufficient explanation of the deficiencies of his criticism of Gray. We may add a further explanation of them which is supplied by Mr Cole's papers. 'When Johnson was publishing his Life of Gray', says Mr Cole, 'I gave him several anecdotes, *but he was very anxious as soon as possible to get to the end of his labours.*' Johnson was not naturally in sympathy with

Gray, whose life he had to write, and when he wrote it he was in a hurry besides. He did Gray injustice, but even Johnson's authority failed to make injustice, in this case, prevail. Lord Macaulay calls the Life of Gray the worst of Johnson's Lives, and it had found many censurers before Macaulay. Gray's poetical reputation grew and flourished in spite of it. The poet Mason, his first biographer, in his epitaph equalled him with Pindar. Britain has known, says Mason,

> . . . a Homer's fire in Milton's strains,
> A Pindar's rapture in the lyre of Gray.

The immense vogue of Pope and of his style of versification had at first prevented the frank reception of Gray by the readers of poetry. The *Elegy* pleased; it could not but please: but Gray's poetry, on the whole, astonished his contemporaries at first more than it pleased them; it was so unfamiliar, so unlike the sort of poetry in vogue. It made its way, however, after his death, with the public as well as with the few; and Gray's second biographer, Mitford, remarks that 'the works which were either neglected or ridiculed by their contemporaries have now raised Gray and Collins to the rank of our two greatest lyric poets'. Their reputation was established, at any rate, and stood extremely high, even if they were not popularly read. Johnson's disparagement of Gray was called 'petulant', and severely blamed. Beattie, at the end of the eighteenth century, writing to Sir William Forbes, says: 'Of all the English poets of this age Mr Gray is most admired, and I think with justice.' Cowper writes: 'I have been reading Gray's works, and think him the only poet since Shakespeare entitled to the character of sublime. Perhaps you will remember that I once had a different opinion of him. I was prejudiced.' Adam Smith says: 'Gray joins to the sublimity of Milton the elegance and harmony of Pope; and nothing is wanting to render him, perhaps, the first poet in the English language, but to have written a little more.' And, to come nearer to our own times, Sir James Mackintosh speaks of Gray thus: 'Of all English poets he was the most finished artist. He attained the highest degree of splendour of which poetical style seemed to be capable.'

In a poet of such magnitude, how shall we explain his scantiness of production? Shall we explain it by saying that to make of Gray a poet of this magnitude is absurd; that his genius and resources were small, and that his production, therefore, was small also, but that the popularity of a single piece, the *Elegy*,— a popularity due in great measure to the subject,—created for Gray a reputation to which he has really no right? He himself was not deceived by the favour shown to the *Elegy*. 'Gray told me with a good deal of acrimony', writes Dr Gregory, 'that the *Elegy* owed its popularity entirely to the subject, and that the public would have received it as well if it had been written in prose.' This is too much to say; the *Elegy* is a beautiful poem, and in admiring it the public showed a true feeling for poetry. But it is true that the *Elegy* owed much of its success to its subject, and that it has received a too unmeasured and unbounded praise.

Gray himself, however, maintained that the *Elegy* was not his best work in poetry, and he was right. High as is the praise due to the *Elegy*, it is yet true that in other productions of Gray he exhibits poetical qualities even higher than those exhibited in the *Elegy*. He deserves, therefore, his extremely high reputation as a poet, although his critics and the public may not always have praised him with perfect judgment. We are brought back, then, to the question: How, in a poet so really considerable, are we to explain his scantiness of production?

Scanty Gray's production, indeed, is; so scanty that to supplement our knowledge of it by a knowledge of the man is in this case of peculiar interest and service. Gray's letters and the record of him by his friends have happily made it possible for us thus to know him, and to appreciate his high qualities of mind and soul. Let us see these in the man first, and then observe how they appear in his poetry; and why they cannot enter into it more freely and inspire it with more strength, render it more abundant.

We will begin with his acquirements. 'Mr Gray was', writes his friend Temple, 'perhaps the most learned man in Europe. He knew every branch of history both natural and civil; had read all the original historians of England, France, and Italy; and was a great antiquarian. Criticism, metaphysics, morals, politics, made a principal part of his study. Voyages and travels of all sorts were his favourite amusements; and he had a fine taste in painting, prints, architecture, and gardening.' The notes in his interleaved copy of Linnaeus remained to show the extent and accuracy of his knowledge in the natural sciences, particularly in botany, zoology, and entomology. Entomologists testified that his account of English insects was more perfect than any that had then appeared. His notes and papers, of which some have been published, others remain still in manuscript, give evidence, besides, of his knowledge of literature ancient and modern, geography and topography, painting, architecture and antiquities, and of his curious researches in heraldry. He was an excellent musician. Sir James Mackintosh reminds us, moreover, that to all the other accomplishments and merits of Gray we are to add this: 'That he was the first discoverer of the beauties of nature in England, and has marked out the course of every picturesque journey that can be made in it.'

Acquirements take all their value and character from the power of the individual storing them. Let us take, from amongst Gray's observations on what he read, enough to show us his power. Here are criticisms on three very different authors, criticisms without any study or pretension, but just thrown out in chance letters to his friends. First, on Aristotle:

In the first place he is the hardest author by far I ever meddled with. Then he has a dry conciseness that makes one imagine one is perusing a table of contents rather than a book; it tastes for all the world like chopped hay, or rather like chopped logic; for he has a violent affection to that art, being in some sort his own invention; so that he often loses himself in little trifling distinctions and verbal niceties, and what is worse, leaves you to extricate yourself as you can. Thirdly, he has suffered vastly by his transcribers, as all authors of great brevity necessarily must. Fourthly and lastly, he has abundance of fine, uncommon things, which make him well worth the pains he gives one. You see what you have to expect.

Next, on Isocrates:

It would be strange if I should find fault with you for reading Isocrates; I did so myself twenty years ago, and in an edition at least as bad as yours. The Panegyric, the De Pace, Areopagitic, and Advice to Philip, are by far the noblest remains we have of this writer, and equal to most things extant in the Greek tongue; but it depends on your judgment to distinguish between his real and occasional opinion of things, as he directly contradicts in one place what he has advanced in another; for example, in the Panathenaic and the De Pace, on the naval power of Athens; the latter of the two is undoubtedly his own undisguised sentiment.

After hearing Gray on Isocrates and Aristotle, let us hear him on Froissart:

> I rejoice you have met with Froissart, he is the Herodotus of a barbarous age; had he but had the luck of writing in as good a language, he might have been immortal. His locomotive disposition (for then there was no other way of learning things), his simple curiosity, his religious credulity, were much like those of the old Grecian. When you have *tant chevauché* as to get to the end of him, there Monstrelet waits to take you up, and will set you down at Philip de Commines; but previous to all these, you should have read Villehardouin and Joinville.

Those judgments, with their true and clear ring, evince the high quality of Gray's mind, his power to command and use his learning. But Gray was a poet; let us hear him on a poet, on Shakespeare. We must place ourselves in the full midst of the eighteenth century and of its criticism; Gray's friend, West, had praised Racine for using in his dramas 'the language of the times and that of the purest sort'; and he had added: 'I will not decide what style is fit for our English stage, but I should rather choose one that bordered upon Cato, than upon Shakespeare.' Gray replies:

> As to matter of style, I have this to say: The language of the age is never the language of poetry; except among the French, whose verse, where the thought does not support it, differs in nothing from prose. Our poetry, on the contrary, has a language peculiar to itself, to which almost everyone that has written has added something. In truth, Shakespeare's language is one of his principal beauties; and he has no less advantage over your Addisons and Rowes in this, than in those other great excellences you mention. Every word in him is a picture. Pray put me the following lines into the tongue of our modern dramatics—
>
>> But I, that am not shaped for sportive tricks,
>> Nor made to court an amorous looking-glass—

and what follows? To me they appear untranslatable; and if this be the case, our language is greatly degenerated.

It is impossible for a poet to lay down the rules of his own art with more insight, soundness, and certainty. Yet at that moment in England there was perhaps not one other man, besides Gray, capable of writing the passage just quoted.

Gray's quality of mind, then, we see; his quality of soul will no less bear inspection. His reserve, his delicacy, his distaste for many of the persons and things surrounding him in the Cambridge of that day,—'this silly, dirty place', as he calls it,—have produced an impression of Gray as being a man falsely fastidious, finical, effeminate. But we have already had that grave testimony to him from the Master of Pembroke Hall: 'The thoughts I have of him will last, and will be useful to me the few years I can expect to live.' And here is another to the same effect from a younger man, from Gray's friend Nicholls:

You know [he writes to his mother, from abroad, when he heard of Gray's death] that I considered Mr Gray as a second parent, that I thought only of him, built all my happiness on him, talked of him for ever, wished him with me whenever I partook of any pleasure, and flew to him for refuge whenever I felt any uneasiness. To whom now shall I talk of all I have seen here? Who will teach me to read, to think, to feel? I protest to you, that whatever I did or thought had a reference to him. If I met with any chagrins, I comforted myself that I had a treasure at home; if all the world had despised and hated me, I should have thought myself perfectly recompensed in his friendship. There remains only one loss more; if I lose you, I am left alone in the world. At present I feel that I have lost half of myself.

Testimonies such as these are not called forth by a fastidious effeminate weakling; they are not called forth, even, by mere qualities of mind; they are called forth by qualities of soul. And of Gray's high qualities of soul, of his σπουδαιότης, his excellent seriousness, we may gather abundant proof from his letters. Writing to Mason, who had just lost his father, he says:

I have seen the scene you describe, and know how dreadful it is; I know too I am the better for it. We are all idle and thoughtless things, and have no sense, no use in the world any longer than that sad impression lasts; the deeper it is engraved the better.

And again, on a like occasion to another friend:

He who best knows our nature (for he made us what we are) by such afflictions recalls us from our wandering thoughts and idle merriment, from the insolence of youth and prosperity, to serious reflection, to our duty, and to himself; nor need we hasten to get rid of these impressions. Time (by appointment of the same Power) will cure the smart and in some hearts soon blot out all the traces of sorrow; but such as preserve them longest (for it is partly left in our own power) do perhaps best acquiesce in the will of the chastiser.

And once more to Mason, in the very hour of his wife's death; Gray was not sure whether or not his letter would reach Mason before the end:

If the worst be not yet past, you will neglect and pardon me; but if the last struggle be over, if the poor object of your long anxieties be no longer sensible to your kindness or to her own sufferings, allow me, at least an idea (for what could I do, were I present, more than this?) to sit by you in silence and pity from her heart not her, who is at rest, but you, who lose her. May he, who made us, the Master of our pleasures and of our pains, support you! Adieu.

Seriousness, character, was the foundation of things with him; where this was lacking he was always severe, whatever might be offered to him in its stead. Voltaire's literary genius charmed him, but the faults of Voltaire's nature he felt so strongly that when his young friend Nicholls was going abroad in 1771, just before Gray's death, he said to him: 'I have one thing to beg of you which you must not refuse.' Nicholls answered: 'You know you have only to command; what is it?'—'Do not go to see Voltaire,' said Gray; and then added: 'No one knows the mischief that man will do.' Nicholls promised compliance with Gray's injunction; 'But what', he asked, 'could a visit from me signify?'—'Every tribute to such a man signifies,' Gray answered. He admired Dryden, admired him, even, too much; had too much felt his influence as a poet. He told Beattie 'that if there was any excellence in his own numbers he had learned it wholly from that great poet'; and writing to Beattie afterwards he recurs to Dryden, whom Beattie, he thought, did not honour enough as a poet: 'Remember Dryden,' he writes, 'and be blind to all his faults.' Yes, his faults as a poet; but on the man Dryden, nevertheless, his sentence is stern. Speaking of the Poet-Laureateship, 'Dryden', he writes to Mason, 'was as disgraceful to the office from his character, as the poorest scribbler could have been from his verses.' Even where crying blemishes were absent, the want of weight and depth of character in a man deprived him, in Gray's judgment, of serious significance. He says of Hume: 'Is not the *naïveté* and good-humour, which his admirers celebrate in him, owing to this, that he has continued all his days an infant, but one that has unhappily been taught to read and write?'

And with altl his strenuous seriousness, a pathetic sentiment, and an element, likewise, of sportive and charming humour. At Keswick, by the lakeside on an autumn evening, he has the accent of the *Rêveries*, or of Obermann, or Wordsworth:

> In the evening walked down alone to the lake by the side of Crow Park after sunset and saw the solemn colouring of light draw on, the last gleam of sunshine fading away on the hill-tops, the deep serene of the waters, and the long shadows of the mountains thrown across them, till they nearly touched the hithermost shore. At distance heard the murmur of many waterfalls, not audible in the daytime. Wished for the Moon, but she was *dark to me and silent, hid in her vacant interlunar cave.*

Of his humour and sportiveness his delightful letters are full; his humour appears in his poetry too, and is by no means to be passed over there. Horace Walpole said that 'Gray never wrote anything easily but things of humour; humour was his natural and original turn.'

Knowledge, penetration, seriousness, sentiment, humour, Gray had them all; he had the equipment and endowment for the office of poet. But very soon in his life appear traces of something obstructing, something disabling; of spirits failing, and health not sound; and the evil increases with years. He writes to West in 1737:

> Low spirits are my true and faithful companions; they get up with me, go to bed with me, make journeys and returns

as I do; nay, and pay visits and will even affect to be jocose and force a feeble laugh with me; but most commonly we sit alone together, and are the prettiest insipid company in the world.

The tone is playful, Gray was not yet twenty-one. 'Mine,' he tells West four or five years later, 'mine, you are to know, is a white Melancholy, or rather *Leucocholy*, for the most part; which, though it seldom laughs or dances, nor ever amounts to what one calls joy or pleasure, yet is a good easy sort of a state.' But, he adds in this same letter:

But there is another sort, black indeed, which I have now and then felt, that has something in it like Tertullian's rule of faith, *Credo quia impossibile est*; for it believes, nay, is sure of everything that is unlikely, so it be but frightful; and on the other hand excludes and shuts its eyes to the most possible hopes, and everything that is pleasurable; from this the Lord deliver us! for none but he and sunshiny weather can do it.

Six or seven years pass, and we find him writing to Wharton from Cambridge thus:

The spirit of laziness (the spirit of this place) begins to possess even me, that have so long declaimed against it. Yet has it not so prevailed, but that I feel that discontent with myself, that *ennui*, that ever accompanies it in its beginnings. Time will settle my conscience, time will reconcile my languid companion to me; we shall smoke, we shall tipple, we shall doze together, we shall have our little jokes, like other people, and our long stories. Brandy will finish what port began; and, a month after the time, you will see in some corner of a London *Evening Post*, 'Yesterday died the Rev. Mr John Gray, Senior-Fellow of Clare Hall, a facetious companion, and well-respected by all who knew him.'

The humorous advertisement ends, in the original letter, with a Hogarthian touch which I must not quote. Is it Leucocholy or is it Melancholy which predominates here? at any rate, this entry in his diary, six years later, is black enough:

Insomnia crebra, atque expergiscenti surdus quidam doloris sensus; frequens etiam in regione sterni oppressio, et cardialgia gravis, fere sempiterna.

And in 1757 he writes to Hurd:

> To be employed is to be happy. This principle of mine (and I am convinced of its truth) has, as usual, no influence on my practice. I am alone, and *ennuyé* to the last degree, yet do nothing. Indeed I have one excuse; my health (which you have so kindly inquired after) is not extraordinary. It is no great malady, but several little ones, that seem brewing no good to me.

From thence to the end his languor and depression, though still often relieved by occupation and travel, keep fatally gaining on him. At last the depression became constant, became mechanical. 'Travel I must,' he writes to Dr Wharton, 'or cease to exist. Till this year I hardly knew what *mechanical* low spirits were; but now I even tremble at an east wind.' Two months afterwards he died.

What wonder, that with this troublous cloud, throughout the whole term of his manhood, brooding over him and weighing him down, Gray, finely endowed though he was, richly stored with knowledge though he was, yet produced so little, found no full and sufficient utterance, '*never*', as the Master of Pembroke Hall said, '*spoke out*'. He knew well enough, himself, how it was with him.

'My *verve* is at best, you know' (he writes to Mason), 'of so delicate a constitution, and has such weak nerves, as not to stir out of its chamber above three days in a year.' And to Horace Walpole he says: 'As to what you say to me civilly, that I ought to write more, I will be candid, and avow to you, that till four-score and upward, whenever the humour takes me, I will write; because I like it, and because I like myself better when I do so. If I do not write much, it is because I cannot.' How simply said and how truly also! Fain would a man like Gray speak out if he could, he 'likes himself better' when he speaks out; if he does not speak out, 'it is because I cannot'.

Bonstetten, that mercurial Swiss who died in 1832 at the age of eighty-seven, having been younger and livelier from his six-tieth year to his eightieth than at any other time in his life, paid a visit in his early days to Cambridge, and saw much of Gray, to whom he attached himself with devotion. Gray, on his part, was charmed with his young friend; 'I never saw such a boy,' he writes; 'our breed is not made on this model.' Long afterwards Bonstetten published his reminiscences of Gray. 'I used to tell Gray', he says, 'about my life and my native country, but *his* life was a sealed book to me; he never would talk of himself, never would allow me to speak to him of his poetry. If I quoted lines of his to him, he kept silence like an obstinate child. I said to him sometimes: "Will you have the goodness to give me an answer?" But not a word issued from his lips.' *He never spoke out.* Bonstetten thinks that Gray's life was poisoned by an un-satisfied sensibility, was withered by his having never loved; by his days being passed in the dismal cloisters of Cambridge, in the company of a set of monastic book-worms, 'whose existence no honest woman ever came to cheer'. Sainte-Beuve, who was much attracted and interested by Gray, doubts whether Bonstetten's explanation of him is admissible; the secret of Gray's melancholy he finds rather in the sterility of his poetic talent, 'so distinguished, so rare, but so stinted'; in the poet's despair at his own unproductiveness.

But to explain Gray, we must do more than allege his sterility, as we must look further than to his reclusion at Cambridge. What caused his sterility? Was it his ill health, his hereditary gout? Certainly we will pay all respect to the powers of hereditary gout for afflicting us poor mortals. But Goethe, after pointing out that Schiller, who was so productive, was 'almost constantly ill', adds the true remark that it is incredible how much the spirit can do, in these cases, to keep up the body. Pope's anima-tion and activity through all the course of what he pathetically calls 'that long disease, my life', is an example presenting itself signally, in Gray's own country and time, to confirm what Goethe here says. What gave the power to Gray's reclusion and ill health to induce his sterility?

The reason, the indubitable reason as I cannot but think it, I have already given elsewhere. Gray, a born poet, fell upon an age of prose. He fell upon an age whose task was such as to call forth in general men's powers of understanding, wit, and clever-ness, rather than their deepest powers of mind and soul. As regards literary production, the task of the eighteenth century in England was not the poetic interpretation of the world, its task was to create a plain, clear, straightforward, efficient prose. Poetry obeyed the bent of mind requisite for the due fulfilment of this task of the century. It was intellectual, argumentative, ingenious; not seeing things in their truth and beauty, not interpretative. Gray, with the qualities of mind and soul of a genuine poet, was isolated in his century. Maintaining and fortifying them by lofty studies, he yet could not fully educe and enjoy them; the want of a genial atmosphere, the failure of sympathy in his contemporaries, were too great. Born in the same year with Milton, Gray would have been another man; born in the same year with Burns, he would have been another man. A man born in 1608 could profit by the larger and more poetic scope of the English spirit in the Elizabethan age; a man born in 1759 could profit by that European renewing of men's minds of which the great historical manifestation is the French Revolution. Gray's alert and brilliant young friend, Bonstetten, who would explain the void in the life of Gray by his having never loved, Bonstetten himself loved, married, and had children. Yet at the age of fifty he was bidding fair to grow old, dismal, and torpid like the rest of us, when he was roused and made young again for some thirty years, says M. Sainte-Beuve, by the events of 1789. If Gray, like Burns, had been just thirty years old when the French Revolution broke out, he would have shown, probably, productiveness and animation in plenty. Coming when he did, and endowed as he was, he was a man born out of date, a man whose full spiritual flowering was impossible. The same thing is to be said of his great contemporary, Butler, the author of the *Analogy*. In the sphere of religion, which touches that of poetry, Butler was impelled by the endowment of his nature to strive for a profound and adequate conception of religious things, which was not pursued by his contemporaries, and which at that time, and in that atmosphere of mind, was not fully attainable. Hence, in Butler too, a dissatisfaction, a weariness, as in Gray; 'great labour and weariness, great disappointment, pain and even vexation of mind'. A sort of spiritual east wind was at that time blowing; neither Butler nor Gray could flower. They *never spoke out*.

Gray's poetry was not only stinted in quantity by reason of the age wherein he lived, it suffered somewhat in quality also. We have seen under what obligation to Dryden Gray professed himself to be—'if there was any excellence in his numbers, he had learned it wholly from that great poet'. It was not for nothing that he came when Dryden had lately 'embellished', as Johnson says, English poetry; had 'found it brick and left it marble'. It was not for nothing that he came just when 'the English ear', to quote Johnson again, 'had been accustomed to the mellifluence of Pope's numbers, and the diction of poetry had grown more splendid'. Of the intellectualities, ingenuities, personifications, of the movement and diction of Dryden and Pope, Gray caught something, caught too much. We have little of Gray's poetry, and that little is not free from the faults of his age. Therefore it was important to go for aid, as we did, to Gray's life and letters, to see his mind and soul there, and to corroborate from thence that high estimate of his quality which his poetry indeed calls forth, but does not establish so amply and irresistibly as one could desire.

For a just criticism it does, however, clearly establish it. The difference between genuine poetry and the poetry of Dryden, Pope, and all their school, is briefly this: their poetry is conceived and composed in their wits, genuine poetry is conceived and composed in the soul. The difference between the two kinds of poetry is immense. They differ profoundly in their modes of language, they differ profoundly in their modes of evolution. The poetic language of our eighteenth century in general is the language of men composing *without their eye on the object*, as Wordsworth excellently said of Dryden; language merely recalling the object, as the common language of prose does, and then dressing it out with a certain smartness and brilliancy for the fancy and understanding. This is called 'splendid diction'. The evolution of the poetry of our eighteenth century is likewise intellectual; it proceeds by ratiocination, antithesis, ingenious turns and conceits. This poetry is often eloquent, and always, in the hands of such masters as Dryden and Pope, clever; but it does not take us much below the surface of things, it does not give us the emotion of seeing things in their truth and beauty. The language of genuine poetry, on the other hand, is the language of one composing with his eye on the object; its evolution is that of a thing which has been plunged in the poet's soul until it comes forth naturally and necessarily. This sort of evolution is infinitely simpler than the other, and infinitely more satisfying; the same thing is true of the genuine poetic language likewise. But they are both of them also infinitely harder of attainment; they come only from those who, as Emerson says, 'live from a great depth of being'.

Goldsmith disparaged Gray who had praised his *Traveller*, and indeed in the poem on the *Alliance of Education and Government* had given him hints which he used for it. In retaliation let us take from Goldsmith himself a specimen of the poetic language of the eighteenth century—

> No cheerful murmurs fluctuate in the gale—

there is exactly the poetic diction of our prose century! rhetorical, ornate,—and, poetically, quite false. Place beside it a line of genuine poetry, such as the

> In cradle of the rude, imperious surge

of Shakespeare; and all its falseness instantly becomes apparent.

Dryden's poem on the death of Mrs Killigrew is, says Johnson, 'undoubtedly the noblest ode that our language ever has produced'. In this vigorous performance Dryden has to say, what is interesting enough, that not only in poetry did Mrs Killigrew excel, but she excelled in painting also. And thus he says it—

> To the next realm she stretch'd her sway,
> For Painture near adjoining lay—
> A plenteous province and alluring prey.
> A Chamber of Dependencies was framed
> (As conquerors will never want pretence
> When arm'd, to justify the offence),
> And the whole fief, in right of Poetry, she claim'd.

The intellectual, ingenious, superficial evolution of poetry of this school could not be better illustrated. Place beside it Pindar's

> αἰὼν ἀσφαλὴς
> οὐκ ἔγεντ' οὔτ' Αἰακίδα παρὰ Πηλεῖ,
> οὔτε παρ' ἀντιθέῳ Κάδμῳ . . .

A secure time fell to the lot neither of Peleus the son of Aeacus, nor of the godlike Cadmus; howbeit these are said to have had, of all mortals, the supreme of happiness, who heard the golden-snooded Muses sing,—on the mountain the one heard them, the other in seven-gated Thebes.

There is the evolution of genuine poetry, and such poetry kills Dryden's the moment it is put near it.

Gray's production was scanty, and scanty, as we have seen,

it could not but be. Even what he produced is not always pure in diction, true in evolution. Still, with whatever drawbacks, he is alone, or almost alone (for Collins has something of the like merit) in his age. Gray said himself that 'the style he aimed at was extreme conciseness of expression, yet pure, perspicuous, and musical'. Compared, not with the work of the masters of the golden ages of poetry, but with the poetry of his own contemporaries in general, Gray's may be said to have reached, in style, the excellence at which he aimed; while the evolution also of such a piece as his *Progress of Poesy* must be accounted not less noble and sound than its style.

IV

JOHN KEATS

POETRY, according to Milton's famous saying, should be 'simple, sensuous, impassioned'. No one can question the eminency, in Keats's poetry, of the quality of sensuousness. Keats as a poet is abundantly and enchantingly sensuous; the question, with some people, will be whether he is anything else. Many things may be brought forward which seem to show him as under the fascination and sole dominion of sense, and desiring nothing better. There is the exclamation in one of his letters: 'O for a life of sensations rather than of thoughts!' There is the thesis, in another, 'that with a great Poet the sense of Beauty overcomes every other consideration, or rather obliterates all consideration'. There is Haydon's story of him, how 'he once covered his tongue and throat as far as he could reach with cayenne pepper, in order to appreciate the delicious coldness of claret in all its glory—his own expression'. One is not much surprised when Haydon further tells us, of the hero of such a story, that once for six weeks together he was hardly ever sober. 'He had no decision of character,' Haydon adds; 'no object upon which to direct his great powers.'

Character and self-control, the *virtus verusque labor* so necessary for every kind of greatness, and for the great artist, too, indispensable, appear to be wanting, certainly, to this Keats of Haydon's portraiture. They are wanting also to the Keats of the *Letters to Fanny Brawne*. These letters make as unpleasing an impression as Haydon's anecdotes. The editor of Haydon's journals could not well omit what Haydon said of his friend, but for the publication of the *Letters to Fanny Brawne* I can see no good reason whatever. Their publication appears to me, I confess, inexcusable; they ought never to have been published. But published they are, and we have to take notice of them. Letters written when Keats was near his end, under the throttling and unmanning grasp of mortal disease, we will not judge. But here is a letter written some months before he was taken ill. It is printed just as Keats wrote it:

> You have absorb'd me. I have a sensation at the present moment as though I was dissolving—I should be exquisitely miserable without the hope of soon seeing you. I should be afraid to separate myself far from you. My sweet Fanny, will your heart never change? My love, will it? I have no limit now to my love. . . . Your note came in just here. I cannot be happier away from you. 'Tis richer than an Argosy of Pearles. Do not threat me even in jest. I have been astonished that Men could die Martyrs for religion—I have shuddered at it. I shudder no more—I could be martyred for my Religion— Love is my religion—I could die for that. I could die for you. My Creed is Love and you are its only tenet. You have ravished me away by a Power I cannot resist; and yet I could resist till I saw you; and even since I have seen you I have endeavoured often 'to reason against the reasons of my Love '. I can do that no more—the pain would be too great. My love is selfish. I cannot breathe without you.

A man who writes love-letters in this strain is probably pre-destined, one may observe, to misfortune in his love-affairs; but that is nothing. The complete enervation of the writer is the real point for remark. We have the tone, or rather the entire want of tone, the abandonment of all reticence and all dignity, of the merely sensuous man, of the man who 'is passion's slave'. Nay, we have them in suchwise that one is tempted to speak even as *Blackwood* or the *Quarterly* were in the old days wont to speak; one is tempted to say that Keats's love-letter is the love-letter of a surgeon's apprentice. It has in its relaxed self-abandonment something underbred and ignoble, as of a youth ill brought up, without the training which teaches us that we must put some constraint upon our feelings and upon the expression of them. It is the sort of love-letter of a surgeon's apprentice which one might hear read out in a breach of promise case, or in the Divorce Court. The sensuous man speaks in it, and the sensuous man of a badly bred and badly trained sort. That many who are themselves also badly bred and badly trained should enjoy it, and should even think it a beautiful and charac-teristic production of him whom they call their 'lovely and beloved Keats', does not make it better. These are the admirers whose pawing and fondness do not good but harm to the fame of Keats; who concentrate attention upon what in him is least wholesome and most questionable; who worship him, and would have the world worship him too, as the poet of

> Light feet, dark violet eyes, and parted hair,
> Soft dimpled hands, white neck, and creamy breast.

This sensuous strain Keats had, and a man of his poetic powers could not, whatever his strain, but show his talent in it. But he has something more, and something better. We who believe Keats to have been by his promise, at any rate, if not fully by his performance, one of the very greatest of English poets, and who believe also that a merely sensuous man cannot either by promise or by performance be a very great poet, because poetry interprets life, and so large and noble a part of life is outside of such a man's ken,—we cannot but look for signs in him of something more than sensuousness, for signs of character and virtue. And indeed the elements of high character Keats undoubtedly has, and the effort to develop them; the effort is frustrated and cut short by misfortune, and disease, and time, but for the due understanding of Keats's worth the recognition of this effort, and of the elements on which it worked, is necessary.

Lord Houghton, who praises very discriminatingly the poetry of Keats, has on his character also a remark full of discrimination. He says: 'The faults of Keats's disposition were precisely the contrary of those attributed to him by common opinion.' And he gives a letter written after the death of Keats by his brother George, in which the writer, speaking of the fantastic *Johnny Keats* invented for common opinion by Lord Byron and by the reviewers, declares indignantly: 'John was the very soul of manliness and courage, and as much like the Holy Ghost as *Johnny Keats*.' It is important to note this testimony, and to look well for whatever illustrates and confirms it.

Great weight is laid by Lord Houghton on such a direct profession of faith as the following: 'That sort of probity and disinterestedness', Keats writes to his brothers, 'which such men as Bailey possess, does hold and grasp the tip-top of any spiritual honours that can be paid to anything in this world.' Lord Houghton says that 'never have words more effectively expressed the conviction of the superiority of virtue above beauty than those'. But merely to make a profession of faith of the kind here made by Keats is not difficult; what we should rather look for is some evidence of the instinct for character, for virtue, passing into the man's life, passing into his work.

Signs of virtue, in the true and large sense of the word, the instinct for virtue passing into the life of Keats and strengthening it, I find in the admirable wisdom and temper of what he says to his friend Bailey on the occasion of a quarrel between Reynolds and Haydon:

> Things have happened lately of great perplexity; you must have heard of them; Reynolds and Haydon retorting and recriminating, and parting for ever. The same thing has happened between Haydon and Hunt. It is unfortunate; men should bear with each other; there lives not the man who may not be cut up, aye, lashed to pieces, on his weakest side. The best of men have but a portion of good in them. . . . The sure way, Bailey, is first to know a man's faults, and then be passive. If, after that, he insensibly draws you towards him, then you have no power to break the link. Before I felt interested in either Reynolds or Haydon, I was well read in their faults; yet, knowing them, I have been cementing gradually with both. I have an affection for them both, for reasons almost opposite; and to both must I of necessity cling, supported always by the hope that when a little time, a few years, shall have tried me more fully in their esteem, I may be able to bring them together.

Butler has well said that 'endeavouring to enforce upon our own minds a practical sense of virtue, or to beget in others that practical sense of it which a man really has himself, is a virtuous *act*'. And such an 'endeavouring' is that of Keats in those words written to Bailey. It is more than mere words; so justly thought and so discreetly urged as it is, it rises to the height of a virtuous *act*. It is proof of character.

The same thing may be said of some words written to his friend Charles Brown, whose kindness, willingly exerted whenever Keats chose to avail himself of it, seemed to free him from any pressing necessity of earning his own living. Keats felt that he must not allow this state of things to continue. He

determined to set himself to 'fag on as others do' at periodical
literature, rather than to endanger his independence and his
self-respect; and he writes to Brown:

> I had got into a habit of mind of looking towards you as a
> help in all difficulties. This very habit would be the parent
> of idleness and difficulties. You will see it is a duty I owe to
> myself to break the neck of it. I do nothing for my subsistence
> —make no exertion. At the end of another year you shall
> applaud me, not for verses, but for conduct.

He had not, alas, another year of health before him when he
announced that wholesome resolve; it then wanted but six
months of the day of his fatal attack. But in the brief time allowed
to him he did what he could to keep his word.

What character, again, what strength and clearness of judgment, in his criticism of his own productions, of the public, and
of 'the literary circles'! His words after the severe reviews of
Endymion have often been quoted; they cannot be quoted too
often:

> Praise or blame has but a momentary effect on the man whose
> love of beauty in the abstract makes him a severe critic of his
> own works. My own criticism has given me pain without com-
> parison beyond what *Blackwood* or the *Quarterly* could possibly
> inflict; and also, when I feel I am right, no external praise can
> give me such a glow as my own solitary reperception and rati-
> fication of what is fine. J. S. is perfectly right in regard to the
> 'slip-shod Endymion'. That it is so is no fault of mine. No!
> though it may sound a little paradoxical, it is as good as I had
> power to make it by myself.

And again, as if he had foreseen certain of his admirers gushing over him, and was resolved to disengage his responsibility:

> I have done nothing, except for the amusement of a few
> people who refine upon their feelings till anything in the un-
> understandable way will go down with them. I have no cause
> to complain, because I am certain anything really fine will in
> these days be felt. I have no doubt that if I had written *Othello*
> I should have been cheered. I shall go on with patience.

Young poets almost inevitably overrate what they call 'the

might of poesy', and its power over the world which now is.
Keats is not a dupe on this matter any more than he is a dupe
about the merit of his own performances:

> I have no trust whatever in poetry. I don't wonder at it;
> the marvel is to me how people read so much of it.

His attitude towards the public is that of a strong man, not of
a weakling avid of praise, and made to 'be snuff'd out by an
article':

> I shall ever consider the public as debtors to me for verses,
> not myself to them for admiration, which I can do without.

And again, in a passage where one may perhaps find fault with
the capital letters, but surely with nothing else:

> I have not the slightest feel of humility towards the public
> or to anything in existence but the Eternal Being, the Principle
> of Beauty, and the Memory of great Men. . . . I would be sub-
> dued before my friends, and thank them for subduing me;
> but among multitudes of men I have no feel of stooping; I
> hate the idea of humility to them. I never wrote one single
> line of poetry with the least shadow of thought about their
> opinion. Forgive me for vexing you, but it eases me to tell
> you: I could not live without the love of my friends; I would
> jump down Etna for any great public good—but I hate a
> mawkish popularity. I cannot be subdued before them. My
> glory would be to daunt and dazzle the thousand jabberers
> about pictures and books.

Against these artistic and literary 'jabberers', amongst whom
Byron fancied Keats, probably, to be always living, flattering
them and flattered by them, he has yet another outburst:

> Just so much as I am humbled by the genius above my
> grasp, am I exalted and look with hate and contempt upon the
> literary world. Who could wish to be among the common-
> place crowd of the little famous, who are each individually
> lost in a throng made up of themselves?

And he loves Fanny Brawne the more, he tells her, because
he believes that she has liked him for his own sake and for nothing
else. 'I have met with women who I really think would like to
be married to a Poem and to be given away by a Novel.'

There is a tone of too much bitterness and defiance in all this, a tone which he with great propriety subdued and corrected when he wrote his beautiful preface to *Endymion*. But the thing to be seized is, that Keats had flint and iron in him, that he had character; that he was, as his brother George says, 'as much like the Holy Ghost as *Johnny Keats*',—as that imagined sensuous weakling, the delight of the literary circles of Hampstead.

It is a pity that Byron, who so misconceived Keats, should never have known how shrewdly Keats, on the other hand, had characterized *him* as 'a fine thing' in the sphere of 'the worldly theatrical, and pantomimical'. But indeed nothing is more remarkable in Keats than his clear-sightedness, his lucidity; and lucidity is in itself akin to character and to high and severe work. In spite, therefore, of his overpowering feeling for beauty, in spite of his sensuousness, in spite of his facility, in spite of his gift of expression, Keats could say resolutely:

> I know nothing, I have read nothing; and I mean to follow Solomon's directions: 'Get learning, get understanding.' There is but one way for me. The road lies through application, study, and thought. I will pursue it.

And of Milton, instead of resting in Milton's incomparable phrases, Keats could say, although indeed all the while 'looking upon fine phrases', as he himself tells us, 'like a lover'—

> Milton had an exquisite passion for what is properly, in the sense of ease and pleasure, poetical luxury; and with that, it appears to me, he would fain have been content, if he could, so doing, preserve his self-respect, and feeling of duty performed; but there was working in him, as it were, that same sort of thing which operates in the great world to the end of a prophecy's being accomplished. Therefore he devoted himself rather to the ardours than the pleasures of song, solacing himself at intervals with cups of old wine.

In his own poetry, too, Keats felt that place must be found for 'the ardours rather than the pleasures of song', although he was aware that he was not yet ripe for it—

> But my flag is not unfurl'd
> On the Admiral-staff, and to philosophise
> I dare not yet.

Even in his pursuit of 'the pleasures of song', however, there is that stamp of high work which is akin to character, which is character passing into intellectual production. *'The best sort of poetry*—that', he truly says, 'is all I care for, all I live for.' It is curious to observe how this severe addiction of his to the best sort of poetry affects him with a certain coldness, as if the addiction had been to mathematics, towards those prime objects of a sensuous and passionate poet's regard, love and women. He speaks of 'the opinion I have formed of the generality of women, who appear to me as children to whom I would rather give a sugar-plum than my time'. He confesses 'a tendency to class women in my books with roses and sweetmeats—they never see themselves dominant'; and he can understand how the unpopularity of his poems may be in part due to 'the offence which the ladies', not unnaturally, 'take at him' from this cause. Even to Fanny Brawne he can write 'a flint-worded letter' when his 'mind is heaped to the full' with poetry:

> I know the generality of women would hate me for this; that I should have so unsoftened, so hard a mind as to forget them; forget the brightest realities for the dull imaginations of my own brain. . . . My heart seems now made of iron— I could not write a proper answer to an invitation to Idalia.

The truth is that 'the yearning passion for the Beautiful', which was with Keats, as he himself truly says, the master-passion, is not a passion of the sensuous or sentimental man, is not a passion of the sensuous or sentimental poet. It is an intellectual and spiritual passion. It is 'connected and made one', as Keats declares that in his case it was, 'with the ambition of the intellect'. It is, as he again says, 'the mighty *abstract idea* of Beauty in all things'. And in his last days Keats wrote: 'If I should die, I have left no immortal work behind me—nothing to make my friends proud of my memory; *but I have loved the principle of beauty in all things,* and if I had had time I would have made myself remembered.' He *has* made himself remembered, and remembered as no merely sensuous poet could be; and he has done it by having 'loved the principle of beauty in all things'.

For to see things in their beauty is to see things in their truth, and Keats knew it. 'What the Imagination seizes as Beauty must be Truth,' he says in prose; and in immortal verse he has said the same thing—

> Beauty is truth, truth beauty,—that is all
> Ye know on earth, and all ye need to know.

No, it is not all; but it is true, deeply true, and we have deep need to know it. And with beauty goes not only truth, joy goes with her also; and this too Keats saw and said, as in the famous first line of his *Endymion* it stands written—

> A thing of beauty is a joy for ever.

It is no small thing to have so loved the principle of beauty as to perceive the necessary relation of beauty with truth, and of both with joy. Keats was a great spirit, and counts for far more than many even of his admirers suppose, because this just and high perception made itself clear to him. Therefore a dignity and a glory shed gleams over his life, and happiness, too, was not a stranger to it. 'Nothing startles me beyond the moment,' he says; 'the setting sun will always set me to rights, or if a sparrow come before my window I take part in its existence and pick about the gravel.' But he had terrible bafflers—consuming disease and early death. 'I think', he writes to Reynolds, 'if I had a free and healthy and lasting organization of heart, and lungs as strong as an ox's, so as to be able to bear unhurt the shock of extreme thought and sensation without weariness, I could pass my life very nearly alone, though it should last eighty years. But I feel my body too weak to support me to the height; I am obliged continually to check myself, and be nothing.' He had against him even more than this; he had against him the blind power which we call Fortune. 'O that something fortunate', he cries in the closing months of his life, 'had ever happened to me or my brothers!—then I might hope,—but despair is forced upon me as a habit.' So baffled and so sorely tried,—while laden, at the same time, with a mighty formative thought requiring health, and many days, and favouring circumstances, for its adequate manifestation,—what wonder if the achievement of Keats be partial and incomplete?

Nevertheless, let and hindered as he was, and with a short term and imperfect experience,—'young', as he says of himself, 'and writing at random, straining after particles of light in the midst of a great darkness, without knowing the bearing of any one assertion, of any one opinion',—notwithstanding all this, by virtue of his feeling for beauty and of his perception of the vital connection of beauty with truth, Keats accomplished so much in poetry, that in one of the two great modes by which poetry interprets, in the faculty of naturalistic interpretation, in what we call natural magic, he ranks with Shakespeare. 'The tongue of Kean,' he says in an admirable criticism of that great actor and of his enchanting elocution, 'the tongue of Kean must seem to have robbed the Hybla bees and left them honeyless. There is an indescribable *gusto* in his voice;—in *Richard*, "Be stirring with the lark to-morrow, gentle Norfolk!" comes from him as through the morning atmosphere towards which he yearns.' This magic, this 'indescribable *gusto* in the voice', Keats himself, too, exhibits in his poetic expression. No one else in English poetry, save Shakespeare, has in expression quite the fascinating felicity of Keats, his perfection of loveliness. 'I think', he said humbly, 'I shall be among the English poets after my death.' He is; he is with Shakespeare.

For the second great half of poetic interpretation, for that faculty of moral interpretation which is in Shakespeare, and is informed by him with the same power of beauty as his naturalistic interpretation, Keats was not ripe. For the architectonics of poetry, the faculty which presides at the evolution of works like the *Agamemnon* or *Lear*, he was not ripe. His *Endymion*, as he himself well saw, is a failure, and his *Hyperion*, fine things as it contains, is not a success. But in shorter things, where the matured power of moral interpretation, and the high architectonics which go with complete poetic development, are not required, he is perfect. The poems which follow prove it,— prove it far better by themselves than anything which can be said about them will prove it. Therefore I have chiefly spoken here of the man, and of the elements in him which explain the production of such work. Shakespearian work it is; not imitative, indeed, of Shakespeare, but Shakespearian, because its expression has that rounded perfection and felicity of loveliness of which Shakespeare is the great master. To show such work is to praise it. Let us now end by delighting ourselves with a fragment of it, too broken to find a place among the pieces which follow,

but far too beautiful to be lost. It is a fragment of an ode for
May-day. O might I, he cries to May, O might I

> . . . thy smiles
> Seek as they once were sought, in Grecian isles,
> By bards who died content on pleasant sward,
> Leaving great verse unto a little clan!
> O, give me their old vigour, and unheard
> Save of the quiet primrose, and the span
>   Of heaven, and few ears,
> Rounded by thee, my song should die away,
>   Content as theirs,
> Rich in the simple worship of a day!

V

WORDSWORTH

I REMEMBER hearing Lord Macaulay say, after Wordsworth's death, when subscriptions were being collected to found a memorial of him, that ten years earlier more money could have been raised in Cambridge alone, to do honour to Wordsworth, than was now raised all through the country. Lord Macaulay, had, as we know, his own heightened and telling way of putting things, and we must always make allowance for it. But probably it is true that Wordsworth has never, either before or since, been so accepted and popular, so established in possession of the minds of all who profess to care for poetry, as he was between the years 1830 and 1840, and at Cambridge. From the very first, no doubt, he had his believers and witnesses. But I myself heard him declare that, for he knew not how many years, his poetry had never brought him in enough to buy his shoe-strings. The poetry-reading public was very slow to recognize him, and was very easily drawn away from him. Scott effaced him with this public, Byron effaced him.

The death of Byron, seemed, however, to make an opening for Wordsworth. Scott, who had for some time ceased to produce poetry himself, and stood before the public as a great novelist; Scott, too genuine himself not to feel the profound genuineness of Wordsworth, and with an instinctive recognition of his firm hold on nature and of his local truth, always admired him sincerely, and praised him generously. The influence of Coleridge upon young men of ability was then powerful, and was still gathering strength; this influence told entirely in favour of Wordsworth's poetry. Cambridge was a place where Coleridge's influence had great action, and where Wordsworth's poetry, therefore, flourished especially. But even amongst the general public its sale grew large, the eminence of its author was widely recognized, and Rydal Mount became an object of pilgrimage.

I remember Wordsworth relating how one of the pilgrims, a clergyman, asked him if he had ever written anything besides the *Guide to the Lakes*. Yes, he answered modestly, he had written verses. Not every pilgrim was a reader, but the vogue was established, and the stream of pilgrims came.

Mr Tennyson's decisive appearance dates from 1842. One cannot say that he effaced Wordsworth as Scott and Byron had effaced him. The poetry of Wordsworth had been so long before the public, the suffrage of good judges was so steady and so strong in its favour, that by 1842 the verdict of posterity, one may almost say, had been already pronounced, and Wordsworth's English fame was secure. But the vogue, the ear and applause of the great body of poetry-readers, never quite thoroughly perhaps his, he gradually lost more and more, and Mr Tennyson gained them. Mr Tennyson drew to himself, and away from Wordsworth, the poetry-reading public, and the new generations. Even in 1850, when Wordsworth died, this diminution of popularity was visible, and occasioned the remark of Lord Macaulay which I quote at starting.

The diminution has continued. The influence of Coleridge has waned, and Wordsworth's poetry can no longer draw succour from this ally. The poetry has not, however, wanted eulogists; and it may be said to have brought its eulogists luck, for almost everyone who has praised Wordsworth's poetry has praised it well. But the public has remained cold, or, at least, undetermined. Even the abundance of Mr Palgrave's fine and skilfully chosen specimens of Wordsworth, in the *Golden Treasury*, surprised many readers, and gave offence to not a few. To tenth-rate critics and compilers, for whom any violent shock to the public taste would be a temerity not to be risked, it is still quite permissible to speak of Wordsworth's poetry, not only with ignorance, but with impertinence. On the Continent he is almost unknown.

I cannot think, then, that Wordsworth has, up to this time, at all obtained his deserts. 'Glory,' said M. Renan the other day, 'glory after all is the thing which has the best chance of not being altogether vanity.' Wordsworth was a homely man, and himself would certainly never have thought of talking of glory as that which, after all, has the best chance of not being altogether vanity. Yet we may well allow that few things are less vain than *real* glory. Let us conceive of the whole group of civilized nations as being, for intellectual and spiritual purposes, one great confederation, bound to a joint action and working towards a common result; a confederation whose members have a due knowledge both of the past, out of which they all proceed, and of one another. This was the ideal of Goethe, and it is an ideal which will impose itself upon the thoughts of our modern societies more and more. Then to be recognized by the verdict of such a confederation as a master, or even as a seriously and eminently worthy workman, in one's own line of intellectual or spiritual activity, is indeed glory; a glory which it would be difficult to rate too highly. For what could be more beneficent, more salutary? The world is forwarded by having its attention fixed on the best things; and here is a tribunal, free from all suspicion of national and provincial partiality, putting a stamp on the best things, and recommending them for general honour and acceptance. A nation, again, is furthered by recognition of its real gifts and successes; it is encouraged to develop them further. And here is an honest verdict, telling us which of our supposed successes are really, in the judgment of the great impartial world, and not in our own private judgment only, successes, and which are not.

It is so easy to feel pride and satisfaction in one's own things, so hard to make sure that one is right in feeling it! We have a great empire. But so had Nebuchadnezzar. We extol the 'unrivalled happiness' of our national civilization. But then comes a candid friend, and remarks that our upper class is materialized, our middle class vulgarized, and our lower class brutalized. We are proud of our painting, our music. But we find that in the judgment of other people our painting is questionable, and our music non-existent. We are proud of our men of science. And here it turns out that the world is with us; we find that in the judgment of other people, too, Newton among the dead, and Mr Darwin among the living, hold as high a place as they hold in our national opinion.

Finally, we are proud of our poets and poetry. Now poetry is nothing less than the most perfect speech of man, that in which he comes nearest to being able to utter the truth. It is no small thing, therefore, to succeed eminently in poetry. And so much is required for duly estimating success here, that about poetry it is perhaps hardest to arrive at a sure general verdict, and takes longest. Meanwhile, our own conviction of the superiority of our national poets is not decisive, is almost certain to be mingled, as we see constantly in English eulogy of Shakespeare, with much of provincial infatuation. And we know what was the opinion current amongst our neighbours the French—people of taste, acuteness, and quick literary tact—not a hundred years ago, about our great poets. The old *Biographie Universelle* notices the pretension of the English to a place for their poets among the chief poets of the world, and says that this is a pretension which to no one but an Englishman can ever seem admissible. And the scornful, disparaging things said by foreigners about Shakespeare and Milton, and about our national overestimate of them, have been often quoted, and will be in everyone's remembrance.

A great change has taken place, and Shakespeare is now generally recognized, even in France, as one of the greatest of poets. Yes, some anti-Gallican cynic will say, the French rank him with Corneille and with Victor Hugo! But let me have the pleasure of quoting a sentence about Shakespeare, which I met with by accident not long ago in the *Correspondant*, a French review which not a dozen English people, I suppose, look at. The writer is praising Shakespeare's prose. With Shakespeare, he says, 'prose comes in whenever the subject, being more familiar, is unsuited to the majestic English iambic'. And he goes on: 'Shakespeare is the king of poetic rhythm and style, as well as the king of the realm of thought; along with his dazzling prose, Shakespeare has succeeded in giving us the most varied, the most harmonious verse which has ever sounded upon the human ear since the verse of the Greeks.' M. Henry Cochin, the writer of this sentence, deserves our gratitude for it; it would not be easy to praise Shakespeare, in a single sentence, more justly. And when a foreigner and a Frenchman writes thus of Shakespeare, and when Goethe says of Milton, in whom there was so much to repel Goethe rather than to attract him, that 'nothing has been ever done so entirely in the sense of the Greeks as *Samson Agonistes*', and that 'Milton is in very truth a poet whom we must treat with all reverence', then we understand what constitutes a European recognition of poets and poetry as contradistinguished from a merely national recognition, and that in favour both of Milton and of Shakespeare the judgment of the high court of appeal has finally gone.

I come back to M. Renan's praise of glory, from which I started. Yes, real glory is a most serious thing, glory authenticated by the Amphictyonic Court of final appeal, definitive glory. And even for poets and poetry, long and difficult as may be the process of arriving at the right award, the right award comes at last, the definitive glory rests where it is deserved. Every establishment of such a real glory is good and wholesome for mankind at large, good and wholesome for the nation which produced the poet crowned with it. To the poet himself it can seldom do harm; for he, poor man, is in his grave, probably, long before his glory crowns him.

Wordsworth has been in his grave for some thirty years, and certainly his lovers and admirers cannot flatter themselves that this great and steady light of glory as yet shines over him. He is not fully recognized at home; he is not recognized at all abroad. Yet I firmly believe that the poetical performance of Wordsworth is, after that of Shakespeare and Milton, of which all the world now recognizes the worth, undoubtedly the most considerable in our language from the Elizabethan age to the present time. Chaucer is anterior; and on other grounds, too, he cannot well be brought into the comparison. But taking the roll of our chief poetical names, besides Shakespeare and Milton, from the age of Elizabeth downwards, and going through it,— Spenser, Dryden, Pope, Gray, Goldsmith, Cowper, Burns, Coleridge, Scott, Campbell, Moore, Byron, Shelley, Keats (I mention only those who are dead),—I think it certain that Wordsworth's name deserves to stand, and will finally stand, above them all. Several of the poets named have gifts and excellences which Wordsworth has not. But taking the performance of each as a whole, I say that Wordsworth seems to me to have left a body of poetical work superior in power, in interest, in the qualities which give enduring freshness, to that which any one of the others has left.

But this is not enough to say. I think it certain, further, that if we take the chief poetical names of the Continent since the death of Molière, and, omitting Goethe, confront the remaining names with that of Wordsworth, the result is the same. Let us take Klopstock, Lessing, Schiller, Uhland, Rückert, and Heine for Germany; Filicaia, Alfieri, Manzoni, and Leopardi for Italy; Racine, Boileau, Voltaire, André Chénier, Béranger, Lamartine, Musset, M. Victor Hugo (he has been so long celebrated that although he still lives I may be permitted to name him) for France. Several of these, again, have evidently gifts and excellences to which Wordsworth can make no pretension. But in real poetical achievement it seems to me indubitable that to Wordsworth, here again, belongs the palm. It seems to me that Wordsworth has left behind him a body of poetical work which wears, and will wear, better on the whole than the performance of any one of these personages, so far more brilliant and celebrated, most of them, than the homely poet of Rydal. Wordsworth's performance in poetry is on the whole, in power, in interest, in the qualities which give enduring freshness, superior to theirs.

This is a high claim to make for Wordsworth. But if it is a just claim, if Wordsworth's place among the poets who have appeared in the last two or three centuries is after Shakespeare, Molière, Milton, Goethe, indeed, but before all the rest, then in time Wordsworth will have his due. We shall recognize him in his place, as we recognize Shakespeare and Milton; and not only we ourselves shall recognize him, but he will be recognized by Europe also. Meanwhile, those who recognize him already may do well, perhaps, to ask themselves whether there are not in the case of Wordsworth certain special obstacles which hinder or delay his due recognition by others, and whether these obstacles are not in some measure removable.

The *Excursion* and the *Prelude*, his poems of greatest bulk, are by no means Wordsworth's best work. His best work is in his shorter pieces, and many indeed are there of these which are of first-rate excellence. But in his seven volumes the pieces of high merit are mingled with a mass of pieces very inferior to them; so inferior to them that it seems wonderful how the same poet should have produced both. Shakespeare frequently has lines and passages in a strain quite false, and which are entirely unworthy of him. But one can imagine his smiling if one could meet him in the Elysian Fields and tell him so; smiling and replying that he knew it perfectly well himself, and what did it matter? But with Wordsworth the case is different. Work altogether inferior, work quite uninspired, flat and dull, is produced by him with evident unconsciousness of its defects, and he presents it to us with the same faith and seriousness as his best work. Now a drama or an epic fill the mind, and one does not look beyond them; but in a collection of short pieces the impression made by one piece requires to be continued and sustained by the piece following. In reading Wordsworth the impression made by one of his fine pieces is too often dulled and spoiled by a very inferior piece coming after it.

Wordsworth composed verses during a space of some sixty years; and it is no exaggeration to say that within one single decade of those years, between 1798 and 1808, almost all his really first-rate work was produced. A mass of inferior work remains, work done before and after this golden prime, imbedding the first-rate work and clogging it, obstructing our approach to it, chilling, not unfrequently, the high-wrought mood with which we leave it. To be recognized far and wide as a great poet, to be possible and receivable as a classic, Wordsworth needs to be relieved of a great deal of the poetical baggage which now encumbers him. To administer this relief is indispensable, unless he is to continue to be poet for the few only,—a poet valued far below his real worth by the world.

There is another thing. Wordsworth classified his poems not according to any commonly received plan of arrangement, but according to a scheme of mental physiology. He has poems of the fancy, poems of the imagination, poems of sentiment and reflection, and so on. His categories are ingenious but far-fetched, and the result of his employment of them is unsatisfactory. Poems are separated one from another which possess a kinship of subject or of treatment far more vital and deep than the supposed unity of mental origin, which was Wordsworth's reason for joining them with others.

The tact of the Greeks in matters of this kind was infallible. We may rely upon it that we shall not improve upon the classification adopted by the Greeks for kinds of poetry; that their categories of epic, dramatic, lyric, and so forth, have a natural propriety, and should be adhered to. It may sometimes seem doubtful to which of two categories a poem belongs; whether this or that poem is to be called, for instance, narrative or lyric, lyric or elegiac. But there is to be found in every good poem a strain, a predominant note, which determines the poem as belonging to one of these kinds rather than the other; and here is the best proof of the value of the classification and of the advantage of adhering to it. Wordsworth's poems will never produce their due effect until they are freed from their present artificial arrangment, and grouped more naturally.

Disengaged from the quantity of inferior work which now obscures them, the best poems of Wordsworth, I hear many people say, would indeed stand out in great beauty, but they would prove to be very few in number, scarcely more than half a dozen. I maintain, on the other hand, that what strikes me with admiration, what establishes in my opinion Wordsworth's superiority, is the great and ample body of powerful work which remains to him, even after all his inferior work has been cleared away. He gives us so much to rest upon, so much which communicates his spirit and engages ours!

This is of very great importance. If it were a comparison of single pieces, or of three or four pieces, by each poet, I do not say that Wordsworth would stand decisively above Gray, or Burns, or Coleridge, or Keats, or Manzoni, or Heine. It is in his ampler body of powerful work that I find his superiority. His good work itself, his work which counts, is not all of it, of course, of equal value. Some kinds of poetry are in themselves lower kinds than others. The ballad kind is a lower kind; the didactic kind, still more, is a lower kind. Poetry of this latter sort counts, too, sometimes, by its biographical interest partly, not by its poetical interest pure and simple; but then this can only be when the poet producing it has the power and importance of Wordsworth, a power and importance which he assuredly did not establish by such didactic poetry alone. Altogether, it is, I say, by the great body of powerful and significant work which remains to him, after every reduction and deduction has been made, that Wordsworth's superiority is proved.

To exhibit this body of Wordsworth's best work, to clear away obstructions from around it, and to let it speak for itself, is what every lover of Wordsworth should desire. Until this has been done, Wordsworth, whom we, to whom he is dear, all of us know and feel to be so great a poet, has not had a fair chance before the world. When once it has been done, he will make his way best, not by our advocacy of him, but by his own worth and power. We may safely leave him to make his way thus, we who believe that a superior worth and power in poetry finds in mankind a sense responsive to it and disposed at last to recognize it. Yet at the outset, before he has been duly known and recognized, we may do Wordsworth a service, perhaps by indicating in what his superior power and worth will be found to consist, and in what it will not.

Long ago, in speaking of Homer, I said that the noble and profound application of ideas to life is the most essential part of poetic greatness. I said that a great poet receives his distinctive character of superiority from his application, under the conditions immutably fixed by the laws of poetic beauty and poetic truth, from his application, I say, to his subject, whatever it may be, of the ideas

On man, on nature, and on human life,

which he has acquired for himself. The line quoted is Wordsworth's own; and his superiority arises from his powerful use, in his best pieces, his powerful application to his subject, of ideas 'on man, on nature, and on human life'.

Voltaire, with his signal acuteness, most truly remarked that 'no nation has treated in poetry moral ideas with more energy and depth than the English nation'. And he adds: 'There, it seems to me, is the great merit of the English poets.' Voltaire does not mean, by 'treating in poetry moral ideas', the composing moral and didactic poems;—that brings us but a very little way in poetry. He means just the same thing as was meant when I spoke above 'of the noble and profound application of ideas to life'; and he means the application of these ideas under the conditions fixed for us by the laws of poetic beauty and poetic truth. If it is said that to call these ideas *moral* ideas is to introduce a strong and injurious limitation, I answer that it is to do nothing of the kind, because moral ideas are really so main a part of human life. The question, *how to live*, is itself a moral idea; and it is the question which most interests every man, and with which, in some way or other, he is perpetually occupied. A large sense is of course to be given to the term *moral*. Whatever bears upon the question, 'how to live', comes under it.

Nor love thy life, nor hate; but, what thou liv'st,
Live well; how long or short, permit to heaven.

In those fine lines Milton utters, as everyone at once perceives, a moral idea. Yes, but so too, when Keats consoles the forward-bending lover on the Grecian Urn, the lover arrested and presented in immortal relief by the sculptor's hand before he can kiss, with the line,

> For ever wilt thou love, and she be fair—

he utters a moral idea. When Shakespeare says that

> We are such stuff
> As dreams are made on, and our little life
> Is rounded with a sleep,

he utters a moral idea.

Voltaire was right in thinking that the energetic and profound treatment of moral ideas, in this large sense, is what distinguishes the English poetry. He sincerely meant praise, not dispraise or hint of limitation; and they err who suppose that poetic limitation is a necessary consequence of the fact, the fact being granted as Voltaire states it. If what distinguishes the greatest poets is their powerful and profound application of ideas to life, which surely no good critic will deny, then to prefix to the term ideas here the term moral makes hardly any difference, because human life itself is in so preponderating a degree moral.

It is important, therefore, to hold fast to this: that poetry is at bottom a criticism of life; that the greatness of a poet lies in his powerful and beautiful application of ideas to life,—to the question: How to live. Morals are often treated in a narrow and false fashion; they are bound up with systems of thought and belief which have had their day; they are fallen into the hands of pedants and professional dealers; they grow tiresome to some of us. We find attraction, at times, even in a poetry of revolt against them; in a poetry which might take for its motto Omar Khayyam's words: 'Let us make up in the tavern for the time which we have wasted in the mosque.' Or we find attractions in a poetry indifferent to them; in a poetry where the contents may be what they will, but where the form is studied and exquisite. We delude ourselves in either case; and the best cure for our delusion is to let our minds rest upon that great and inexhaustible word *life*, until we learn to enter into its meaning. A poetry of revolt against moral ideas is a poetry of revolt against *life*; a poetry of indifference towards moral ideas is a poetry of indifference towards *life*.

Epictetus had a happy figure for things like the play of the senses, or literary form and finish, or argumentative ingenuity, in comparison with 'the best and master thing', for us, as he called it, the concern, how to live. Some people were afraid of them, he said, or they disliked and undervalued them. Such people were wrong; they were unthankful or cowardly. But the things might also be over-prized, and treated as final when they are not. They bear to life the relation which inns bear to home. 'As if a man, journeying home, and finding a nice inn on the road, and liking it, were to stay for ever at the inn! Man, thou hast forgotten thine object; thy journey was not *to* this, but *through* this. "But this inn is taking." And how many other inns, too, are taking, and how many fields and meadows! but as places of passage merely. You have an object, which is this: to get home, to do your duty to your family, friends, and fellow countrymen, to attain inward freedom, serenity, happiness, contentment. Style takes your fancy, arguing takes your fancy, and you forget your home and want to make your abode with them and to stay with them, on the plea that they are taking. Who denies that they are taking? but as places of passage, as inns. And when I say this, you suppose me to be attacking the care for style, the care for argument. I am not; I attack the resting in them, the not looking to the end which is beyond them.'

Now, when we come across a poet like Théophile Gautier, we have a poet who has taken up his abode at an inn, and never got farther. There may be inducements to this or that one of us, at this or that moment, to find delight in him, to cleave to him; but after all, we do not change the truth about him,—we only stay ourselves in his inn along with him. And when we come across a poet like Wordsworth, who sings

> Of truth, of grandeur, beauty, love and hope,
> And melancholy fear subdued by faith,
> Of blessed consolations in distress,
> Or moral strength and intellectual power,
> Of joy in widest commonalty spread—

then we have a poet intent on 'the best and master thing', and who prosecutes his journey home. We say, for brevity's sake, that he deals with *life*, because he deals with that in which life really consists. This is what Voltaire means to praise in the English poets,—this dealing with what is really life. But always it is the mark of the greatest poets that they deal with it; and to say that the English poets are remarkable for dealing with it, is only another way of saying what is true, that in poetry the English genius has especially shown its power.

Wordsworth deals with it, and his greatness lies in his dealing with it so powerfully. I have named a number of celebrated poets above all of whom he, in my opinion, deserves to be placed. He is to be placed above poets like Voltaire, Dryden, Pope, Lessing, Schiller, because these famous personages, with a thousand gifts and merits, never, or scarcely ever, attain the distinctive accent and utterance of the high and genuine poets—

Quique pii vates et Phoebo digna locuti,

at all. Burns, Keats, Heine, not to speak of others in our list, have this accent;—who can doubt it? And at the same time they have treasures of humour, felicity, passion, for which in Wordsworth we shall look in vain. Where, then, is Wordsworth's superiority? It is here; he deals with more of *life* than they do; he deals with *life*, as a whole, more powerfully.

No Wordsworthian will doubt this. Nay, the fervent Wordsworthian will add, as Mr Leslie Stephen does, that Wordsworth's poetry is precious because his philosophy is sound; that his 'ethical system is as distinctive and capable of systematical exposition as Bishop Butler's'; that his poetry is informed by ideas which 'fall spontaneously into a scientific system of thought'. But we must be on our guard against the Wordsworthians, if we want to secure for Wordsworth his due rank as a poet. The Wordsworthians are apt to praise him for the wrong things, and to lay far too much stress upon what they call his philosophy. His poetry is the reality, his philosophy,—so far, at least, as it may put on the form and habit of 'a scientific system of thought', and the more that it puts them on,—is the illusion. Perhaps we shall one day learn to make this proposition general, and to say: Poetry is the reality, philosophy the illusion. But in Wordsworth's case, at any rate, we cannot do him justice until we dismiss his formal philosophy.

The *Excursion* abounds with philosophy, and therefore the

Excursion is to the Wordsworthian what it never can be to the disinterested lover of poetry,—a satisfactory work. 'Duty exists,' says Wordsworth, in the *Excursion*; and then he proceeds thus—

> . . . Immutably survive,
> For our support, the measures and the forms,
> Which an abstract Intelligence supplies,
> Whose kingdom is, where time and space are not.

And the Wordsworthian is delighted, and thinks that here is a sweet union of philosophy and poetry. But the disinterested lover of poetry will feel that the lines carry us really not a step further than the proposition which they would interpret; that they are a tissue of elevated but abstract verbiage, alien to the very nature of poetry.

Or let us come direct to the centre of Wordsworth's philosophy, as 'an ethical system, as distinctive and capable of systematical exposition as Bishop Butler's'—

> . . . One adequate support
> For the calamities of mortal life
> Exists, one only;—an assured belief
> That the procession of our fate, howe'er
> Sad or disturbed, is ordered by a Being
> Of infinite benevolence and power;
> Whose everlasting purposes embrace
> All accidents, converting them to good.

That is doctrine such as we hear in church too, religious and philosophic doctrine; and the attached Wordsworthian loves passages of such doctrine, and brings them forward in proof of his poet's excellence. But however true the doctrine may be, it has, as here presented, none of the characters of *poetic* truth, the kind of truth which we require from a poet, and in which Wordsworth is really strong.

Even the 'intimations' of the famous Ode, those cornerstones of the supposed philosophic system of Wordsworth,—idea of the high instincts and affections coming out in childhood, testifying of a divine home recently left, and fading away as our life proceeds,—this idea, of undeniable beauty as a play of fancy, has itself not the character of poetic truth of the best kind; it has no real solidity. The instinct of delight in Nature and her beauty had no doubt extraordinary strength in Wordsworth himself as a child. But to say that universally this instinct is mighty in childhood, and tends to die away afterwards, is to say what is extremely doubtful. In many people, perhaps with the majority of educated persons, the love of nature is nearly imperceptible at ten years old, but strong and operative at thirty. In general we may say of these high instincts of early childhood, the base of the alleged systematic philosophy of Wordsworth, what Thucydides says of the early achievements of the Greek race: 'It is impossible to speak with certainty of what is so remote; but from all that we can really investigate, I should say that they were no very great things.'

Finally, the 'scientific system of thought' in Wordsworth gives us at last such poetry as this, which the devout Wordsworthian accepts—

> O for the coming of that glorious time
> When, prizing knowledge as her noblest wealth
> And best protection, this Imperial Realm,
> While she exacts allegiance, shall admit
> An obligation, on her part, to *teach*
> Them who are born to serve her and obey;
> Binding herself by statute to secure,
> For all the children whom her soil maintains,
> The rudiments of letters, and inform
> The mind with moral and religious truth.

Wordsworth calls Voltaire dull, and surely the production of these un-Voltairian lines must have been imposed on him as a judgment! One can hear them being quoted at a Social Science Congress; one can call up the whole scene. A great room in one of our dismal provincial towns; dusty air and jaded afternoon daylight; benches full of men with bald heads and women in spectacles; an orator lifting up his face from a manuscript written within and without to declaim these lines of Wordsworth; and in the soul of any poor child of nature who may have wandered in thither, an unutterable sense of lamentation, and mourning, and woe!

'But turn we', as Wordsworth says, 'from these bold, bad men,' the haunters of Social Science Congresses. And let us be on our guard, too, against the exhibitors and extollers of a 'scientific system of thought' in Wordsworth's poetry. The poetry will never be seen aright while they thus exhibit it. The cause of its greatness is simple, and may be told quite simply. Wordsworth's poetry is great because of the extraordinary power with which Wordsworth feels the joy offered to us in nature, the joy offered to us in the simple primary affections and duties; and because of the extraordinary power with which, in case after case, he shows us this joy, and renders it so as to make us share it.

The source of joy from which he thus draws is the truest and most unfailing source of joy accessible to man. It is also accessible universally. Wordsworth brings us word, therefore, according to his own strong and characteristic line, he brings us word

Of joy in widest commonalty spread.

Here is an immense advantage for a poet. Wordsworth tells of what all seek, and tells of it at its truest and best source, and yet a source where all may go and draw for it.

Nevertheless, we are not to suppose that everything is precious which Wordsworth, standing even at this perennial and beautiful source, may give us. Wordsworthians are apt to talk as if it must be. They will speak with the same reverence of *The Sailor's Mother*, for example, as of *Lucy Gray*. They do their master harm by such lack of discrimination. *Lucy Gray* is a beautiful success; *The Sailor's Mother* is a failure. To give aright what he wishes to give, to interpret and render successfully, is not always within Wordsworth's own command. It is within no poet's command; here is the part of the Muse, the inspiration, the God, the 'not ourselves'. In Wordsworth's case, the accident, for so it may almost be called, of inspiration, is of peculiar importance. No poet, perhaps, is so evidently filled with a new and sacred energy when the inspiration is upon him; no poet, when it fails him, is so left 'weak as is a breaking wave'. I remember hearing him say that 'Goethe's poetry was not inevitable enough'. The remark is striking and true; no line in Goethe, as Goethe said himself, but its maker knew well how it came there. Wordsworth is right, Goethe's poetry is not inevitable; not inevitable enough. But Wordsworth's poetry, when he is at his best, is inevitable, as inevitable as Nature herself. It might seem that Nature not only gave him the matter for his poem, but wrote his poem for him. He has no style. He was too conversant with Milton not to catch at times his master's manner, and he has fine Miltonic lines; but he has no assured poetic style of his own like Milton. When he seeks to have a style he falls into ponderosity and pomposity. In the *Excursion* we have his style, as an artistic product of his own creation; and although Jeffrey completely failed to recognize Wordsworth's real greatness, he was yet not wrong in saying of the *Excursion*, as a work of poetic style: 'This will never do.' And yet magical as is that power, which Wordsworth has not, of assured and possessed poetic style, he has something which is an equivalent for it.

Everyone who has any sense for these things feels the subtle turn, the heightening, which is given to a poet's verse by his genius for style. We can feel it in the

> After life's fitful fever he sleeps well—

of Shakespeare; in the

> . . . though fall'n on evil days,
> On evil days though fall'n, and evil tongues—

of Milton. It is the incomparable charm of Milton's power of poetic style which gives such worth to *Paradise Regained*, and makes a great poem of a work in which Milton's imagination does not soar high. Wordsworth has in constant possession, and at command, no style of this kind; but he had too poetic a nature, and had read the great poets too well, not to catch, as I have already remarked, something of it occasionally. We find it not only in his Miltonic lines; we find it in such a phrase as this, where the manner is his own, not Milton's—

> . . . the fierce confederate storm
> Of sorrow barricadoed evermore
> Within the walls of cities;

although even here, perhaps, the power of style, which is undeniable, is more properly that of eloquent prose than the subtle heightening and change wrought by genuine poetic style. It is style, again, and the elevation given by style, which chiefly make the effectiveness of *Laodameia*. Still the right sort of verse to choose from Wordsworth, if we are to seize his true and most characteristic form of expression, is a line like this from *Michael*—

> And never lifted up a single stone.

There is nothing subtle in it, no heightening, no study of poetic style, strictly so called, at all; yet it is expression of the highest and most truly expressive kind.

Wordsworth owed much to Burns, and a style of perfect plainness, relying for effect solely on the weight and force of that which with entire fidelity it utters, Burns could show him:

> The poor inhabitant below
> Was quick to learn and wise to know,
> And keenly felt the friendly glow
>   And softer flame;
> But thoughtless follies laid him low
>   And stain'd his name.

Everyone will be conscious of a likeness here to Wordsworth; and if Wordsworth did great things with this nobly plain manner, we must remember, what indeed he himself would always have been forward to acknowledge, that Burns used it before him.

Still Wordsworth's use of it has something unique and unmatchable. Nature herself seems, I say, to take the pen out of his hand, and to write for him with her own bare, sheer, penetrating power. This arises from two causes; from the profound sincereness with which Wordsworth feels his subject, and also from the profoundly sincere and natural character of his subject itself. He can and will treat such a subject with nothing but the most plain, first-hand, almost austere naturalness. His expression may often be called bald, as, for instance, in the poem of *Resolution and Independence*; but it is bald as the bare mountain tops are bald, with a baldness which is full of grandeur.

Wherever we meet with the successful balance, in Wordsworth, of profound truth of subject with profound truth of execution, he is unique. His best poems are those which most perfectly exhibit this balance. I have a warm admiration for *Laodameia* and for the great *Ode*; but if I am to tell the very truth, I find *Laodameia* not wholly free from something artificial, and the great *Ode* not wholly free from something declamatory. If I had to pick out poems of a kind most perfectly to show Wordsworth's unique power, I should rather choose poems such as *Michael*, *The Fountain*, *The Highland Reaper*. And poems with the peculiar and unique beauty which distinguishes these, Wordsworth produced in considerable number; besides very many other poems of which the worth, although not so rare as the worth of these, is still exceedingly high.

On the whole, then, as I said at the beginning, not only is Wordsworth eminent by reason of the goodness of his best work, but he is eminent also by reason of the great body of good work which he has left to us. With the ancients I will not compare him. In many respects the ancients are far above us, and yet there is something that we demand which they can never give. Leaving the ancients, let us come to the poets and poetry of Christendom. Dante, Shakespeare, Molière, Milton, Goethe, are altogether larger and more splendid luminaries in the poetical heaven than Wordsworth. But I know not where else, among the moderns, we are to find his superiors.

To disengage the poems which show his power, and to present them to the English-speaking public and to the world, is the object of this volume[1]. I by no means say that it contains all which in Wordsworth's poems is interesting. Except in the case of *Margaret*, a story composed separately from the rest of the *Excursion*, and which belongs to a different part of England, I have not ventured on detaching portions of poems, or on giving any piece otherwise than as Wordsworth himself gave it. But under the conditions imposed by this reserve, the volume contains, I think, everything, or nearly everything, which may best serve him with the majority of lovers of poetry, nothing which may disserve him.

I have spoken lightly of Wordsworthians; and if we are to get Wordsworth recognized by the public and by the world, we must recommend him not in the spirit of a clique, but in the spirit of disinterested lovers of poetry. But I am a Wordsworthian myself. I can read with pleasure and edification *Peter Bell*, and the whole series of *Ecclesiastical Sonnets*, and the address to Mr Wilkinson's spade, and even the *Thanksgiving Ode*;—everything of Wordsworth, I think, except *Vaudracour and Julia*. It is not for nothing that one has been brought up in the veneration of a man so truly worthy of homage; that one has seen him and heard him, lived in his neighbourhood, and been familiar with his country. No Wordsworthian has a tenderer affection for this pure and sage master than I, or is less really offended by his

---

[1] The present essay formed the Introduction to *Poems of Wordsworth*, a volume of selections edited by Matthew Arnold in 1879.—PUBLISHER.

defects. But Wordsworth is something more than the pure and sage master of a small band of devoted followers, and we ought not to rest satisfied until he is seen to be what he is. He is one of the very chief glories of English Poetry; and by nothing is England so glorious as by her poetry. Let us lay aside every weight which hinders our getting him recognized as this, and let our one study be to bring to pass, as widely as possible and as truly as possible, his own word concerning his poems: 'They will co-operate with the benign tendencies in human nature and society, and will, in their degree, be efficacious in making men wiser, better, and happier.'

VI

BYRON

WHEN at last I held in my hand the volume of poems which I had chosen from Wordsworth, and began to turn over its pages, there arose in me almost immediately the desire to see beside it, as a companion volume, a like collection of the best poetry of Byron. Alone amongst our poets of the earlier part of this century, Byron and Wordsworth not only furnish material enough for a volume of this kind, but also, as it seems to me, they both of them gain considerably by being thus exhibited. There are poems of Coleridge and of Keats equal, if not superior, to anything of Byron or Wordsworth; but a dozen pages or two will contain them, and the remaining poetry is of a quality much inferior. Scott never, I think, rises as a poet to the level of Byron and Wordsworth. On the other hand, he never falls below his own usual level very far; and by a volume of selections from him, therefore, his effectiveness is not increased. As to Shelley there will be more question; and indeed Mr Stopford Brooke, whose accomplishments, eloquence, and love of poetry we must all recognize and admire, has actually given us Shelley in such a volume. But for my own part I cannot think that Shelley's poetry, except by snatches and fragments, has the value of the good work of Wordsworth and Byron; or that it is possible for even Mr Stopford Brooke to make up a volume of selections from him which, for real substance, power, and worth, can at all take rank with a like volume from Byron or Wordsworth.

Shelley knew quite well the difference between the achievement of such a poet as Byron and his own. He praises Byron too unreservedly, but he sincerely felt, and he was right in feeling, that Byron was a greater poetical power than himself. As a man, Shelley is at a number of points immeasurably Byron's superior; he is a beautiful and enchanting spirit, whose vision, when we call it up, has far more loveliness, more charm for our soul, than the vision of Byron. But all the personal charm of Shelley cannot hinder us from at last discovering in his poetry the incurable want, in general, of a sound subject matter, and the incurable fault, in consequence, of unsubstantiality. Those who extol him as the poet of clouds, the poet of sunsets, are only saying that he did not, in fact, lay hold upon the poet's right subject matter; and in honest truth, with all his charm of soul and spirit, and with all his gift of musical diction and movement, he never, or hardly ever, did. Except, as I have said, for a few short things and single stanzas, his original poetry is less satisfactory than his translations, for in these the subject matter was found for him. Nay, I doubt whether his delightful Essays and Letters, which deserve to be far more read than they are now, will not resist the wear and tear of time better, and finally, come to stand higher, than his poetry.

There remain to be considered Byron and Wordsworth. That Wordsworth affords good material for a volume of selections, and that he gains by having his poetry thus presented, is an old belief of mine which led me lately to make up a volume of poems chosen out of Wordsworth, and to bring it before the public. By its kind reception of the volume, the public seems to show itself a partaker in my belief. Now Byron also supplies plenty of material for a like volume, and he too gains, I think, by being so presented. Mr Swinburne urges, indeed, that 'Byron, who rarely wrote anything either worthless or faultless, can only be judged or appreciated in the mass; the greatest of his works was his whole work taken together'. It is quite true that Byron rarely wrote anything either worthless or faultless; it is quite true also that in the appreciation of Byron's power a sense of the amount and variety of his work, defective though much of his work is, enters justly into our estimate. But although there may be little in Byron's poetry which can be pronounced either worthless or faultless, there are portions of it which are far higher in worth and far more free from fault than others. And although, again, the abundance and variety of his production is undoubtedly a proof of his power, yet I question whether by reading everything which he gives us we are so likely to acquire an admiring sense even of his variety and abundance, as by reading what he gives us at his happier moments. Varied and abundant he amply proves himself even by this taken alone. Receive him absolutely without omission or compression, follow his whole outpouring stanza by stanza and line by line from the very commencement to the very end, and he is capable of being tiresome.

Byron has told us himself that the *Giaour* 'is but a string of passages'. He has made full confession of his own negligence. 'No one', says he, 'has done more through negligence to corrupt the language.' This accusation brought by himself against his poems is not just; but when he goes on to say of them, that 'their faults, whatever they may be, are those of negligence and not of labour', he says what is perfectly true. '*Lara*', he declares, 'I wrote while undressing after coming home from balls and masquerades, in the year of revelry, 1814. The *Bride* was written in four, the *Corsair* in ten days.' He calls this 'a humiliating confession, as it proves my own want of judgment in publishing, and the public's in reading, things which cannot have stamina for permanence'. Again he does his poems injustice; the producer of such poems could not but publish them, the public could not but read them. Nor could Byron have produced his work in any other fashion; his poetic work could not have first grown and matured in his own mind, and then come forth as an organic whole; Byron had not enough of the artist in him for this, nor enough of self-command. He wrote, as he truly tells us, to relieve himself, and he went on writing because he found the relief become indispensable. But it was inevitable that works so produced should be, in general, 'a string of passages', poured out, as he describes them, with rapidity and excitement, and with new passages constantly suggesting themselves, and added while his work was going through the press. It is evident that we have here neither deliberate scientific construction, nor yet the instinctive artistic creation of poetic wholes; and that to take passages from work produced as Byron's was is a very different thing from taking passages out of the *Oedipus* or the *Tempest*, and deprives the poetry far less of its advantage.

Nay, it gives advantage to the poetry, instead of depriving it of any. Byron, I said, has not a great artist's profound and patient skill in combining an action or in developing a character,—a skill which we must watch and follow if we are to do justice to it. But he has a wonderful power of vividly conceiving a single incident, a single situation; of throwing himself upon it, grasping it as if it were real and he saw and felt it, and of making us see and feel it too. The *Giaour* is, as he truly called it, 'a string of passages', not a work moving by a deep internal law of development to a necessary end; and our total impression from it cannot but receive from this, its inherent defect, a certain dimness and indistinctness. But the incidents of the journey and death of Hassan, in that poem, are conceived and presented with a vividness not to be surpassed; and our impression from them is correspondingly clear and powerful. In *Lara*, again, there is no adequate development either of the character of the chief personage or of the action of the poem; our total impression from the work is a confused one. Yet such an incident as the disposal of the slain Ezzelin's body passes before our eyes as if we actually saw it. And in the same way as these bursts of incident, bursts of sentiment also, living and vigorous, often occur in the midst of poems which must be admitted to be but weakly-conceived and loosely-combined wholes. Byron cannot but be a gainer by having attention concentrated upon what is vivid, powerful, effective in his work, and withdrawn from what is not so.

Byron, I say, cannot but be gainer by this, just as Wordsworth is a gainer by a like proceeding. I esteem Wordsworth's poetry so highly, and the world, in my opinion, has done it such scant justice, that I could not rest satisfied until I had fulfilled, on Wordsworth's behalf, a long-cherished desire;—had disengaged, to the best of my power, his good work from the inferior work joined with it, and had placed before the public the body of his good work by itself. To the poetry of Byron the world has ardently paid homage; full justice from his contemporaries, perhaps even more than justice, his torrent of poetry received. His poetry was admired, adored, 'with all its imperfections on its head',—in spite of negligence, in spite of diffuseness, in spite of repetitions, in spite of whatever faults it possessed. His name is still great and brilliant. Nevertheless the hour of irresistible vogue has passed away for him; even for Byron it could not but pass away. The time has come for him, as it comes for all poets, when he must take his real and permanent place, no longer depending upon the vogue of his own day and upon the enthusiasm of his contemporaries. Whatever we may think of him, we shall not be subjugated by him as they were; for, as he cannot be for us what he was for them, we cannot admire him so hotly and indiscriminately as they. His faults of negligence, of diffuseness, of repetition, his faults of whatever kind, we shall abundantly feel and unsparingly criticize; the mere interval of time between us and him makes disillusion of this kind inevitable. But how then will Byron stand, if we relieve him too, so far as we can, of the encumbrance of his inferior and weakest work, and if we bring before us his best and strongest work in one body together? That is the question which I, who can even remember the latter years of Byron's vogue, and have myself felt the expiring wave of that mighty influence, but who certainly also regard him, and have long regarded him, without illusion, cannot but ask myself, cannot but seek to answer.

Byron has been over-praised, no doubt. 'Byron is one of our French superstitions,' says M. Edmond Scherer; but where has Byron, not been a superstition? He pays now the penalty of this exaggerated worship. 'Alone among the English poets his contemporaries, Byron', said M. Taine, '*atteint à la cime*,—gets to the top of the poetic mountain.' But the idol that M. Taine had thus adored M. Scherer is almost for burning. 'In Byron', he declares, 'there is a remarkable inability ever to lift himself into the region of real poetic art,—art impersonal and disinterested,— at all. He has fecundity, eloquence, wit, but even these qualities themselves are confined within somewhat narrow limits. He has treated hardly any subject but one,—himself; now the man, in Byron, is of a nature even less sincere than the poet. This beautiful and blighted being is at bottom a coxcomb. He posed all his life long'.

Our poet could not well meet with more severe and unsympathetic criticism. However, the praise often given to Byron has been so exaggerated as to provoke, perhaps, a reaction in which he is unduly disparaged. 'As various in composition as Shakespeare himself, Lord Byron has embraced', says Sir Walter Scott, 'every topic of human life, and sounded every string on the divine harp, from its slightest to its most powerful and heart-astounding tones.' It is not surprising that someone with a cool head should retaliate, on such provocation as this, by saying: 'He has treated hardly any subject but one, *himself*.' 'In the very grand and tremendous drama of *Cain*', says Scott, 'Lord Byron has certainly matched Milton on his own ground.' And Lord Byron has done all this, Scott adds, 'while managing his pen with the careless and negligent ease of a man of quality'.

Alas, 'managing his pen with the careless and negligent ease of a man of quality', Byron wrote in his *Cain*—

> Souls that dare look the Omnipotent tyrant in
> His everlasting face, and tell him that
> His evil is not good;

or he wrote—

> . . . And *thou* would'st go on aspiring
> To the great double Mysteries! the *two Principles*![1]

One has only to repeat to oneself a line from *Paradise Lost* in order to feel the difference.

Sainte-Beuve, speaking of that exquisite master of language, the Italian poet Leopardi, remarks how often we see the alliance, singular though it may at first sight appear, of the poetical genius with the genius for scholarship and philology. Dante and Milton are instances which will occur to everyone's mind. Byron is so negligent in his poetical style, he is often, to say the truth, so slovenly, slipshod, and infelicitous, he is so little haunted by the true artist's fine passion for the correct use and consummate management of words, that he may be described as having for this artistic gift the insensibility of the barbarian;—which is perhaps only another and a less flattering way of saying, with Scott, that he 'manages his pen with the careless and negligent ease of a man of quality'. Just of a piece with the rhythm of

> Dare you await the event of a few minutes'
> Deliberation?

or of

> All shall be void—
> Destroy'd!

is the diction of

> Which now is painful to these eyes,
> Which have not seen the sun to rise;

or of

> . . . there let him lay!

or of the famous passage beginning

> He who hath bent him o'er the dead;

[1] The italics are in the original.

with those trailing relatives, that crying grammatical solecism, that inextricable anacoluthon! To class the work of the author of such things with the work of the authors of such verse as

> In the dark backward and abysm of time—

or as

> Presenting Thebes, or Pelops' line,
> Or the tale of Troy divine—

is ridiculous. Shakespeare and Milton, with their secret of consummate felicity in diction and movement, are of another and an altogether higher order from Byron, nay, for that matter, from Wordsworth also; from the author of such verse as

> Sol hath dropt into his harbour—

or (if Mr Ruskin pleases) as

> Parching summer hath no warrant—

as from the author of

> All shall be void—
> Destroy'd!

With a poetical gift and a poetical performance of the very highest order, the slovenliness and tunelessness of much of Byron's production, the pompousness and ponderousness of much of Wordsworth's, are incompatible. Let us admit this to the full.

Moreover, while we are hearkening to M. Scherer, and going along with him in his fault-finding, let us admit, too, that the man in Byron is in many respects as unsatisfactory as the poet. And, putting aside all direct moral criticism of him,—with which we need not concern ourselves here,—we shall find that he is unsatisfactory in the same way. Some of Byron's most crying faults as a man,—his vulgarity, his affectation,—are really akin to the faults of commonness, of want of art, in his workmanship as a poet. The ideal nature for the poet and artist is that of the finely touched and finely gifted man, the εὐφυής of the Greeks; now, Byron's nature was in substance not that of the εὐφυής at all, but rather, as I have said, of the barbarian. The want of fine perception which made it possible for him to formulate either the comparison between himself and Rousseau, or his reason for getting Lord Delawarr excused from a 'licking' at Harrow, is exactly what made possible for him also his terrible dealings in, *An ye wool*; *I have redde thee*; *Sunburn me*; *Oons, and it is excellent well*. It is exactly, again, what made possible for him his precious dictum that Pope is a Greek temple, and a string of other criticisms of the like force; it is exactly, in fine, what deteriorated the quality of his poetic production. If we think of a good representative of that finely touched and exquisitely gifted nature which is the ideal nature for the poet and artist,—if we think of Raphael, for instance, who truly is εὐφυής just as Byron is not,—we shall bring into clearer light the connection in Byron between the faults of the man and the faults of the poet. With Raphael's character Byron's sins of vulgarity and false criticism would have been impossible, just as with Raphael's art Byron's sins of common and bad workmanship.

Yes, all this is true, but it is not the whole truth about Byron nevertheless; very far from it. The severe criticism of M. Scherer by no means gives us the whole truth about Byron, and we have not yet got it in what has been added to that criticism here. The negative part of the true criticism of him we perhaps have; the positive part, by far the more important, we have not. Byron's admirers appeal eagerly to foreign testimonies in his favour. Some of these testimonies do not much move me; but one testimony there is among them which will always carry, with me at any rate, very great weight,—the testimony of Goethe. Goethe's sayings about Byron were uttered, it must however be remembered, at the height of Byron's vogue, when that puissant and splendid personality was exercising its full power of attraction. In Goethe's own household there was an atmosphere of glowing Byron-worship; his daughter-in-law was a passionate admirer of Byron, nay, she enjoyed and prized his poetry, as did Tieck and so many others in Germany at that time, much above the poetry of Goethe himself. Instead of being irritated and rendered jealous by this, a nature like Goethe's was inevitably led by it to heighten, not lower, the note of his praise. The Time-Spirit, or *Zeit-Geist*, he would himself have said, was working just then for Byron. This working of the *Zeit-Geist* in his favour was an advantage added to Byron's other advantages, an advantage of which he had a right to get the benefit. This is what Goethe would have thought and said to himself; and so he would have been led even to heighten somewhat his estimate of Byron, and to accentuate the emphasis of praise. Goethe speaking of Byron at that moment was not and could not be quite the same cool critic as Goethe speaking of Dante, or Molière, or Milton. This, I say, we ought to remember in reading Goethe's judgments on Byron and his poetry. Still, if we are careful to bear this in mind, and if we quote Goethe's praise correctly, which is not always done by those who in this country quote it,—and if we add to it that great and due qualification added to it by Goethe himself,—which so far as I have seen has never yet been done by his quoters in this country at all,—then we shall have a judgment on Byron, which comes, I think, very near to the truth, and which may well command our adherence.

In his judicious and interesting Life of Byron, Professor Nichol quotes Goethe as saying that Byron 'is undoubtedly to be regarded as the greatest genius of our century'. What Goethe did really say was 'the greatest *talent*', not 'the greatest *genius*'. The difference is important, because, while talent gives the notion of power in a man's performance, genius gives rather the notion of felicity and perfection in it; and this divine gift of consummate felicity by no means, as we have seen, belongs to Byron and to his poetry. Goethe said that Byron 'must unquestionably be regarded as the greatest talent of the century'. [1] He said of him moreover: 'The English may think of Byron what they please, but it is certain that they can point to no poet who is his like. He is different from all the rest, and in the main greater.' Here, again, Professor Nichol translates: 'They can show no (living) poet who is to be compared to him';—inserting the word *living*, I suppose, to prevent its being thought that Goethe would have ranked Byron, as a poet, above Shakespeare and Milton. But Goethe did not use, or, I think, mean to imply, any limitation such as is added by Professor Nichol. Goethe said simply, and he meant to say, '*no* poet'. Only the words which follow [2] ought not, I think, to be rendered, 'who is to be compared to him', that is to say, '*who is his equal as a poet*'.

[1] 'Der ohne Frage als das grösste Talent des Jahrhunderts anzusehen ist.'
[2] 'Der ihm zu vergleichen wäre.'

They mean rather, 'who may properly be compared with him', '*who is his parallel*'. And when Goethe said that Byron was 'in the main greater' than all the rest of the English poets, he was not so much thinking of the strict rank, as poetry, of Byron's production; he was thinking of that wonderful personality of Byron which so enters into his poetry, and which Goethe called 'a personality such, for its eminence, as has never been yet, and such as is not likely to come again'. He was thinking of that 'daring, dash, and grandiosity',[1] of Byron, which are indeed so splendid; and which were, so Goethe maintained, of a character to do good, because 'everything great is formative', and what is thus formative does us good.

The faults which went with this greatness, and which impaired Byron's poetical work, Goethe saw very well. He saw the constant state of warfare and combat, the 'negative and polemical work-ing', which makes Byron's poetry a poetry in which we can so little find rest; he saw the *Hang zum Unbegrenzten*, the straining after the unlimited, which made it impossible for Byron to pro-duce poetic wholes such as the *Tempest* or *Lear*; he saw the *zu viel Empirie*, the promiscuous adoption of all the matter offered to the poet by life, just as it was offered, without thought or patience for the mysterious transmutation to be operated on this matter by poetic form. But in a sentence which I cannot, as I say, remember to have yet seen quoted in any English criticism of Byron, Goethe lays his finger on the cause of all these defects in Byron, and on his real source of weakness both as a man and as a poet. 'The moment he reflects, he is a child,' says Goethe—'*sobald er reflectirt, ist er ein Kind*'.

Now if we take the two parts of Goethe's criticism of Byron, the favourable and the unfavourable, and put them together, we shall have, I think, the truth. On the one hand, a splendid and puissant personality—a personality 'in eminence such as has never been yet, and is not likely to come again'; of which the like, therefore, is not to be found among the poets of our nation, by which Byron 'is different from all the rest, and in the main greater'. Byron is, moreover, 'the greatest talent of our century'. On the other hand, this splendid personality and un-matched talent, this unique Byron, 'is quite too much in the

[1] 'Byrons Kühnheit, Keckheit und Grandiosität, ist das nicht alles bildend? —Alles Grosse bildet, sobald wir es gewahr werden.'

dark about himself;' [1] nay, 'the moment he begins to reflect, he is a child'. There we have, I think, Byron complete; and in estimating him and ranking him we have to strike a balance between the gain which accrues to his poetry, as compared with the productions of other poets, from his superiority, and the loss which accrues to it from his defects.

A balance of this kind has to be struck in the case of all poets except the few supreme masters in whom a profound criticism of life exhibits itself in indissoluble connection with the laws of poetic truth and beauty. I have seen it said that I allege poetry to have for its characteristic this: that it is a criticism of life; and that I make it to be thereby distinguished from prose, which is something else. So far from it, that when I first used this expression, *a criticism of life*, now many years ago, it was to literature in general that I applied it, and not to poetry in especial. 'The end and aim of all literature', I said, 'is, if one considers it attentively, nothing but that: *a criticism of life*.' And so it surely is; the main end and aim of all our utterance, whether in prose or in verse, is surely a criticism of life. We are not brought much on our way, I admit, towards an adequate definition of poetry as distinguished from prose by that truth; still a truth it is, and poetry can never prosper if it is forgotten. In poetry, however, the criticism of life has to be made conformably to the laws of poetic truth and poetic beauty. Truth and seriousness of substance and matter, felicity and perfection of diction and manner, as these are exhibited in the best poets, are what constitute a criticism of life made in conformity with the laws of poetic truth and poetic beauty; and it is by knowing and feeling the work of those poets, that we learn to recognize the fulfilment and non-fulfilment of such conditions.

The moment, however, that we leave the small band of the very best poets, the true classics, and deal with poets of the next rank, we shall find that perfect truth and seriousness of matter, in close alliance with perfect truth and felicity of manner, is the rule no longer. We have now to take what we can get, to forego something here, to admit compensation for it there; to strike a balance, and to see how our poets stand in respect to one another when that balance has been struck. Let us observe how this is so.

[1] 'Gar zu dunkel über sich selbst.'

We will take three poets, among the most considerable of our century: Leopardi, Byron, Wordsworth. Giacomo Leopardi was ten years younger than Byron, and he died thirteen years after him; both of them, therefore, died young—Byron at the age of thirty-six, Leopardi at the age of thirty-nine. Both of them were of noble birth, both of them suffered from physical defect, both of them were in revolt against the established facts and beliefs of their age; but here the likeness between them ends. The stricken poet of Recanati had no country, for an Italy in his day did not exist; he had no audience, no celebrity. The volume of his poems, published in the very year of Byron's death, hardly sold, I suppose, its tens, while the volumes of Byron's poetry were selling their tens of thousands. And yet Leopardi has the very qualities which we have found wanting to Byron; he has the sense for form and style, the passion for just expression, the sure and firm touch of the true artist. Nay, more, he has a grave fulness of knowledge, an insight into the real bearings of the questions which as a sceptical poet he raises, a power of seizing the real point, a lucidity, with which the author of *Cain* has nothing to compare. I can hardly imagine Leopardi reading the

> . . . And *thou* would'st go on aspiring
> To the great double Mysteries! the *two Principles*!

or following Byron in his theological controversy with Dr Kennedy, without having his features overspread by a calm and fine smile, and remarking of his brilliant contemporary as Goethe did, that 'the moment he begins to reflect, he is a child'. But indeed whoever wishes to feel the full superiority of Leopardi over Byron in philosophic thought, and in the expression of it, has only to read one paragraph of one poem, the paragraph of *La Ginestra*, beginning

> Sovente in queste piagge,

and ending

> Non so se il riso o la pietà prevale.

In like manner, Leopardi is at many points the poetic superior of Wordsworth too. He has a far wider culture than Wordsworth, more mental lucidity, more freedom from illusions as to the real character of the established fact and of reigning conventions;

above all, this Italian, with his pure and sure touch, with his fineness of perception, is far more of the artist. Such a piece of pompous dulness as

> O for the coming of that glorious time,

and all the rest of it, or such lumbering verse as Mr Ruskin's enemy,

> Parching summer hath no warrant—

would have been as impossible to Leopardi as to Dante. Where then, is Wordsworth's superiority? for the worth of what he has given us in poetry I hold to be greater, on the whole, than the worth of what Leopardi has given us. It is in Wordsworth's sound and profound sense

> Of joy in widest commonalty spread;

whereas Leopardi remains with his thoughts ever fixed upon the *essenza insanabile*, upon the *acerbo indegno mistero delle cose*. It is in the power with which Wordsworth feels the resources of joy offered to us in nature, offered to us in the primary human affections and duties, and in the power with which, in his moments of inspiration, he renders this joy, and makes us, too, feel it; a force greater than himself seeming to lift him and to prompt his tongue, so that he speaks in a style far above any style of which he has the constant command, and with a truth far beyond any philosophic truth of which he has the conscious and assured possession. Neither Leopardi nor Wordsworth are of the same order with the great poets who made such verse as

> Τλητὸν γὰρ Μοῖραι θυμὸν θέσαν ἀνθρώποισιν·

or as

> In la sua volontade è nostra pace;

or as

> . . . Men must endure
> Their going hence, even as their coming hither;
> Ripeness is all.

But as compared with Leopardi, Wordsworth, though at many points less lucid, though far less a master of style, far less of an artist, gains so much by his criticism of life being, in certain matters of profound importance, healthful and true, whereas Leopardi's pessimism is not, that the value of Wordsworth's poetry, on the whole, stands higher for us than that of Leopardi's, as it stands higher for us, I think, than that of any modern poetry except Goethe's.

Byron's poetic value is also greater, on the whole, than Leopardi's; and his superiority turns in the same way upon the surpassing worth of something which he had and was, after all deduction has been made for his shortcomings. We talk of Byron's *personality*, 'a personality in eminence such as has never been yet, and is not likely to come again'; and we say that by this personality Byron is 'different from all the rest of English poets, and in the main greater'. But can we not be a little more circumstantial, and name that in which the wonderful power of this personality consisted? We can; with the instinct of a poet Mr Swinburne has seized upon it and named it for us. The power of Byron's personality lies in 'the splendid and imperishable excellence which covers all his offences and outweighs all his defects: *the excellence of sincerity and strength*'.

Byron found our nation, after its long and victorious struggle with revolutionary France, fixed in a system of established facts and dominant ideas which revolted him. The mental bondage of the most powerful part of our nation, of its strong middle-class, to a narrow and false system of this kind, is what we call British Philistinism. That bondage is unbroken to this hour, but in Byron's time it was even far more deep and dark than it is now. Byron was an aristocrat, and it is not difficult for an aristocrat to look on the prejudices and habits of the British Philistine with scepticism and disdain. Plenty of young men of his own class Byron met at Almack's or at Lady Jersey's, who regarded the established facts and reigning beliefs of the England of that day with as little reverence as he did. But these men, disbelievers in British Philistinism in private, entered English public life, the most conventional in the world, and at once they saluted with respect the habits and ideas of British Philistinism as if they were a part of the order of creation, and as if in public no sane man would think of warring against them. With Byron it was different. What he called the *cant* of the great middle part of the English nation, what we call its Philistinism, revolted him;

but the cant of his own class, deferring to this Philistinism and profiting by it, while they disbelieved in it, revolted him even more. 'Come what may', are his own words, 'I will never flatter the million's canting in any shape.' His class in general, on the other hand, shrugged their shoulders at this cant, laughed at it, pandered to it, and ruled by it. The falsehood, cynicism, insolence, misgovernment, oppression, with their consequent unfailing crop of human misery, which were produced by this state of things, roused Byron to irreconcilable revolt and battle. They made him indignant, they infuriated him; they were so strong, so defiant, so maleficent,—and yet he felt that they were doomed. 'You have seen every trampler down in turn,' he comforts himself with saying, 'from Buonaparte to the simplest individuals.' The old order, as after 1815 it stood victorious, with its ignorance and misery below, its cant, selfishness, and cynicism above, was at home and abroad equally hateful to him. 'I have simplified my politics', he writes, 'into an utter detestation of all existing governments.' And again: 'Give me a republic. The king-times are fast finishing; there will be blood shed like water and tears like mist, but the peoples will conquer in the end. I shall not live to see it, but I foresee it.'

Byron himself gave the preference, he tells us, to politicians and doers, far above writers and singers. But the politics of his own day and of his own class,—even of the Liberals of his own class,—were impossible for him. Nature had not formed him for a Liberal peer, proper to move the Address in the House of Lords, to pay compliments to the energy and self-reliance of British middle-class Liberalism, and to adapt his politics to suit it. Unfitted for such politics, he threw himself upon poetry as his organ; and in poetry his topics were not Queen Mab, and the Witch of Atlas, and the Sensitive Plant—they were the upholders of the old order, George the Third, and Lord Castlereagh and the Duke of Wellington and Southey, and they were the canters and tramplers of the great world, and they were his enemies and himself.

Such was Byron's personality, by which 'he is different from all the rest of English poets, and in the main greater'. But he posed all his life, says M. Scherer. Let us distinguish. There is the Byron who posed, there is the Byron with his affectations and silliness, the Byron whose weakness Lady Blessington, with a woman's acuteness, so admirably seized: 'His great defect is flippancy and a total want of self-possession.' But when this theatrical and easily criticized personage betook himself to poetry, and when he had fairly warmed to his work, then he became another man; then the theatrical personage passed away; then a higher power took possession of him and filled him; then at last came forth into light that true and puissant personality, with its direct strokes, its ever-welling force, its satire, its energy, and its agony. This is the real Byron; whoever stops at the theatrical preludings does not know him. And this real Byron may well be superior to the stricken Leopardi, he may well be declared 'different from all the rest of English poets, and in the main greater', in so far as it is true of him, as M. Taine well says, that 'all other souls, in comparison with his, seem inert'; in so far as it is true of him that with superb, exhaustless energy, he maintained, as Professor Nichol well says, 'the struggle that keeps alive, if it does not save, the soul'; in so far, finally, as he deserves (and he does deserve) the noble praise of him which I have already quoted from Mr Swinburne; the praise for 'the splendid and imperishable excellence which covers all his offences and outweighs all his defects: *the excellence of sincerity and strength*'.

True, as a man, Byron could not manage himself, could not guide his ways aright, but was all astray. True, he has no light, cannot lead us from the past to the future; 'the moment he reflects, he is a child'. The way out of the false state of things which enraged him he did not see,—the slow and laborious way upward; he had not the patience, knowledge, self-discipline, virtue, requisite for seeing it. True, also, as a poet, he has no fine and exact sense for word and structure and rhythm; he has not the artist's nature and gifts. Yet a personality of Byron's force counts for so much in life, and a rhetorician of Byron's force counts for so much in literature! But it would be most unjust to label Byron, as M. Scherer is disposed to label him, as a rhetorician only. Along with his astounding power and passion he had a strong and deep sense for what is beautiful in nature, and for what is beautiful in human action and suffering. When he warms to his work, when he is inspired, Nature herself seems to take the pen from him as she took it from Wordsworth, and to write for him as she wrote for Wordsworth, though in a different fashion, with her own penetrating simplicity. Goethe has well observed of Byron, that when he is at his happiest his representation of things is as easy and real as if he were improvising. It is so; and his verse then exhibits quite another and a higher quality from the rhetorical quality,—admirable as this also in its own kind of merit is,—of such verse as

> Minions of splendour shrinking from distress,

and of so much more verse of Byron's of that stamp. Nature, I say, takes the pen for him; and then, assured master of a true poetic style though he is not, any more than Wordsworth, yet as from Wordsworth at his best there will come such verse as

> Will no one tell me what she sings?

so from Byron, too, at his best, there will come such verse as

> He heard it, but he heeded not; his eyes
> Were with his heart, and that was far away.

Of verse of this high quality, Byron has much; of verse of a quality lower than this, of a quality rather rhetorical than truly poetic, yet still of extraordinary power and merit, he has still more. To separate, from the mass of poetry which Byron poured forth, all this higher portion, so superior to the mass, and still so considerable in quantity, and to present it in one body by itself, is to do a service, I believe, to Byron's reputation, and to the poetic glory of our country.

Such a service I have in the present volume attempted to perform. To Byron, after all the tributes which have been paid to him, here is yet one tribute more—

> Among thy mightier offerings here are mine!

Not a tribute of boundless homage certainly, but sincere; a tribute which consists not in covering the poet with eloquent eulogy of our own, but in letting him, at his best and greatest, speak for himself. Surely the critic who does most for his author is the critic who gains readers for his author himself, not for any lucubrations on his author;—gains more readers for him, and enables those readers to read him with more admiration.

And in spite of his prodigious vogue, Byron has never yet, perhaps, had the serious admiration which he deserves. Society read him and talked about him, as it reads and talks about *Endymion* today; and with the same sort of result. It looked in Byron's glass as it looks in Lord Beaconsfield's, and sees, or fancies that it sees, its own face there; and then it goes its way, and straightway forgets what manner of man it saw. Even of his passionate admirers, how many never got beyond the theatrical Byron, from whom they caught the fashion of deranging their hair, or of knotting their neck-handkerchief, or of leaving their shirt-collar unbuttoned; how few profoundly felt his vital influence, the influence of his splendid and imperishable excellence of sincerity and strength!

His own aristocratic class, whose cynical make-believe drove him to fury; the great middle-class, on whose impregnable Philistinism he shattered himself to pieces,—how little have either of these felt Byron's vital influence! As the inevitable break-up of the old order comes, as the English middle-class slowly awakens from its intellectual sleep of two centuries, as our actual present world, to which this sleep has condemned us, shows itself more clearly,—our world of an aristocracy materialized and null, a middle-class purblind and hideous, a lower class crude and brutal,—we shall turn our eyes again, and to more purpose, upon this passionate and dauntless soldier of a forlorn hope, who, ignorant of the future and unconsoled by its promises, nevertheless waged against the conservation of the old impossible world so fiery battle; waged it till he fell,—waged it with such splendid and imperishable excellence of sincerity and strength.

Wordsworth's value is of another kind. Wordsworth has an insight into permanent sources of joy and consolation for mankind which Byron has not; his poetry gives us more which we may rest upon than Byron's,—more which we can rest upon now, and which men may rest upon always. I place Wordsworth's poetry, therefore, above Byron's on the whole, although in some points he was greatly Byron's inferior, and although Byron's poetry will always, probably, find more readers than Wordsworth's, and will give pleasure more easily. But these two, Wordsworth and Byron, stand, it seems to me, first and preeminent in actual performance, a glorious pair, among the English poets of this century. Keats had probably, indeed, a more consummate poetic gift than either of them; but he died having produced too little and being as yet too immature to rival them. I for my part can never even think of equalling with them any other of their contemporaries;—either Coleridge, poet and philosopher wrecked in a mist of opium; or Shelley, beautiful and ineffectual angel, beating in the void his luminous wings in vain. Wordsworth and Byron stand out by themselves. When the year 1900 is turned, and our nation comes to recount her poetic glories in the century which has then just ended, the first names with her will be these.

VII

SHELLEY

Nowadays all things appear in print sooner or later; but I have heard from a lady who knew Mrs Shelley a story of her which, so far as I know, has not appeared in print hitherto. Mrs Shelley was choosing a school for her son, and asked the advice of this lady, who gave for advice—to use her own words to me—'Just the sort of banality, you know, one does come out with: Oh, send him somewhere where they will teach him to think for himself!' I have had far too long a training as a school inspector to presume to call an utterance of this kind a *banality*; however, it is not on this advice that I now wish to lay stress, but upon Mrs Shelley's reply to it. Mrs Shelley answered: 'Teach him to think for himself? Oh, my God, teach him rather to think like other people!'

To the lips of many and many a reader of Professor Dowden's volumes a cry of this sort will surely rise, called forth by Shelley's life as there delineated. I have read those volumes with the deepest interest, but I regret their publication, and am surprised, I confess, that Shelley's family should have desired or assisted it. For my own part, at any rate, I would gladly have been left with the impression, the ineffaceable impression, made upon me by Mrs Shelley's first edition of her husband's collected poems. Medwin and Hogg and Trelawny had done little to change the impression made by those four delightful volumes of the original edition of 1839. The text of the poems has in some places been mended since; but Shelley is not a classic, whose various readings are to be noted with earnest attention. The charm of the poems flowed in upon us from that edition and the charm of the character. Mrs Shelley had done her work admirably; her introductions to the poems of each year, with Shelley's prefaces and passages from his letters, supplied the very picture of Shelley to be desired. Somewhat idealized by tender regret and exalted memory Mrs Shelley's representation no doubt was. But without sharing her conviction that Shelley's character, impartially judged, 'would stand in fairer and brighter light than that of any contemporary', we learned from her to know the soul of affection, of 'gentle and cordial goodness', of eagerness and ardour for human happiness, which was in this rare spirit—so mere a monster unto many. Mrs Shelley said in her general preface to her husband's poems: 'I abstain from any remark on the occurrences of his private life, except inasmuch as the passions which they engendered inspired his poetry; this is not the time to relate the truth.' I for my part could wish, I repeat, that that time had never come.

But come it has, and Professor Dowden has given us the Life of Percy Bysshe Shelley in two very thick volumes. If the work was to be done, Professor Dowden has indeed done it thoroughly. One or two things in his biography of Shelley I could wish different, even waiving the question whether it was desirable to relate in full the occurrences of Shelley's private life. Professor Dowden holds a brief for Shelley; he pleads for Shelley as an advocate pleads for his client, and this strain of pleading, united with an attitude of adoration which in Mrs Shelley had its charm, but which Professor Dowden was not bound to adopt from her, is unserviceable to Shelley, nay, injurious to him, because it inevitably begets, in many readers of the story which Professor Dowden has to tell, impatience and revolt. Further, let me remark that the biography before us is of prodigious length, although its hero died before he was thirty years old, and that it might have been considerably shortened if it had been more plainly and simply written. I see that one of Professor Dowden's critics, while praising his style for 'a certain poetic quality of fervour and picturesqueness', laments that in some important passages Professor Dowden 'fritters away great opportunities for sustained and impassioned narrative'. I am inclined much rather to lament that Professor Dowden has not steadily kept his poetic quality of fervour and picturesqueness more under control. Is it that the Home Rulers have so loaded the language that even an Irishman who is not one of them catches something of their full habit of style? No, it is rather, I believe, that Professor Dowden, of poetic nature himself, and dealing with a poetic nature like Shelley, is so steeped in sentiment by his subject that in almost every page of the biography the sentiment runs over. A curious note of his style, suffused with sentiment, is that it seems incapable of using the common word *child*. A great many births are mentioned in the biography, but always it is a poetic *babe* that is born, not a prosaic *child*. And so, again, André Chénier is not guillotined, but 'too foully done to death'. Again, Shelley after his runaway marriage with Harriet West-brook was in Edinburgh without money and full of anxieties for the future, and complained of his hard lot in being unable to get away, in being 'chained to the filth and commerce of Edinburgh'. Natural enough; but why should Professor Dowden improve the occasion as follows? 'The most romantic of northern cities could lay no spell upon his spirit. His eye was not fascinated by the presences of mountains and the sea, by the fantastic outlines of aërial piles seen amid the wreathing smoke of Auld Reekie, by the gloom of the Canongate illuminated with shafts of sunlight streaming from its interesting wynds and alleys; nor was his imagination kindled by storied house or palace, and the voices of old, forgotten, far-off things, which haunt their walls.' If Professor Dowden, writing a book in prose, could have brought himself to eschew poetic excursions of this kind and to tell his story in a plain way, lovers of simplicity, of whom there are some still left in the world, would have been gratified, and at the same time his book would have been the shorter by scores of pages.

These reserves being made, I have little except praise for the manner in which Professor Dowden has performed his task; whether it was a task which ought to be performed at all, probably did not lie with him to decide. His ample materials are used with order and judgment; the history of Shelley's life develops itself clearly before our eyes; the documents of importance for it are given with sufficient fulness, nothing essential seems to have been kept back, although I would gladly, I confess, have seen more of Miss Clairmont's journal, whatever arrangements she may in her later life have chosen to exercise upon it. In general all documents are so fairly and fully cited, that Professor Dowden's pleadings for Shelley, though they may sometimes indispose and irritate the reader, produce no obscuring of the truth; the documents manifest it of themselves. Last but not least of Professor Dowden's merits, he has provided his book with an excellent index.

Undoubtedly this biography, with its full account of the occurrences of Shelley's private life, compels one to review one's former impression of him. Undoubtedly the brilliant and attaching rebel who in thinking for himself had of old our sympathy so passionately with him, when we come to read his full biography makes us often and often inclined to cry out: 'My God! he had far better have thought like other people.' There is a passage in Hogg's capitally written and most interesting account of Shelley which I wrote down when I first read it and have borne in mind ever since; so beautifully it seemed to render the true Shelley. Hogg has been speaking of the intellectual expression of Shelley's features, and he goes on: 'Nor was the moral expression less beautiful than the intellectual; for there was a softness, a delicacy, a gentleness, and especially (though this will surprise many) that air of profound religious veneration that characterizes the best works and chiefly the frescoes (and into these they infused their whole souls) of the great masters of Florence and of Rome.' What we have of Shelley in poetry and prose suited with this charming picture of him; Mrs Shelley's account suited with it; it was a possession which one would gladly have kept unimpaired. It still subsists, I must now add; it subsists even after one has read the present biography; it subsists, but so as by fire. It subsists with many a scar and stain; never again will it have the same pureness and beauty which it had formerly. I regret this, as I have said, and I confess I do not see what has been gained. Our ideal Shelley was the true Shelley after all; what has been gained by making us at moments doubt it? What has been gained by forcing upon us so much in him which is ridiculous and odious, by compelling any fair mind, if it is to retain with a good conscience its ideal Shelley, to do that which I propose to do now? I propose to mark firmly what is ridiculous and odious in the Shelley brought to our knowledge by the new materials, and then to show that our former beautiful and lovable Shelley nevertheless survives.

Almost everybody knows the main outline of the events of Shelley's life. It will be necessary for me, however, up to the date of his second marriage, to go through them here. Percy Bysshe Shelley was born at Field Place, near Horsham, in Sussex, on the 4th of August 1792. He was of an old family of country gentlemen, and the heir to a baronetcy. He had one brother and five sisters, but the brother was so much younger than himself as to be no companion for him in his boyhood at home, and after he was separated from home and England he never saw him. Shelley was brought up at Field Place with his sisters. At ten years old he was sent to a private school at Isleworth, where he read Mrs Radcliffe's romances and was fascinated by a popular scientific lecturer. After two years of private school he went in 1804 to Eton. Here he took no part in cricket or football, refused to fag, was known as 'mad Shelley' and much tormented; when tormented beyond endurance he could be dangerous. Certainly he was not happy at Eton; but he had friends, he boated, he rambled about the country. His school lessons were easy to him, and his reading extended far beyond them; he read books on chemistry, he read Pliny's *Natural History*, Godwin's *Political Justice*, Lucretius, Franklin, Condorcet. It is said he was called 'atheist Shelley' at Eton, but this is not so well established as his having been called 'mad Shelley'. He was full, at any rate, of new and revolutionary ideas, and he declared at a later time that he was twice expelled from the school but recalled through the interference of his father.

In the spring of 1810 Shelley, now in his eighteenth year, entered University College, Oxford, as an exhibitioner. He had already written novels and poems; a poem on the Wandering Jew, in seven or eight cantos, he sent to Campbell, and was told by Campbell that there were but two good lines in it. He had solicited the correspondence of Mrs Hemans, then Felicia Browne and unmarried; he had fallen in love with a charming cousin, Harriet Grove. In the autumn of 1810 he found a publisher for his verse; he also found a friend in a very clever and free-minded commoner of his college, Thomas Jefferson Hogg, who has admirably described the Shelley of those Oxford days, with his chemistry, his eccentric habits, his charm of look and character, his conversation, his shrill discordant voice. Shelley read incessantly. Hume's *Essays* produced a powerful impression on him; his free speculation led him to what his father, and worse still his cousin Harriet, thought, 'detestable principles'; his cousin and his family became estranged from him. He, on his part, became more and more incensed against the 'bigotry' and 'intolerance' which produced such estrangement. 'Here I swear, and as I break my oaths, may Infinity, Eternity, blast me—here I swear that never will I forgive intolerance.' At the beginning of 1811 he prepared and published what he called a 'leaflet for letters', having for its title *The Necessity of Atheism*. He sent copies to all the bishops, to the Vice-Chancellor of Oxford, and to the heads of houses. On Lady Day he was summoned before the authorities of his College, refused to answer the question whether he had written *The Necessity of Atheism*, told the Master and Fellows that 'their proceedings would become a court of inquisitors but not free men in a free country', and was expelled for contumacy. Hogg wrote a letter of remonstrance to the authorities, was in his turn summoned before them and questioned as to his share in the 'leaflet', and, refusing to answer, he also was expelled.

Shelley settled with Hogg in lodgings in London. His father, excusably indignant, was not a wise man and managed his son ill. His plan of recommending Shelley to read Paley's *Natural Theology*, and of *reading it with him himself*, makes us smile. Shelley, who about this time wrote of his younger sister, then at school at Clapham, 'There are some hopes of this dear little girl, she would be a divine little scion of infidelity if I could get hold of her', was not to have been cured by Paley's *Natural Theology* administered through Mr Timothy Shelley. But by the middle of May Shelley's father had agreed to allow him two hundred pounds a year. Meanwhile in visiting his sisters at their school in Clapham, Shelley made the acquaintance of a schoolfellow of theirs, Harriet Westbrook. She was a beautiful and lively girl, with a father who had kept a tavern in Mount Street, but had now retired from business, and one sister much older than herself, who encouraged in every possible way the acquaintance of her sister of sixteen with the heir to a baronetcy and a great estate. Soon Shelley heard that Harriet met with cold looks at her school for associating with an atheist; his generosity and his ready indignation against 'intolerance' were roused. In the summer Harriet wrote to him that she was persecuted not at school only but at home also, that she was lonely and miserable, and would gladly put an end to her life. Shelley went to see her; she owned her love for him, and he engaged himself to her. He told his cousin Charles Grove that his happiness had been blighted when the other Harriet, Charles's sister, cast him off; that now the only thing worth living for was self-sacrifice. Harriet's persecutors became yet more troublesome, and Shelley, at the end of August, went off with her to

Edinburgh and they were married. The entry in the register is this:

August 28, 1811.—Percy Bysshe Shelley, farmer, Sussex, and Miss Harriet Westbrook, St Andrew Church Parish, daughter of Mr John Westbrook, London.

After five weeks in Edinburgh the young farmer and his wife came southwards and took lodgings at York, under the shadow of what Shelley calls that 'gigantic pile of superstition', the Minster. But his friend Hogg was in a lawyer's office in York, and Hogg's society made the Minster endurable. Mr Timothy Shelley's happiness in his son was naturally not increased by the runaway marriage; he stopped his allowance, and Shelley determined to visit 'this thoughtless man', as he calls his parent, and to 'try the force of truth' upon him. Nothing could be effected; Shelley's mother, too, was now against him. He returned to York to find that in his absence his friend Hogg had been making love to Harriet, who had indignantly repulsed him. Shelley was shocked, but after a 'terrible day' of explanation from Hogg, he 'fully, freely pardoned him', promised to retain him still as 'his friend, his bosom friend', and 'hoped soon to convince him how lovely virtue was'. But for the present it seemed better to separate. In November he and Harriet, with his sister Eliza, took a cottage at Keswick. Shelley was now in great straits for money; the great Sussex neighbour of the Shelleys, the Duke of Norfolk, interposed in his favour, and his father and grandfather seem to have offered him at this time an income of £2,000 a year, if he would consent to entail the family estate. Shelley indignantly refused to 'forswear his principles', by accepting 'a proposal so insultingly hateful'. But in December his father agreed, though with an ill grace, to grant him his allowance of £200 a year again, and Mr Westbrook promised to allow a like sum to his daughter. So after four months of marriage the Shelleys began 1812 with an income of £400 a year.

Early in February they left Keswick and proceeded to Dublin, where Shelley, who had prepared an address to the Catholics, meant to 'devote himself towards forwarding the great ends of virtue and happiness in Ireland'. Before leaving Keswick he wrote to William Godwin, 'the regulator and former of his mind', making profession of his mental obligations to him, of his respect

and veneration, and soliciting Godwin's friendship. A correspondence followed; Godwin pronounced his young disciple's
plans for 'disseminating the doctrines of philanthropy and
freedom' in Ireland to be unwise; Shelley bowed to his mentor's
decision and gave up his Irish campaign, quitting Dublin on
the 4th of April 1812. He and Harriet wandered first to Nant-
Gwillt in South Wales, near the upper Wye, and from thence
after a month or two to Lynmouth in North Devon, where he
busied himself with his poem of *Queen Mab*, and with sending
to sea boxes and bottles containing a *Declaration of Rights* by
him, in the hope that the winds and waves might carry his
doctrines where they would do good. But his Irish servant,
bearing the prophetic name of Healy, posted the *Declaration*
on the walls of Barnstaple and was taken up; Shelley found
himself watched and no longer able to enjoy Lynmouth in peace.
He moved in September 1812 to Tremadoc, in North Wales,
where he threw himself ardently into an enterprise for recover-
ing a great stretch of drowned land from the sea. But at the
beginning of October he and Harriet visited London, and Shelley
grasped Godwin by the hand at last. At once an intimacy arose,
but the future Mary Shelley—Godwin's daughter by his first
wife, Mary Wollstonecraft—was absent on a visit in Scotland
when the Shelleys arrived in London. They became acquainted,
however, with the second Mrs Godwin, on whom we have
Charles Lamb's friendly comment: 'A very disgusting woman,
and wears green spectacles!' with the amiable Fanny, Mary
Wollstonecraft's daughter by Imlay, before her marriage with
Godwin; and probably also with Jane Clairmont, the second
Mrs Godwin's daughter by a first marriage, and herself afterwards the mother of Byron's Allegra. Complicated relationships,
as in the Theban story! and there will be not wanting, presently,
something of the Theban horrors. During this visit of six weeks
to London Shelley renewed his intimacy with Hogg; in the
middle of November he returned to Tremadoc. There he remained until the end of February 1813, perfectly happy with
Harriet, reading widely, and working at his *Queen Mab* and at
the notes to that poem. On the 26th of February an attempt was
made, or so he fancied, to assassinate him, and in high nervous
excitement he hurriedly left Tremadoc and repaired with
Harriet to Dublin again. On this visit to Ireland he saw

Killarney, but early in April he and Harriet were back again in London.

There in June 1813 their daughter Ianthe was born; at the end of July they moved to Bracknell, in Berkshire. They had for neighbours there a Mrs Boinville and her married daughter, whom Shelley found to be fascinating women, with a culture which to his wife was altogether wanting. Cornelia Turner, Mrs Boinville's daughter, was melancholy, required consolation, and found it, Hogg tells us, in Petrarch's poetry; 'Bysshe entered at once fully into her views and caught the soft infection, breathing the tenderest and sweetest melancholy as every true poet ought'. Peacock, a man of keen and cultivated mind, joined the circle at Bracknell. He and Harriet, not yet eighteen, used sometimes to laugh at the gushing sentiment and enthusiasm of the Bracknell circle; Harriet had also given offence to Shelley by getting a wet-nurse for her child; in Professor Dowden's words, 'the beauty of Harriet's motherly relation to her babe was marred in Shelley's eyes by the introduction into his home of a hireling nurse to whom was delegated the mother's tenderest office'. But in September Shelley wrote a sonnet to his child which expresses his deep love for the mother also, to whom in March 1814 he was remarried in London, lest the Scotch marriage should prove to have been in any point irregular. Harriet's sister Eliza, however, whom Shelley had at first treated with excessive deference, had now become hateful to him. And in the very month of the London marriage we find him writing to Hogg that he is staying with the Boinvilles, having 'escaped, in the society of all that philosophy and friendship combine, from the dismaying solitude of myself'. Cornelia Turner, he adds, whom he once thought cold and reserved, 'is the reverse of this, as she is the reverse of everything bad; she inherits all the divinity of her mother'. Then comes a stanza, beginning

> Thy dewy looks sink in my breast,
> Thy gentle words stir poison there.

It has no meaning, he says; it is only written in thought. 'It is evident from this pathetic letter', says Professor Dowden, 'that Shelley's happiness in his home had been fatally stricken.' This is a curious way of putting the matter. To me what is evident is rather that Shelley had, to use Professor Dowden's words again—for in these things of high sentiment I gladly let him speak for me—'a too vivid sense that here (in the society of the Boinville family) were peace and joy and gentleness and love'. In April come some more verses to the Boinvilles, which contain the first good stanza that Shelley wrote. In May comes a poem to Harriet, of which Professor Dowden's prose analysis is as poetic as the poem itself. 'If she has something to endure (from the Boinville attachment), it is not much, and all her husband's weal hangs upon her loving endurance, for see how pale and wildered anguish has made him!' Harriet, unconvinced, seems to have gone off to Bath in resentment, from whence, however, she kept up a constant correspondence with Shelley, who was now of age, and busy in London raising money on post-obit bonds for his own wants and those of the friend and former of his mind, Godwin.

And now, indeed, it was to become true that if from the inflammable Shelley's devotion to the Boinville family poor Harriet had had 'something to endure', yet this was 'not much' compared with what was to follow. At Godwin's house Shelley met Mary Wollstonecraft Godwin, his future wife, then in her seventeenth year. She was a gifted person, but, as Professor Dowden says, she 'had breathed during her entire life an atmosphere of free thought'. On the 8th of June Hogg called at Godwin's with Shelley; Godwin was out, but 'a door was partially and softly opened, a thrilling voice called "Shelley!" a thrilling voice answered "Mary!" Shelley's summoner was 'a very young female, fair and fair-haired, pale indeed, and with a piercing look, wearing a frock of tartan'. Already they were 'Shelley' and 'Mary' to one another; 'before the close of June they knew and felt', says Professor Dowden, 'that each was to the other inexpressibly dear'. The churchyard of St Pancras, where her mother was buried, became 'a place now doubly sacred to Mary, since on one eventful day Bysshe here poured forth his griefs, his hopes, his love, and she, in sign of everlasting union, placed her hand in his'. In June Shelley gave her a copy of *Queen Mab*, printed but not published, and under the tender dedication to Harriet he wrote: 'Count Slobendorf was about to marry a woman who, attracted solely by his fortune, proved her selfishness by deserting him in prison.' Mary added an inscription on her part: 'I love the author beyond all powers of expression . . .

by that love we have promised to each other, although I may not be yours I can never be another's,'—and a good deal more to the same effect.

Amid these excitements Shelley was for some days without writing to Harriet, who applied to Hookham the publisher to know what had happened. She was expecting her confinement; 'I always fancy something dreadful has happened', she wrote, 'if I do not hear from him . . . I cannot endure this dreadful state of suspense.' Shelley then wrote to her, begging her to come to London; and when she arrived there, he told her the state of his feelings, and proposed separation. The shock made Harriet ill; and Shelley, says Peacock, 'between his old feelings towards Harriet, and his new passion for Mary, showed in his looks, in his gestures, in his speech, the state of a mind, 'suffering, like a little kingdom, the nature of an insurrection'. Godwin grew uneasy about his daughter, and after a serious talk with her, wrote to Shelley. Under such circumstances, Professor Dowden tells us, 'to youth, swift and decisive measures seem the best'. In the early morning of the 28th of July 1814 'Mary Godwin stepped across her father's threshold into the summer air', she and Shelley went off together in a post-chaise to Dover, and from thence crossed to the Continent.

On the 14th of August the fugitives were at Troyes on their way to Switzerland. From Troyes Shelley addressed a letter to Harriet, of which the best description I can give is that it is precisely the letter which a man in the writer's circumstances should not have written.

MY DEAREST HARRIET (he begins),—I write to you from this detestable town; I write to show that I do not forget you; I write to urge you to come to Switzerland, where you will at last find one firm and constant friend to whom your interests will be always dear—by whom your feelings will never wilfully be injured. From none can you expect this but me—all else are either unfeeling or selfish, or have beloved friends of their own.

Then follows a description of his journey with Mary from Paris, 'through a fertile country, neither interesting from the character of its inhabitants nor the beauty of the scenery, with a mule to carry our baggage, as Mary, who has not been sufficiently well to walk, fears the fatigue of walking'. Like St Paul to Timothy, he ends with commissions:

> I wish you to bring with you the two deeds which Tahourdin has to prepare for you, as also a copy of the settlement. Do not part with any of your money. But what shall be done about the books? You can consult on the spot. With love to my sweet little Ianthe, ever most affectionately yours,   S.
>
> I write in great haste; we depart directly.

Professor Dowden's flow of sentiment is here so agitating, that I relieve myself by resorting to a drier world. Certainly my comment on this letter shall not be his, that it 'assures Harriet that her interests were still dear to Shelley, though now their lives had moved apart'. But neither will I call the letter an odious letter, a hideous letter. I prefer to call it, applying an untranslatable French word, a *bête* letter. And it is *bête* from what is the signal, the disastrous want and weakness of Shelley, with all his fine intellectual gifts—his utter deficiency in humour.

Harriet did not accept Shelley's invitation to join him and Mary in Switzerland. Money difficulties drove the travellers back to England in September. Godwin would not see Shelley, but he sorely needed, continually demanded, and eagerly accepted, pecuniary help from his erring 'spiritual son'. Between Godwin's wants and his own, Shelley was hard pressed. He got from Harriet, who still believed that he would return to her, twenty pounds which remained in her hands. In November she was confined; a son and heir was born to Shelley. He went to see Harriet, but 'the interview left husband and wife each embittered against the other'. Friends were severe; 'when Mrs Boinville wrote, her letter seemed cold and even sarcastic', says Professor Dowden. 'Solitude,' he continues, 'unharassed by debts and duns, with Mary's companionship, the society of a few friends, and the delights of study and authorship, would have made these winter months to Shelley months of unusual happiness and calm.' But, alas! creditors were pestering, and even Harriet gave trouble. In January 1815 Mary had to write in her journal this entry: 'Harriet sends her creditors here; nasty woman. Now we must change our lodgings.'

One day about this time Shelley asked Peacock, 'Do you think Wordsworth could have written such poetry if he ever had

dealings with money-lenders?' Not only had Shelley dealings
with money-lenders, he now had dealings with bailiffs also.
But still he continued to read largely. In January 1815 his
grandfather, Sir Bysshe Shelley, died. Shelley went down into
Sussex; his father would not suffer him to enter the house, but
he sat outside the door and read *Comus*, while the reading of his
grandfather's will went on inside. In February was born Mary's
first child, a girl, who lived but a few days. All the spring Shelley
was ill and harassed, but by June it was settled that he should
have an allowance from his father of £1,000 a year, and that his
debts (including £1,200 promised by him to Godwin) should be
paid. He on his part paid Harriet's debts and allowed her £200
a year. In August he took a house on the borders of Windsor
Park, and made a boating excursion up the Thames as far as
Lechlade, an excursion which produced his first poem of value,
the beautiful *Stanzas in Lechlade Churchyard*. They were followed, later in the autumn, by *Alastor*. Henceforth, from this
winter of 1815 until he was drowned between Leghorn and
Spezia in July 1822, Shelley's literary history is sufficiently
given in the delightful introductions prefixed by Mrs Shelley
to the poems of each year. Much of the history of his life is there
given also; but with some of those 'occurrences of his private
life' on which Mrs Shelley forbore to touch, and which are now
made known to us in Professor Dowden's book, we have still
to deal.

Mary's first son, William, was born in January 1816, and in
February we find Shelley declaring himself 'strongly urged,
by the perpetual experience of neglect or enmity from almost
everyone but those who are supported by my resources, to
desert my native country, hiding myself and Mary from the
contempt which we so unjustly endure'. Early in May he left
England with Mary and Miss Clairmont; they met Lord Byron
at Geneva and passed the summer by the Lake of Geneva in his
company. Miss Clairmont had already stayed in London, without
the knowledge of the Shelleys, made Byron's acquaintance and
become his mistress. Shelley determined, in the course of the
summer, to go back to England, and, after all, 'to make that
most excellent of nations my perpetual resting-place'. In
September he and his ladies returned; Miss Clairmont was then
expecting her confinement. Of her being Byron's mistress the

Shelleys were now aware; but 'the moral indignation', says Professor Dowden, 'which Byron's act might justly arouse, seems to have been felt by neither Shelley nor Mary'. If Byron and Claire Clairmont, as she was now called, loved and were happy, all was well.

The eldest daughter of the Godwin household, the amiable Fanny, was unhappy at home and in deep dejection of spirits. Godwin was, as usual, in terrible straits for money. The Shelleys and Miss Clairmont settled themselves at Bath; early in October Fanny Godwin passed through Bath without their knowing it, travelled on to Swansea, took a bedroom at the hotel there, and was found in the morning dead, with a bottle of laudanum on the table beside her and these words in her handwriting:

I have long determined that the best thing I could do was to put an end to the existence of a being whose birth was unfortunate,[1] and whose life has only been a series of pain to those persons who have hurt their health in endeavouring to promote her welfare. Perhaps to hear of my death will give you pain, but you will soon have the blessing of forgetting that such a creature ever existed as . . .

There is no signature.

A sterner tragedy followed. On the 9th of November 1816 Harriet Shelley left the house in Brompton where she was then living, and did not return. On the 10th of December her body was found in the Serpentine; she had drowned herself. In one respect Professor Dowden resembles Providence: his ways are inscrutable. His comment on Harriet's death is: 'There is no doubt she wandered from the ways of upright living.' But, he adds: 'That no act of Shelley's during the two years which immediately preceded her death, tended to cause the rash act which brought her life to its close, seems certain.' Shelley had been living with Mary all the time; only that!

On the 30th of December 1816 Mary Godwin and Shelley were married. I shall pursue 'the occurrences of Shelley's private life' no further. For the five years and a half which remain, Professor Dowden's book adds to our knowledge of Shelley's life much that is interesting; but what was chiefly important we knew already. The new and grave matter which

---

[1] She was Mary Wollstonecraft's natural daughter by Imlay.

we did not know, or knew in the vaguest way only, but which Shelley's family and Professor Dowden have now thought it well to give us in full, ends with Shelley's second marriage.

I regret, I say once more, that it has been given. It is a sore trial for our love of Shelley. What a set! what a world! is the exclamation that breaks from us as we come to an end of this history of 'the occurrences of Shelley's private life'. I used the French word *bête* for a letter of Shelley's; for the world in which we find him I can only use another French word, *sale*. Godwin's house of sordid horror, and Godwin preaching and holding the hat, and the green-spectacled Mrs Godwin, and Hogg the faithful friend, and Hunt the Horace of this precious world, and, to go up higher, Sir Timothy Shelley, a great country gentleman, feeling himself safe while 'the exalted mind of the Duke of Norfolk [the drinking Duke] protects me with the world', and Lord Byron with his deep grain of coarseness and commonness, his affectation, his brutal selfishness—what a set! The history carries us to Oxford, and I think of the clerical and respectable Oxford of those old times, the Oxford of Copleston and the Kebles and Hawkins, and a hundred more, with the relief Keble declares himself to experience from Izaak Walton:

> When, wearied with the tale thy times disclose,
> The eye first finds thee out in thy secure repose.

I am not only thinking of morals and the house of Godwin, I am thinking also of tone, bearing, dignity. I appeal to Cardinal Newman, if perchance he does me the honour to read these words, is it possible to imagine Copleston or Hawkins declaring himself safe 'while the exalted mind of the Duke of Norfolk protects me with the world'?

Mrs Shelley, after her marriage and during Shelley's closing years, becomes attractive; up to her marriage her letters and journal do not please. Her ability is manifest, but she is not attractive. In the world discovered to us by Professor Dowden as surrounding Shelley up to 1817, the most pleasing figure is poor Fanny Godwin; after Fanny Godwin the most pleasing figure is Harriet Shelley herself.

Professor Dowden's treatment of Harriet is not worthy—so much he must allow me in all kindness, but also in all serious-ness, to say—of either his taste or his judgment. His pleading for Shelley is constant, and he does more harm than good to Shelley by it. But here his championship of Shelley makes him very unjust to a cruelly used and unhappy girl. For several pages he balances the question whether or not Harriet was unfaithful to Shelley before he left her for Mary, and he leaves the question unsettled. As usual Professor Dowden (and it is his signal merit) supplies the evidence decisive against himself. Thornton, Hunt, not well disposed to Harriet, Hogg, Peacock, Trelawny, Hookham, and a member of Godwin's own family, are all clear in their evidence that up to her parting from Shelley Harriet was perfectly innocent. But that precious witness, Godwin, wrote in 1817 that 'she had proved herself unfaithful to her husband before their separation. . . . Peace be to her shade!' Why, Godwin was the father of Harriet's successor. But Mary believed the same thing. She was Harriet's successor. But Shelley believed it too. He had it from Godwin. But he was convinced of it earlier. The evidence for this is, that, in writing to Southey in 1820, Shelley declares that 'the single passage of a life, otherwise not only spotless but spent in an impassioned pursuit of virtue, which looks like a blot', bears that appearance 'merely because I regulated my domestic arrangements without deferring to the notions of the vulgar, although I might have done so quite as conveniently had I descended to their base thoughts'. From this Professor Dowden concludes that Shelley believed he could have got a divorce from Harriet had he so wished. The conclusion is not clear. But even were the evidence perfectly clear that Shelley believed Harriet unfaithful when he parted from her, we should have to take into account Mrs Shelley's most true sentence in her introduction to *Alastor*: 'In all Shelley did, he, at the time of doing it, believed himself justified to his own conscience.'

Shelley's asserting a thing vehemently does not prove more than that he chose to believe it and did believe it. His extreme and violent changes of opinion about people show this sufficiently. Eliza Westbrook is at one time 'a diamond not so large' as her sister Harriet but 'more highly polished'; and then: 'I certainly hate her with all my heart and soul. I sometimes feel faint with the fatigue of checking the overflowings of my unbounded abhorrence for this miserable wretch.' The antipathy, Hogg tells us, was as unreasonable as the former excess of deference. To his friend Miss Hitchener he says: 'Never shall that intercourse cease, which has been the day-dawn of my existence, the sun which has shed warmth on the cold drear length of the anticipated prospect of life.' A little later, and she has become 'the Brown Demon, a woman of desperate views and dreadful passions, but of cool and undeviating revenge'. Even Professor Dowden admits that this is absurd: that the real Miss Hitchener was not seen by Shelley, either when he adored or when he detested.

Shelley's power of persuading himself was equal to any occasion; but would not his conscientiousness and high feeling have prevented his exerting this power at poor Harriet's expense? To abandon her as he did, must he not have known her to be false? Professor Dowden insists always on Shelley's 'conscientiousness'. Shelley himself speaks of his 'impassioned pursuit of virtue'. Leigh Hunt compared his life to that of 'Plato himself, or, still more, a Pythagorean', and added that he 'never met a being who came nearer, perhaps so near, to the height of humanity', to being an 'angel of charity'. In many respects Shelley really resembled both a Pythagorean and an angel of charity. He loved high thoughts, he cared nothing for sumptuous lodging, fare, and raiment, he was poignantly afflicted at the sight of misery, he would have given away his last farthing, would have suffered in his own person, to relieve it. But in one important point he was like neither a Pythagorean nor an angel: he was extremely inflammable. Professor Dowden leaves no doubt on the matter. After reading his book, one feels sickened for ever of the subject of irregular relations; God forbid that I should go into the scandals about Shelley's 'Neapolitan charge', about Shelley and Emilia Viviani, about Shelley and Miss Clairmont, and the rest of it! I will say only that it is visible enough that when the passion of love was aroused in Shelley (and it was aroused easily) one could not be sure of him, his friends could not trust him. We have seen him with the Boinville family. With Emilia Viviani he is the same. If he is left much alone with Miss Clairmont, he evidently makes Mary uneasy; nay, he makes Professor Dowden himself uneasy. And I conclude that an entirely human inflammability, joined to an inhuman want of humour and a superhuman power of self-deception, are the causes which chiefly explain Shelley's abandonment of Harriet in the first place, and then his behaviour to her and his defence of himself afterwards.

His misconduct to Harriet, his want of humour, his self-deception, are fully brought before us for the first time by Professor Dowden's book. Good morals and good criticism alike forbid that when all this is laid bare to us we should deny, or hide, or extenuate it. Nevertheless I go back after all to what I said at the beginning; still our ideal Shelley, the angelic Shelley, subsists. Unhappily the data for this Shelley we had and knew long ago, while the data for the unattractive Shelley are fresh; and what is fresh is likely to fix our attention more than what is familiar. But Professor Dowden's volumes, which give so much, which give too much, also afford data for picturing anew the Shelley who delights, as well as for picturing for the first time a Shelley who, to speak plainly, disgusts; and with what may renew and restore our impression of the delightful Shelley I shall end.

The winter at Marlow, and the ophthalmia caught among the cottages of the poor, we knew, but we have from Professor Dowden more details of this winter and of Shelley's work among the poor; we have above all, for the first time I believe, a line of verse of Shelley's own which sums up truly and perfectly this most attractive side of him—

I am the friend of the unfriended poor.

But that in Shelley on which I would especially dwell is that in him which contrasts most with the ignobleness of the world in which we have seen him living, and with the pernicious nonsense which we have found him talking. The Shelley of 'marvellous gentleness', of feminine refinement, with gracious and considerate manners, 'a perfect gentleman, entirely without arrogance or aggressive egotism', completely devoid of the proverbial and ferocious vanity of authors and poets, always disposed to make little of his own work and to prefer that of others, of reverent enthusiasm for the great and wise, of high and tender seriousness, of heroic generosity, and of a delicacy in rendering services which was equal to his generosity—the Shelley who was all this is the Shelley with whom I wish to end. He may talk nonsense about tyrants and priests, but what a high and noble ring in such a sentence as the following, written by a young man who is refusing £2,000 a year rather than consent to entail a great property!

That I should entail £120,000 of command over labour, of power to remit this, to employ it for benevolent purposes, on one whom I know not—who might, instead of being the benefactor of mankind, be its bane, or use this for the worst purposes, which the real delegates of my chance-given property might convert into a most useful instrument of benevolence! No! this you will not suspect me of.

And again:—

I desire money because I think I know the use of it. It commands labour, it gives leisure; and to give leisure to those who will employ it in the forwarding of truth is the noblest present an individual can make to the whole.

If there is extravagance here, it is extravagance of a beautiful and rare sort, like Shelley's 'underhand ways' also, which differed singularly, the cynic Hogg tells us, from the underhand ways of other people; 'the latter were concealed because they were mean, selfish, sordid; Shelley's secrets, on the contrary (kindnesses done by stealth), were hidden through modesty, delicacy, generosity, refinement of soul'.

His forbearance to Godwin, to Godwin lecturing and renouncing him and at the same time holding out, as I have said, his hat to him for alms, is wonderful; but the dignity with which he at last, in a letter perfect for propriety of tone, reads a lesson to his ignoble father-in-law, is in the best possible style:

Perhaps it is well that you should be informed that I consider your last letter to be written in a style of haughtiness and encroachment which neither awes nor imposes on me; but I have no desire to transgress the limits which you place to our intercourse, nor in any future instance will I made any remarks but such as arise from the strict question in discussion.

And again:—

My astonishment, and, I will confess, when I have been treated with most harshness and cruelty by you, my indignation, has been extreme, that, knowing as you do my nature, any considerations should have prevailed on you to have been thus harsh and cruel. I lamented also over my ruined hopes of all that your genius once taught me to expect from your virtue, when I found that for yourself, your family, and your creditors, you would submit to that communication with me which you once rejected and abhorred, and which no pity for my poverty or sufferings, assumed willingly for you, could avail to extort.

Moreover, though Shelley has no humour, he can show as quick and sharp a tact as the most practised man of the world. He has been with Byron and the Countess Guicciolo, and he writes of the latter:

La Guiccioli is a very pretty, sentimental, innocent Italian, who has sacrificed an immense future for the sake of Lord Byron, and who, if I know anything of my friend, of her, and of human nature, will hereafter have plenty of opportunity to repent her rashness.

Tact also, and something better than tact, he shows in his dealings, in order to befriend Leigh Hunt, with Lord Byron. He writes to Hunt:

Particular circumstances, or rather, I should say, particular dispositions in Lord Byron's character, render the close and exclusive intimacy with him, in which I find myself, intolerable to me; thus much, my best friend, I will confess and confide to you. No feelings of my own shall injure or interfere with what is now nearest to them—your interest; and I will take care to preserve the little influence I may have over this Proteus, in whom such strange extremes are reconciled, until we meet.

And so we have come back again, at last, to our original Shelley—to the Shelley of the lovely and well-known picture, to the Shelley with 'flushed, feminine, artless face', the Shelley 'blushing like a girl', of Trelawny. Professor Dowden gives us some further attempts at portraiture. One by a Miss Rose, of Shelley at Marlow:

He was the most interesting figure I ever saw; his eyes like a deer's, bright but rather wild; his white throat unfettered; his slender but to me almost faultless shape; his brown long coat with curling lambs' wool collar and cuffs—in fact, his whole appearance—are as fresh in my recollection as an occurrence of yesterday.'

Feminine enthusiasm may be deemed suspicious, but a Captain Kennedy must surely be able to keep his head. Captain Kennedy was quartered at Horsham in 1813, and saw Shelley when he was on a stolen visit, in his father's absence, at Field Place:

> He received me with frankness and kindliness, as if he had known me from childhood, and at once won my heart. I fancy I see him now as he sate by the window, and hear his voice, the tones of which impressed me with his sincerity and simplicity. His resemblance to his sister Elizabeth was as striking as if they had been twins. His eyes were most expressive; his complexion beautifully fair, his features exquisitely fine; his hair was dark, and no peculiar attention to its arrangement was manifest. In person he was slender and gentlemanlike, but inclined to stoop; his gait was decidedly not military. The general appearance indicated great delicacy of constitution. One would at once pronounce of him that he was different from other men. There was an earnestness in his manner and such perfect gentleness of breeding and freedom from everything artificial as charmed every one. I never met a man who so immediately won upon me.

Mrs Gisborne's son, who knew Shelley well at Leghorn, declared Captain Kennedy's description of him to be 'the best and most truthful I have ever seen'.

To all this we have to add the charm of the man's writings—of Shelley's poetry. It is his poetry, above everything else, which for many people establishes that he is an angel. Of his poetry I have not space now to speak. But let no one suppose that a want of humour and a self-delusion such as Shelley's have no effect upon a man's poetry. The man Shelley, in very truth, is not entirely sane, and Shelley's poetry is not entirely sane either. The Shelley of actual life is a vision of beauty and radiance, indeed, but availing nothing, effecting nothing. And in poetry, no less than in life, he is 'a beautiful *and ineffectual* angel, beating in the void his luminous wings in vain'.

VIII
COUNT LEO TOLSTOI

IN REVIEWING at the time of its first publication, thirty years ago, Flaubert's remarkable novel of *Madame Bovary*, Sainte-Beuve observed that in Flaubert we come to another manner, another kind of inspiration, from those which had prevailed hitherto; we find ourselves, he said, with a man of a new and different generation from novelists like George Sand. The ideal has ceased, the lyric vein is dried up; the new men are cured of lyricism and the ideal; 'a severe and pitiless truth has made its entry, as the last word of experience, even into art itself'. The characters of the new literature of fiction are 'science, a spirit of observation, maturity, force, a touch of hardness'. *L'idéal a cessé, le lyrique a tari.*

The spirit of observation and the touch of hardness (let us retain these mild and inoffensive terms) have since been carried in the French novel very far. So far have they been carried, indeed, that in spite of the advantage which the French language, familiar to the cultivated classes everywhere, confers on the French novel, this novel has lost much of its attraction for those classes; it no longer commands their attention as it did formerly. The famous English novelists have passed away, and have left no successors of like fame. It is not the English novel, therefore, which has inherited the vogue lost by the French novel. It is the novel of a country new to literature, or at any rate unregarded, till lately, by the general public of readers: it is the novel of Russia. The Russian novel has now the vogue, and deserves to have it. If fresh literary productions maintain this vogue and enhance it, we shall all be learning Russian.

The Slav nature, or at any rate the Russian nature, the Russian nature as it shows itself in the Russian novels, seems marked by an extreme sensitiveness, a consciousness most quick and acute both for what the man's self is experiencing, and also for what others in contact with him are thinking and feeling. In a nation full of life, but young, and newly in contact with an old and powerful civilization, this sensitiveness and self-consciousness are prompt to appear. In the Americans, as well as in the Russians, we see them active in a high degree. They are somewhat agitating and disquieting agents to their possessor, but they have, if they get fair play, great powers for evoking and enriching a literature. But the Americans, as we know, are apt to set them at rest in the manner of my friend Colonel Higginson of Boston. 'As I take it, Nature said, some years since: "Thus far the English is my best race; but we have had Englishmen enough; we need something with a little more buoyancy than the Englishman; let us lighten the structure, even at some peril in the process. Put in one drop more of nervous fluid, and make the American." With that drop, a new range of promise opened on the human race, and a lighter, finer, more highly organized type of mankind was born.' People who by this sort of thing give rest to their sensitive and busy self-consciousness may very well, perhaps, be on their way to great material prosperity, to great political power; but they are scarcely on the right way to a great literature, a serious art.

The Russian does not assuage his sensitiveness in this fashion. The Russian man of letters does not make Nature say: 'The Russian is my best race.' He finds relief to his sensitiveness in letting his perceptions have perfectly free play, and in recording their reports with perfect fidelity. The sincereness with which the reports are given has even something childlike and touching. In the novel of which I am going to speak there is not a line, not a trait, brought in for the glorification of Russia, or to feed vanity; things and characters go as nature takes them, and the author is absorbed in seeing how nature takes them and in relating it. But we have here a condition of things which is highly favourable to the production of good literature, of good art. We have great sensitiveness, subtlety, and finesse, addressing themselves with entire disinterestedness and simplicity to the representation of human life. The Russian novelist is thus master of a spell to which the secrets of nature—both what is external and what is internal, gesture and manner no less than thought and feeling—willingly make themselves known. The crown of literature is poetry, and the Russians have not yet had a great poet. But in that form of imaginative literature which in our day is the most popular and the most possible, the Russians at the present moment seem to me to hold, as Mr Gladstone would say, the field. They have great novelists, and of one of their great novelists I wish now to speak.

Count Leo Tolstoi is about sixty years old, and tells us that he shall write novels no more. He is now occupied with religion and with the Christian life. His writings concerning these great matters are not allowed, I believe, to obtain publication in Russia, but instalments of them in French and English reach us from time to time. I find them very interesting, but I find his novel of *Anna Karénine* more interesting still. I believe that many readers prefer to *Anna Karénine* Count Tolstoi's other great novel, *La Guerre et la Paix*. But in the novel one prefers, I think, to have the novelist dealing with the life which he knows from having lived it, rather than with the life which he knows from books or hearsay. If one has to choose a representative work of Thackeray, it is *Vanity Fair* which one would take rather than *The Virginians*. In like manner I take *Anna Karénine* as the novel best representing Count Tolstoi. I use the French translation; in general, as I long ago said, work of this kind is better done in France than in England, and *Anna Karénine* is perhaps also a novel which goes better into French than into English, just as Frederika Bremer's *Home* goes into English better than into French. After I have done with *Anna Karénine* I must say something of Count Tolstoi's religious writings. Of these too I use the French translation, so far as it is available. The English translation, however, which came into my hands late, seems to be in general clear and good. Let me say in passing that it has neither the same arrangement, nor the same titles, nor altogether the same contents, with the French translation.

There are many characters in *Anna Karénine*—too many if we look in it for a work of art in which the action shall be vigorously one, and to that one action everything shall converge. There are even two main actions extending throughout the book, and we keep passing from one of them to the other—from the affairs of Anna and Wronsky to the affairs of Kitty and Levine. People appear in connection with these two main actions whose appearance and proceedings do not in the least contribute to develop them; incidents are multiplied which we expect are to lead to something important, but which do not. What, for instance, does the episode of Kitty's friend Warinka and Levine's brother Serge Ivanitch, their inclination for one another and its failure to come to anything, contribute to the development of either the character or the fortunes of Kitty and Levine? What does the incident of Levine's long delay in getting to church to be married, a delay which as we read of it seems to have significance, really import? It turns out to import absolutely nothing, and to be introduced solely to give the author the pleasure of telling us that all Levine's shirts had been packed up.

But the truth is we are not to take *Anna Karénine* as a work of art; we are to take it as a piece of life. A piece of life it is. The author has not invented and combined it, he has seen it; it has all happened before his inward eye, and it was in this wise that it happened. Levine's shirts were packed up, and he was late for his wedding in consequence; Warinka and Serge Ivanitch met at Levine's country-house and went out walking together; Serge was very near proposing, but did not. The author saw it all happening so—saw it, and therefore relates it; and what his novel in this way loses in art it gains in reality.

For this is the result which, by his extraordinary fineness of perception, and by his sincere fidelity to it, the author achieves; he works in us a sense of the absolute reality of his personages and their doings. Anna's shoulders, and masses of hair, and half-shut eyes; Alexis Karénine's updrawn eyebrows, and tired smile, and cracking finger-joints; Stiva's eyes suffused with facile moisture—these are as real to us as any of those outward peculiarities which in our own circle of acquaintance we are noticing daily, while the inner man of our own circle of acquaintance, happily or unhappily, lies a great deal less clearly revealed to us than that of Count Tolstoi's creations.

I must speak of only a few of these creations, the chief personages and no more. The book opens with 'Stiva', and who that has once made Stiva's acquaintance will ever forget him? We are living, in Count Tolstoi's novel, among the great people of Moscow and St Petersburg, the nobles and the high functionaries, the governing class of Russia. Stépane Arcadiévitch—'Stiva'—is Prince Oblonsky, and descended from Rurik, although to think of him as anything except 'Stiva' is difficult. His *air souriant*, his good looks, his satisfaction; his 'ray', which made the Tartar waiter at the club joyful in contemplating it;

his pleasure in oysters and champagne, his pleasure in making people happy and in rendering services; his need of money, his attachment to the French governess, his distress at his wife's distress, his affection for her and the children; his emotion and suffused eyes, while he quite dismisses the care of providing funds for household expenses and education; and the French attachment, contritely given up today only to be succeeded by some other attachment tomorrow—no, never, certainly, shall we come to forget Stiva. Anna, the heroine, is Stiva's sister. His wife Dolly (these English diminutives are common among Count Tolstoi's ladies) is daughter of the Prince and Princess Cherbatzky, grandees who show us Russian high life by its most respectable side; the Prince, in particular, is excellent—simple, sensible, right-feeling; a man of dignity and honour. His daughters, Dolly and Kitty, are charming. Dolly, Stiva's wife, is sorely tried by her husband, full of anxieties for the children, with no money to spend on them or herself, poorly dressed, worn and aged before her time. She has moments of despairing doubt whether the gay people may not be after all in the right, whether virtue and principle answer; whether happiness does not dwell with adventuresses and profligates, brilliant and perfectly dressed adventuresses and profligates, in a land flowing with roubles and champagne. But in a quarter of an hour she comes right again and is herself—a nature straight, honest, faithful, loving, sound to the core; such she is and such she remains; she can be no other. Her sister Kitty is at bottom of the same temper, but she has her experience to get, while Dolly, when the book begins, has already acquired hers. Kitty is adored by Levine, in whom we are told that many traits are to be found of the character and history of Count Tolstoi himself. Levine belongs to the world of great people by his birth and property, but he is not at all a man of the world. He had been a reader and thinker, he has a conscience, he has public spirit and would ameliorate the condition of the people, he lives on his estate in the country, and occupies himself zealously with local business, schools, and agriculture. But he is shy, apt to suspect and to take offence, somewhat impracticable, out of his element in the gay world of Moscow. Kitty likes him, but her fancy has been taken by a brilliant guardsman, Count Wronsky, who has paid her attentions. Wronsky is described to us by Stiva; he is 'one of the finest specimens of the *jeunesse dorée* of St Petersburg; immensely rich, handsome, aide-de-camp to the emperor, great interest at his back, and a good fellow notwithstanding; more than a good fellow, intelligent besides and well read—a man who has a splendid career before him'. Let us complete the picture by adding that Wronsky is a powerful man, over thirty, bald at the top of his head, with irreproachable manners, cool and calm, but a little haughty. A hero, one murmurs to oneself, too much of the Guy Livingstone type, though without the bravado and exaggeration. And such is, justly enough perhaps, the first impression, an impression which continues all through the first volume; but Wronsky, as we shall see, improves towards the end.

Kitty discourages Levine, who retires in misery and confusion. But Wronsky is attracted by Anna Karénine, and ceases his attentions to Kitty. The impression made on her heart by Wronsky was not deep; but she is so keenly mortified with herself, so ashamed, and so upset, that she falls ill, and is sent with her family to winter abroad. There she regains health and mental composure, and discovers at the same time that her liking for Levine was deeper than she knew, that it was a genuine feeling, a strong and lasting one. On her return they meet, their hearts come together, they are married; and in spite of Levine's waywardness, irritability, and unsettlement of mind, of which I shall have more to say presently, they are profoundly happy. Well, and who could help being happy with Kitty? So I find myself adding impatiently. Count Tolstoi's heroines are really so living and charming that one takes them, fiction though they are, too seriously.

But the interest of the book centres in Anna Karénine. She is Stiva's sister, married to a high official at St Petersburg, Alexis Karénine. She has been married to him nine years, and has one child, a boy named Serge. The marriage had not brought happiness to her, she had found in it no satisfaction to her heart and soul, she had a sense of want and isolation; but she is devoted to her boy, occupied, calm. The charm of her personality is felt even before she appears, from the moment when we hear of her being sent for as the good angel to reconcile Dolly with Stiva. Then she arrives at the Moscow station from St Petersburg, and we see the gray eyes with their long eyelashes, the graceful carriage, the gentle and caressing smile on the fresh lips, the vivacity restrained but waiting to break through, the fulness of life, the softness and strength joined, the harmony, the bloom, the charm. She goes to Dolly, and achieves, with infinite tact and tenderness, the task of reconciliation. At a ball a few days later, we add to our first impression of Anna's beauty, dark hair, a quantity of little curls over her temples and at the back of her neck, sculptural shoulders, firm throat, and beautiful arms. She is in a plain dress of black velvet with a pearl necklace, a bunch of forget-me-nots in the front of her dress, another in her hair. This is Anna Karénine.

She had travelled from St Petersburg with Wronsky's mother; had seen him at the Moscow station, where he came to meet his mother; had been struck with his looks and manner, and touched by his behaviour in an accident which happened, while they were in the station, to a poor workman crushed by a train. At the ball she meets him again; she is fascinated by him and he by her. She had been told of Kitty's fancy, and had gone to the ball meaning to help Kitty; but Kitty is forgotten, or at any rate neglected; the spell which draws Wronsky and Anna is irresistible. Kitty finds herself opposite to them in a quadrille together:

> She seemed to remark in Anna the symptoms of an over-excitement which she herself knew from experience—that of success. Anna appeared to her as if intoxicated with it. Kitty knew to what to attribute that brilliant and animated look, that happy and triumphant smile, those half-parted lips, those movements full of grace and harmony.

Anna returns to St Petersburg, and Wronsky returns there at the same time; they meet on the journey, they keep meeting in society, and Anna begins to find her husband, who before had not been sympathetic, intolerable. Alexis Karénine is much older than herself, a bureaucrat, a formalist, a poor creature; he has conscience, there is a root of goodness in him, but on the surface and until deeply stirred he is tiresome, pedantic, vain, exasperating. The change in Anna is not in the slightest degree comprehended by him; he sees nothing which an intelligent man might in such a case see, and does nothing which an intelligent man would do. Anna abandons herself to her passion for Wronsky.

I remember M. Nisard saying to me many years ago at the École Normale in Paris, that he respected the English because they are *une nation qui sait se gêner*—people who can put constraint on themselves and go through what is disagreeable. Perhaps in the Slav nature this valuable faculty is somewhat wanting; a very strong impulse is too much regarded as irresistible, too little as what can be resisted and ought to be resisted, however, difficult and disagreeable the resistance may be. In our high society with its pleasure and dissipation, laxer notions may to some extent prevail; but in general an English mind will be startled by Anna's suffering herself to be so overwhelmed and irretrievably carried away by her passion, by her almost at once regarding it, apparently, as something which it was hopeless to fight against. And this I say irrespectively of the worth of her lover. Wronsky's gifts and graces hardly qualify him, one might think, to be the object of so instantaneous and mighty a passion on the part of a woman like Anna. But that is not the question. Let us allow that these passions are incalculable; let us allow that one of the male sex scarcely does justice, perhaps, to the powerful and handsome guardsman and his attractions. But if Wronsky had been even such a lover as Alcibiades or the Master of Ravenswood, still that Anna, being what she is and her circumstances being what they are, should show not a hope, hardly a thought, of conquering her passion, of escaping from its fatal power, is to our notions strange and a little bewildering.

I state the objection; let me add that it is the triumph of Anna's charm that it remains paramount for us nevertheless; that throughout her course, with its failures, errors, and miseries, still the impression of her large, fresh, rich, generous, delightful nature never leaves us—keeps our sympathy, keeps even, I had almost said, our respect.

To return to the story. Soon enough poor Anna begins to experience the truth of what the Wise Man told us long ago, that 'the way of transgressors is hard'. Her agitation at a steeplechase where Wronsky is in danger attracts her husband's notice and provokes his remonstrance. He is bitter and contemptuous. In a transport of passion Anna declares to him that she is his wife no longer; that she loves Wronsky, belongs to Wronsky. Hard at first, formal, cruel, thinking only of himself, Karénine, who, as I have said, has a conscience, is touched by grace at the moment when Anna's troubles reach their height. He returns to her to find her with a child just born to her and Wronsky, the lover in the house and Anna apparently dying. Karénine has words of kindness and forgiveness only. The noble and victorious effort transfigures him, and all that her husband gains in the eyes of Anna, her lover Wronsky loses. Wronsky comes to Anna's bedside, and standing there by Karénine, buries his face in his hands. Anna says to him, in the hurried voice of fever:

'Uncover your face; look at that man; he is a saint. Yes, uncover your face; uncover it,' she repeated with an angry air. 'Alexis, uncover his face; I want to see him.'

Alexis took the hands of Wronsky and uncovered his face, disfigured by suffering and humiliation.

'Give him your hand; pardon him.'

Alexis stretched out his hand without even seeking to restrain his tears.

'Thank God, thank God!' she said; 'all is ready now. How ugly those flowers are,' she went on, pointing to the wallpaper; 'they are not a bit like violets. My God, my God! when will all this end? Give me morphine, doctor—I want morphine. Oh, my God, my God!'

She seems dying, and Wronsky rushes out and shoots himself. And so, in a common novel, the story would end: Anna would die, Wronsky would commit suicide, Karénine would survive, in possession of our admiration and sympathy. But the story does not always end so in life; neither does it end so in Count Tolstoï's novel. Anna recovers from her fever, Wronsky from his wound. Anna's passion for Wronsky reawakens, her estrangement from Karénine returns. Nor does Karénine remain at the height at which in the forgiveness scene we saw him. He is formal, pedantic, irritating. Alas! even if he were not all these, perhaps even his *pince-nez*, and his rising eyebrows, and his cracking finger-joints, would have been provocation enough. Anna and Wronsky depart together. They stay for a time in Italy, then return to Russia. But her position is false, her disquietude incessant, and happiness is impossible for her. She takes opium every night, only to find that 'not poppy nor mandragora shall ever medicine her to that sweet sleep which she owed yesterday'. Jealousy and irritability grow upon her; she tortures Wronsky, she tortures herself. Under these trials Wronsky, it must be said, comes out well, and rises in our esteem. His love for Anna endures; he behaves, as our English phrase is, 'like a gentleman'; his patience is in general exemplary. But then Anna, let us remember, is to the last, through all the fret and misery, still Anna; always with something which charms; nay, with something, even, something in her nature, which consoles and does good. Her life, however, was becoming impossible under its existing conditions. A trifling misunderstanding brought the inevitable end. After a quarrel with Anna, Wronsky had gone one morning into the country to see his mother; Anna summons him by telegraph to return at once, and receives an answer from him that he cannot return before ten at night. She follows him to her mother's place in the country, and at the station hears what leads her to believe that he is not coming back. Maddened with jealousy and misery, she descends the platform and throws herself under the wheels of a goods train passing through the station. It is over—the graceful head is untouched, but all the rest is a crushed, formless heap. Poor Anna!

We have been in a world which misconducts itself nearly as much as the world of a French novel all palpitating with 'modernity'. But there are two things in which the Russian novel—Count Tolstoi's novel at any rate—is very advantageously distinguished from the type of novel now so much in request in France. In the first place, there is no fine sentiment, at once tiresome and false. We are not told to believe, for example, that Anna is wonderfully exalted and ennobled by her passion for Wronsky. The English reader is thus saved from many a groan of impatience. The other thing is yet more important. Our Russian novelist deals abundantly with criminal passion and with adultery, but he does not seem to feel himself owing any service to the goddess Lubricity, or bound to put in touches at this goddess's dictation. Much in *Anna Karénine* is painful, much is unpleasant, but nothing is of a nature to trouble the senses, or to please those who wish their senses troubled. This taint is wholly absent. In the French novels where it is so abundantly present its baneful effects do not end with itself. Burns long ago remarked with deep truth that it *petrifies feeling*. Let us revert for a moment to the powerful novel of which I spoke at the outset, *Madame Bovary*. Undoubtedly the taint in question is present in *Madame Bovary*, although to a much less degree than in more recent French novels which will be in everyone's mind. But *Madame Bovary*, with this taint, is a work of *petrified feeling;* over it hangs an atmosphere of bitterness, irony, impotence; not a personage in the book to rejoice or console us; the springs of freshness and feeling are not there to create such personages. Emma Bovary follows a course in some respects like that of Anna, but where, in Emma Bovary, is Anna's charm? The treasures of compassion, tenderness, insight, which alone, amid such guilt and misery, can enable charm to subsist and to emerge, are wanting to Flaubert. He is cruel, with the cruelty of petrified feeling, to his poor heroine; he pursues her without pity or pause, as with malignity; he is harder upon her himself than any reader even, I think, will be inclined to be.

But where the springs of feeling have carried Count Tolstoi, since he created Anna ten or twelve years ago, we have now to see.

We must return to Constantine Dmitrich Levine. Levine, as I have already said, thinks. Between the age of twenty and that of thirty-five he had lost, he tells us, the Christian belief in which he had been brought up, a loss of which examples nowadays abound certainly everywhere, but which in Russia, as in France, is among all young men of the upper and cultivated classes more a matter of course, perhaps, more universal, more avowed, than it is with us. Levine had adopted the scientific notions current all round him; talked of cells, organisms, the indestructibility of matter, the conservation of force, and was of opinion, with his comrades of the university, that religion no longer existed. But he was of a serious nature, and the question what his life meant, whence it came, whither it tended, presented themselves to him in moments of crisis and affliction with irresistible importunity, and getting no answer, haunted him, tortured him, made him think of suicide.

Two things, meanwhile, he noticed. One was, that he and his university friends had been mistaken in supposing that Christian belief no longer existed; they had lost it, but they were not all the world. Levine observed that the persons to whom he was most attached, his own wife Kitty amongst the number, retained it and drew comfort from it; that the women generally, and almost the whole of the Russian common people, retained it and drew comfort from it. The other was, that his scientific friends, though not troubled like himself by questionings about the meaning of human life, were untroubled by such questionings, not because they had got an answer to them, but because, entertaining themselves intellectually with the consideration of the cell theory, and evolution, and the indestructibility of matter, and the conservation of force, and the like, they were satisfied with this entertainment, and did not perplex themselves with investigating the meaning and object of their own life at all.

But Levine noticed further that he himself did not actually proceed to commit suicide; on the contrary, he lived on his lands as his father had done before him, busied himself with all the duties of his station, married Kitty, was delighted when a son was born to him. Nevertheless he was indubitably not happy at bottom, restless and disquieted, his disquietude sometimes amounting to agony.

Now on one of his bad days he was in the field with his peasants and one of them happened to say to him, in answer to a question from Levine why one farmer should in a certain case act more humanely than another: 'Men are not all alike; one man lives for his belly, like Mitiovuck, another for his soul, for God, like old Plato.' [1]—'What do you call', cried Levine, 'living for his soul, for God?' The peasant answered: 'It's quite simple—living by the rule of God, of the truth. All men are not the same, that's certain. You yourself, for instance, Constantine Dmitrich, you wouldn't do wrong by a poor man.' Levine gave no answer, but turned away with the phrase, *living by the rule of God, of the truth*, sounding in his ears.

Then he reflected that he had been born of parents professing this rule, as their parents again had professed it before them; that he had sucked it in with his mother's milk; that some sense of it, some strength and nourishment from it, had been ever with him although he knew it not; that if he had tried to do the duties of his station it was by help of the secret support ministered by this rule; that if in his moments of despairing restlessness and agony, when he was driven to think of suicide, he had yet not committed suicide, it was because this rule had silently enabled

_____
[1] A common name among Russian peasants.

him to do his duty in some degree, and had given him some hold upon life and happiness in consequence.

The words came to him as a clue of which he could never again lose sight, and which with full consciousness and strenuous endeavour he must henceforth follow. He sees his nephews and nieces throwing their milk at one another and scolded by Dolly for it. He says to himself that these children are wasting their subsistence because they have not to earn it for themselves and do not know its value, and he exclaims inwardly: 'I, a Christian, brought up in the faith, my life filled with the benefits of Christianity, living on these benefits without being conscious of it, I, like these children, I have been trying to destroy what makes and builds up my life.' But now the feeling has been borne in upon him, clear and precious, that what he has to do is to *be good*; he has 'cried to *Him*'. What will come of it?

> I shall probably continue to get out of temper with my coachman, to go into useless arguments, to air my ideas unseasonably; I shall always feel a barrier between the sanctuary of my soul and the soul of other people, even that of my wife; I shall always be holding her responsible for my annoyances and feeling sorry for it directly afterwards. I shall continue to pray without being able to explain to myself why I pray; but my inner life has won its liberty; it will no longer be at the mercy of events, and every minute of my existence will have a meaning sure and profound which it will be in my power to impress on every single one of my actions, that of *being good*.

With these words the novel of *Anna Karénine* ends. But in Levine's religious experiences Count Tolstoi was relating his own, and the history is continued in three autobiographical works translated from him, which have within the last two or three years been published in Paris: *Ma Confession, Ma Religion*, and *Que Faire*. Our author announces further, 'two great works', on which he has spent six years: one a criticism of dogmatic theology, the other a new translation of the four Gospels, with a concordance of his own arranging. The results which he claims to have established in these two works are, however, indicated sufficiently in the three published volumes which I have named above.

These autobiographical volumes show the same extraordinary

penetration, the same perfect sincerity, which are exhibited in the author's novel. As autobiography they are of profound interest, and they are full, moreover, of acute and fruitful remarks. I have spoken of the advantages which the Russian genius possesses for imaginative literature. Perhaps for Biblical exegesis, for the criticism of religion, and its documents the advantage lies more with the older nations of the West. They will have more of the experience, width of knowledge, patience, sobriety, requisite for these studies; they may probably be less impulsive, less heady.

Count Tolstoi regards the change accomplished in himself during the last half-dozen years, he regards his recent studies and the ideas which he has acquired through them, as epoch-making in his life and of capital importance:

> Five years ago faith came to me; I believed in the doctrine of Jesus, and all my life suddenly changed. I ceased to desire that which previously I desired, and, on the other hand, I took to desiring what I had never desired before. That which formerly used to appear good in my eyes appeared evil, that which used to appear evil appeared good.

The novel of *Anna Karénine* belongs to that past which Count Tolstoi has left behind him; his new studies and the works founded on them are what is important; light and salvation are there. Yet I will venture to express my doubt whether these works contain, as their contribution to the cause of religion and to the establishment of the true mind and message of Jesus, much that had not already been given or indicated by Count Tolstoi in relating, in *Anna Karénine*, Levine's mental history. Points raised in that history are developed and enforced; there is an abundant and admirable exhibition of knowledge of human nature, penetrating insight, fearless sincerity, wit, sarcasm, eloquence, style. And we have too the direct autobiography of a man not only interesting to us from his soul and talent, but highly interesting also from his nationality, position, and course of proceeding. But to light and salvation in the Christian religion we are not, I think, brought very much nearer than in Levine's history. I ought to add that what was already present in that history seems to me of high importance and value. Let us see what it amounts to.

I must be general and I must be brief; neither my limits nor my purpose permit the introduction of what is abstract. But in Count Tolstoi's religious philosophy there is very little which is abstract, arid. The idea of *life* is his master idea in studying and establishing religion. He speaks impatiently of St Paul as a source, in common with the Fathers and the Reformers, of that ecclesiastical theology which misses the essential and fails to present Christ's Gospel aright. Yet Paul's 'law of the spirit of life in Christ Jesus freeing me from the law of sin and death' is the pith and ground of all Count Tolstoi's theology. Moral life is the gift of God, is God, and this true life, this union with God to which we aspire, we reach through Jesus. We reach it through union with Jesus and by adopting his life. This doctrine is proved true for us by the life in God, to be acquired through Jesus, being what our nature feels after and moves to, by the warning of misery if we are severed from it, the sanction of happiness if we find it. Of the access for *us*, at any rate, to the spirit of life, us who are born in Christendom, are in touch, conscious or unconscious, with Christianity, this is the true account. Questions over which the churches spend so much labour and time—questions about the Trinity, about the godhead of Christ, about the procession of the Holy Ghost, are not vital; what is vital is the doctrine of access to the spirit of life through Jesus.

Sound and saving doctrine, in my opinion, this is. It may be gathered in a great degree from what Count Tolstoi had already given us in the novel of *Anna Karénine*. But of course it is greatly developed in the special works which have followed. Many of these developments are, I will repeat, of striking force, interest, and value. In *Anna Karénine* we had been told of the scepticism of the upper and educated classes in Russia. But what reality is added by such an anecdote as the following from *Ma Confession*:

I remember that when I was about eleven years old we had a visit one Sunday from a boy, since dead, who announced to my brother and me, as great news, a discovery just made at his public school. This discovery was to the effect that God had no existence; and that everything which we were taught about Him was pure invention.

Count Tolstoi touched, in *Anna Karénine*, on the failure of science to tell a man what his life means. Many a sharp stroke does he add in his latter writings:

> Development is going on, and there are laws which guide it. You yourself are a part of the whole. Having come to understand the whole so far as is possible, and having comprehended the law of development, you will comprehend also your place in that whole, you will understand yourself.
>
> In spite of all the shame the confession costs me, there was a time, I declare, when I tried to look as if I was satisfied with this sort of thing!

But the men of science may take comfort from hearing that Count Tolstoi treats the men of letters no better than them, although he is a man of letters himself:

> The judgment which my literary companions passed on life was to the effect that life in general is in a state of progress, and that in this development we, the men of letters, take the principal part. The vocation of us artists and poets is to instruct the world; and to prevent my coming out with the natural question, 'What am I, and what am I to teach?' it was explained to me that it was useless to know that, and that the artist and the poet taught without perceiving how. I passed for a superb artist, a great poet, and consequently it was but natural I should appropriate this theory. I, the artist, the poet —I wrote, I taught, without myself knowing what. I was paid for what I did. I had everything: splendid fare and lodging, women, society; I had *la gloire*. Consequently, what I taught was very good. This faith in the importance of poetry and of the development of life was a religion, and I was one of its priests—a very agreeable and advantageous office.
>
> And I lived ever so long in this belief, never doubting but that it was true!

The adepts of this literary and scientific religion are not numerous, to be sure, in comparison with the mass of the people, and the mass of the people, as Levine had remarked, find comfort still in the old religion of Christendom; but of the mass of the people our literary and scientific instructors make no account. Like Solomon and Schopenhauer, these gentlemen, and 'society' along with them, are, moreover, apt to say that life is, after all, vanity: but then they all know of no life except their own.

It used to appear to me that the small number of cultivated, rich, and idle men, of whom I was one, composed the whole of humanity, and that the millions and millions of other men who had lived and are still living were not in reality men at all. Incomprehensible as it now seems to me, that I should have gone on considering life without seeing the life which was surrounding me on all sides, the life of humanity; strange as it is to think that I should have been so mistaken, and have fancied my life, the life of the Solomons and the Schopenhauers, to be the veritable and normal life, while the life of the masses was but a matter of no importance—strangely odd as this seems to me now, so it was, notwithstanding.

And this pretentious minority, who call themselves 'society', 'the world', and to whom their own life, the life of 'the world', seems the only life worth naming, are all the while miserable! Our author found it so in his own experience:

In my life, an exceptionally happy one from a worldly point of view, I can number such a quantity of sufferings endured for the sake of 'the world', that they would be enough to furnish a martyr for Jesus. All the most painful passages in my life, beginning with the orgies and duels of my student days, the wars I have been in, the illnesses, and the abnormal and unbearable conditions in which I am living now—all this is but one martyrdom endured in the name of the doctrine of the world. Yes, and I speak of my own life, exceptionally happy from the world's point of view.

Let any sincere man pass his life in review, and he will perceive that never, not once, has he suffered through practising the doctrine of Jesus; the chief part of the miseries of his life have proceeded solely from his following, contrary to his inclination, the spell of the doctrine of the world.

On the other hand, the simple, the multitudes, outside of this spell, are comparatively contented:

In opposition to what I saw in our circle, where life without faith is possible, and where I doubt whether one in a thousand would confess himself a believer, I conceive that among the people (in Russia) there is not one sceptic to many thousands of believers. Just contrary to what I saw in our circle, where life passes in idleness, amusements, and discontent with life, I saw that of these men of the people the whole life was passed in severe labour, and yet they were contented with life. Instead of complaining like the persons in our world of the hardship of their lot, these poor people received sickness and disappointments without any revolt, without opposition, but with a firm and tranquil confidence that so it was to be, that it could not be otherwise, and that it was all right.

All this is but development, sometimes rather surprising, but always powerful and interesting, of what we have already had in the pages of *Anna Karénine*. And like Levine in that novel, Count Tolstoi was driven by his inward struggle and misery very near to suicide. What is new in the recent books is the solution and cure announced. Levine had accepted a provisional solution of the difficulties oppressing him; he had lived right on, so to speak, obeying his conscience, but not asking how far all his actions hung together and were consistent:

He advanced money to a peasant to get him out of the clutches of a money-lender, but did not give up the arrears due to himself; he punished thefts of wood strictly, but would have scrupled to impound a peasant's cattle trespassing on his fields; he did not pay the wages of a labourer whose father's death caused him to leave work in the middle of harvest, but he pensioned and maintained his old servants; he let his peasants wait while he went to give his wife a kiss after he came home, but would not have made them wait while he went to visit his bees.

Count Tolstoi has since advanced to a far more definite and stringent rule of life—the positive doctrine, he thinks, of Jesus. It is the determination and promulgation of this rule which is the novelty in our author's recent works. He extracts this essential doctrine, or rule of Jesus, from the Sermon on the Mount, and presents it in a body of commandments—Christ's commandments; the pith, he says, of the New Testament, as the Decalogue is the pith of the Old. These all-important commandments of Christ are 'commandments of peace', and five in number. The first commandment is: 'Live in peace with all men; treat no one as contemptible and beneath you. Not only allow yourself no anger, but do not rest until you have dissipated even unreasonable anger in others against yourself.' The second is: 'No libertinage and no divorce; let every man have one wife and every woman one husband.' The third: 'Never on any pretext take an oath of service of any kind; all such oaths are imposed for a bad purpose.' The fourth: 'Never employ force against the evildoer; bear whatever wrong is done to you without opposing the wrongdoer or seeking to have him punished.' The fifth and last: 'Renounce all distinction of nationality; do not admit that men of another nation may ever be treated by you as enemies; love all men alike as alike near to you; do good to all alike.'

If these five commandments were generally observed, says Count Tolstoi, all men would become brothers. Certainly the actual society in which we live would be changed and dissolved. Armies and wars would be renounced; courts of justice, police, property, would be renounced also. And whatever the rest of us may do, Count Tolstoi at least will do his duty and follow Christ's commandments sincerely. He has given up rank, office, and property, and earns his bread by the labour of his own hands. 'I believe in Christ's commandments,' he says, 'and this faith changes my whole former estimate of what is good and great, bad and low, in human life.' At present—'Everything which I used to think bad and low—the rusticity of the peasant, the plainness of lodging, food, clothing, manners—all this has become good and great in my eyes. At present I can no longer contribute to anything which raises me externally above others, which separates me from them. I cannot, as formerly, recognize either in my own case or in that of others any title, rank, or quality beyond the title and quality of man. I cannot seek fame and praise; I cannot seek a culture which separates me from men. I cannot refrain from seeking in my whole existence—in my lodging, my food, my clothing, and my ways of going on with people—whatever, far from separating me from the mass of mankind, draws me nearer to them.'

Whatever else we have or have not in Count Tolstoi, we have at least a great soul and a great writer. In his Biblical exegesis, in the criticism by which he extracts and constructs his Five

Commandments of Christ which are to be the rule of our lives, I find much which is questionable along with much which is ingenious and powerful. But I have neither space, nor, indeed, inclination, to criticize his exegesis here. The right moment, besides, for criticizing this will come when the 'two great works,' which are in preparation, shall have appeared.

For the present I limit myself to a single criticism only—a general one. Christianity cannot be packed into any set of commandments. As I have somewhere or other said, 'Christianity is a *source*; no one supply of water and refreshment that comes from it can be called the sum of Christianity. It is a mistake, and may lead to much error, to exhibit any series of maxims, even those of the Sermon on the Mount, as the ultimate sum and formula into which Christianity may be run up.'

And the reason mainly lies in the character of the Founder of Christianity and in the nature of his utterances. Not less important than the teachings given by Jesus is the *temper* of their giver, his temper of sweetness and reasonableness, of ἐπιείκεια. Goethe calls him a *Schwärmer*, a fanatic; he may much more rightly be called an opportunist. But he is an opportunist of an opposite kind from those who in politics, that 'wild and dreamlike trade' of insincerity, give themselves this name. They push or slacken, press their points or let them be, as may best suit the interests of their self-aggrandizement and of their party. Jesus has in view simply 'the rule of God, of the truth'. But this is served by waiting as well as by hasting forward, and sometimes served better.

Count Tolstoi sees rightly that whatever the propertied and satisfied classes may think, the world, ever since Jesus Christ came, is judged; 'a new earth' is in prospect. It was ever in prospect with Jesus, and should be ever in prospect with his followers. And the ideal in prospect has to be realized. 'If ye know these things, happy are ye if ye do them.' But they are to be done through a great and widespread and long-continued change, and a change of the inner man to begin with. The most important and fruitful utterances of Jesus, therefore, are not things which can be drawn up as a table of stiff and stark external commands, but the things which have most soul in them; because these can best sink down into our soul, work there, set up an influence, form habits of conduct, and prepare the future.

The Beatitudes are on this account more helpful than the utterances from which Count Tolstoi builds up his Five Commandments. The very *secret* of Jesus, 'He that loveth his life shall lose it, he that will lose his life shall save it', does not give us a command to be taken and followed in the letter, but an idea to work in our mind and soul, and of inexhaustible value there.

Jesus paid tribute to the government and dined with the publicans, although neither the empire of Rome nor the high finance of Judaea were compatible with his ideal and with the 'new earth' which that ideal must in the end create. Perhaps Levine's provincial solution, in a society like ours, was nearer to 'the rule of God, of the truth', than the more trenchant solution which Count Tolstoi has adopted for himself since. It seems calculated to be of more use. I do not know how it is in Russia, but in an English village the determination of 'our circle' to earn their bread by the work of their hands would produce only dismay, not fraternal joy, amongst that 'majority' who are so earning it already. 'There are plenty of us to compete as things stand,' the gardeners, carpenters, and smiths would say; 'pray stick to your articles, your poetry, and nonsense; in manual labour you will interfere with us, and be taking the bread out of our mouths.'

So I arrive at the conclusion that Count Tolstoi has perhaps not done well in abandoning the work of the poet and artist, and that he might with advantage return to it. But whatever he may do in the future, the work which he has already done, and his work in religion as well as his work in imaginative literature, is more than sufficient to signalize him as one of the most marking, interesting, and sympathy-inspiring men of our time—an honour, I must add, to Russia, although he forbids us to heed nationality.

IX

AMIEL

IT IS somewhat late to speak of Amiel, but I was late in reading him. Goethe says that in seasons of cholera one should read no books but such as are tonic, and certainly in the season of old age this precaution is as salutary as in seasons of cholera. From what I heard I could clearly make out that Amiel's Journal was not a tonic book: the extracts from it which here and there I fell in with did not much please me; and for a good while I left the book unread.

But what M. Edmond Scherer writes I do not easily resist reading, and I found that M. Scherer had prefixed to Amiel's Journal a long and important introduction. This I read; and was not less charmed by the *mitis sapientia*, the understanding, kindness and tenderness, with which the character of Amiel himself, whom M. Scherer had known in youth, was handled, than interested by the criticism on the Journal. Then I read Mrs Humphry Ward's interesting notice, and then—for all biography is attractive, and of Amiel's life and circumstances I had by this time become desirous of knowing more—the *Étude Biographique* of Mademoiselle Berthe Vadier.

Of Amiel's cultivation, refinement, and high feeling, of his singular graces of spirit and character, there could be no doubt. But the specimens of his work given by his critics left me hesitating. A poetess herself, Mademoiselle Berthe Vadier is much occupied with Amiel's poetry, and quotes it abundantly. Even Victor Hugo's poetry leaves me cold, I am so unhappy as not to be able to admire *Olympio*; what am I to say, then, to Amiel's

> Journeé
> Illuminée,
> Riant solei! d'avril,
> En quel songe
> Se plonge
> Mon cœur, et que veut-il?

373

But M. Scherer and other critics, who do not require us to admire Amiel's poetry, maintain that in his Journal he has left 'a book which will not die', a book describing a malady of which 'the secret is sublime and the expression wonderful'; a marvel of 'speculative intuition', a 'psychological experience of the utmost value'. M. Scherer and Mrs Humphry Ward give Amiel's Journal very decidedly the preference over the letters of an old friend of mine, Obermann. The quotations made from Amiel's Journal by his critics failed, I say, to enable me quite to understand this high praise. But I remember the time when a new publication by George Sand or by Sainte-Beuve was an event bringing to me a shock of pleasure, and a French book capable of renewing that sensation is seldom produced now. If Amiel's Journal was of the high quality alleged, what a pleasure to make acquaintance with it, what a loss to miss it! In spite, therefore, of the unfitness of old age to bear atonic influences, I at last read Amiel's Journal—read it carefully through. Tonic it is not; but it is to be read with profit, and shows, moreover, powers of great force and value, though not quite, I am inclined to think, in the exact line which his critics with one consent indicate.

In speaking of Amiel at present, after so much has been written about him, I may assume that the main outlines of his life are known to my readers: that they know him to have been born in 1821 and to have died in 1881, to have passed the three or four best years of his youth at the University of Berlin, and the remainder of his life mostly at Geneva, as a professor, first of aesthetics, afterwards of philosophy. They know that his publications and lectures, during his lifetime, disappointed his friends, who expected much from his acquirements, talents, and vivacity; and that his fame rests upon two volumes of extracts from many thousand pages of a private journal, *Journal Intime*, extending over more than thirty years, from 1848 to 1881, which he left behind him at his death. This Journal explains his sterility; and displays in explaining it, say his critics, such sincerity, with such gifts of expression and eloquence, of profound analysis and speculative intuition, as to make it most surely 'one of those books which will not die'.

The sincerity is unquestionable. As to the gifts of eloquence and expression, what are we to say? M. Scherer speaks of an 'ever new eloquence' pouring itself in the pages of the Journal;

M. Paul Bourget, of 'marvellous pages' where the feeling for nature finds an expression worthy of Shelley or Wordsworth: Mrs Humphry Ward, of 'magic of style', of 'glow and splendour of expression', of the 'poet and artist' who fascinates us in Amiel's prose. I cannot quite agree. Obermann has been mentioned: it seems to me that we have only to place a passage from Sénancour beside a passage from Amiel, to perceive the difference between a feeling for nature which gives magic to style and one which does not. Here and throughout I am to use as far as possible Mrs Humphry Ward's translation, at once spirited and faithful, of Amiel's Journal. I will take a passage where Amiel has evidently some reminiscence of Sénancour (whose work he knew well), is inspired by Sénancour—a passage which has been extolled by M. Paul Bourget:

Shall I ever enjoy again those marvellous reveries of past days,—as, for instance, once, when I was still quite a youth in the early dawn sitting amongst the ruins of the castle of Faucigny; another time in the mountains above Lancy, under the midday sun, lying under a tree and visited by three butterflies; and again another night on the sandy shore of the North Sea, stretched full length upon the beach, my eyes wandering over the Milky Way? Will they ever return to me, those grandiose, immortal, cosmogonic dreams in which one seems to carry the world in one's breast, to touch the stars, to possess the infinite? Divine moments, hours of ecstasy, when thought flies from world to world, penetrates the great enigma, breathes with a respiration large, tranquil, and profound like that of the ocean, and hovers serene and boundless like the blue heaven! Visits from the Muse Urania, who traces around the foreheads of those she loves the phosphorescent nimbus of contemplative power, and who pours into their hearts the tranquil intoxication, if not the authority of genius,—moments of irresistible intuition in which a man feels himself great as the universe and calm like God! . . . What hours, what memories!

And now for Obermann's turn, Obermann by the Lake of Bienne:

My path lay beside the green waters of the Thiele. Feeling inclined to muse, and finding the night so warm that there was no hardship in being all night out of doors, I took the road to Saint Blaise. I descended a steep bank, and got upon the shore of the lake where its ripple came up and expired. The air was calm; everyone was at rest; I remained there for hours. Towards morning the moon shed over the earth and waters the ineffable melancholy of her last gleams. Nature seems unspeakably grand, when, plunged in a long reverie, one hears the rippling of the waters upon a solitary strand, in the calm of a night still enkindled and luminous with the setting moon.

Sensibility beyond utterance, charm and torment of our vain years; vast consciousness of a nature everywhere greater than we are, and everywhere impenetrable; all-embracing passion, ripened wisdom, delicious self-abandonment—everything that a mortal heart can contain of life-weariness and yearning, I felt it all, I experienced it all, in this memorable night. I have made a grave step towards the age of decline, I have swallowed up ten years of life at once. Happy the simple, whose heart is always young!

No translation can render adequately the cadence of diction, the 'dying fall' of reveries like those of Sénancour or Rousseau. But even in a translation we must surely perceive that the magic of style is with Sénancour's feeling for nature, not Amiel's; and in the original this is far more manifest still.

Magic of style is creative: its possessor himself creates, and he inspires and enables his reader in some sort to create after him. And creation gives the sense of life and joy; hence its extraordinary value. But eloquence may exist without magic of style, and this eloquence, accompanying thoughts of rare worth and depth, may heighten their effect greatly. And M. Scherer says that Amiel's speculative philosophy is 'on a far other scale of vastness' than Sénancour's, and therefore he gives the preference to the eloquence of Amiel, which clothes and conveys this vaster philosophy. Amiel was no doubt greatly Sénancour's superior in culture and instruction generally; in philosophical reading and what is called philosophical thought he was immensely his superior. My sense for philosophy, I know, is as far from satisfying Mr Frederic Harrison as my sense for Hugo's poetry is from satisfying Mr Swinburne. But I am too old to change and too hardened to hide what I think; and when I am

presented with philosophical speculations and told that they are
'on a high scale of vastness', I persist in looking closely at them
and in honestly asking myself what I find to be their positive
value. And we get from Amiel's powers of 'speculativeint uition'
things like this:

> Created spirits in the accomplishment of their destinies
> tend, so to speak, to form constellations and milky ways
> within the empyrean of the divinity; in becoming gods, they
> surround the throne of the sovereign with a sparkling court.

Or this:

> Is not mind the universal virtuality, the universe latent? If
> so, its zero would be the germ of the infinite, which is expressed
> mathematically by the double zero (∞).

Or, to let our philosopher develop himself at more length, let
us take this return to the zero, which Mrs Humphry Ward
prefers here to render by *nothingness*:

> This psychological reinvolution is an anticipation of death;
> it represents the life beyond the grave, the return to Scheol,
> the soul fading into the world of ghosts or descending into the
> region of *Die Mütter*; it implies the simplification of the
> individual who, allowing all the accidents of personality to
> evaporate, exists henceforward only in the invisible state, the
> state of point, of potentiality, of pregnant nothingness. Is not
> this the true definition of mind? is not mind, dissociated from
> space and time, just this? Its development, past or future, is
> contained in it just as a curve is contained in its algebraical
> formula. This nothing is an all. This *punctum* without dimen-
> sions is a *punctum saliens*.

French critics throw up their hands in dismay at the violence
which the Germanized Amiel, propounding his speculative
philosophy, often does to the French language. My objection is
rather that such speculative philosophy as that of which I have
been quoting specimens has no value, is perfectly futile. And
Amiel's Journal contains far too much of it.

What is futile we may throw aside; but when Amiel tells us
of his 'protean nature essentially metamorphosable, polarizable,
and virtual', when he tells us of his longing for 'totality', we

must listen, although these phrases may in France, as M. Paul Bourget says, 'raise a shudder in a humanist trained on Livy and Pascal'. But these phrases stood for ideas which did practically rule, in a great degree, Amiel's life, which he often develops not only with great subtlety, but also with force, clearness, and eloquence, making it both easy and interesting to us to follow him. But still, when we have the ideas present before us, I shall ask, what is their value, what does Amiel obtain in them for the service of either himself or other people?

Let us take first what, adopting his own phrase, we may call his 'bedazzlement with the infinite', his thirst for 'totality'. *Omnis determinatio est negatio.* Amiel has the gift and the bent for making his soul 'the capacity for all form, not *a* soul but *the* soul'. He finds it easier and more natural 'to be *man* than *a* man'. His permanent instinct is to be 'a subtle and fugitive spirit which no base can absorb or fix entirely'. It costs him an effort to affirm his own personality: 'the infinite draws me to it, the *Henosis* of Plotinus intoxicates me like a philtre'.

It intoxicates him until the thought of absorption and extinction, the *Nirvana* of Buddhism, becomes his thought of refuge:

> The individual life is a nothing ignorant of itself, and as soon as this nothing knows itself, individual life is abolished in principle. For as soon as the illusion vanishes, Nothingness resumes its eternal sway, the suffering of life is over, error has disappeared, time and form have for this enfranchised individuality ceased to be; the coloured air-bubble has burst in infinite space, and the misery of thought has sunk to rest in the changeless repose of all-embracing Nothing.

With this bedazzlement with the infinite and this drift towards Buddhism comes the impatience with all production, with even poetry and art themselves, because of their necessary limits and imperfection:

> Composition demands a concentration, decision, and pliancy which I no longer possess. I cannot fuse together materials and ideals. If we are to give anything a form we must, so to speak, be the tyrants of it. We must treat our subject brutally and not be always trembling lest we should be doing it a wrong. We must be able to transmute and absorb it into our own substance. This sort of confident effrontery is beyond

me; my whole nature tends to that impersonality which respects and subordinates itself to the object; it is love of truth which holds me back from concluding and deciding.

The desire for the all, the impatience with what is partial and limited, the fascination of the infinite, are the topics of page after page in the Journal. It is a prosaic mind which has never been in contact with ideas of this sort, never felt their charm. They lend themselves well to poetry, but what are we to say of their value as ideas to be lived with, dilated on, made the governing ideas of life? Except for use in passing, and with the power to dismiss them again, they are unprofitable. Shelley's

> Life like a dome of many-coloured glass
> Stains the white radiance of eternity
> Until death tramples it to fragments

has value as a splendid image nobly introduced in a beautiful and impassioned poem. But Amiel's 'coloured air-bubble', as a positive piece of 'speculative intuition', has no value whatever. Nay, the thoughts which have positive truth and value, the thoughts to be lived with and dwelt upon, the thoughts which are a real acquisition for our minds, are precisely thoughts which counterect the 'vague aspiration and indeterminate desire' possessing Amiel and filling his Journal: they are thoughts insisting on the need of limit, the feasibility of performance. Goethe says admirably—

> Wer grosses will, muss sich zusammenraffen:
> In der Beschränkung zeigt sich erst der Meister.

He who will do great things must pull himself together: it is in working within limits that the master comes out.

Buffon says not less admirably:

> Tout sujet est un; et quelque vaste qu'il soit, il peut être renfermé dans un seul discours.

Every subject is one; and however vast it may be is capable of being contained in a single discourse.

The ideas to live with, the ideas of sterling value to us, are, I repeat, ideas of this kind: ideas staunchly counteracting and reducing the power of the infinite and indeterminate, not paralysing us with it.

And indeed we have not to go beyond Amiel himself for proof of this. Amiel was paralysed by living in these ideas of 'vague aspiration and indeterminate desire', of 'confounding his personal life in the general life', by feeding on these ideas, treating them as august and precious, and filling hundreds of pages of Journal with them. He was paralysed by it, he became impotent and miserable. And he knew it, and tells us of it himself with a power of analysis and with a sad eloquence which to me are much more interesting and valuable than his philosophy of Maïa and the Great Wheel. 'By your natural tendency', he says to himself, 'you arrive at disgust with life, despair, pessimism.' And again: 'Melancholy outlook on all sides. Disgust with myself.' And again: 'I cannot deceive myself as to the fate in store for me: increasing isolation, inward disappointment, enduring regrets, a melancholy neither to be consoled nor confessed, a mournful old age, a slow agony, a death in the desert.' And all this misery by his own fault, his own mistakes. 'To live is to conquer incessantly; one must have the courage to be happy. I turn in a vicious circle; I have never had clear sight of my true vocation.'

I cannot, therefore, fall in with that particular line of admiration which critics, praising Amiel's Journal, have commonly followed. I cannot join in celebrating his prodigies of speculative intuition, the glow and splendour of his beatific vision of absolute knowledge, the marvellous pages in which his deep and vast philosophic thought is laid bare, the secret of his sublime malady is expressed. I hesitate to admit that all this part of the Journal has even a very profound psychological interest: its interest is rather pathological. In reading it we are pursuing not so much a study of psychology as a study of morbid pathology.

But the Journal reveals a side in Amiel which his critics, so far as I have seen, have hardly noticed, a side of real power, originality, and value. He says himself that he never had clear sight of his true vocation: well, his true vocation, it seems to me, was that of a literary critic. Here he is admirable: M. Scherer was a true friend when he offered to introduce him to an editor, and suggested an article on Uhland. There is hardly a literary criticism in these two volumes which is not masterly, and which does not make one desire more of the same kind. And not Amiel's literary criticism only, but his criticism of society, politics, national character, religion, is in general well informed, just, and penetrating in an eminent degree. Any one single page of this criticism is worth, in my opinion, a hundred of Amiel's pages about the Infinite Illusion and the Great Wheel. It is to this side in Amiel that I desire now to draw attention. I would have abstained from writing about him if I had only to disparage and to find fault, only to say that he had been overpraised, and that his dealings with Maïa seemed to me profitable neither for himself nor for others.

Let me first take Amiel as a critic of literature, and of the literature which he naturally knew best—French literature. Hear him as critic on that best of critics, Sainte-Beuve, of whose death (1869) he had just heard:

> The fact is, Sainte-Beuve leaves a greater void behind him than either Béranger or Lamartine; their greatness was already distant, historical; he was still helping us to think. The true critic supplies all the world with a basis. He represents the public judgment, that is to say, the public reason, the touchstone, the scales, the crucible, which tests the value of each man and the merit of each work. Infallibility of judgment is perhaps rarer than anything else, so fine a balance of qualities does it demand—qualities both natural and acquired, qualities of both mind and heart. What years of labour, what study and comparison, are needed to bring the critical judgment to maturity! Like Plato's sage, it is only at fifty that the critic is risen to the true height of his literary priesthood, or, to put it less pompously, of his social function. Not till then has he compassed all modes of being, and made every shade of appreciation his own. And Sainte-Beuve joined to this infinitely refined culture a prodigious memory and an incredible multitude of facts and anecdotes stored up for the service of his thought.

The criticism is so sound, so admirably put, and so charming, that one wishes Sainte-Beuve could have read it himself.

Try Amiel next on the touchstone afforded by that 'half genius, half charlatan', Victor Hugo:

> I have been again looking through Victor Hugo's *Paris* (1867). For ten years event after event has given the lie to the

prophet, but the confidence of the prophet in his own imaginings is not therefore a whit diminished. Humility and common sense are only fit for Lilliputians. Victor Hugo superbly ignores everything which he has not foreseen. He does not know that pride limits the mind, and that a limitless pride is a littleness of soul. If he could but learn to rank himself with other men and France with other nations, he would see things more truly, and would not fall into his insane exaggerations, his extravagant oracles. But proportion and justness his chords will never know. He is vowed to the Titanic; his gold is always mixed with lead, his insight with childishness, his reason with madness. He cannot be simple; like the blaze of a house on fire, his light is blinding. In short, he astonishes but provokes, he stirs but annoys. His note is always half or two-thirds false, and that is why he perpetually makes us feel uncomfortable. The great poet in him cannot get clear of the charlatan. A few pricks of Voltaire's irony would have made the inflation of this genius collapse, and rendered him stronger by rendering him saner. It is public misfortune that the most powerful poet of France should not have better understood his role, and that, unlike the Hebrew prophets who chastised because they loved, he flatters his fellow-citizens from system and from pride. France is the world, Paris is France, Hugo is Paris. Bow down and worship, ye nations!

Finally, we will hear Amiel on a consummate and supreme French classic, as perfect as Hugo is flawed—La Fontaine:

Went through my La Fontaine yesterday, and remarked his omissions. . . . He has not an echo of chivalry haunting him. His French history dates from Louis XIV. His geography extends in reality but a few square miles, and reaches neither the Rhine nor the Loire, neither the mountains nor the sea. He never invents his subjects, but indolently takes them ready-made from elsewhere. But with all this, what an adorable writer, what a painter, what an observer, what a master of the comic and the satirical, what a teller of a story! I am never tired of him, though I know half his fables by heart. In the matter of vocabulary, turns of expression, tones, idioms, his language is perhaps the richest of the great period, for it combines skilfully the archaic with the classical, the Gaulish element with what is French. Variety, finesse, sly fun, sensibility, rapidity, conciseness, suavity, grace, gaiety—when necessary nobleness, seriousness, grandeur—you find everything in our fabulist. And the happy epithets, and the telling proverbs, and the sketches dashed off, and the unexpected audacities, and the point driven well home! One cannot say what he had not, so many diverse aptitudes he has.

Compare his *Woodcutter and Death* with Boileau's, and you can measure the prodigious difference between the artist and the critic who wanted to teach him better. La Fontaine brings visibly before you the poor peasant under the monarchy, Boileau but exhibits a drudge sweating under his load. The first is a historic witness, the second a school-versifier. La Fontaine enables you to reconstruct the whole society of his age; the pleasant old soul from Champagne, with his animals, turns out to be the one and only Homer of France.

His weak side is his epicureanism, with its tinge of grossness. This, no doubt, was what made Larmartine dislike him. The religious string is wanting to his lyre, he has nothing which shows him to have known either Christianity or the high tragedies of the soul. Kind Nature is his goddess, Horace his prophet, and Montaigne his gospel. In other words, his horizon is that of the Renascence. This islet of paganism in the midst of a Catholic society is very curious; the paganism is perfectly simple and frank.

These are but notes, jottings in his Journal, and Amiel passed from them to broodings over the infinite, and personality, and totality. Probably the literary criticism which he did so well, and for which he shows a true vocation, gave him nevertheless but little pleasure because he did it thus fragmentarily and by fits and starts. To do it thoroughly, to make his fragments into wholes, to fit them for coming before the public, composition with its toils and limits was necessary. Toils and limits composition indeed has; yet all composition is a kind of creation. Creation gives, as I have already said, pleasure, and, when successful and sustained, more than pleasure, joy. Amiel, had he tried the experiment with literary criticism, where lay his true vocation, would have found it so. Sainte-Beuve, whom he so much admires, would have been the most miserable of men if his production had been but a volume or two of middling poems and a journal. But Sainte-Beuve's motto, as Amiel himself notices, was that of the Emperor Severus: *Laboremus*. 'Work', Sainte-Beuve confesses to a friend, 'is my sore burden, but it is also my great resource. I eat my heart out when I am not up to the neck in work; there you have the secret of the life I lead.' If M. Scherer's introduction to the *Revue Germanique* could but have been used, if Amiel could but have written the article on Uhland, and followed it up by plenty of articles more!

I have quoted largely from Amiel's literary criticism, because this side of him has, so far as I have observed, received so little attention, and yet deserves attention so eminently. But his more general criticism, too, shows, as I have said, the same high qualities as his criticism of authors and books. I must quote one or two of his aphorisms: *L'esprit sert bien à tout, mais ne suffit à rien:* 'Wits are of use for everything, sufficient for nothing.' *Une société vit de sa foi et se développe par la science:* 'A society lives on its faith and develops itself by science.' *L'État libéral est irréalisable avec une religion antilibérale, et presque irréalisable avec l'absence de religion:* 'Liberal communities are impossible with an anti-liberal religion, and almost impossible with the absence of religion.' But epigrammatic sentences of this sort are perhaps not so very difficult to produce, in French at any rate. Let us take Amiel when he has room and verge enough to show what he can really say which is important about society, religion, national life and character. We have seen what an influence his years passed in Germany had upon him: we have seen how severely he judges Victor Hugo's faults: the faults of the French nation at large he judges with a like severity. But what a fine and just perception does the following passage show of the deficiencies of Germany, the advantage which the western nations have in their more finished civilization:

It is in the novel that the average vulgarity of German society and its inferiority to the societies of France and Emgland are most clearly visible. The notion of a thing's *jarring on the taste* is wanting to German aesthetics. Their elegance knows nothing of grace; they have no sense of the enormous distance between distinction (gentlemanly, lady-like) and their stiff *Vornehmlichkeit*. Their imagination lacks style, training, education, and knowledge of the world; it is stamped with an ill-bred air even in its Sunday clothes. The race is practical and intelligent, but common and ill-mannered. Ease, amiability, manners, wit, animation, dignity, charm, are qualities which belong to others.

Will that inner freedom of soul, that profound harmony of all the faculties, which I have so often observed among the best Germans, ever come to the surface? Will the conquerors of today ever civilize their forms of life? It is by their future novels that we shall be able to judge. As soon as the German novel can give us quite good society, the Germans will be in the raw stage no longer.

And this pupil of Berlin, this devourer of German books, this victim, say the French critics, to the contagion of German style, after three hours, one day, of a *Geschichte der Aesthetik in Deutschland*, breaks out:

Learning and even thought are not everything. A little *esprit*, point, vivacity, imagination, grace, would do no harm. Do these pedantic books leave a single image or sentence, a single striking or new fact, in the memory when one lays them down? No, nothing but fatigue and confusion. Oh, for clearness, terseness, brevity! Diderot, Voltaire, or even Galiani! A short article by Sainte-Beuve, Scherer, Renan, Victor Cherbuliez, gives one more pleasure, and makes one ponder and reflect more, than a thousand of these German pages crammed to the margin and showing the work itself rather than its result. The Germans heap the faggots for the pile, the French being the fire. Spare me your lucubrations, give me facts or ideas. Keep your vats, your must, your dregs, to yourselves; I want wine fully made, wine which will sparkle in the glass, and kindle my spirits instead of oppressing them.

Amiel may have been led away *deteriora sequi*: he may have Germanized until he has become capable of the verb *déperson-naliser* and the noun *réimplication*; but after all, his heart is in the right place: *videt meliora probatque*. He remains at bottom the man who said: *Le livre serait mon ambition*. He adds, to be sure, that it would be *son ambition*, 'if ambition were not vanity, and vanity of vanities'.

Yet this disenchanted brooder, 'full of a tranquil disgust at the futility of our ambitions, the void of our existence', bedazzled with the infinite, can observe the world and society with consummate keenness and shrewdness, and at the same time with a delicacy which to the man of the world is in general wanting. Is it possible to analyse *le grand monde*, high society, as the Old World knows it and America knows it not, more acutely than Amiel does in what follows?

> In society people are expected to behave as if they lived on ambrosia and concerned themselves with no interests but such as are noble. Care, need, passion do not exist. All realism is suppressed as brutal. In a word, what is called *le grand monde* gives itself for the moment the flattering illusion that it is moving in an ethereal atmosphere and breathing the air of the gods. For this reason all vehemence, any cry of nature, all real suffering, all heedless familiarity, any genuine sign of passion, are startling and distasteful in this delicate *milieu*, and at once destroy the collective work, the cloud-palace, the imposing architectural creation raised by common consent. It is like the shrill cock-crow which breaks the spell of all enchantments, and puts the fairies to flight. These select gatherings produce without intending it a sort of concert for eye and ear, an improvising work of art. By the instinctive collaboration of everybody concerned, wit and taste hold festival, and the associations of reality are exchanged for the associations of imagination. So understood, society is a form of poetry; the cultivated classes deliberately recompose the idyll of the past, and the buried world of Astraea. Paradox or not, I believe that these fugitive attempts to reconstruct a dream, whose only end is beauty, represent confused reminiscences of an age of gold haunting the human heart; or rather, aspirations towards a harmony of things which everyday reality denies to us, and of which art alone gives us a glimpse.

I remember reading in an American newspaper a solemn letter by an excellent republican, asking what were a shopman's or a labourer's feelings when he walked through Eaton or Chatsworth. Amiel will tell him: they are 'reminiscences of an age of gold haunting the human heart, aspirations towards a harmony of things which everyday reality denies to us'. I appeal to my

friend, the author of *Triumphant Democracy* himself, to say
whether these are to be had in walking through Pittsburg.

Indeed it is by contrast with American life that *Nirvana*
appears to Amiel so desirable:

> For the Americans, life means devouring, incessant activity.
> They must win gold, predominance, power; they must crush
> rivals, subdue nature. They have their heart set on the means,
> and never for an instant think of the end. They confound
> being with individual being, and the expansion of self with
> happiness. This means that they do not live by the soul, that
> they ignore the immutable and eternal, bustle at the circum-
> ference of their existence because they cannot penetrate to its
> centre. They are restless, eager, positive, because they are
> superficial. To what end all this stir, noise, greed, struggle?
> It is all a mere being stunned and deafened!

Space is failing me, but I must yet find room for a less indirect
criticism of democracy than the foregoing remarks on American
life:

> *Each function to the most worthy :* this maxim is the professed
> rule of all constitutions, and serves to test them. Democracy
> is not forbidden to apply it; but Democracy rarely does apply
> it, because she holds, for example, that the most worthy man
> is the man who pleases her, whereas he who pleases her is not
> always the most worthy; and because she supposes that reason
> guides the masses, whereas in reality they are most commonly
> led by passion. And in the end every falsehood has to be
> expiated, for truth always takes its revenge.

What publicists and politicians have to learn is, that 'the
ultimate ground upon which every civilization rests is the
average morality of the masses and a sufficient amount of practical righteousness'. But where does duty find its inspiration and
sanctions? In religion. And what does Amiel think of the traditional religion of Christendom, the Christianity of the Churches?
He tells us repeatedly; but a month or two before his death, with
death in full view, he tells us with peculiar impressiveness:

> The whole Semitic dramaturgy has come to seem to me a
> work of the imagination. The apostolic documents have
> changed in value and meaning to my eyes. The distinction
> between belief and truth has grown clearer and clearer to me.

Religious psychology has become a simple phenomenon, and has lost its fixed and absolute value. The apologetics of Pascal, Leibnitz, Secrétan, appear to me no more convincing than those of the Middle Age, for they assume that which is in question—a revealed doctrine, a definite and unchangeable Christianity.

Is it possible, he asks, to receive at this day the common doctrine of a Divine Providence directing all the circumstances of our life, and consequently inflicting upon us our miseries as means of education?

Is this heroic faith compatible with our actual knowledge of the laws of nature? Hardly. But what this faith makes objective we may take subjectively. The moral being may moralize his suffering in turning the natural fact to account for the education of his inner man. What he cannot change he calls the will of God, and to will what God wills brings him peace.

But can a religion, Amiel asks again, without miracles, without unverifiable mystery, be efficacious, have influence with the many? And again he answers:

Pious fiction is still fiction. Truth has superior rights. The world must adapt itself to truth, not truth to the world. Copernicus upset the astronomy of the Middle Age; so much the worse for the astronomy. The Everlasting Gospel is revolutionizing the Churches; what does it matter?

This is water to our mill, as the Germans say, indeed. But I have come even thus late in the day to speak of Amiel, not because I found him supplying water for any particular mill, either mine or any other, but because it seemed to me that by a whole important side he was eminently worth knowing, and that to this side of him the public, here in England at any rate, had not had its attention sufficiently drawn. If in the seventeen thousand pages of the Journal there are many pages still unpublished in which Amiel exercises his true vocation of critic, of literary critic more especially, let his friends give them to us, let M. Sherer introduce them to us, let Mrs Humphry Ward translate them for us. But *sat patriae Priamoque datum*: Maïa has had her full share of space already: I will not ask for a word more about the infinite illusion, or the double zero, or the Great Wheel.

Charlotte Brontë's SHIRLEY. *The heroine is drawn from the character of Emily Brontë.* 528 pages. No. 1288.

Charlotte Brontë's THE PROFESSOR. *Largely autobiographical novel of the author's early life as a pupil teacher, and the professor she secretly adored.* 256 pages. No. 1417.

Charlotte Brontë's VILLETTE. *'. . . so full of riches, its emotional truth is so deep, its prose so majestically matched to a moving theme'* MARGARET LANE. 480 pages. No. 1351.

Emily Brontë's WUTHERING HEIGHTS. *Tale of an elemental and passionate love set in the loneliness of the Yorkshire moors; also contains 64 of her poems.* 384 pages. No. 1243.

Bunyan's PILGRIM'S PROGRESS. *Containing both parts of the great Christian allegory. With Notes.* 352 pages. No. 1204.

Samuel Butler's THE WAY OF ALL FLESH. *A milestone in the English novel on the divisions between the generations.* 360 pages. No. 1895.

Lewis Carroll's ALICE IN WONDERLAND. *With the author's original illustrations.* 112 pages. No. 1836.

G. K. Chesterton's STORIES, ESSAYS AND POEMS.
352 pages. No. 1913.

Wilkie Collins's THE WOMAN IN WHITE. *Uniquely combines melodrama with realism.* 584 pages. No. 1464.

Wilkie Collins's THE MOONSTONE. *Another classic story of detection.*
448 pages. No. 1979.

Joseph Conrad's LORD JIM. *A man's struggle with life on the lonely Isle of Patusan under an acute consciousness of lost honour.*
320 pages. No. 1925.

Joseph Conrad's THE NIGGER OF THE ' NARCISSUS '; TYPHOON; and **THE SHADOW LINE.** *Three of the author's best-known sea stories.*
320 pages. No. 1980.

Joseph Conrad's THE SECRET AGENT. *Anarchists in Edwardian London.* 328 pages. No. 1282.

Joseph Conrad's VICTORY: An Island Tale. *Solitary Axel Heyst on his island aided by a girl he has rescued foils the schemes of a brutal gang.*
432 pages. No. 1228.

Sir Edward Creasy's FIFTEEN DECISIVE BATTLES OF THE WORLD. *From Marathon to Waterloo.* 432 pages. No. 1300.

Dante's THE DIVINE COMEDY. *Translated by H. F. Cary. A standard reading that has stood the test of time.* 480 pages. No. 1308.

Darwin's THE VOYAGE OF THE ' BEAGLE '. *The flora and fauna of South America, Australia and elsewhere through the youthful eyes of a great naturalist and scientist.* 512 pages. No. 1104.

Daniel Defoe's CAPTAIN SINGLETON. *A pirate yarn which includes a remarkable journey across unexplored Africa, anticipating later discoveries.* 352 pages. No. 1074.

Defoe's MOLL FLANDERS. *A low-life heroine, 'five times a wife, twelve years a thief, eight years a transported felon', who died honest and a penitent.* 320 pages. No. 1837.

Defoe's A JOURNAL OF THE PLAGUE YEAR. *A realistic novel of plague-stricken London.* 320 pages. No. 1289.

Defoe's ROBINSON CRUSOE and **THE FARTHER ADVENTURES OF ROBINSON CRUSOE.** 448 pages. No. 1059.

Charles Dickens's BARNABY RUDGE. *The 'Gordon' or 'No Popery' riots form the historical background.* 640 pages. No. 1076.

Dickens's A CHRISTMAS CAROL and **OTHER CHRISTMAS BOOKS.** (*'The Battle of Life'*, *'The Chimes'*, *'The Cricket on the Hearth'*, *'The Haunted Man'*.) 432 pages. No. 1239.

Dickens's GREAT EXPECTATIONS. *The author's most economically written novel.* 480 pages. No. 1234.

Dickens's HARD TIMES. *The early industrial North, kingdom of the Gradgrinds and Bounderbys whose rule seemed destined to last for ever.* 288 pages. No. 1292.

Dickens's OLIVER TWIST. 448 pages. No. 1233.

Dickens's THE PICKWICK PAPERS. *The whole of the Pickwickian extravaganza in an inexpensive edition.* 832 pages. No. 1235.

Dickens's A TALE OF TWO CITIES. *Sydney Carton cheats Madame Guillotine of a precious victim.* 384 pages. No. 1102.

Dostoyevsky's CRIME AND PUNISHMENT. *Constance Garnett translation. One of the world's great novels.* 512 pages. No. 1501.

Dostoyevsky's THE IDIOT. *Vast canvas of St Petersburg life in the last century, revolving round the magnetic Prince Muishkin.* 608 pages. No. 1682.

Dostoyevsky's LETTERS FROM THE UNDERWORLD, THE GENTLE MAIDEN and **THE LANDLADY.** *Three shorter novels, revealing his irresistible humour and irony.* 320 pages. No. 1654.

Dostoyevsky's POOR FOLK and **THE GAMBLER.** *Two stories, the first a love idyll of the St Petersburg slums; the second revealing the author's passion for gambling.* 320 pages. No. 1711.

Dumas's THE BLACK TULIP. *The fall of the brothers de Witt in seventeenth-century Holland.* 272 pages. No. 1174.

George Eliot's ADAM BEDE. *Her first full-scale novel.* 528 pages. No. 1027.

George Eliot's MILL ON THE FLOSS. *A pastoral.* 512 pages. No. 1325.

George Eliot's SILAS MARNER. *A notable picture of Midland village life a century ago.* 256 pages. No. 1121.

ENGLISH SHORT STORIES. *Thirty-six stories from the fifteenth to the twentieth centuries.* 384 pages. No. 1743.

Fieldings's JONATHAN WILD and **JOURNAL OF A VOYAGE TO LISBON.** *The former is a satirical novel on hero worship; the Journal narrates the incidents of Fielding's last voyage.* 304 pages. No. 1877.

Fielding's JOSEPH ANDREWS. *'Writ in the manner of Cervantes.'* 304 pages. No. 1467.

Fielding's TOM JONES. *'The life of the average natural man'—with vagabond and nobleman, soldier and chambermaid.* 2 vols. 896 pages. Nos. 1355–6.

Flaubert's MADAME BOVARY. *One of the great psychological novels, telling of a provincial doctor's wife's agonizing choice between loyalty and adultery.* 304 pages. No. 1808.

Flaubert's SENTIMENTAL EDUCATION. *A lyrically tender love story set in the Paris of the 1840's.* 416 pages. No. 1969.

FRENCH SHORT STORIES *by Balzac, Baudelaire, Gautier, Maupassant, etc. etc.* 368 pages. No. 1896.

Mrs Gaskell's CRANFORD. *Flutterings and tea-time gossip around the adorable Miss Matty.* 256 pages. No. 1083.

Mrs Gaskell's MARY BARTON. *Powerful emotional novel, set against the industrial distress of the north in the 1840's.* 384 pages. No. 1598.

John Gay's THE BEGGAR'S OPERA. *The volume also contains a selection of other eighteenth-century plays by Colman and Garrick, Cumberland, Fielding, Nicholas Rowe, etc.* 432 pages. No. 1818.

GHOST STORIES. *Eighteen stories from such masters of the genre as Algernon Blackwood, Walter de la Mare, Lord Dunsany, etc. etc.* 384 pages. No. 1952.

Gogol's TARAS BULBA. *Epic novel of the Cossacks, living picturesquely and dangerously under open skies in the Ukraine.* 144 pages. No. 1740.

THE GOLDEN TREASURY OF LONGER POEMS. *Now includes section by twentieth-century poets.* 448 pages. No. 1746.

Goldsmith's THE VICAR OF WAKEFIELD. *The Primrose family must have come straight from Goldsmith's heart.* 240 pages. No. 1295.

Gorky's THROUGH RUSSIA. *Ten representative stories by the great naturalistic writer.* 288 pages. No. 1741.

G. and W. Grossmith's THE DIARY OF A NOBODY. *Nostalgic evocation of a London of yesteryear.* 288 pages. No. 1963.

Hawthorne's THE HOUSE OF THE SEVEN GABLES. *As the clock ticks and a leaf falls a life may be passing too.* 336 pages. No. 1176.

Hawthorne's THE SCARLET LETTER. *Hester Prynne finds her true self after her adultery in a narrow seventeenth-century American community.* 328 pages. No. 1122.

Victor Hugo's THE HUNCHBACK OF NOTRE DAME. *Swinburne called this 'the greatest of all tragic romances'—set in medieval Paris.* 480 pages. No. 1422.

Ibsen's A DOLL'S HOUSE, THE LADY FROM THE SEA, THE WILD DUCK. 256 pages. No. 1494.

Ibsen's GHOSTS, THE WARRIORS AT HELGELAND, AN ENEMY OF THE PEOPLE. 264 pages. No. 1552.

INTERNATIONAL MODERN PLAYS. *Plays by Strindberg, the Brothers Capek and Luigi Chiarelli are included.* 320 pages. No. 1989.

Henry James's THE TURN OF THE SCREW and **THE ASPERN PAPERS.** *Two of the author's most famous novels.* 320 pages. No. 1912.

Jerome K. Jerome's THREE MEN IN A BOAT and THREE MEN ON THE BUMMEL. *Two comic masterpieces from an author who created his own brand of humour. (With original illustrations from A. Fredericks and L. Raven Hill.)* 384 pages. No. 1118.

Keats's POEMS. *Contains everything by Keats published in the poet's lifetime, and practically everything discovered since.*

384 pages. No. 1101.

Lamb's ESSAYS OF ELIA. *The volume is edited from the original edition.* 192 pages. No. 1014.

Lamb's TALES OF SHAKESPEARE. *Excellent prose versions of the plot and characters, offering introductions to twenty of the plays.*

320 pages. No. 1008.

Law's A SERIOUS CALL TO A DEVOUT AND HOLY LIFE. *A plea for practical Christianity. The standard text for those entering the ministry.*

384 pages. No. 1091.

Lytton's THE LAST DAYS OF POMPEII. *The terrible end of a noble city* (A.D. 79). 416 pages. No. 1080.

Machiavelli's THE PRINCE. *The first book to consider seriously scientific method in statecraft.* 256 pages. No. 1280.

Manzoni's THE BETROTHED. *One of the world's great novels, set in seventeenth-century Milan.* 576 pages. No. 1999.

Maupassant's SHORT STORIES. *Thirty-two stories.* 352 pages. No. 1907.

Melville's MOBY DICK: or The White Whale. *A cosmic allegory, whose basic theme is the corrosive nature of evil.* 528 pages. No. 1179.

MODERN PLAYS. (*R. C. Sherriff's 'Journey's End'; Maugham's 'For Services Rendered'; Noël Coward's 'Hay Fever'; A. A. Milne's 'The Dover Road'; Arnold Bennett's and Edward Knoblock's 'Milestones').* 368 pages. No. 1942.

MODERN SHORT STORIES. *Twenty masterly examples, including examples from P. G. Wodehouse, T. F. Powys, D. H. Lawrence, William Saroyan, H. E. Bates, etc. etc.* 352 pages. No. 1954.

Palgrave's GOLDEN TREASURY. 352 pages. No. 1096.

Peacock's HEADLONG HALL and **NIGHTMARE ABBEY.** *Two novels combining the author's rare satire with brilliant conversation.*

272 pages. No. 1327.

Poe's TALES OF MYSTERY AND IMAGINATION. *Forty-five classic spine-chillers.* 554 pages. No. 1336.

POEMS OF OUR TIME, 1900-1960. *400 poems by some 150 twentieth-century poets, ranging from Hardy to Dylan Thomas.*

384 pages. No. 1981.

Prescott's HISTORY OF THE CONQUEST OF PERU. *The Inca civilization at the time of its tragic subjugation by Spanish invaders.*

708 pages. No. 1301.

RESTORATION PLAYS (Dryden, Wycherley, Vanbrugh, etc.). *Includes 'The Country Wife'.*
528 pages. No. 1604.

De Quincey's CONFESSIONS OF AN ENGLISH OPIUM-EATER. *This classic reminiscence of drug addiction contains some of de Quincey's finest writing.*
288 pages. No. 1223.

READER'S GUIDE TO EVERYMAN'S LIBRARY by A. J. Hoppé, *with notes to each volume, authors' dates of birth and death.*
448 pages. No. 1889.

RUSSIAN SHORT STORIES. *Stories by Pushkin, Gogol, Tolstoy, Korolenko, Chehov, Chirikov, Andreyev, Kuprin, Gorky and Sologub.*
296 pages. No. 1758.

Scott's THE BRIDE OF LAMMERMOOR. *The penurious Master of Ravenswood's tragic love for the fair Lucy Ashton, whose father is the proprietor of Ravenswood's property.*
352 pages. No. 1129.

Scott's GUY MANNERING. *A romance of Scottish life in the time of George III.*
448 pages. No. 1133.

Scott's HEART OF MIDLOTHIAN.
The Porteous Riots, 1736.
576 pages. No. 1134.

Scott's KENILWORTH. *A romance of Elizabeth I and the Earl of Leicester, and his clandestine marriage to Amy Robsart.*
480 pages. No. 1135.

Scott's REDGAUNTLET. *Adventures in eighteenth-century Cumberland.*
480 pages. No. 1141.

Scott's ROB ROY. *The fortunes of the notorious chief of clan MacGregor during the 1715 rebellion. (With Glossary.)*
480 pages. No. 1142.

Scott's THE TALISMAN. *A romance of the Third Crusade (Syria, 1191–2).*
336 pages. No. 1144.

Mary Shelley's FRANKENSTEIN. *The classic masterpiece of the macabre.*
256 pages. No. 1616.

SHORTER NOVELS: ELIZABETHAN. *Introduction by George Saintsbury and Notes by Philip Henderson. Contains: Deloney's 'Jack of Newberie' and 'Thomas of Reading'; Nashe's 'The Unfortunate Traveller'; Greene's 'Carde of Fancie'.*
384 pages. No. 1824.

SHORTER NOVELS: SEVENTEENTH CENTURY. *Edited, with Introduction by Philip Henderson. Contains: Emanual Ford's 'Ornatus and Artesia'; Aphra Behn's 'Oroonoko'; Neville's 'The Isle of Pines'; Congreve's 'Incognita'.*
320 pages. No. 1841.

SHORTER NOVELS: EIGHTEENTH CENTURY. *Edited, with Introduction by Philip Henderson. Contains: Beckford's 'Vathek'; Horace Walpole's 'The Castle of Otranto'; Dr Johnson's 'Rasselas'.*
304 pages. No. 1856.